**Research & Education Association**

The Best Teachers' Test Preparation for the

OGET™/OSAT™

Oklahoma General Education Test™
(Field 74)

Oklahoma Subject Area Tests™
(Fields 50 & 51)

Staff of
Research & Education Association

Foreword by
David Rosen, M.A.

Former Program Director
Oklahoma Teacher's Recruitment Program

Visit our Educator Support Center at:
www.REA.com/teacher

The OGET/OSAT Test Objectives presented in this book were created and implemented by the Oklahoma Commission for Teacher Preparation (OCTP) and NES. For further information visit the OCTP website at *www.octp.org*.

For all references in this book, Oklahoma General Education Test™, Oklahoma Subject Area Tests™, OGET™, and OSAT™ are trademarks of the Oklahoma Commission for Teacher Preparation and National Evaluation Systems, Inc.™ NES® is a registered trademark of National Evaluation Systems, Inc.™

Research & Education Association
61 Ethel Road West
Piscataway, New Jersey 08854
E-mail: info@rea.com

The Best Teachers' Test Preparation for the OGET™/OSAT™ (Oklahoma General Education Test™ and Oklahoma Subject Area Tests™)

Printed in the United States of America

Library of Congress Control Number 2005906662

International Standard Book Number 0-7386-0149-7

REA® is a registered trademark of
Research & Education Association, Inc.

CONTENTS

GENERAL EDUCATION REVIEW

CHAPTER 1: CRITICAL THINKING SKILLS: READING AND COMMUNICATIONS   3

CHAPTER 2: COMMUNICATION SKILLS   33

CHAPTER 3: CRITICAL THINKING SKILLS: MATHEMATICS   79

OSAT SUBTEST 1

OSAT SUBTEST 2

Foreword

It is my pleasure to welcome you to the extraordinary, extra-ordinary, world of education. As a tenured English Instructor and former Program Director for the Oklahoma Teacher's Recruitment Program, I can assure you that the key to success in academia, as in any field of endeavor, lies in your preparation and practice. Whether it is in the preparation of your daily lesson plans, or in your preparation to enter the discipline, becoming familiar with the appropriate materials will greatly enhance your chances for success. Preparation and practice are what REA's *The Best Teachers' Test Preparation for the OGET/OSAT* is all about.

This comprehensive guidebook will familiarize you with everything you will need to successfully complete the Oklahoma General Education/Subject Area Test. From how to prepare for the actual exam, to detailed explanations of how the test's questions and answers sections are scored, as well as the criteria that will be used when scoring them, this is your opportunity to "take the test," before you actually do. Once you're acquainted with the style, structure, and overall concepts of the *OGET/OSAT*, the stress of the unknown will be eliminated and the more you'll relax on test day. Preparation will help you to answer the questions with more confidence, and this confidence will translate into higher test scores and greater academic opportunities down the road.

A key factor in preparation for the *OGET/OSAT* is practice. Face it, the more you practice at something, whether it's playing the piano, throwing a football, or taking a certification exam, the better you get. So, it goes without saying that the more time you spend with this book, the better prepared you'll be and the better prepared you are, the higher your test scores will be.

Since REA's study guides contain a wealth of information, I suggest that rather than trying to cram it all into your brain at once, you review small sections at a time. Spend a few minutes at various times during the day with the guide, thumbing through the various sections not only for the information, but also for practice. You can answer several questions, then check yourself with the accompanying details section. Working back and forth like this will allow you to monitor your progress while you take note of subject areas where you need to improve. After a few practice sections, you'll know your strengths and weaknesses. Then, of course, you can devote additional study time and energy to the areas of the test that give you the most headaches. By the time you take the actual test, you'll have a clear understanding of what is required and how to deal with each section.

Oklahoma is a wonderful place to live and teach. It is a combination of agrarian beauty and high academic standards. Combine the information in this guidebook with your own dedication to practice and preparation, and you'll never find a place or an occupation more rewarding. Good luck, and again to all my new colleagues, welcome to the extra-ordinary world of education.

—*Prof. David M. Rosen*

About Research & Education Association

Founded in 1959, Research & Education Association is dedicated to publishing the finest and most effective educational materials—including software, study guides, and test preps—for students in middle school, high school, college, graduate school, and beyond.

REA's Test Preparation series includes books and software for all academic levels in almost all disciplines. Research & Education Association publishes test preps for students who have not yet completed high school, as well as for high school students preparing to enter college. Students from countries around the world seeking to attend college in the United States will find the assistance they need in REA's publications. For college students seeking advanced degrees, REA publishes test preps for many major graduate school admission examinations in a wide variety of disciplines, including engineering, law, and medicine. Students at every level, in every field, with every ambition can find what they are looking for among REA's publications.

REA's practice tests are always based upon the most recently administered exams and include every type of question that you can expect on the actual exams.

REA's publications and educational materials are highly regarded and continually receive an unprecedented amount of praise from professionals, instructors, librarians, parents, and students. Our authors are as diverse as the fields represented in the books we publish. They are well-known in their respective disciplines and serve on the faculties of prestigious high schools, colleges, and universities throughout the United States and Canada.

Today, REA's wide-ranging catalog is a leading resource for teachers, students, and professionals.

We invite you to visit us at *www.rea.com* to find out how "REA is making the world smarter."

Acknowledgments

We would like to thank REA's Larry B. Kling, Vice President, Editorial, for supervising development; Pam Weston, Vice President, Publishing, for setting the quality standards for production integrity and managing the publication to completion; Christine Reilley, Senior Editor, for project management and preflight editorial review; Diane Goldschmidt, Associate Editor, for post-production quality assurance; Jeremy Rech, Graphic Artist, for interior page design; Christine Saul, Senior Graphic Artist, for cover design; and Jeff LoBalbo, Senior Graphic Artist, for post-production file mapping.

We gratefully acknowledge David M. Myton, Ph.D., Renay M. Scott, Ph.D., Karen Bondarchuk, M.F.A., John A. Lychner, Ph.D., Janet E. Rubin, Ph.D., Ellen R. Van't Hof, M.A., Nelson Maylone, Ph.D., and Ginny Mullen, Ph.D., for providing foundational material for this book. We also thank Al Davis, M.A, M.S., for editing this book in accordance with Oklahoma's OGET/OSAT standards.

We also gratefully acknowledge the team at Publication Services for editing, proofreading, and page composition.

Teach...
Lead...
Inspire...

INTRODUCTION

With this book in hand, you've taken an important step toward becoming a certified teacher in the state of Oklahoma. REA's all-new **OGET/OSAT** teacher certification test prep is designed to help you get into an Oklahoma classroom. The instructive chapters in this book provide complete coverage of the **Oklahoma OGET** and **OSAT** tests with in-depth reviews of every topic and area appearing on the exam. Full-length practice tests carefully derived from actual OGET (Field 74) and OSAT (Fields 50 and 51) exams will hone your test-taking skills. All practice test answers are explained in thorough detail to provide you with a greater understanding of the exam's content and difficulty. When you finish preparing with this book, you will be well-equipped with all the knowledge, practice, and strategies needed to succeed on these important exams.

ABOUT THE TESTS

What are the OGET and OSAT used for?

The Oklahoma General Education Test (OGET) is designed to assess state core general education knowledge and skills, including critical thinking, computation, and communication. The Oklahoma Subject Area Tests (OSAT) are designed to assess subject-matter knowledge and skills. The OSAT Elementary Education test consists of two subtests: One is for reading, language arts, and social studies, while the second covers math, science, health, and fine arts.

Am I required to take these tests if I hold a teaching certificate from another state?

Comparable test evaluation is now available for out-of-state candidates. Contact the State Director of Assessment at the Oklahoma Commission for Teacher Preparation, (405) 525-2612, for more information.

How is the test content determined?

The Oklahoma Commission for Teacher Preparation (OCTP) has the responsibility of developing a competency-based testing program for teacher candidates. The assessment was designed to examine competency in the following areas: general education, subject area, and professional teaching knowledge. Candidates for teacher licensure/certification are required to successfully complete the Oklahoma General Education Test (OGET), the Oklahoma Subject Area Test (OSAT), and the Oklahoma Professional Teaching Examination (OPTE).

Who administers the OGET and OSAT?

OCTP has contracted with National Evaluation Systems (NES) and the Buros Center for Testing to assist in the development, validation, and administration of the assessments included in the Certification Examinations for Oklahoma Educators (CEOE) program.

When are the OGET and OSAT tests offered? How long is the testing time?

The OGET and OSAT tests are offered five times a year. Test sessions are determined by the type of test you are taking. The OGET is only given in the morning. OSATs are given in both the morning and the afternoon. Additional information is available from the Oklahoma Commission for Teacher Preparation. The department can be contacted as follows:

Oklahoma Commission for Teacher Preparation
4545 N. Lincoln Blvd., Suite 275
Oklahoma City, OK 73105-3418
Phone: 405-525-2612
Fax: 405-525-0373
E-mail: octp@octp.org
Website: *www.octp.org*

Is there a registration fee?

Yes. Only cashiers' checks, money orders, or credit cards (Visa and MasterCard) are accepted for test fee payment. Information on testing fees and registration can be found in the CEOE Registration Bulletin available online at *www.ceoe.nesinc.com*.

HOW TO USE THIS BOOK

What do I study first?

We recommend beginning your study with the comprehensive chapter reviews. It is important to read over each review, noting crucial test-taking suggestions and insights. By studying each review thoroughly, you will reinforce basic skills that are vital to performing well on the OGET and OSAT. After reviewing, take the practice tests. This will familiarize you with the actual exam's format, procedures, and level of difficulty. An added bonus to taking these practice tests is knowing what to expect on exam day.

Wisely scheduling your study time is also a key component to your success on the OGET/OSAT. To best utilize your study time, follow our flexible study schedule at the end of this chapter. The schedule is based ideally on a seven-week program, but can be condensed if needed.

When should I start studying for the OGET/OSAT tests?

It is never too early to start studying for your test. Time is your ally here. The earlier you begin, the more time you will have to sharpen your skills and focus your efforts. Do not procrastinate! Cramming is not an effective way to study, since it does not allow you enough time to learn what will be required of you. It takes time to learn the tested areas and test format. Make the most of your time while you have it. Use it well to master the essentials necessary to pass.

FORMAT OF THE OGET/OSAT TESTS

What is the basic format of the OGET/OSAT?

The OGET includes both selected-response questions and a single constructed-response (writing assignment) question. There are approximately 80–100 selected-response (multiple-choice) questions that account for approximately 80% of the test's scaled score. Each constructed-response question offers four possible answer choices. The writing assignment accounts for 20% of the total scaled test score.

The OSAT Elementary Education subtest 1 focuses on reading, language arts, and social studies. Subtest 1 contains approximately 40 selected-responses that account for 85% of your score. As with the OGET, the OSAT's selected-response questions offer four possible answers. Subtest 1's single constructed-response assignment accounts for 15% of your total scaled test score. The OSAT Elementary Education subtest 2 focuses on mathematics, science, health and fitness, and fine arts. Subtest 2 contains approximately 40 selected-response questions.

The constructed-response assignment is intended to assess subject knowledge and skills, not writing ability. However, your response must be communicated clearly enough to be scored. Your response to the constructed-response assignment will be evaluated on the basis of the following criteria:

- The extent to which your response answers the question

- The accuracy and appropriateness of subject matter knowledge

- The quality and relevance of your supporting details

- The soundness of your argument and your understanding of the subject matter

About the Subject Reviews

The subject reviews in this book are designed purposefully to provide you critical insight into the content and form of the OGET and OSAT. For smarter study, we break down this part of test preparation into more manageable "chunks." Before you begin reviewing, it is important to note that your own schooling experience has taught you most of what is needed to answer the questions on the actual tests. Our review is written to help you fit and shape information acquired over the years into a context ideally suited for taking the OGET and OSAT.

You may also be taking test preparation classes for the OGET and OSAT, or have purchased other study guides and textbooks. Reviewing class notes and textbooks along with our subject reviews will provide you with an even better foundation for passing the OGET and OSAT.

SCORING THE OGET/OSAT

Your test score report will be mailed to you and to the Oklahoma Commission for Teacher Preparation approximately four weeks after you take the test. Unofficial scores will be available for online access by 5 p.m. CT on the official score report mailing date for each test administration. To access your unofficial scores, go to *www.ceoe.nesinc.com* and follow the score retrieval instructions.

Total test scores are reported as scaled scores. For the OGET and OSAT, scaled scores are reported using a range from 100 to 300, with 240 as the minimum passing scaled score. Your score report will indicate whether you have passed the test and will include your total test score and a description of your performance on the major content subareas of the test. These scores will provide you with valuable information for identifying the strengths and weaknesses in your content preparation.

And finally, if you do not do well on test day, don't panic! Each test can be taken again, so you can work on improving your score on your next test. A score on the OGET or OSAT that does not match your expectations does not mean you should change your plans about teaching.

Test-Taking Strategies

Although you may not be familiar with tests like the OGET/OSAT, this book will help acquaint you with this type of exam and help alleviate test-taking anxieties. Here are the key ways you can more easily get into an OGET/OSAT state of mind:

Become comfortable with the format of the OGET/OSAT. Practice tests are the best way to learn the format of the OGET/OSAT. When you take a practice test, try to simulate the environmental conditions of the actual testing facility. Remember, you are in training for the OGET/OSAT, and simulated testing conditions will only help you perform better. Stay calm and pace yourself. After simulating a test even once, you boost your chances of doing well, and you will be able to sit down for the actual OGET/OSAT with much more confidence.

Read all the possible answers. Examine each answer choice to ensure that you are not making a mistake. Jumping to conclusions without considering all the answers is a common test-taking error.

Use the process of elimination. GUESS if you do not know. If you do not know the answer immediately after reading the answer choices, try to eliminate as many of the answers as possible. Eliminating just one or two answer choices gives you a far better chance of selecting the right answer.

Do not leave an answer blank. There is no penalty for wrong answers, and you might even get it right if you had to guess at the answer.

Familiarize yourself with the test's directions and content. Familiarizing yourself with the directions and content of the OGET/OSAT not only saves you valuable time, but can also aid in reducing anxiety before the test. Many mistakes are caused by anxiety. It's simply better to go in knowing what you will face.

Mark it right! Be sure that the answer oval you mark corresponds to the appropriate number in the test booklet. The test is multiple-choice and is graded by machine. Marking just one answer in the wrong place can throw off the rest of the test. Correcting an error like this will deprive you of precious test time.

The Day of the Test

Your admission ticket lists your test site, test date, and reporting time. Report to the test site no later than 7:30 a.m. for the morning session or 12:30 p.m. for the afternoon session. Testing is scheduled to begin approximately one half hour after the reporting time. If you arrive late to a test session, you may not be admitted. If you are admitted late, you will not be given any additional time beyond the scheduled ending time for the test session, and you will be required to sign a statement acknowledging this.

You **must** bring the following with you to the test site on test day:

- Your official admission ticket or a printout of your e-mail admission information (I-Ticket).

- Several sharpened No. 2 pencils with erasers (no pens); pencils will not be supplied at the test site.

- Two pieces of personal identification; one must contain a recent photograph.

After the Test

When you finish your test, hand in your materials and you will be dismissed. Then, you are free. Go home and relax. Meet with friends. Go out to dinner. Or go shopping. Whatever you do, make it a great day! After all you have done to get this far, you deserve it!

OGET/OSAT Study Schedule

The following study schedule allows for thorough preparation to pass the OGET/OSAT. This is a suggested seven-week course of study. This schedule can, however, be condensed if you have less time available to study, or expanded if you have more time. Whatever the length of your available study time, be sure to keep a structured schedule by setting aside ample time each day to study. Depending on your schedule, you may find it easier to study throughout the weekend. No matter which schedule works best for you, the more time you devote to studying for the OGET/OSAT, the more prepared and confident you will be on the day of the test.

Week	Activity
1	Take the practice test as a diagnostic exam. Your score will indicate where your strengths and weaknesses lie. Try to take the test under simulated exam conditions, and review the explanations for the questions you answered incorrectly.
2	Study the OGET/OSAT test objectives to get a better idea of the content on which you will be tested. You should make a list of the objectives that you know you will have the most trouble mastering so that you can concentrate your study on those areas.
3	Study *The Best Teachers' Test Preparation for the OGET/OSAT*. Take notes on the sections as you work through them, as writing will aid in your retention of information. Keep a list of the subject areas for which you may need additional aid.
4	Identify and review references and sources. Textbooks for college composition, science, social studies, arts, and mathematics courses will help in your preparation. You may also want to consult the Oklahoma curriculum website at *www.sde.state.ok.us*.
5	Condense your notes and findings. You should develop a structured outline detailing specific facts. You may want to use index cards to aid you in memorizing important facts and concepts.
6	Test yourself using the index cards. You may want to have a friend or colleague quiz you on key facts and items. Then, retake the drills and tests. Review the explanations for the questions you answered incorrectly.
7	Study any areas you consider to be your weaknesses by using your study materials, references, and notes. You may want to retake some tests.

OGET

Oklahoma General Education Test

Review

Critical Thinking Skills: Reading and Communications

The reading portion of the OGET asks you to utilize critical reading and reading comprehension skills. The objectives for this section of the test are to understand the main ideas of the passage based on the supporting evidence or details and to understand the author's purpose, point of view, and/or intended meaning.

You will be asked to read a passage and answer questions about the material included in that passage. The reading section is entirely multiple choice. It will be to your benefit to read the questions about the particular passage first. This will give you an idea of what to look for and focus on as you are reading. It is also crucial that you understand the passage as a whole and comprehend the overall intention, meaning, or main idea of the material you have read.

This review was developed to prepare you for the reading section of the OGET. You will be guided through a step-by-step approach to attacking reading passages and questions. Also included are tips to help you quickly and accurately answer the questions that will appear in this section. By studying this review, you will greatly increase your chances of achieving a good score on the reading section of the OGET.

Fast Facts

The more you know about the skills tested, the better you will perform on the test.

Remember, the more you know about the skills tested, the better you will perform on the test. In this section, the objectives you will be tested on are contained in the following list:

SUBAREA I—CRITICAL THINKING SKILLS: READING AND COMMUNICATIONS

Competency 0001

Identify a writer's point of view and intended meaning.

The following topics are examples of content that may be covered under this competency.
- Identify the statement that best expresses the main idea of a paragraph or passage.
- Recognize ideas that support, illustrate, or elaborate the main idea of a paragraph or passage.
- Use the content, word choice, and phrasing of a passage to determine a writer's opinions or point of view (e.g., belief, position on an issue).

Competency 0002

Analyze the relationship among ideas in written material.

The following topics are examples of content that may be covered under this competency.
- Identify the sequence of events or steps presented in technical, scientific, or research material.
- Identify cause-effect relationships from information in a passage.
- Analyze relationships between ideas in opposition (e.g., pro and con).
- Identify a solution to a problem presented in a passage.
- Draw conclusions inductively and deductively from information stated or implied in a passage.

Competency 0003

Use critical reasoning skills to evaluate written material.

The following topics are examples of content that may be covered under this competency.
- Draw valid conclusions using information from written communications.
- Recognize the stated or implied assumptions on which the validity of an argument depends.
- Determine the relevance or importance of particular facts, examples, or graphic data to a writer's argument.
- Use inductive and deductive reasoning to recognize fallacies in the logic of a writer's argument.
- Evaluate the validity of analogies used in written material.
- Distinguish between fact and opinion in written material.
- Assess the credibility, objectivity, or bias of the writer or source of written material.

Competency 0004

Recognize the roles of purpose and audience in written communication.

The following topics are examples of content that may be covered under this competency.
- Recognize a writer's stated or implied purpose for writing (e.g., to persuade, to describe).
- Evaluate the appropriateness of written material for a specific purpose or audience.
- Recognize the likely effect on an audience of a writer's choice of a particular word or words (e.g., to evoke sympathy, to undermine an opposing point of view).

Competency 0005

Recognize unity, focus, and development in writing.

The following topics are examples of content that may be covered under this competency.
- Recognize unnecessary shifts in point of view (e.g., shifts from first to third person) or distracting details that impair the development of the main idea in a piece of writing.
- Recognize revisions that improve the unity and focus of a piece of writing.
- Recognize examples of well-developed writing.

To help you master these skills, we present examples of the types of questions you will encounter and explanations of how to answer them.

The Passages

The reading passages in the reading section are designed to be on the level of the type of material encountered in college textbooks. They will present you with very diverse subjects. Although you will not be expected to have prior knowledge of the information presented in the passages, you will be expected to know the fundamental reading comprehension techniques presented in this chapter. Only your ability to read and comprehend material will be tested.

The Questions

Each passage will be followed by a number of questions. The questions will ask you to make determinations based on what you have read. You will commonly encounter questions that will ask you to:

- Determine which of the given answer choices best expresses the main idea of the passage.

- Determine the author's purpose in writing the passage.

- Determine which fact best supports the writer's main idea.

- Know the difference between fact and opinion in a statement.

- Organize the information in the passage.

- Determine which of the answer choices best summarizes the information presented in the passage.

- Recall information from the passage.

- Analyze cause-and-effect relationships based on information in the passage.

- Determine the definition of a word as it is used in the passage.

- Answer a question based on information presented in graphic form.

- Answer a question based on an excerpt from a table of contents or an index.

Strategies for the Reading Section

The following is a recommended plan of attack to follow when answering the questions in the reading section.

When reading the passage,

Step 1: Read quickly while keeping in mind that questions will follow.
Step 2: Uncover the main idea or theme of the passage. Many times it is contained within the first few lines of the passage.
Step 3: Uncover the main idea of each paragraph. Usually it is contained in either the first or last sentence of the paragraph.
Step 4: Skim over the detailed points of the passage while circling key words or phrases. These are words or phrases such as *but*, *on the other hand*, *although*, *however*, *yet*, and *except*.

When answering the questions,

Step 1: Approach each question one at a time. Read it carefully.

Step 2: Uncover the main idea or theme of the passage. Many times it is contained within the first few lines of the passage.

Step 3: If the question is asking for an answer that can only be found in a specific place in the passage, save it for last since this type of question requires you to go back to the passage and therefore takes more of your time.

Additional Tips

- Read over the questions before reading the passage. This will give you an idea of what you are reading for.

- Look over all the passages first and then attack the passages that seem easiest and most interesting.

- Identify and underline what sentences are the main ideas of each paragraph.

- If a question asks you to draw inferences, your answer should reflect what is implied in the passage, rather than what is directly stated.

- Use the context of the sentence to find the meaning of an unfamiliar word.

- Identify which sentences are example sentences and label them with an "E." Determine whether or not the writer is using facts or opinions.

- Circle key transitions and identify dominant patterns of organization.

- Make your final response and move on. Don't dawdle or get frustrated by the really troubling passages. If you haven't gotten answers after two attempts, answer as best you can and move on.

- If you have time at the end, go back to the passages that were difficult and review them.

A Four-Step Approach

When you take the reading section of the OGET, you will have two tasks: to read the passage, and to answer the questions.

Of the two, carefully reading the passage is the more important; answering the questions is based on an understanding of the passage. What follows is a four-step approach to reading:

> Step 1: preview
> Step 2: read actively
> Step 3: review the passage
> Step 4: answer the questions

You should study the following exercises and use these four steps when you complete the reading section of the OGET.

Step 1: Preview

A preview of the reading passage will give you a purpose and a reason for reading; previewing is a good strategy to use when taking a test. Before beginning to read the passage (usually a four-minute activity if you preview and review), you should take about thirty seconds to look over the passage and questions. An effective way to preview the passage is to quickly read the first sentence of each paragraph, the concluding sentence of the passage, and the questions—but not the answers—following the passage. A passage follows; practice previewing the passage by reading the first sentence of each paragraph and the last line of the passage.

A preview of the reading passage will give you a purpose and a reason for reading.

Fast Facts

Passage

That the area of obscenity and pornography is a difficult one for the Supreme Court is well documented. The Court's numerous attempts to define obscenity have proven unworkable and left the decision to the subjective preferences of the justices. Perhaps Justice Stewart put it best when, after refusing to define obscenity, he declared, but "I know it when I see it." Does the Court literally have to see it to know it? Specifically, what role does the fact-pattern, including the materials' medium, play in the Court's decision?

Several recent studies employ fact-pattern analysis in modeling the Court's decision making. These studies examine the fact-pattern or case characteristics, often with ideological and attitudinal factors, as a determinant of the decision reached by the Court. In broad terms, these studies owe their theoretical underpinnings to attitude theory. As the name suggests, attitude theory views the Court's attitudes as an explanation of its decisions.

These attitudes, however, do not operate in a vacuum. As Spaeth explains, "the activation of an attitude involves both an object and the situation in which that object is encountered." The objects to which the court directs its attitudes are litigants. The situation—the subject matter of the case—can be defined in broad or narrow terms. One may define the situation as an entire area of the law (e.g., civil liberties issues). On an even broader scale, the situation may be defined as the decision to grant certiorari or whether to defect from a minimum-winning coalition.

Defining the situation with such broad strokes, however, does not allow one to control for case content. In many specific issue areas, the cases present strikingly similar patterns. In examining the Court's search and seizure decisions, Segal found that a relatively small number of situational and case characteristic variables explain a high proportion of the Court's decisions.

Despite Segal's success, efforts to verify the applicability of fact-pattern analysis in other issue areas and using broad-based factors have been slow in forthcoming. Renewed interest in obscenity and pornography by federal and state governments as a result of lobbying campaigns by fundamentalist groups, the academic community, and other antipornography interest groups pro and con indicate the Court's decisions in this area deserve closer examination.

The Court's obscenity and pornography decisions also present an opportunity to study the Court's behavior in an area where the Court has granted significant decision-making authority to the states. In *Miller v. California* (1973) the Court announced the importance of local community standards in obscenity determinations. The Court's subsequent behavior may suggest how the Court will react in other areas where it has chosen to defer to the states (e.g., abortion).

Questions

1. The main idea of the passage is best stated in which of the following?

   A. The Supreme Court has difficulty convicting those who violate obscenity laws.

   B. The current definitions for obscenity and pornography provided by the Supreme Court are unworkable.

   C. Fact-pattern analysis is insufficient for determining the attitude of the Court toward the issues of obscenity and pornography.

   D. Despite the difficulties presented by fact-pattern analysis, Justice Segal found the solution in the patterns of search and seizure decisions.

2. The main purpose of the writer in this passage is to

    A. convince the reader that the Supreme Court is making decisions about obscenity based on their subjective views alone.

    B. explain to the reader how fact-pattern analysis works with respect to cases of obscenity and pornography.

    C. define obscenity and pornography for the layperson.

    D. demonstrate the role fact-pattern analysis plays in determining the Supreme Court's attitude about cases in obscenity and pornography.

3. Of the following, which fact best supports the writer's contention that the Court's decisions in the areas of obscenity and pornography deserve closer scrutiny?

    A. The fact that a Supreme Court Justice said, "I know it when I see it."

    B. Recent studies that employ fact-pattern analysis in modeling the Court's decision-making process.

    C. The fact that attitudes do not operate in a vacuum.

    D. The fact that federal and state governments, interested groups, and the academic community show renewed interest in the obscenity and pornography decisions by the Supreme Court.

4. Among the following statements, which states an opinion expressed by the writer rather than a fact?

    A. It is well documented that the area of obscenity and pornography is a difficult one for the Supreme Court.

    B. The objects to which a court directs its attitudes are the litigants.

    C. In many specific issue areas, the cases present strikingly similar fact-patterns.

    D. The Court's subsequent behavior may suggest how the Court will react in other legal areas.

5.   The group of topics in the list that follows that best reflects the organization of the topics of the passage is

A.   I.   The difficulties of the Supreme Court
     II.   Several recent studies
     III.   Spaeth's definition of *attitude*
     IV.   The similar patterns of cases
     V.   Other issue areas
     VI.   The case of *Miller v. California*

B.   I.   The Supreme Court, obscenity, and fact-pattern analysis
     II.   Fact-pattern analyses and attitude theory
     III.   The definition of *attitude* for the Court
     IV.   The definition of *situation*
     V.   The breakdown in fact-pattern analysis
     VI.   Studying Court behavior

C.   I.   Justice Stewart's view of pornography
     II.   Theoretical underpinnings
     III.   A minimum-winning coalition
     IV.   Search and seizure decisions
     V.   Renewed interest in obscenity and pornography
     VI.   The importance of local community standards

D.   I.   The Court's numerous attempts to define obscenity
     II.   Case characteristics
     III.   The subject matter of cases
     IV.   The Court's proportion of decisions
     V.   Broad-based factors
     VI.   Obscenity determination

6. Which paragraph among those that follow is the best summary of the passage?

    A. The Supreme Court's decision-making process with respect to obscenity and pornography has become too subjective. Fact-pattern analyses used to determine the overall attitude of the Court reveal only broad-based attitudes on the part of the Court toward the situations of obscenity cases. But these patterns cannot fully account for the Court's attitudes toward case content. Research is not conclusive on whether fact-pattern analyses work when applied to legal areas. Renewed public and local interest suggests continued study and close examination of how the Court makes decisions. Delegating authority to the states may reflect patterns for Court decisions in other socially sensitive areas.

    B. Though subjective, the Supreme Court decisions are well documented. Fact-pattern analyses reveal the attitude of the Supreme Court toward its decisions in cases. Spaeth explains that an attitude involves both an object and a situation. For the Court, the situation may be defined as the decision to grant certiorari. Cases present strikingly similar patterns, and a small number of variables explain a high proportion of the Court's decisions. Segal has made an effort to verify the applicability of fact-pattern analysis with some success. The Court's decisions on obscenity and pornography suggest weak Court behavior, such as in *Miller v. California*.

    C. To determine what obscenity and pornography mean to the Supreme Court, we must use fact-pattern analysis. Fact-pattern analysis reveals the ideas that the Court uses to operate in a vacuum. The litigants and the subject matter of cases are defined in broad terms (such as an entire area of law) to reveal the Court's decision-making process. Search and seizure cases reveal strikingly similar patterns, leaving the Court open to grant certiorari effectively. Renewed public interest in the Court's decisions proves how the Court will react in the future.

    D. Supreme Court decisions about pornography and obscenity are under examination and are out of control. The Court has to see the case to know it. Fact-pattern analyses reveal that the Court can only define cases in narrow terms, thus revealing individual egotism on the part of the Justices. As a result of strikingly similar patterns in search and seizure cases, the Court should be studied further for its weakness in delegating authority to state courts, as in the case of *Miller v. California*.

7. Based on the passage, the rationale for fact-pattern analyses arises out of what theoretical groundwork?

    A. Subjectivity theory

    B. The study of cultural norms

    C. Attitude theory

    D. Cybernetics

8. Based on data in the passage, what would most likely be the major cause for the difficulty in pinning down the Supreme Court's attitude toward cases of obscenity and pornography?

    A. The personal opinions of the Court Justices

    B. The broad nature of the situations of the cases

    C. The ineffective logistics of certiorari

    D. The inability of the Court to resolve the variables presented by individual case content

9. In the context of the passage, *subjective* might be most nearly defined as

    A. personal.

    B. wrong.

    C. focused.

    D. objective.

By previewing the passage, you should have read the following:

*   It is well documented that the areas of obscenity and pornography are difficult ones for the Supreme Court.

*   Several recent studies employ fact-pattern analysis in modeling the Court's decision making.

*   These attitudes, however, do not operate in a vacuum.

*   Defining the situation with such broad strokes, however, does not allow one to control for case content.

*   Despite Segal's success, efforts to verify the applicability of fact-pattern analysis in other issue areas and using broad-based factors have been slow in coming.

*   The Court's obscenity and pornography decisions also present an opportunity to study the Court's behavior in an area where the Court has granted significant decision-making authority to the states.

*   The Court's subsequent behavior may suggest how the Court will react in other areas where it has chosen to defer to the states (e.g., abortion).

These few sentences tell you much about the entire passage. As you begin to examine the passage, you should first determine the main idea of the passage and underline it so you can easily refer to it if a question requires you to do so (see question 1). The main idea should be found in the first paragraph of the passage, and may even be the first sentence. From what you have read thus far, you now know that the main idea of this passage is that the Supreme Court has difficulty in making static decisions about obscenity and pornography.

In addition, you also know that recent studies have used fact-pattern analysis in modeling the Court's decision. You have learned that attitudes do not operate independently and that case content is important. The feasibility of using fact-pattern analysis in other areas and broad-based factors have not been quickly verified. To study the behavior of the Court in an area in which they have granted significant decision-making authority to the states, one has only to consider the obscenity and pornography decisions. In summary, the author suggests that the Court's subsequent behavior may suggest how the Court will react in those other areas in which decision-making authority has previously been ceded to the states. As you can see, having this information will make the reading of the passage much easier.

You should have also looked at the stem of the question in your preview. You do not necessarily need to spend time reading the answers to each question in your preview. The stem alone can help to guide you as you read.

The stems in this case are

1.   The main idea of the passage is best stated in which of the following?

2.   The main purpose of the writer in this passage is to _____?

3.   Of the following, which fact best supports the writer's contention that the Court's decisions in the areas of obscenity and pornography deserve closer scrutiny?

4.   Among the following statements, which states an opinion expressed by the writer rather than a fact?

5.   The group of topics in the list that follows that best reflects the organization of the topics of the passage is _____.

6.   Which paragraph among those that follow is the best summary of the passage?

7.   Based on the passage, the rationale for fact-pattern analyses arises out of what theoretical groundwork?

8.   Based on data in the passage, what would most likely be the major cause for the difficulty in pinning down the Supreme Court's attitude toward cases of obscenity and pornography?

9.   In the context of the passage, *subjective* might be most nearly defined as _____.

Step 2: Read Actively

After your preview, you are now ready to read actively. This means that, as you read, you will be engaged in such things as underlining important words, topic sentences, main ideas, and words denoting the tone of a passage. If you think underlining can help you save time and help you remember the main ideas, feel free to use your pencil.

Read the first sentence of each paragraph carefully, since this often contains the topic of the paragraph. You may wish to underline each topic sentence.

During this stage, you should also determine the writer's purpose in writing the passage (see question 2), as this will help you focus on the main points and the writer's key points in the organization of a passage.

You can determine the author's purpose by asking yourself whether the relationship between the writer's main idea and evidence the writer uses answer one of the following four questions:

- What is the writer's primary goal or overall objective?

- Is the writer trying to persuade you by proving or using facts to make a case for an idea?

- Is the writer trying only to inform and enlighten you about an idea, object, or event?

- Is the writer attempting to amuse you? To keep you fascinated or laughing?

Read these examples and see whether you can decide what the primary purpose of the statements that follow might be.

(A) Jogging too late in life can cause more health problems than it solves. I will allow that the benefits of jogging are many: lowered blood pressure, increased vitality, better cardiovascular health, and better muscle tone. However, an older person may have a history of injury or chronic ailments that makes jogging counterproductive. For example, the elderly jogger may have hardening of the arteries, emphysema, or undiscovered aneurysms just waiting to burst and cause stroke or death. Chronic arthritis in the joints will only be aggravated by persistent irritation and use. Moreover, for those of us with injuries sustained in our youth—such as torn Achilles tendons or knee cartilage—jogging might just make a painful life more painful, cancelling out the benefits the exercise is intended to produce.

(B) Jogging is a sporting activity that exercises all the main muscle groups of the body. That the arms, legs, buttocks, and torso voluntary muscles are engaged goes without question. Running down a path makes you move your upper body as well as your lower body muscles. People do not often take into account, however, how the involuntary muscle system is also put through its paces. The heart, diaphragm, and even the eye and facial muscles take part as we hurl our bodies through space at speeds up to five miles per hour over distances as long as twenty-six miles and more for some.

(C) It seems to me that jogging styles are as identifying as fingerprints! People seem to be as individual in the way they run as they are in personality. Here comes the Duck, waddling down the track, little wings going twice as fast as the feet in an effort to stay upright. At about the quarter-mile mark, I see the Penguin, quite natty in the latest jogging suit, body stiff as a board from neck to ankles and the ankles flexing a mile a minute to cover the yards. And down there at the half-mile post—there goes the Giraffe—a tall fellow in a spotted electric yellow outfit, whose long strides cover about a dozen yards each, and whose neck waves around under some old army camouflage hat that may have served its time in a surplus store in the Bronx or in the Arabian desert. If you see the animals in the jogger woods once, you can identify them from miles away just by seeing their gait. And, by the way, be careful whose hoof you're stepping on, it may be mine!

In (A) the writer makes a statement that a number of people would debate and which isn't clearly demonstrated by science or considered common knowledge. In fact, common wisdom usually maintains the opposite thesis. Many would say that jogging improves the health of the aging—even to the point of slowing the aging process. As soon as you see a writer point to or identify *an issue open to debate* that stands in need of proof, he or she is setting out to persuade you that one side or the other is the more justified position. You'll notice, too, that the writer in this case takes a stand here. It's almost as if he or she is saying, "I have concluded that . . ." But a thesis or arguable idea is only a *hypothesis* until evidence is summoned by the writer to prove it. Effective arguments are based on serious, factual, or demonstrable evidence, not merely opinion.

In (B) the writer is just stating a fact. This is not a matter for debate. From here, the writer's evidence is to *explain* and *describe* what is meant by the fact. This is accomplished by *analyzing* (breaking down into its constituent elements) the way the different muscle groups come into play or do work when jogging, thus explaining the fact stated as a main point in the opening sentence. The assertion that jogging exercises all the muscle groups is not in question or a matter of debate. Besides taking the form of explaining how something works or what parts it comprises (for example, the basic parts of a bicycle are . . .), writers may show how the idea, object, or event functions. A writer may use this information to prove something. But if the writer doesn't argue to prove a debatable point one way or the other, then the purpose must be either to inform (as here) or to entertain.

In (C) the writer is taking a stand yet not attempting to prove anything; a lighthearted observation is made instead and nothing more. In addition, all of the examples used to support the statement are fanciful, funny, odd, or peculiar to the writer's particular vision. Joggers aren't *really* animals, after all.

Make sure to examine all the facts that the author uses to support the main idea. This will allow you to decide whether or not the writer has made a case, and what sort of purpose it supports. Look for supporting details—facts, examples, illustrations, the testimony or research of experts—that are relevant to the topic in question and show what the writer says is so. In fact, paragraphs and theses consist of *show* and *tell*. The writer *tells* you something is so or not so and then *shows* you facts, illustrations, expert testimony, or experiences to back up whatever is assertedly the case or is not the case. As you determine where the author's supporting details are, you may want to label them with an "S" so that you can refer back to them easily when answering questions (see question 3).

It is also important for you to be able to recognize the difference between the statements of fact presented versus statements of the author's opinion. You will be tested on this skill in this section of the test (see question 4). Look at the following examples. In each case ask yourself whether you are reading a fact or an opinion.

1.   Some roses are red.

2.   Roses are the most beautiful flower on Earth.

3.   After humans smell roses, they fall in love.

4.   Roses are the worst plants to grow in your backyard.

Item 1 is a fact. All you have to do is look at the evidence. Go to a florist. You will see that item 1 is true. A fact is anything that can be demonstrated to be objectively true in reality or which has been demonstrated to be true in reality and is documented by others. For example, the moon is orbiting about 250,000 miles from the Earth.

Item 2 is an opinion. The writer claims this as truth, but since it is a subjective quality (beauty), it remains to be seen. Others may hold different opinions. This is a matter of taste, not fact.

Item 3 is an opinion. There is probably some time-related coincidence between these two, but there is no verifiable, repeatable, or observable evidence that this is always true—at least not the way it is true that if you throw a ball into the air, it will come back down to Earth if left on its own without interference. Opinions have a way of sounding absolute; they are held by the writer with confidence, but are not facts that provide evidence.

Item 4, though perhaps sometimes true, is nevertheless a matter of opinion. Many variables contribute to the health of a plant in a garden: soil, temperature range, amount of moisture, and number and kinds of bugs. This is a debatable point for which the writer would have to provide evidence.

As you read, you should note the structure of the passage. There are several common structures for the passages. Some of these structures are described below.

Main Types of Paragraph Structures

1. The structure is a main idea plus supporting arguments.

2. The structure is a main idea plus examples.

3. The structure includes comparisons or contrasts.

4. There is a pro and a con structure.

5. The structure is chronological.

6. The structure has several different aspects of one idea.

For example, a passage on education in the United States in the 1600s and 1700s might first define education, then describe colonial education, then give information about separation of church and state, and then outline the opposing and supporting arguments regarding taxation as a source of educational funding. Being able to recognize these structures will help you recognize how the author has organized the passage.

Examining the structure of the passage will help you answer questions that ask you to organize (see question 5) the information in the passage or to summarize (see question 6) the information presented in that passage.

For example, if you see a writer using a transitional pattern that reflects a sequence moving forward in time, such as "In 1982 . . . Then, in the next five years . . . A decade later, in 1997, the . . .," chances are the writer is telling a story, history, or the like. Writers often use transitions of classification to analyze an idea, object, or event. They may say something like, "The first part . . . Secondly . . . Thirdly . . . Finally . . ." You may then ask yourself what the analysis is for. Is it to explain or to persuade you of something? These transitional patterns may also help reveal the relationship of one part of a passage to another. For example, a writer may be writing, "On the one hand . . . On the other hand . . ." This should alert you to the fact that the writer is comparing two things or contrasting them. What for? Is one better than the other? Worse?

By understanding the *relationship* among the main point, transitions, and supporting information, you may more readily determine the pattern of organization as well as the writer's purpose in a given piece of writing.

As with the paragraph examples above showing the difference among possible purposes, you must look at the relationship between the facts or information presented (that's the show part) and what the writer is trying to point out to you (that's the tell part) with that data. For example, a discussion presented about education in the 1600s might be used

- to prove that it was a failure (a form of argument).

- to show that it consisted of these elements (an analysis of the status of education during that time).

- to show that education during that time was silly.

To understand the author's purpose, the main point and the evidence that supports it must be considered together to be understood. To be meaningful, a controlling or main point is needed. You need to know if that main point is missing. You need to be able to distinguish between the writer showing data and the writer making a point.

In the two paragraphs that follow, consider the different relationship between the same data above and the controlling statement, and how that controlling statement changes the discussion from explanation to argument.

(A) Colonial education was different than today's education and consisted of several elements. Education in those days meant primarily studying the three "R's" (Reading, 'Riting, and 'Rithmetic) and the Bible. The church and state were more closely aligned with one another—education was, after all, for the purpose of serving God better, not to make more money.

(B) Colonial "education" was really just a way to create a captive audience for churches. Education in those days meant studying the three "R's" in order to learn God's word— the Bible—not commerce. The churches and the state were closely aligned with one another, and what was good for the church was good for the state—or else you were excommunicated, which kept you out of Heaven for sure.

The same informational areas are brought up in both cases, but in choice A the writer treats it more analytically ("consisted of several elements"), not taking as debatable a stand on the issue. However, the controlling statement in choice B puts forth a more volatile hypothesis, and then uses the same information to support that hypothesis.

Step 3: Review the Passage

After you finish reading actively, take ten or twenty seconds to look over the main idea and the topic sentences that you have underlined, and the key words and phrases you have marked. Now you are ready to enter Step 4 and answer the questions.

Step 4: Answer the Questions

In Step 2, you gathered enough information from the passage to answer questions dealing with main idea, purpose, support, fact vs. opinion, organization, and summarization. Let's look again at these questions.

Main Idea Questions

Looking back at the questions that follow the passage, you should see that question 1 is a *main idea* question.

1.   The main idea of the passage is best stated in which of the following?

    A.   The Supreme Court has difficulty convicting those who violate obscenity laws.

    B.   The current definitions for obscenity and pornography provided by the Supreme Court are unworkable.

    C.   Fact-pattern analysis is insufficient for determining the attitude of the Court toward the issues of obscenity and pornography.

    D.   Despite the difficulties presented by fact-pattern analysis, Justice Segal found the solution in the patterns of search and seizure decisions.

In answering the question, you see that answer choice C is correct. The writer uses the second, third, fourth, and fifth paragraphs to show how fact-pattern analysis is an ineffective determinant of the Supreme Court's attitudes toward obscenity and pornography.

Choice A is incorrect. Nothing is ever said directly about *convicting* persons accused of obscenity, only that the Court has difficulty defining it.

Choice B is also incorrect. Though the writer states it as a fact, it is only used as an effect that leads the writer to examine how fact-pattern analysis does or does not work to reveal the "cause" or attitude of the Court toward obscenity and pornography.

Also, answer choice D is incorrect. The statement is contrary to what Segal found when he examined search and seizure cases.

Purpose Questions

In examining question 2, you see that you must determine the author's purpose in writing the passage:

2.   The main purpose of the writer in this passage is to

   A.   convince the reader that the Supreme Court is making decisions about obscenity based on their subjective views alone.

   B.   explain to the reader how fact-pattern analysis works with respect to cases of obscenity and pornography.

   C.   define obscenity and pornography for the layperson.

   D.   demonstrate the role fact-pattern analysis plays in determining the Supreme Court's attitude about cases in obscenity and pornography.

Looking at the answer choices, you should see that choice D is correct. Though the writer never states it directly, the data is consistently summoned to show that fact-pattern analysis only gives us part of the picture, or "broad strokes" about the Court's attitude, but cannot account for the attitude toward individual cases.

Choice A is incorrect. The writer doesn't try to convince us of this fact, but merely states it as an opinion resulting from the evidence derived from the "well-documented" background of the problem.

B is also incorrect. The writer not only explains the role of fact-pattern analysis but also rather shows how it cannot fully apply.

The passage is about the Court's difficulty in defining these terms, not the man or woman in the street. Nowhere do definitions for these terms appear. Therefore, choice C is incorrect.

Support Questions

Question 3 requires you to analyze the author's supporting details.

3.   Of the following, which fact best supports the writer's contention that the Court's decisions in the areas of obscenity and pornography deserve closer scrutiny?

   A.   The fact that a Supreme Court Justice said, "I know it when I see it."

   B.   Recent studies that employ fact-pattern analysis in modeling the Court's decision-making process.

   C.   The fact that attitudes do not operate in a vacuum.

   D.   The fact that federal and state governments, interested groups, and the academic community show renewed interest in the obscenity and pornography decisions by the Supreme Court.

Look at the answer choices to answer this question. Choice D must be correct. In the fifth paragraph, the writer states that the "renewed interest"—a real and observable fact—from these groups "indicates the Court's decisions . . . deserve closer examination," another way of saying scrutiny.

Choice A is incorrect. The writer uses this remark to show how the Court cannot effectively define obscenity and pornography, relying on "subjective preferences" to resolve issues.

In addition, choice B is incorrect because the writer points to the data in D, not fact-pattern analyses, to prove this. C, too, is incorrect. Although it is true, the writer makes this point to show how fact-pattern analysis doesn't help clear up the real-world situations in which the Court must make its decisions.

Fact vs. Opinion Questions

By examining question 4, you can see that you are required to know the difference between fact and opinion.

4.   Among the following statements, which states an opinion expressed by the writer rather than a fact?

   A.   It is well documented that the area of obscenity and pornography is a difficult one for the Supreme Court.

   B.   The objects to which a court directs its attitudes are the litigants.

   C.   In many specific issue areas, the cases present strikingly similar fact-patterns.

   D.   The Court's subsequent behavior may suggest how the Court will react in other legal areas.

Keeping in mind that an opinion is something that is yet to be proven to be the case, you can determine that choice D is correct. It is the only statement among the four for which evidence is yet to be gathered. It is the writer's opinion that this may be a way to predict the Court's attitudes.

A, B, and C are all derived from verifiable data or documentation, and are therefore incorrect.

Organization Questions

Question 5 asks you to organize given topics to reflect the organization of the passage.

5.   The group of topics in the list that follows that best reflects the organization of the topics of the passage is

   A.   I. The difficulties of the Supreme Court
   II. Several recent studies
   III. Spaeth's definition of *attitude*
   IV. The similar patterns of cases
   V. Other issue areas
   VI. The case of *Miller v. California*

   B.   I. The Supreme Court, obscenity, and fact-pattern analysis
   II. Fact-pattern analyses and attitude theory
   III. The definition of *attitude* for the Court
   IV. The definition of *situation*
   V. The breakdown in fact-pattern analysis
   VI. Studying Court behavior

   C.   I. Justice Stewart's view of pornography
   II. Theoretical underpinnings
   III. A minimum-winning coalition
   IV. Search and seizure decisions
   V. Renewed interest in obscenity and pornography
   VI. The importance of local community standards

   D.   I. The Court's numerous attempts to define obscenity
   II. Case characteristics
   III. The subject matter of cases
   IV. The Court's proportion of decisions
   V. Broad-based factors
   VI. Obscenity determination

After examining all of the choices, you will determine that choice B is the correct response. These topical areas lead directly to the implied thesis that the "role" of fact-pattern analysis is insufficient to determine the attitude of the Supreme Court in the areas of obscenity and pornography.

Choice A is incorrect because the first topic stated in the list is not the topic of the first paragraph. It is too global. The first paragraph is about the difficulties the Court has with defining obscenity and how fact-pattern analysis might be used to determine the Court's attitude and clear up the problem.

C is incorrect because each of the items listed in this topic list represents supporting evidence or data for the real topic of each paragraph. (See the list in B for correct topics.) For example, Justice Stewart's statement about pornography is only cited to indicate the nature of the problem the Court has with obscenity. It is not the focus of the paragraph itself.

Finally, D is incorrect. As with choice C, these are all incidental pieces of information or data used to support broader points.

Summarization Questions

To answer question 6, you must be able to summarize the passage.

6.   Which paragraph among those that follow is the best summary of the passage?

A.   The Supreme Court's decision-making process with respect to obscenity and pornography has become too subjective. Fact-pattern analyses used to determine the overall attitude of the Court reveal only broad-based attitudes on the part of the Court toward the situations of obscenity cases. But these patterns cannot fully account for the Court's attitudes toward case content. Research is not conclusive on whether fact-pattern analyses work when applied to legal areas. Renewed public and local interest suggests continued study and close examination of how the Court makes decisions. Delegating authority to the states may reflect patterns for Court decisions in other socially sensitive areas.

B.   Though subjective, the Supreme Court decisions are well documented. Fact-pattern analyses reveal the attitude of the Supreme Court toward its decisions in cases. Spaeth explains that an attitude involves both an object and a situation. For the Court, the situation may be defined as the decision to grant certiorari. Cases present strikingly similar patterns, and a small number of variables explain a high proportion of the Court's decisions. Segal has made an effort to verify the applicability of fact-pattern analysis with some success. The Court's decisions on obscenity and pornography suggest weak Court behavior, such as in *Miller v. California*.

C.   To determine what obscenity and pornography mean to the Supreme Court, we must use fact-pattern analysis. Fact-pattern analysis reveals the ideas that the Court uses to operate in a vacuum. The litigants and the subject matter of cases are defined in broad terms (such as an entire area of law) to reveal the Court's decision-making process. Search and seizure cases reveal strikingly similar patterns, leaving the Court open to grant certiorari effectively. Renewed public interest in the Court's decisions proves how the Court will react in the future.

D.   Supreme Court decisions about pornography and obscenity are under examination and are out of control. The Court has to see the case to know it. Fact-pattern analyses reveal that the Court can only define cases in narrow terms, thus revealing individual egotism on the part of the Justices. As a result of strikingly similar patterns in search and seizure cases, the Court should be studied further for its weakness in delegating authority to state courts, as in the case of *Miller v. California*.

The paragraph that best and most accurately reports what the writer demonstrated based on the implied thesis is answer choice C, which is correct.

Choice A is incorrect because, while it reflects some of the evidence presented in the passage, the passage does not imply that all Court decisions are subjective, just the ones about pornography and obscenity. Similarly, the writer does not suggest that ceding authority to the states (as in *Miller v. California*) is a sign of some weakness, but merely that it is worthy of study as a tool for predicting or identifying the Court attitudes.

Response B is also incorrect. The writer summons information over and over to show how fact-pattern analysis cannot pin down the Court's attitude toward case content.

D is incorrect. Nowhere does the writer say or suggest that the justice system is "out of control" or that the justices are "egotists," only that they are liable to be reduced to being "subjective" rather than having a cogent and identifiable shared standard.

At this point, the three remaining question types must be discussed: recall questions (see question 7), cause/effect questions (see question 8), and definition questions (question 9). They are as follows.

Recall Questions

To answer question 7, you must be able to recall information from the passage.

7. Based on the passage, the rationale for fact-pattern analyses arises out of what theoretical groundwork?

    A. Subjectivity theory

    B. The study of cultural norms

    C. Attitude theory

    D. Cybernetics

The easiest way to answer this question is to refer back to the passage. In the second paragraph, the writer states that recent studies using fact-pattern analyses "owe their theoretical underpinnings to attitude theory." Therefore, we can conclude that response C is correct.

Answer choices A, B, and D are incorrect, as they are never discussed or mentioned by the writer.

Cause/Effect Questions

Question 8 requires you to analyze a cause-and-effect relationship.

8. Based on data in the passage, what would most likely be the major cause for the difficulty in pinning down the Supreme Court's attitude toward cases of obscenity and pornography?

   A. The personal opinions of the Court Justices

   B. The broad nature of the situations of the cases

   C. The ineffective logistics of certiorari

   D. The inability of the Court to resolve the variables presented by individual case content

Choice D is correct, as it is precisely what fact-pattern analyses cannot resolve.

Response A is incorrect because no evidence is presented for it; all that is mentioned is that they do make personal decisions. Answer choice B is incorrect because it is one way in which fact-pattern analysis can be helpful. Finally, C is only a statement about certiorari being difficult to administer, and this was never claimed about them by the writer in the first place.

Definition Questions

Returning to question 9, we can now determine an answer.

9. In the context of the passage, *subjective* might be most nearly defined as

   A. personal.

   B. wrong.

   C. focused.

   D. objective.

Choice A is best. By taking in and noting the example of Justice Stewart provided by the writer, we can see that Justice Stewart's comment is not an example of right or wrong. Most of the time, if we are talking about people's "preferences," they are usually about taste or quality, and they are usually not a result of scientific study or clear reasoning, but arise out of personal taste, idiosyncratic intuitions, et cetera. Thus, A is the most likely choice.

C is incorrect because the Court's focus is already in place: on obscenity and pornography. Choice B is incorrect. Nothing is implied or stated about the tightness or wrongness of the decisions themselves. Rather it is the definition of obscenity that seems "unworkable." D is also incorrect. Objective is an antonym of subjective in this context. To reason based on the object of study is the opposite of reasoning based upon the beliefs, opinions, or ideas of the one viewing the object, rather than the evidence presented by the object itself, independent of the observer.

You may not have been familiar with the word subjective, but from your understanding of the writer's intent, you should have been able to figure out what was being sought. Surrounding words and phrases almost always offer you some clues in determining the meaning of a word. In addition, any examples that appear in the text may also provide some hints.

Interpretation of Graphic Information Questions

Graphs, charts, and tables may play a large part on the OGET, and you should be familiar with them. More than likely, you will encounter at least one passage that is accompanied by some form of graphic information. You will then be required to answer any question(s) based on the interpretation of the information presented in the graph, chart, or table.

Graphs are used to produce visual aids for sets of information. Often, the impact of numbers and statistics is diminished by an overabundance of tedious numbers. A graph helps a reader rapidly visualize or organize irregular information, as well as trace long periods of decline or increase. The following is a guide to reading the three principal graphic forms that you will encounter when taking the OGET.

Line Graphs

IMMIGRATION TO THE UNITED STATES, 1820–1930

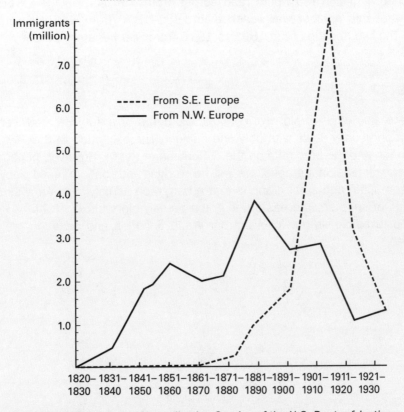

Source: Immigration and Naturalization Service of the U.S. Dept. of Justice

Line graphs are used to track multiple elements of one or more subjects. One element is usually a time factor, over whose span the other element increases, decreases, or remains static. The lines that compose such graphs are connected points that are displayed on the chart through each integral stage. For example, look at the preceding immigration graph.

The average number of immigrants from 1820 to 1830 is represented at one point; the average number of immigrants from 1831 to 1840 is represented at the next. The line that connects these points is used only to ease the visual gradation between the points. It is not meant to give a strictly accurate representation for every year between the two decades. If this were so, the line would hardly be straight, even progression from year to year. The sharp directness of the lines reveals otherwise. The purpose of the graph is to plot the average increases or decreases from point to point. When dealing with more than one subject, a line graph must use either differently colored lines or different types of lines if the graph is black-and-white. In the graph, the dark bold line represents immigration from Northwestern Europe; the broken line represents immigration from Southeastern Europe.

To read a line graph, find the point of change that interests you. For example, if you want to trace immigration from Northwestern Europe from 1861 to 1870, you would find the position of the dark line on that point. Next, trace the position to the vertical information on the chart. In this instance, one would discover that approximately 2 million immigrants arrived from Northwestern Europe in the period of time from 1861 to 1870. If wishing to discover when the number of immigrants reached 4 million you would read across from 4 million on the vertical side of the graph, and see that this number was reached in 1881–1890 from Northwestern Europe, and somewhere over the two decades from 1891 to 1910 from Southeastern Europe.

Bar Graphs

Bar graphs are also used to plot two dynamic elements of a subject. However, unlike a line graph, the bar graph usually deals with only one subject. The exception to this is when the graph is three-dimensional, and the bars take on the dimension of depth. However, because we will only be dealing with two-dimensional graphs, we will be working with only a single subject. The other difference between a line and a bar graph is that a bar graph usually calls for a single element to be traced in terms of another, whereas a line graph usually plots either of the two elements with equal interest. For example, in the following bar graph, inflation and deflation are being marked over a span of years.

INFLATION

Inflation is a rise in the general level of prices.
Deflation is a decline in the general level of prices.

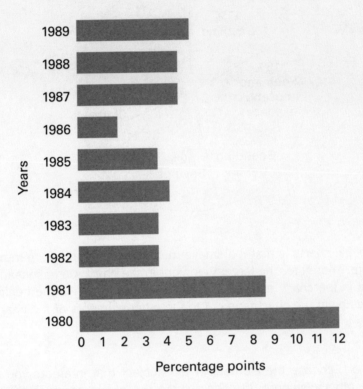

Percentage points are assigned to each year's level of prices, and that percentage decreases (deflation) from 1980 to 1981, and from 1981 to 1982. The price level is static from 1982 to 1983. The price level then increases (inflation) from 1983 to 1984. Therefore, it is obvious that the bar graph is read strictly in terms of the changes exhibited over a period of time or against some other element. Conversely, a line graph is used to plot two dynamic elements of equal interest to the reader (e.g., either number of immigrants or the particular decade in question).

To read a bar graph, simply begin with the element at the base of a bar and trace the bar to its full length. Once reaching its length, cross-reference the other element of information that matches the length of the bar.

Pie Charts

Pie charts differ greatly from line or bar graphs. Pie charts are used to help a reader visualize percentages of information with many elements to the subject. An entire "pie" represents 100 percent of a given quantity of information. The pie is then sliced into measurements that correspond to their respective shares of the 100 percent. For example, in the pie chart that follows, Myrna's rent occupies a slice greater than any other in the pie, because no other element equals or exceeds 25 percent of Myrna's monthly budget.

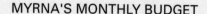

MYRNA'S MONTHLY BUDGET

Another aspect of pie charts is that the smaller percentage elements are moved consecutively to the larger elements. Therefore, the largest element in the chart will necessarily be adjacent to the smallest element in the chart, and the line that separates them is the beginning or endpoint of the chart. From this point the chart fans out to the other elements of the chart, going from the smallest percentages to the largest.

To read a pie chart, choose the element of the subject that interests you and compare its size to those of the other elements. In cases where the elements are similar in size, do not assume that they are equal. The exact percentage of the element will be listed within that slice of the chart. For example, Myrna's utilities, savings, and spending money are all similar in size, but it is clear when reading the chart that each possesses a different value.

Reading Tables

Tables are useful because they relate to large bodies of information within a confined area. To read a table, cross-reference the column headings that run horizontally across the top of the table with the row headings that run vertically down the left side of the table. Scanning the table for the overall information within is usually done by reading line by line, as if reading regular text, while referring to the appropriate headings of the table to interpret the information listed. Note that some tables possess horizontal subheadings, which further ease the separation of different areas of information.

Effects of Common Drugs

Drug	Psychological Dependence	Physical Dependence	Physical Withdrawal Effects	Development of Tolerance
Depressants				
Alcohol	Mild to very strong	Very strong	Severe/dangerous	Minimal
Barbiturates	Develops slowly	Develops slowly	Death possible	Minimal
Narcotics				
Opiates (heroin, morphine)	Very strong; develops rapidly	Rapid/increases with dosage	Frightening symptoms but not dangerous	Very high; Goes down quickly after withdrawal (Danger if user returns to original dose)
Stimulants				
Amphetamines	Strong	Not in formal sense, but body seeks "rush"	Mild	Extremely high
Cocaine	Very strong	None	None (can cause heart spasms and instant death even if healthy)	None
Crack	Strong	Strong	Mild	High
Psychedelics				
LSD	Unpredictable	None	None	Extremely high
Marijuana	Mild to strong	Some, in high doses	None	None (Some to high doses)

To use the preceding table, one should simply choose a particular drug, and then find the appropriate information needed about that drug through the headings listed at the top of the table. For example, the physical withdrawal effects of amphetamines, a stimulant drug, are mild in effect.

Helpful Hints

You should approach any graphic information you encounter as a key to a larger body of information in abbreviated form. Be sure to use the visual aids of the graphics (e.g., the size of slices on pie charts) as aids only; do not ignore the written information listed on the graph, table, et cetera.

Note especially the title and headings so that you know exactly what it is at which you are looking. Also, be aware of the source of the information, where applicable. Know what each element of the graphic information represents; this will help you compare how drastic or subtle any changes are, and over what span of time they take place. Be sure you realize what the actual numbers represent, whether it is dollars, so many thousands of people, millions of shares, and so forth. Finally, note the way in which the graphic information relates to the text it seeks to illustrate; know in what ways the graphic information supports the arguments of the author of the given passage.

Communication Skills

The communication skills portion of the OGET asks the test taker to use skills in the areas of grammar and composition. The objectives for this section of the test are to recognize correct and incorrect grammar and usage and to recognize good and bad features of various kinds of writing.

Test takers will be asked to read a passage and answer questions about the words or punctuation included in that passage. You may also be asked to fill in a blank with a sentence or phrase that makes the passage more effective. When taking the test, you should skip ahead to read the questions about the particular passage first. This will give you an idea of what to look for and focus on as you are reading. It is also important that you understand the passage as a whole and comprehend its overall intention, meaning, or main idea.

This review was developed to prepare you for the communication skills section of the OGET. You will be guided through a step-by-step approach to attacking reading passages and questions. Also included are tips to help you quickly and accurately answer the questions. By studying this review, you will greatly increase your chances of achieving a good score on the communication skills section of the OGET.

SUBAREA II—COMMUNICATION SKILLS

Competency 0006

Recognize effective organization in writing.

The following topics are examples of content that may be covered under this competency.
- Recognize methods of paragraph organization.
- Reorganize sentences to improve cohesion and the effective sequence of ideas.
- Recognize the appropriate use of transitional words or phrases to convey text structure (e.g., however, therefore).

Competency 0007

Recognize sentences that effectively communicate intended messages.

The following topics are examples of content that may be covered under this competency.
- Recognize ineffective repetition and inefficiency in sentence construction.
- Identify effective placement of modifiers, parallel structure, and use of negatives in sentence formation.
- Recognize imprecise and inappropriate word choices.

Competency 0008

Recognize standard conventions of formal written English usage in the United States.

The following topics are examples of content that may be covered under this competency.
- Recognize the standard use of verb forms.
- Recognize the standard use of pronouns.
- Recognize the standard formation and use of adverbs, adjectives, comparatives and superlatives, and plural and possessive forms of nouns.
- Recognize standard punctuation.
- Identify sentence fragments and run-on sentences (e.g., fused sentences, comma splices).
- Identify standard subject-verb agreement.

To help you master these skills, we present examples of the types of questions you will encounter and explanations of how to answer them. A drill section is also provided for further practice. Even if you are sure you will perform well on this section, be sure to complete the drills, as they will help sharpen your skills.

The Reading Passages

The reading passages in this section are designed for several different audiences. The readings will present you with very diverse subjects. Although you will not be expected to have prior knowledge of the information presented in the passages, you will be expected to know the fundamental writing techniques needed to convey the passage's message to its intended audience. Only your ability to write standard English for a specific audience will be tested. For example, you may get a passage like this one, written for a high-school history textbook:

[1]After the Civil War, raw cotton regained its traditional role as America's largest export good. [2]From 1803 to 1937, the Civil War and two other years excluded, unprocessed cotton was America's largest merchandise export. [3]The United States was also an important exporter of grain and mineral products. [4]What most characterized the growth of American exports in the late nineteenth century, _____, was the rise of manufactured goods exports: refined petroleum, machinery, and other manufactured goods. [5]Most of these goods were mass-produced products made by methods that were not used abroad, such as sewing machines, harvesters, and, later, automobiles). [6]Exports, increased rapidly, as American goods became highly competitive in world markets.

[7]Exports rose even faster than imports, with the consequence that exports always exceeded imports until 1971. [8]When the balance of trade remained consistently positive, Americans gradually recognized that a high tariff policy was no longer necessary or even desirable. [9]In 1913, with traditionally low-tariff Democrats in control of Congress, the Underwood Tariff lowered duties substantially. [10]International commerce expanded faster in the late nineteenth and early twentieth centuries than did worldwide output, with the gold standard aiding in this growth.

The Questions

Each passage will be followed by a number of questions. Some questions may ask you to find mistakes in standard English usage; others may ask you to supply appropriate words or phrases in blanks. You will commonly encounter questions that will ask you to:

- Identify the incorrect use of words.

- Identify the incorrect use of punctuation.

- Determine which sentence best makes the transition from one thought to another.

- Determine which word or phrase would be best for a specific audience.

- Determine the type of organization the author of the passage is using.

For example, questions for the passage above might be like these:

1. Which of the following parts does not use standard punctuation?

    A. Part 2

    B. Part 6

    C. Part 8

    D. Part 9

2. Which of the following words used in the blank in Part 4 would make a good transition from the previous sentence?

    A. consequently

    B. moreover

    C. nevertheless

    D. however

(Note that superscripted numbers in the passage are referred to in the answers as "Part X.")

Sentence Structure

Parallelism

Sentences should use the same kind of grammatical construction for all items in a series—those usually joined by a coordinating conjunction (*and, but, or,* and *nor*). "No smoking, eating, or drinking" is parallel; "No smoking, food, or drinking" is not, because *food* is not a verb form. Making elements parallel also requires knowledge of parallel correlative pairs, that is, the use of appropriate pairs together: *neither* and *nor, either* and *or, both* with *and, whether* with *or,* and *not only* with *but also.*

Parallel structure is used to express matching ideas. It refers to the grammatical balance of a series of any of the following:

> **Phrases.** The squirrel ran *along the fence, up the tree,* and *into his hole* with a mouthful of acorns.

> **Adjectives.** The job market is flooded with *very talented, highly motivated,* and *well-educated* young people.

Nouns. You will need a *notebook, pencil,* and *dictionary* for the test.

Clauses. The children were told to decide *which toy they would keep* and *which toy they would give away.*

Verbs. The farmer *plowed, planted,* and *harvested* his corn in record time.

Verbals. *Reading, writing,* and *calculating* are fundamental skills we should all possess.

Correlative Conjunctions. *Either* you will do your homework *or* you will fail. ***Note:*** Correlative conjunctions must be used as pairs and not mixed with other conjunctions, such as *neither* with *or* or *not only* with *also.*

Near-parallelisms. Sometimes a string of seemingly parallel thoughts are not in fact parallel. Consider this sentence: "I *have quit* my job, *enrolled* in school, and *am looking* for a reliable babysitter." In this sentence the writer has already *quit* and *enrolled* but is still looking for a babysitter; therefore she cannot include all three in a parallel structure. A good revision of this sentence is, "I have quit my job and enrolled in school, and I am looking for a babysitter."

Misplaced and Dangling Modifiers

Many people, probably including at least some parents of your students, consider misplaced and dangling modifiers to be a sure sign of ignorance about the English language. Although this belief on their part may be unfair, teachers need to be aware that it is firmly held. As the name suggests, a misplaced modifier is one that is in the wrong place in the sentence. Misplaced modifiers come in all forms—words, phrases, and clauses. Sentences containing misplaced modifiers are often very comical: *Mom made me eat the spinach instead of my brother.* Misplaced modifiers, like the one in this sentence, are usually too far away from the word or words they modify. This sentence should read *Mom made me, instead of my brother, eat the spinach.*

Such modifiers as *only, nearly,* and *almost* should be placed next to the word they modify and not in front of some other word, especially a verb, that they are not intended to modify. For example, *I only sang for one reason* is wrong if the writer means to say that there was *only one* reason for singing.

A modifier is misplaced if it appears to modify the wrong part of the sentence or if the reader cannot be certain what part of the sentence the writer intended it to modify. To correct a misplaced modifier, move the modifier next to the word it describes.

UNREVISED: She served hamburgers to the men on paper plates.

REVISED: She served hamburgers on paper plates to the men.

A **squinting modifier** is one that may refer to either a preceding or a following word, leaving the reader uncertain about what it is intended to modify. Correct a squinting modifier by moving it next to the word it is intended to modify.

UNREVISED: Snipers who fired on the soldiers often escaped capture.

REVISED: Snipers who often fired on the soldiers escaped capture. OR
Snipers who fired on the soldiers escaped capture often.

A **dangling modifier** is a modifier or verb in search of a subject: the modifying phrase (usually a participle phrase—an -ing word group or an -ed or an -en word group—or an infinitive phrase—a to + verb word group) has nothing to modify. It is figuratively dangling at the beginning or the end of a sentence. The sentences often look and sound correct at first glance: To be a student government officer, your grades must be above average. However, the verbal modifier has nothing to describe. You are supposed to be a student government officer; your grades cannot become an officer.

To correct a dangling modifier, reword the sentence by either (1) changing the modifying phrase to a clause with a subject, or (2) changing the subject of the sentence to the word that should be modified. Here are some other examples of correct revision of dangling modifiers:

UNREVISED: Shortly after leaving home, the accident occurred.

REVISED: Shortly after we left home, the accident occurred.

UNREVISED: To get up on time, a great effort was needed.

REVISED: To get up on time, I made a great effort.

Sentence Fragments

A fragment is an incomplete construction that either (1) lacks a subject or a verb or (2) is preceded by a subordinating conjunction (e.g., *because, which, when, although*). A complete construction, such as a sentence or an independent clause, expresses a complete thought.

UNREVISED: Traffic was stalled for ten miles on the freeway. Because repairs were being made on potholes. (The second "sentence" is a dependent, or subordinate, clause.)

REVISED: Traffic was stalled for ten miles on the freeway because repairs were being made on potholes.

UNREVISED: It was a funny story. One that I had never heard before. (The second "sentence" has no verb for its subject, "One.")

REVISED: It was a funny story, one that I had never heard.

Run-On/Fused Sentences

A run-on, or fused, sentence is not necessarily a long sentence or a sentence that the reader considers too long; in fact, a run-on might consist of two short sentences: *Dry ice does not melt it evaporates.* A run-on results when the writer fuses, or runs together, two separate sentences without any correct mark of punctuation separating them.

UNREVISED: Knowing how to use a dictionary is no problem each dictionary has a section in the front of the book that tells you how.

REVISED: Knowing how to use a dictionary is no problem. Each dictionary has a section in the front of the book that tells you how.

The most common type of run-on sentence is characterized by a comma splice—the incorrect use of only a comma to separate what are really two separate sentences. There are three quick ways to fix a comma splice: (1) replace the comma with a period and start a new sentence; (2) replace the comma with a semicolon; and (3) add a coordinating conjunction, such as *and* or *but,* after the comma.

UNREVISED: Bob bought dress shoes, a suit, and a nice shirt, he needed them for his sister's wedding.

REVISED: Bob bought dress shoes, a suit, and a nice shirt. He needed them for his sister's wedding.

UNREVISED: One common error in writing is incorrect spelling, the other is the occasional use of faulty diction.

REVISED: One common error in writing is incorrect spelling; the other is the occasional use of faulty diction.

UNREVISED: We have never won the track championship, we have won the cross-country title.

REVISED: We have never won the track championship, but we have won the cross-country title.

If one of the complete thoughts is subordinate to the other, you may also use a subordinate conjunction to connect the two:

UNREVISED: Neal won the award, he had the highest score.

REVISED: Neal won the award because he had the highest score.

Subordination, Coordination, and Predication

Suppose that you wanted to combine the information in these two sentences to create one statement: *I studied a foreign language. I found English quite easy.* How you decide to combine this information should be determined by the relationship you'd like to show between the two facts. *I studied a foreign language, and I found English quite easy* adds little or nothing to the original meaning. The **coordination** of the two ideas (connecting them with the coordinating conjunction *and*) is therefore ineffective. Using **subordination** instead (connecting the sentences with a subordinating conjunction) clearly shows the relationship between the expressed ideas:

After I studied a foreign language, I found English quite easy. OR

Because I studied a foreign language, I found English quite easy.

When using any conjunction—coordinating or subordinating—be sure that the sentence parts you are joining are in agreement:

UNREVISED: She loved him dearly but not his dog.

REVISED: She loved him dearly, but she did not love his dog. OR She loved him, but not his dog, dearly.

Another common mistake is to forget that each member of the pair must be followed by the same kind of construction.

UNREVISED: She complimented her friends both for their bravery and thanked them for their kindness.

REVISED: She both complimented her friends for their bravery and thanked them for their kindness.

While refers to time and should not be used as a substitute for *though, and,* or *but.*

UNREVISED: While I'm usually interested in Fellini movies, I'd rather not go tonight.

REVISED: Although I'm usually interested in Fellini movies, I'd rather not go tonight.

Where refers to a place and should not be used as a substitute for *that.*

UNREVISED: We read in the paper where they are making strides in DNA research.

REVISED: We read in the paper that they are making great strides in DNA research.

After words such as *reason* and *explanation,* use *that,* not *because.*

UNREVISED: His explanation for his tardiness was because his alarm did not go off.

REVISED: His explanation for his tardiness was that his alarm did not go off.

Punctuation and Capitalization

Commas

Commas should be placed according to standard rules of punctuation for purpose, clarity, and effect. On the test, you will be given choices that require your knowledge of such rules. The proper use of commas is explained in the following rules and examples.

In **a series**:

> When more than one adjective describes a noun, use a comma to separate and emphasize each adjective. The comma takes the place of the word **and** in the series.

> the long, dark passageway

> another confusing, sleepless night

> an elaborate, complex, brilliant plan

> Some adjective-noun combinations are thought of as one word. In these cases, the adjective in front of the adjective-noun combination needs no comma. (If you inserted **and** between the adjective-noun combination, it would not make sense.)

> a stately oak tree

> a superior elementary school

> The comma is also used to separate words, phrases, and whole ideas (clauses); it still takes the place of **and** when used this way.

> a lovely lady, an elegant dress, and many admirers

> She lowered the shade, closed the curtain, turned off the light, and went to bed.

> One question that exists about the use of commas in a series is whether one should be used before the final item. It is standard usage to do so, although newspapers and many magazines do not use the final comma. Occasionally, the omission of the comma can be confusing.

With a **long introductory phrase**:

Usually if a phrase of more than five or six words or if a dependent clause precedes the subject at the beginning of a sentence, a comma is used to set it off:

After last night's fiasco at the disco, she couldn't bear the thought of looking at him again.

Whenever I try to talk about politics, my wife leaves the room.

If an introductory phrase includes a verb form that is being used as another part of speech (a **verbal**), it must be followed by a comma:

UNREVISED: When eating Mary never looked up from her plate.

REVISED: When eating, Mary never looked up from her plate.

UNREVISED: Having decided to leave Mary James wrote her a long email.

REVISED: Having decided to leave Mary, James wrote her a long email.

To separate sentences with **two main ideas**:

To understand this use of the comma, you need to be able to recognize compound sentences. When a sentence contains more than two subjects and verbs (clauses), and the two clauses are joined by a coordinating conjunction (**and, but, or, nor, for, yet**), use a comma before the conjunction to show that another independent clause is coming.

I thought I knew the poem by heart, but he showed me some lines I had forgotten.

He is supposed to leave tomorrow, but he is not ready to go.

Jim knows you are disappointed, and he has known it for a long time.

If the two parts of the sentence are short and closely related, it is not necessary to use a comma.

He threw the ball and the dog ran after it.

Be careful not to confuse a sentence that has a compound verb and a single subject with a compound sentence. If the subject is the same for both verbs, there is no need for a comma.

UNREVISED: Charles sent some flowers, and wrote a long note explaining why he had not been able to attend.

REVISED: Charles sent some flowers and wrote a long note explaining why he had not been able to attend.

UNREVISED: Last Thursday we went to the concert with Julia, and afterwards dined at an old Italian restaurant.

REVISED: Last Thursday we went to the concert with Julia and afterwards dined at an old Italian restaurant.

In general, words and phrases that stop the flow of the sentence or are unnecessary for the main idea are set off by commas.

Abbreviations after names

Martha Harris, Ph.D., will be the speaker tonight.

Interjections (An exclamation without added grammatical connection)

Oh, I'm so glad to see you!

Hey, let us out of here!

Direct address

Roy, won't you open the door for the dog?

Hey, lady, watch out for that car!

Tag questions

Jerry looks like his father, doesn't he?

Geographical names and addresses

The concert will be held in Chicago, Illinois, on August 12. [**Note:** Punctuation must always follow a state name when that name follows a city—except in postal addresses, as illustrated in the next item.]

The letter was addressed to Mrs. Marion Heartwell, 1881 Pine Lane, Palo Alto, California 95824.

Transitional words and phrases

On the other hand, I hope he gets better.

I've always found, however, that the climate is better in the mountains.

Parenthetical words and phrases

In fact, I planted corn last summer.

The Mannes affair was, to put it mildly, a surprise.

With **nonrestrictive elements**:

Parts of a sentence that modify other parts are sometimes essential to the meaning of the sentence and sometimes not. When a modifying word or phrase is not vital to the meaning of the sentence, it is set off by commas. Because it does not restrict the meaning of the words it modifies, it is called **nonrestrictive**. Modifiers that are essential to the meaning of the sentence are **restrictive**; they are not set off by commas.

ESSENTIAL: The girl *who wrote the story* is my sister.

NONESSENTIAL: My sister, *the girl who wrote the story,* has always loved to write.

ESSENTIAL: The man who is wearing the red sweater is the best-dressed person in the class.

NONESSENTIAL: Jorge, who is wearing the red sweater, is the best-dressed person in the class.

To set off **direct quotations**:

Most direct quotes or quoted materials are set off from rest of the sentence by commas.

"Please read your part more loudly," the director insisted.

"I won't know what to do," said Michael, "if you ever leave me alone."

Who was it who said, "Do not ask for whom the bell tolls; it tolls for thee"?

Note: In American English, commas always go inside the closing quotation mark, even if the comma is not part of the material being quoted.

To set off **contrasting elements**:

Her intelligence, not her beauty, got her the job.

It was a reasonable, though not appealing, idea.

In **dates**:

In the month-day-year form, commas follow the day and year.

She will arrive April 6, 2006, on the *Queen Elizabeth*.

If only the month and year are given, no commas are necessary.

The minister's January 1967 resignation was unexpected.

The day-month-year form requires no punctuation.

The events of 14 April 1865 were unprecedented.

Because a specific date makes a descriptive phrase following it nonessential, that phrase will be nonrestrictive and therefore set off by a comma.

He was married on 7 October 1988, which fell five days after his forty-third birthday.

When a subordinate clause is at the end of a sentence, a comma preceding the clause is optional. However, when a subordinate clause introduces a sentence, a comma should be used after the clause. Here are some common subordinating conjunctions:

after	even though	till
although	if	unless
as	inasmuch as	until
as if	since	when
because	so that	whenever
before	though	while

Semicolons

This review section covers the basic uses of the semicolon: to separate independent clauses not joined by a coordinating conjunction, to separate independent clauses separated by a conjunctive adverb, and to separate items in a series with internal commas.

Use the **semicolon** in the following cases:

To separate independent clauses that are not joined by a coordinating conjunction.

I understand how to use commas; the semicolon I have yet to master.

To separate two independent clauses connected by a conjunctive adverb.

He took great care with his work; therefore, he was very successful.

Usually a comma follows the conjunctive adverb. Note also that a period can be used to separate two sentences joined by a conjunctive adverb. Here are some common conjunctive adverbs:

accordingly	indeed	now
besides	in fact	on the other hand
consequently	moreover	otherwise
finally	nevertheless	perhaps
furthermore	next	still
however	nonetheless	therefore

Then is also used as a conjunctive adverb, but it is not usually followed by a comma.

To combine two independent clauses connected by a coordinating conjunction if either or both of the clauses contain other internal punctuation:

> Success in college, some maintain, requires intelligence, industry, and perseverance; *but* others, fewer in number, assert that only geniality is important.

To separate items in a series when each item has internal punctuation. It is important to be consistent; if you use a semicolon between *any* of the items in the series, you must use semicolons to separate *all* of the items in the series.

> I bought an old, dilapidated chair; an antique table that was in beautiful condition; and a new, ugly, blue and white rug.

Do *not* use the semicolon in any other cases, especially as a substitute for a comma. Here are some examples of nonstandard semicolon use; all of them should be replaced with a comma:

> You should never make such statements; even though they are correct.

> My roommate also likes sports; particularly football, basketball, and baseball.

> Being of a cynical mind; I should ask for a recount of the ballots.

Note: The semicolon is not a terminal mark of punctuation; therefore, it should not be followed by a capital letter unless the first word in the second clause ordinarily requires capitalization.

Colons

The difference between the colon and the semicolon and between the colon and the period is that the colon is an introductory mark, not a terminal mark. The colon signals the reader that a list, explanation, or restatement of the preceding thought will follow. It is like an arrow, indicating that something is to follow.

Here are some examples of colons used to introduce lists. Note that some lists may have only one item.

> I hate just one course: English.

Three plays by William Shakespeare will be presented in repertory this summer at Illinois State: *Hamlet*, *Macbeth*, and *Othello*.

The reasons he cited for his success are as follows: honesty, industry, and a pleasant disposition.

A colon should also be used to separate two independent clauses when the second clause is a restatement or explanation of the first:

All of my high school teachers said one thing in particular: college would be difficult.

You should also use a colon to introduce a word or word group that is a restatement, explanation, or summary of the first sentence:

The first week of camping was wonderful: we lived in cabins instead of tents.

In standard English the colon should only be used after statements that are grammatically complete. Do *not*, for example, use a colon after a verb or a preposition.

UNREVISED: My favorite holidays are: Christmas, New Year's Eve, and Halloween.

REVISED: My favorite holidays are Christmas, New Year's Eve, and Halloween.

UNREVISED: I enjoy different ethnic dishes, such as those from: Greece, China, Provence, and Italy.

REVISED: I enjoy different ethnic dishes, such as those from Greece, China, Provence, and Italy.

However, the use of a colon to set off a *displayed* list is becoming more common and may now be considered standard.

Apostrophes

Apostrophes are used to make a noun possessive, not plural. Remember the following rules when considering how to show possession:

Add **'s** to singular nouns and indefinite pronouns:

Tiffany's flowers

at the owner's expense

a dog's bark

Add **'s** to singular nouns ending in *s*, unless this distorts the pronunciation:

Delores's paper

the boss's pen

Dr. Yots' class or Dr. Yots's class (depending on pronunciation)

for righteousness' sake

Add **an apostrophe** to plural nouns ending in *s* or *es*:

two cents' worth

three weeks' pay

ladies' night

Add **'s** to plural nouns not ending in *s*:

men's room

children's toys

Add **'s** to the last word in compound words or groups:

> brother-in-law's car

> someone else's paper

Add **'s** to the last name when indicating joint ownership:

> Joe and Edna's home

> Ted and Jane's marriage

Add **'s** to both names if you intend to show ownership by each person:

> Joe's and Edna's trucks

> Ted's and Jane's marriage vows

Possessive pronouns change their forms *without* the addition of an apostrophe:

> hers, his, its, yours, theirs

Quotation Marks and Italics

The most common use of double quotation marks (") is to set off quoted words, phrases, and sentences.

> "If everybody minded their own business," said Mrs. O'Leary in a huff, "the world would be a much nicer place."

Single quotation marks are used to set off quoted material within a quote.

> "Shall I bring 'Rhyme of the Ancient Mariner' along with us?" asked her brother.

> "If she said that to me," Katherine insisted, "I would tell her, 'I never intend to speak to you again! Goodbye, Susan!'"

To set off titles of poems, stories, and book chapters, use quotation marks. Book, motion picture, newspaper, and magazine titles are italicized when printed.

> The article "Moving South in the Southern Rain," by Jergen Smith, appeared in the *Southern News*.

> The assignment is "Childhood Development," which is Chapter 18 of *Abnormal Behavior*.

Remember that commas and periods at the end of quotations are *always* placed inside the quotation marks even if they are not actually part of the quote. Semicolons and colons are always placed outside. Question marks are placed inside or outside, depending on whether the quotation is a question.

> UNREVISED: "If my dog could talk", Mary mused, "I'll bet he'd say, 'Take me for a walk right this minute'".

> REVISED: "If my dog could talk," Mary mused, "I'll bet he'd say, 'Take me for a walk right this minute.'"

> UNREVISED: She called down the stairs, "When are you going"?

> REVISED: She called down the stairs, "When are you going?"

> UNREVISED: We have to "pull ourselves up by our bootstraps;" we can't just talk about our plans.

> REVISED: We have to "pull ourselves up by our bootstraps"; we can't just talk about our plans.

Remember to use only one mark of punctuation at the end of sentence ending with a quotation mark.

> UNREVISED: She thought out loud, "Will I ever finish this project in time for that class?".

> REVISED: She thought out loud, "Will I ever finish this project in time for that class?"

Capitalization

There are many conventions for beginning words with capital letters; this section will review just a few of the more common ones. In general, capitalize (1) all proper nouns and adjectives, (2) the first word of a sentence, and (3) the first word of a direct quotation. Points (2) and (3) are easy to figure out, but knowing which nouns and adjectives are "proper" is sometimes difficult. Here is a brief list that will help you remember what words to capitalize.

Names of persons, geographical places, and organizations:

Kelvim Escobar is a pitcher for the Anaheim Angels, who play in the American League.

Titles of books, poems, songs, TV shows, newspapers, and the like:

The *Washington Post* ran an interesting review of Frost's *Collected Poems*; its opinions about "Mending Wall" were especially interesting.

Geographical regions, but not compass directions:

Many movies are set in the West.

The Northern Hemisphere is the part of the earth that lies north of the equator.

The cultural division between East and West has persisted throughout modern times.

Titles of persons, if they appear immediately before the person's name:

President George W. Bush held a press conference last week.

George W. Bush, president of the United States, visited our town twice during his first term.

Political parties and philosophy, but not systems of government or individual adherents to a political philosophy:

The problems within the Communist Party foreshadowed the difficulties that communism would have in establishing itself.

The Republicans and Democrats often argue about how best to spread democracy to other countries.

Pronouns

Pronoun Case

One of the most embarrassing mistakes you can make in written English is confusing the spelling of common pronouns: "its" and "it's" and "your" and "you're." The words "its" and "your" are possessive pronouns, meaning "belonging to it" and "belonging to you," respectively. "It's" and "you're" are contractions for "it is" and "you are."

Watch *your* step; if you don't, you might break *your* neck.

It's not likely that the company will give back *its* windfall profits.

Other commonly asked questions regarding the use of pronouns are about the confusion of nominative case pronouns with objective case pronouns.

Nominative Case	Objective Case
I	me
he	him
she	her
we	us
they	them
who	whom

Use the nominative case (subject of pronouns) in the following:

Subject of a sentence:

We students studied until early morning.

Alan and *I* "burned the midnight oil" too.

Pronouns in apposition to the subject:

Only two students, Alex and *I*, were asked to comment.

Predicate nominative/subject complement:

> The cast members nominated for the award were *she* and *I*.

The subject of a subordinate clause:

> Robert is the driver *who* reported the accident.

The only pronouns that are acceptable in standard English after prepositions are the objective case pronouns. When deciding between *who* and *whom* in the sentence "We're having difficulty deciding *who* we can trust," try substituting *he* for *who* and *him* for *whom*; then follow these transformation steps:

1. Isolate the *who* or *whom* clause: who we can trust.

2. Invert the natural word order if necessary, to the normal English subject–verb order: we can trust who

3. Read the final form with the *he* or *him* inserted: we can trust ~~who~~-*him*. The correct pronoun is thus *whom*.

Use the objective case (subject of pronouns) for the following:

Direct object of a verb:

> Mary invited *us* to her party.

Object of a preposition:

> The torn books belonged to *her*.

> Just between you and *me*, I'm bored.

Indirect object of a verb:

> Soren gave *her* a dozen roses.

Appositive of an object:

> The committee selected two delegates, Barbara and *me*.

Object of an infinitive:

The young boy wanted to help *us* paint the fence.

Subject of an infinitive:

The boss told *him* to work late.

Object of a gerund:

Enlisting *him* was surprisingly easy.

When a conjunction connects two pronouns or a pronoun and a noun, one good way to determine the case of a pronoun is to remove the "and" and the noun or other pronoun:

Mom gave ~~Tom and~~ myself a piece of cake.

Mom gave ~~Tom and~~ I a piece of cake.

Mom gave ~~Tom and~~ me a piece of cake.

Removal of the crossed-out words reveals that the correct pronoun should be *me*.

Pronoun-Antecedent Agreement

Some questions might ask you about *pronoun-antecedent agreement*. These kinds of questions test your knowledge of using an appropriate pronoun to agree with its antecedent in number (singular or plural form) and gender (masculine, feminine, or neuter). An *antecedent* is a noun or pronoun to which another noun or pronoun refers.

Here are the two basic rules for pronoun reference-antecedent agreement:

1.   Every pronoun must have a conspicuous antecedent.

2.   Every pronoun must agree with its antecedent in number, gender, and person.

When an antecedent is one of dual gender—such as *student, singer, person,* or *citizen*—use **his** or **her.** Some careful writers change the antecedent to a plural noun to avoid using the sexist, singular masculine pronoun.

UNREVISED: Everyone hopes that they will win the lottery.

CORRECT BUT AMBIGUOUS: Everyone hopes that he will win the lottery.

CORRECT BUT AWKWARD: Everyone hopes that he or she will win the lottery.

REVISED: Most people hope that they will win the lottery.

Ordinarily, the relative pronoun **who** is used to refer to people, **which** to refer to things and places, **where** to refer to places, and **that** to refer to places or things. The distinction between **that** and **which** is a grammatical distinction (see the section on Word Choice Skills). Many writers prefer to use **that** to refer to collective nouns, even for people: A family that traces its lineage is usually proud of its roots.

Many writers, especially students, are not sure when to use the *reflexive case* pronoun and when to use the *possessive case* pronoun. The rules governing the usage of the reflexive case and the possessive case are simple.

Use the **possessive case**:

Before a noun in a sentence:

My dog has fleas, but *her* dog doesn't.

Before a gerund in a sentence:

Her running helps to relieve stress.

As a noun in a sentence:

Mine was the last test graded that day.

To indicate possession:

Brad thought the book was *his,* but it was someone else's.

Use the **reflexive** case:

As a direct object to rename the subject:

I kicked *myself.*

As an indirect object to rename the subject:

Henry bought *himself* a tie.

As an object of a prepositional phrase:

Tom and Lillie baked the pie for *themselves.*

As a predicate pronoun:

She hasn't been *herself lately.*

Do not use the reflexive in place of the nominative pronoun:

UNREVISED: Both Randy and *myself* plan to go.

REVISED: Both Randy and *I* plan to go.

UNREVISED: *Yourself* will take on the challenges of college.

REVISED: *You* will take on the challenges of college *yourself.*

Watch out for careless use of the pronoun form:

UNREVISED: George *hisself* told me it was true.

REVISED: George *himself* told me it was true.

UNREVISED: They washed the car *theirselves.*

REVISED: They washed the car *themselves.*

Notice that reflexive pronouns are not set off by commas:

UNREVISED: Mary, *herself,* gave him the diploma.

REVISED: Mary *herself* gave him the diploma.

Pronoun Reference

Pronoun reference questions require you to determine whether the antecedent is conspicuously written in the sentence or whether it is remote, implied, ambiguous, or vague, none of which results in clear writing. In the following, make sure that every italicized pronoun has a conspicuous antecedent and that one pronoun substitutes only for another noun or pronoun, not for an idea or a sentence.

Pronoun reference problems occur in the following instances:

1.   When a pronoun refers to either of two antecedents.

UNREVISED: Joanna told Tina that *she* was getting fat.

REVISED: Joanna told Tina, "I'm getting fat." OR Joanna told Tina, "You're getting fat."

2.   When a pronoun refers to a nonexistent antecedent.

UNREVISED: A strange car followed us closely, and *he* kept blinking his lights at us.

REVISED: A strange car followed us closely, and its driver kept blinking his lights at us.

3.   When **this, that,** and **which** refer to the general idea of the preceding clause or sentence rather than the preceding word.

UNREVISED: The students could not understand the pronoun reference handout, *which* annoyed them very much.

REVISED: The students could not understand the pronoun reference handout, *a fact that* annoyed them very much. OR The students were annoyed because they could not understand the pronoun reference handout.

4. When a pronoun refers to an unexpressed but implied noun.

UNREVISED: My husband wants me to knit a blanket, but I'm not interested in *it*.

REVISED: My husband wants me to knit a blanket, but I'm not interested in *knitting*.

5. When **it** is used as something other than an expletive to postpone a subject.

UNREVISED: The football game was canceled because it was bad weather.

REVISED: The football game was canceled because the weather was bad.

6. When **they** or **it** is used to refer to something or someone indefinitely, and there is no definite antecedent.

UNREVISED: At the job placement office, *they* told me to stop wearing ripped jeans to my interviews.

REVISED: At the job placement office, I was told to stop wearing ripped jeans to my interviews.

7. When the pronoun does not agree with its antecedent in number, gender, or person.

UNREVISED: Any graduate student, if *they* are interested, may tend the lecture.

REVISED: Any graduate student, if *he or she* is interested, may attend the lecture.

REVISED: All graduate *students*, if *they* are interested, may tend the lecture.

Verbs

This section covers the principal parts of some irregular verbs, including such troublesome verbs as *lie* and *lay*. The use of regular verbs, such as *look* and *receive*, poses little problem for most writers, because the past and past participle forms end in *-ed*; it is the irregular forms that pose the most serious problems—for example, *seen, written,* and *begun.*

Verb Tenses

Tense sequence indicates a logical time sequence.

Use **present tense**:

In statements of universal truth:

I learned that the sun *is* ninety-million miles from the earth.

In statements about the contents of literature and other published work:

In this book, Sandy *becomes* a nun and *writes* a book about psychology.

Use **past tense**:

In statements or questions about action that happened in the past and is now finished:

I *fell* over the limb and *broke* my arm.

How *did* you break your arm?

In statements concerning writing or publication of a book:

He *wrote* his first book in 1949, and it *was published* in 1956.

Use **present perfect tense**:

For an action that began in the past but continues into the future:

I *have lived* here all my life.

Use **past perfect tense**:

For an earlier action that is mentioned in relation to a later action:

Cindy ate the apple that she *had picked*.

(First she picked it; then she ate it.)

Use **future perfect tense**:

For an action that will have been completed at a specific future time:

You *will have graduated* by the time we next meet.

Use **a present participle**:

For action that occurs at the same time as the verb:

Speeding down the interstate, I saw a cop's flashing lights.

Use **a perfect participle**:

For action that occurred before the main verb:

Having read the directions, I started the test.

Use the **subjunctive mood**:

To express a wish or state a condition contrary to fact:

If it were not raining, we could have a picnic.

In "that" clauses after such verbs as **request, recommend, suggest, ask, require,** and **insist**; and after such expressions as **it is important** and **it is necessary**:

It is necessary that all papers *be* submitted on time.

Subject-Verb Agreement

Agreement is the grammatical correspondence between the subject and the verb of a sentence or clause: *I do; you do; we do; they do; he, she, it does.* One source of confusion for many students is which verb form is singular and which forms are plural, so this section begins by focusing on making that distinction and then tackles the task of identifying the real subject of a sentence. Finally, this section deals with subjects that are commonly construed as singular and those that are construed as plural.

Every English verb has five forms, two of which are the bare form (plural) and the **-s** form (singular). Simply put, singular verb forms end in **–s**; plural forms do not.

Study these rules governing subject-verb agreement:

A verb must agree with its subject, not with any additional phrase in the sentence such as a prepositional or verbal phrase.

Your *copy* of the rules *is* on the desk.

Ms. Craig's *record* of community service and outstanding teaching *qualifies* her for a promotion.

In an inverted sentence beginning with a prepositional phrase, the verb must still agree with its subject.

At the end of the summer *come* the best *sales.* Under the house *are* some old Mason *jars.*

Prepositional phrases beginning with compound prepositions such as **along with, together with, in addition to, and as well as** should be ignored, for they do not affect subject-verb agreement.

Gladys Knight, along with the Pips, *is* riding the midnight train to Georgia.

A verb must agree with its subject, not its subject complement.

Taxes are a problem.

One *problem is* taxes.

His main *source* of pleasure *is* food and women.

Food and women are his main source of pleasure.

When a sentence begins with an expletive such as **there**, **here**, or **it**, the verb agrees with the subject, not the expletive.

Surely there *are* several *alumni* who would be interested in starting a group.

There *are* 50 *students* in my English class.

There *is* a horrifying *study* on child abuse in *Psychology Today*.

Indefinite pronouns such as **each**, **either**, **one**, **everyone**, **everybody**, and **everything** are singular.

Somebody in Detroit *loves* me.

Does either [one] of you have a pencil?

Neither of my brothers *has* a car.

Indefinite pronouns such as **several**, **few**, **both**, and **many** are considered plural.

Both of my sorority sisters *have* decided to live off campus.

Few seek the enlightenment of transcendental meditation.

Indefinite pronouns such as **all**, **some**, **most**, and **none** may be singular or plural, depending on their referents.

Some of the food *is* cold.

Some of the vegetables *are* cold.

I can think of some retorts, but *none seem* appropriate.

None of the children *is* as sweet as Sally.

Fractions such as **one-half** and **one-third** may be singular or plural, depending on the referent.

Half of the mail *has* been delivered.

Half of the letters *have* been read.

Subjects joined by **and** take a plural verb unless the subjects are commonly thought of as one item or unit.

Jim and *Tammy were* televangelists.

Guns and Roses is my favorite group.

In cases when the subjects are joined by **or**, **nor**, **either . . . or**, or **neither . . . nor**, the verb must agree with the subject closer to it.

Either the teacher or the *students are* responsible.

Neither the students nor the *teacher is* responsible.

Relative pronouns—such as **who**, **which**, or **that**—require plural verbs if they refer to plural antecedents. However, when the relative pronoun refers to a singular subject, the pronoun takes a singular verb.

She is one of the best *cheerleaders who have* ever attended our school.

She is the only *cheerleader who has* a broken leg.

Subjects preceded by **every** and **each** are singular.

Every man, woman, and child *was* given a life preserver.

Each undergraduate *is* required to pass a proficiency exam.

A collective noun, such as **audience**, **faculty**, and **jury**, requires a singular verb when the group is regarded as a whole, and a plural when the members of the group are regarded as individuals.

The *jury has* made its decision.

The faculty are preparing their grade rosters.

Subjects preceded by **the number of** or **the percentage of** are singular; subjects preceded by **a number of** or **a percentage of** are plural.

The number of vacationers in Florida *increases* every year.

A number of vacationers *are* young couples.

Certain nouns of Latin and Greek origin have unusual plural forms.

Singular	**Plural**
criterion	criteria
alumnus	alumni
datum	data
medium	media

The *data are* available for inspection.

The only *criterion* for membership *is* a high GPA.

Some nouns, such as *deer*, *shrimp*, and *sheep*, have the same spelling for both their singular and plural forms. In these cases, the meaning of the sentence will determine whether they are singular or plural.

Deer are beautiful animals.

The spotted *deer is* licking the salt block.

Some nouns ending in *-ics*, such as *economics* and *ethics*, take singular verbs when they refer to principles or a field of study; however, when they refer to individual practices, they usually take plural verbs.

Ethics is being taught in the spring.

His unusual business *ethics are* what got him into trouble.

Some nouns that end in **-s** may appear to be plural but are not; examples are *measles* and *news*.

Measles is a very contagious disease.

News of her arrival *was* not welcome.

A verbal noun (infinitive or gerund) serving as a subject is treated as singular, even if the object of the verbal phrase is plural.

Hiding your mistakes *does* not make them go away.

A plural subject followed by a singular appositive requires a plural verb; similarly, a singular subject followed by a plural appositive requires a singular verb.

When the girls throw a party, *they* each bring a *gift*.

The *board*, all ten members, *is* meeting today.

Adjectives and Adverbs

Correct Usage

Be careful and *Drive carefully* are sentences that illustrate the differences that this section discusses: the proper use of an adjective or an adverb, including distinctions between *bad* and *badly* and *good* and *well*.

Adjectives are words that modify nouns or pronouns by defining, describing, limiting, or qualifying those nouns or pronouns.

Adverbs are words that modify verbs, adjectives, or other adverbs and that express such ideas as time, place, manner, cause, and degree. In general, use adjectives as subject complements with linking verbs; use adverbs with action verbs.

The old man's speech was *eloquent*.	ADJECTIVE
Mr. Brown speaks *eloquently*.	ADVERB
Please be *careful*.	ADJECTIVE
Please drive *carefully*.	ADVERB

Good and Well

Good is an adjective; its use as an adverb is colloquial and nonstandard.

> NONSTANDARD: He plays *good*.

> STANDARD: He plays *well*.

> STANDARD: He looks *good* to be an octogenarian.

Well may be either an adverb or an adjective. As an adjective it means "in good health."

> He plays *well*.   ADVERB
> My mother is not *well*.   ADJECTIVE

Do not confuse *good* and *well* when used with *feel*. If you say "*I feel good*," you're referring to your general health or mood, whereas "*I feel well*" refers only to your sense of touch.

Bad or Badly

Bad is an adjective used after sense verbs, such as *look*, *smell*, *taste*, *feel*, or *sound*, or after linking verbs (is, am, are, was, were).

> UNREVISED: I feel *badly* about the delay.

> REVISED: I feel *bad* about the delay.

Badly is an adverb used after all other verbs.

> UNREVISED: It doesn't hurt very *bad*.

> REVISED: It doesn't hurt very *badly*.

Real or Really

Real is an adjective; its use as an adverb is colloquial and nonstandard. It means "genuine."

> NONSTANDARD: He writes *real* well.

> STANDARD: This is *real* leather.

Really is an adverb meaning "very."

NONSTANDARD: This is *really* diamond.

STANDARD: Have a *really* nice day.

This is *real* amethyst.	ADJECTIVE
This is *really* difficult.	ADVERB
This is a *real* crisis	ADJECTIVE
This is *really* important.	ADVERB

Faulty Comparisons

This section covers comparisons that use adjectives and adverbs with certain conjunctions, such as *than* and *as,* to indicate a greater or lesser degree of what is specified in the main part of the sentence. Errors occur when the comparison being made is illogical, redundant, or incomplete. Watch for **-er** and **-est** forms of words meaning *more* and *most,* and correlative pairs like *as . . . as.* Other clues are *than* and *other.* Often, sentences containing a faulty comparison sound correct because their problem is not one of grammar but of logic. Read such sentences closely to make sure that like things are being compared, that the comparisons are complete, and that the comparisons are logical.

When comparing two persons or things, use the comparative (**-er**), not the superlative (**-est**) form, of an adjective or an adverb. Use the superlative form for comparison of more than two persons or things. Use *any, other,* or *else* when comparing one thing or person with a group of which it, he, or she is a part.

Most one- and two-syllable words form their comparative and superlative forms with **-er** and **-est** suffixes. Adjectives and adverbs of more than two syllables form their comparatives and superlatives with the addition of *more* and *most.*

Word	Comparative	Superlative
good	better	best
old	older	oldest
friendly	friendlier	friendliest
lonely	lonelier	loneliest
talented	more talented	most talented
beautiful	more beautiful	most beautiful

When in doubt, consult a dictionary; most of them give the comparative and superlative forms.

Here are examples of some common types of faulty comparison:

Double comparison

UNREVISED: He is the *most nicest* brother.

REVISED: He is the *nicest* brother.

UNREVISED: She is the *more meaner* of the sisters.

REVISED: She is the *meaner* sister.

Illogical comparison

UNREVISED: The interest at a loan company is higher *than* a bank.

CORRECT: The interest at a loan company is higher *than at* a bank.

Ambiguous comparison

UNREVISED: I like Mary *better than* you. (than you *what*?)

REVISED: I like Mary *better than* I like you. OR I like Mary *better than* you do.

Incomplete comparison

UNREVISED: Skywriting is *more* spectacular.

REVISED: Skywriting is *more* spectacular *than* billboard advertising.

Omission of words **other**, **any**, or **else** when comparing one thing or person with a group of which it, he, or she is a part

UNREVISED: Joan writes better *than any* student in her class.

REVISED: Joan writes better *than any other* student in her class.

Omission of the second *as* in an **as . . . as** construction

UNREVISED: The University of West Florida is *as large* or larger than the University of North Florida.

REVISED: The University of West Florida is *as large as* or larger than the University of Northern Florida.

Word Choice

Usage

Consider this sentence: The high school *principal* resigned for two *principal* reasons. If you think that the second *principal* is the wrong word (that it should be *principle*), think again. This usage is correct. You may be asked about words that are commonly confused and misused, as well as the use of words based on their grammatical appropriateness in a sentence, such as the distinction between *principal* and *principle*, *fewer* and *less*, and *lie* and *lay*. Here are some commonly confused pairs:

principal—as an adjective, most important; as a noun, the chief authority.

principle—always a noun: a fundamental law. "We hold these principles to be self-evident."

affect—usually a verb, meaning to *influence*; sometimes a noun, with a specific meaning in psychology. "Her performance was adversely affected by the heat."

effect—usually a noun, meaning something that results from something else; occasionally a verb, meaning *to cause to come into being*. "The heat had no effect on his performance." "Her persistence helped to effect the new zoning ordinance."

Connotative and Denotative Meanings

The denotative meaning of a word is its *literal*, dictionary definition: what the word denotes, or "means." The connotative meaning of a word is what the word connotes, or "suggests"; it is a meaning apart from what the word literally means. A writer should choose a word based on the tone and context of the sentence; this ensures that a word bears the appropriate connotation while still conveying some exactness in denotation. For example, a gift might be described as "cheap," but the directness of the word has a negative connotation—something cheap is something of little or no value. The word "inexpensive" has a more positive connotation, although "cheap" is a synonym for "inexpensive." You may very well have to make a decision regarding the appropriateness of words and phrases within the context of a sentence.

Wordiness and Conciseness

Some questions will test your ability to detect redundancies (unnecessary repetitions), circumlocution (failure to get to the point), and padding with loose synonyms. These questions require you to select sentences that use as few words as possible to convey a message clearly, economically, and effectively.

Effective writing is concise. Wordiness, on the other hand, decreases the clarity of expression by cluttering sentences with unnecessary words. Of course, not all short sentences are better than long ones simply because they are brief. As long as a word serves a function, it should remain in the sentence. However, repetition of words, sounds, and phrases should be used only for emphasis or other stylistic reasons. Editing your writing will make a difference in its impact. Notice what revision does here:

UNREVISED: The medical exam that he gave me was entirely complete.

REVISED: The medical exam he gave me was complete.

UNREVISED: Larry asked his friend John, who was a good, old friend, if he would join him and go along with him to see the foreign film made in Japan.

REVISED: Larry asked his good, old friend John if he would join him in seeing the Japanese film.

UNREVISED: I was absolutely, totally happy with the present that my parents gave to me at 7 AM on the morning of my birthday.

REVISED: I was happy with the present my parents gave me on the morning of my birthday.

UNREVISED: It seems perfectly clear to me that although he went and got permission from the professor, he still should not have played that awful, terrible joke on the dean.

REVISED: It seems clear that, although he got permission from the professor, he should not have played that terrible joke on the dean.

Drill: Editing Skills

> **DIRECTIONS: Select the sentence that clearly and effectively states the idea and has no structural errors.**

(A)   South of Richmond, the two roads converge together to form a single highway.

(B)   South of Richmond, the two roads converge together to form an interstate highway.

(C)   South of Richmond, the two roads converge to form an interstate highway.

(D)   South of Richmond, the two roads converge to form a single interstate highway.

The correct answer is (C); *together* is not needed after *converge*, and *single* is not needed to modify *highway*.

(A)   Vincent van Gogh and Paul Gauguin were close personal friends and companions who enjoyed each other's company and frequently worked together on their artwork.

(B)   Vincent van Gogh and Paul Gauguin were friends who frequently painted together.

(C)   Vincent van Gogh was a close personal friend of Paul Gauguin, and the two of them often worked together on their artwork because they enjoyed each other's company.

(D)   Vincent van Gogh, a close personal friend of Paul Gauguin, often worked with him on their artwork.

The correct answer is (B). Choices (A) and (C) pad the sentences with loose synonyms that are redundant. Choice (D), although a short sentence, does not convey the meaning as clearly as choice (B).

Transitions and Coherence

On the Communication Skills portion of the OGET, you will be asked tell whether a particular passage develops its ideas well. You will also be asked to supply missing words, phrases, or sentences that would make a particular passage develop more logically. Let's look at the following passage, which is adapted from a similar passage that appeared in Chapter 1.

Passage

[1]That the area of obscenity and pornography is a difficult one for the Supreme Court is well documented. [2]The Court's numerous attempts to define obscenity have proven unworkable and left the decision to the

subjective preferences of the justices. [3]Perhaps Justice Stewart put it best when, after refusing to define obscenity, he declared, but "I know it when I see it." [4]Does the Court literally have to see it to know it? [5]Specifically, what role does the fact-pattern, including the materials' medium, play in the Court's decision?

[6]Several recent studies employ fact-pattern analysis in modeling the Court's decision making. [7]These studies examine the fact-pattern or case characteristics, often with ideological and attitudinal factors, as a determinant of the decision reached by the Court. [8]In broad terms, these studies owe their theoretical underpinnings to attitude theory. [9]As the name suggests, attitude theory views the Court's attitudes as an explanation of its decisions.

[10]These attitudes, however, do not operate in a vacuum. [11]As Spaeth explains, "the activation of an attitude involves both an object and the situation in which that object is encountered." [12]The objects to which the court directs its attitudes are litigants. [13]The situation—the subject matter of the case—can be defined in broad or narrow terms. [14]One may define the situation as an entire area of the law (e.g., civil liberties issues). [15]On an even broader scale, the situation may be defined as the decision to grant certiorari or whether to defect from a minimum-winning coalition.

[16]Defining the situation with such broad strokes, _____, does not allow one to control for case content. [17]In many specific issue areas, the cases present strikingly similar patterns. [18]In examining the Court's search and seizure decisions, Segal found that a relatively small number of situational and case characteristic variables explain a high proportion of the Court's decisions.

[19]Despite Segal's success, efforts to verify the applicability of fact-pattern analysis in other issue areas and using broad-based factors have been slow in forthcoming. [20]Renewed interest in obscenity and pornography by federal and state governments as a result of lobbying campaigns by fundamentalist groups, the academic community, and other antipornography interest groups pro and con indicate the Court's decisions in this area will get closer examination.

[21]The Court's obscenity and pornography decisions _____ present an opportunity to study the Court's behavior in an area where the Court has granted significant decision-making authority to the states. [22]In *Miller v. California* (1973) the Court announced the importance of local community standards in obscenity determinations. [23]The Court's _____ behavior may suggest how the Court will react in other areas where it has chosen to defer to the states (e.g., abortion).

Questions

1. This passage would be most appropriate in which type of publication?

   A. A popular magazine such as *Time* or *Newsweek*

   B. An editorial about pornography in a newspaper

   C. A chapter on pornography in a sociology textbook

   D. An article in a law journal

2. Which of the following phrases, if inserted in the blank in Part 16, would best help the reader under the author's progression of ideas.

   A. consequently

   B. however

   C. nevertheless

   D. furthermore

3. In the final paragraph, which words or phrases, if inserted in order in the blanks, help the reader understand the author's logical sequence?

   A. in fact; foolish

   B. will; later

   C. also; subsequent

   D. theoretically; firm

4. Which of the following best describes the method of organization used by the author of this passage?

   A. problem and solution

   B. chronological order

   C. order of importance

   D. comparison and contrast

5. Which of the following sentences, if added between Parts 10 and 11, would be most consistent with the writer's purpose and intended audience?

   A. Situations with which the Court is faced are often quite complex.

   B. Supreme Court justices have been known to read newspapers as well as law journals.

   C. Pornography has been a point of public dispute for many decades now.

   D. If they did operate in a vacuum, predicting a justice's vote on a particular issue from his record before his appointment would be somewhat straightforward.

6.   Which word would best replace the underlined words in Part 20?

A.   deserve

B.   are garnering

C.   will continue to elude

D.   have avoided

Answers

Keep in mind that the first step to answering these types of questions involves applying the Four-Step Approach discussed in Chapter 1. You cannot answer questions about the purpose, audience, or organization of a passage without first having analyzed it through the four-step approach. You will see that, in the practice test in this book and in the actual examination, passages are generally shorter than this passage; this one has been included so that you can review the Four-Step Approach while answering these questions.

The answer to Question 1 is **D**. The quotes from scholars eliminate A and B from consideration, because newspapers and magazines for general readers do not usually quote experts without identifying why they are worthy of being experts. Choice B is further eliminated by the fact that the passage takes no position that the average newspaper reader might act upon. The tone of the passage might conceivably be appropriate to choice C, but the passage focuses on law rather than pornography.

The correct answer to Question 2 is **B**. The previous paragraph ended with a statement about a "broad scale," and the new paragraph begins by saying that looking at the broad scale is inadequate. This sentence, then, must convey that contrast, so choices A and D are immediately eliminated. Choice C conveys the correct general meaning, but the use of *nevertheless* directly before a negative—*does not*—would be confusing to a reader.

The correct answer to Question 3 is **C**. To find this answer, you will first have to notice that the author is switching topics from obscenity to states' rights; therefore, the choice A is eliminated, because *in fact* is a transition that signals an example of what has just been discussed. (In addition, nothing in the passage indicates that the author regards the Court's behavior as "foolish.") Choice B is wrong simply because the word "will" is not accurate: the decisions *already do* present an opportunity for further analysis. Choice D's "theoretically" is plausible, but "firm" is definitely wrong because it does not describe the author's opinion of the Court's 1973 decision, which just announces the importance of local standards rather than making firm law regarding them.

Question 4's answer is **D**. Although a problem and solution are implied in the passage, there is no direct statement of the problem followed by a solution. Chronological order and order of importance are clearly not present here, but the writer does compare and contrast analytical methods and attempts to explicate their strengths and weaknesses.

The best answer to Question 5 is **D**. Choices A and C are far from the point of the paragraph, which concerns how justices reach decisions. The choice of D over B depends on the tone of the two sentences as well as the specific content. The content of the two sentences is similar, although the content of D is somewhat more on message. The tone of choice B, however, is a bit flippant and would undoubtedly be out of place in most articles aimed at law scholars.

The best answer to Question 6 is **A**. Choice D contradicts the facts as presented in the paragraph, and choice C is out of line with the entire passage, which does give close examination to the subject. Choice B is technically correct (although not very informative for a final thought in a paragraph), but the word *garner* would be more at home in a newspaper article ("Duncan Garners Another Award") than in an article like this one.

Critical Thinking Skills: Mathematics

Questions from this sub-area of the OGET will ask you to analyze situations and to find solutions to problems that require some mathematical knowledge. This chapter will help you review data representation and analysis, and it will go over some basic ways to solve problems. The chapter will close with a review of how to set up solutions to problems that involve one or two variables.

Data Interpretation and Analysis

Competency 0009

Solve problems involving data interpretation and analysis.

The following topics are examples of content that may be covered under this competency:
- Interpret information from line graphs, bar graphs, histograms, pictographs, and pie charts.
- Interpret data from tables.
- Recognize appropriate representations of various data in graphic form.

Interpret Information from Graphs, Tables, or Charts

Graphs, tables, and charts come in many different forms; most simply represent numerical data in neat visual formats. A bar graph, like the one below, typically shows "how much" for each of many categories (or persons, or time periods, or whatever).

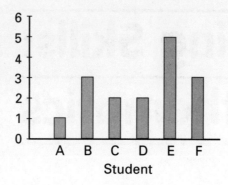

Broken line graphs, like the one below, are reserved for indicating *change over time*. Do not use broken line graphs unless one of the axes (usually the bottom or horizontal axis) indicates time. *Trends* are often revealed by broken line graphs.

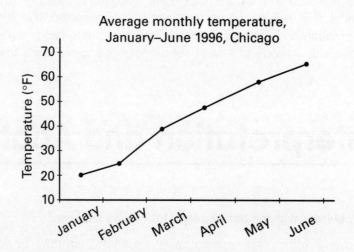

Pie graphs (also known as circle graphs or pie charts) often show how finite quantities are "split up." As with the example below, pie graphs may not necessarily be accompanied by specific numeric values. They are especially good for showing relative amounts or allotments at a glance.

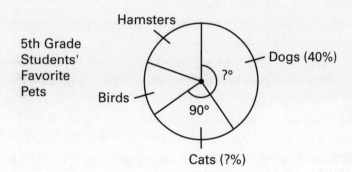

Because pie graphs are circles, the angle formed at the center by the boundaries of each catagory can be determined from the fact that the circle contains 360°. For example, if dogs are the favorite pets of 40% of fifth graders, what is the central angle? (**Answer:** 40% × 360° = .4 × 360° = 144°.) If the central angle of the "Cats" portion of the graph is 90°, what percentage of fifth graders prefer cats? (**Answer:** 90/360 = 1/4 = 25%.)

A key to interpretation of graphs, tables, and charts is to pay close attention to labels. Specific axis labels are also important. Don't assume anything about what a graph, table, or chart might be saying without carefully reading all labeled elements.

Statistical Concepts

The term *data* refers to numerical information acquired by counting or measuring. The number of students in a class, their test scores on a test, and their individual heights are all examples of data.

Data can be represented in *discrete* or *continuous* form, depending on what they represent. If data are discrete, they have gaps between them. The bar graph is a common way to depict discrete data. For example, the bar graph on page 80 represents the number of books read by each of six separate students. Discrete data are generally obtained from counting rather than measuring. Continuous data are usually represented by an unbroken line on a graph, and they are usually obtained by measuring rather than counting. The data shown in the graph at the bottom of 80 are continuous because there are no gaps between the months.

Here is a list of other statistical concepts that you might have to know for the test:

mean   The mean is the sum of a set of numbers divided by the quantity of numbers n in the set. It gives the *average value* of a data set.

range   The range is the measure of spread (*variation*) that is the difference between the largest value and the smallest value in a set of data.

sample survey   This is a survey of a population, usually human, made by taking a sample judged to be representative of the population. Use of a random mechanism for choosing the sample is essential for validity and believability.

spread of data   Spread, or **variation**, describes the degree to which data are spread out around their center. Useful measures of spread include the standard deviation and range.

standard deviation   This is the most commonly used expression of spread, or variation, of data. The higher the standard deviation, the higher is the degree of spread around the center of the data (that is, the data are more inconsistent with each other).

median   The median is the center value in a set of numbers: there are an equal number of values above and below it.

percentiles   These are the measures of where a piece of data stands in relation to the other data in its set. Perhaps best known from standardized tests, percentiles tell how many other data are lower in value. For instance, a test taker might have a raw score of 82% (that is, 82% of the answers correct) but rank in the 91st percentile, meaning that 90% of all test takers received lower raw scores. The median occurs at the 50th percentile.

frequency distributions   These represent the probability that a statistic of interest will fall in a certain interval; for example, the height of a person chosen at random may follow the *normal distribution*. Following are some samples of kinds of distributions, with location of the means and medians indicated:

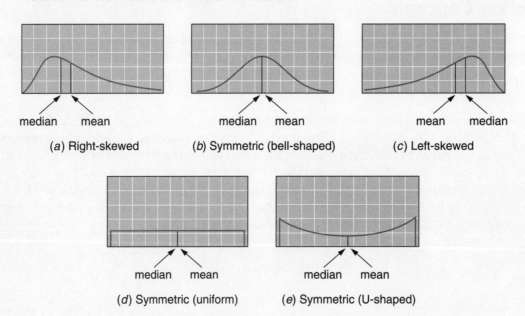

(*a*) Right-skewed   (*b*) Symmetric (bell-shaped)   (*c*) Left-skewed

(*d*) Symmetric (uniform)   (*e*) Symmetric (U-shaped)

Distribution (*b*) in the figure is the famous normal, or bell-shaped, curve on which tests are often said to be graded. Notice that more scores fall in the middle here than on the high or low ends. In the right-skewed distribution, shown in (*a*), more of the scores are low, and in (*c*) more of the scores are high (assuming that all of these graphs represent test scores). The distribution in (*d*) shows that all scores are distributed equally from high to low, and (*e*) shows a distribution in which most scores were either high or low, with very few being average. Notice that in (*a*), the right-skewed distribution, the mean is higher than the median, and in (*c*) the median is higher than the mean.

correlation   Correlation is the relationship between two variables. For example, a graph of tar and nicotine in cigarettes might look like this:

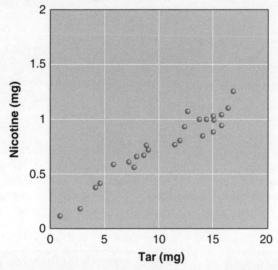

Each dot represents a particular cigarette, and the placement of the dot depends on the amounts of its tar (*x*-axis) and nicotine (*y*-axis). Drawings like this are called *scatterplots*. You could draw a straight line through this scatterplot, and it would go up and to the right, because, in general, the higher the amount of tar, the higher the amount of nicotine. The amounts of tar and nicotine are thus *positively correlated*. Some variables are *negatively correlated*; for instance, the weight of a vehicle would be negatively correlated with gas mileage if several models of vehicle were plotted in a scatterplot.

Here are some other scatterplots with varying kinds of correlation:

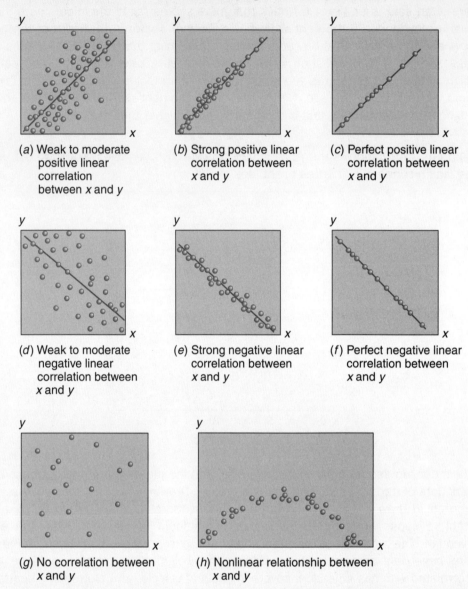

(a) Weak to moderate positive linear correlation between x and y

(b) Strong positive linear correlation between x and y

(c) Perfect positive linear correlation between x and y

(d) Weak to moderate negative linear correlation between x and y

(e) Strong negative linear correlation between x and y

(f) Perfect negative linear correlation between x and y

(g) No correlation between x and y

(h) Nonlinear relationship between x and y

When a correlation is linear or almost linear, you can use the graph to make predictions. For example, in the graph of tar and nicotine above, you could predict with a fair amount of certainty that a cigarette with 10 mg of tar would have between 0.7 and 0.8 mg of nicotine. In scatterplots without a linear correlation [(g) and (h) above], it's much harder to predict what y would be given x; in fact, in graph (g) it's nearly impossible.

Mathematical Reasoning

Competency 0010

Apply mathematical reasoning skills to analyze patterns and solve problems.

The following topics are examples of content that may be covered under this competency.
*   Draw conclusions using inductive reasoning.
*   Draw conclusions using deductive reasoning.

When presented with math or logic problems, including geometry problems, *deductive reasoning* may be helpful. Deductive reasoning is reasoning from the general to the specific, and is supported by deductive logic. Here is an example of deductive reasoning:

> All humans who have walked on the moon are males (a general proposition). Neil Armstrong walked on the moon, therefore he is a male (a specific proposition.)

Note that conclusions reached via deductive reasoning are sound only if the original assumptions are actually true.

With *inductive* reasoning, a general rule is inferred from specific observations (which may be limited). Moving from the statement "All fish I have ever seen have fins" (specific but limited observations) to "All fish have fins" (a general proposition) is an example of inductive reasoning. Conclusions arrived at via inductive reasoning are not necessarily true.

An example of how logical reasoning can be used to solve a geometry problem is given hereafter. (In this case *deductive* reasoning is used to find the measure of ∠J.)

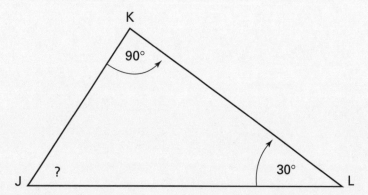

The sum of the measures of the three angles of any triangle is 180° (a general proposition). The sum of the measures of ∠K and ∠L is 120°, therefore the measure of ∠L is 60° (a specific proposition).

Mathematical Induction

A special case of inductive reasoning is *mathematical induction*. With mathematical induction, we can actually prove mathematical propositions about positive integers (i.e., all *n* natural numbers) that we derive from specific observations. In order to prove something by mathematical induction, we need to do the following:

1. Show that the proposition holds when $n = 0$.
2. Show that if the proposition is true when $n = m$, then it is also true when $n = m + 1$.

For example, you might notice that the sum of consecutive integers $1 + 2 + 3 = 6$, and that $1 + 2 + 3 + 4 + 5 = 15$. From these facts, you might conclude (after a bit of algebraic wrangling, which we won't go into here) that the sum of the first *n* positive integers in $n(n + 1)/2$—which does fit our two examples, and which we could easily show fits $1 + 2 + 3 + 4 = 10$ and $1 + 2 + 3 + 4 + 5 + 6 + 7 = 28$. But would it also work for $n = 952$? We can prove that it does by mathematical induction.

First we have to demonstrate that if n = 0, the proposition holds. Clearly it does, since $0 = 0(0 + 1)/2$. Then we can prove the validity of the proposition by proving that if *m* works, then so does *m* +1. Thus, we assume that $1 + 2 + 3 + ... + m = m(m + 1)/2$. Adding $m + 1$ to the sum, we get

$$1 + 2 + 3 + ... + m + m +1 = m(m + 1)/2 + m + 1$$
$$= m(m + 1)/2 + 2(m + 1)/2$$
$$= (m^2 + m + 2m +2)/2$$

By factoring the numerator on the right side of the equation, we get $(m + 1)(m + 2)/2$, or $(m + 1)((m + 1) + 1)/2$, which shows that, starting at zero, we can go up one by one to prove that each succeeding sum follows the same pattern. Thus, the sum of natural numbers 1 through 952 is truly $(952)(953)/2$.

Using Algebra in Deductive Reasoning

On the OGET, you may have to answer a question that gives you general statements that are known to be true. From those you must deduce which of four other statements is also true. For example, consider the following question:

Ghita grows daffodils, crocuses, and tulips in her garden. When asked about how many daffodils she has, she replies that she has at least as many daffodils as she has tulips, and she also says that she has at least as many tulips as crocuses. Assuming her statements are true, which of the following statements is also true?

A.   She has exactly as many crocuses as daffodils.

B.   She has at least as many crocuses as daffodils.

C.   She has at least as many daffodils as crocuses.

D.   She has more daffodils than crocuses.

To answer this question, let d equal the number of daffodils, t be the number of tulips, and c be the number of crocuses. Thus we know that $d \geq t$ and that $t \geq c$. Thus $d \geq t \geq c$, which means that she has *at least* as many daffodils as crocuses (choice C). She may have more daffodils than crocuses (choice D), but we can't be sure of that. The inequalities comparing c to d would be reversed, and neither choice A nor choice B would be true.

Word Problems and Algebraic Methods

Competency 0011

Solve applied problems using a combination of mathematical skills (including word problems involving one and two variables).

The following topics are examples of content that may be covered under this competency.
* Apply combinations of algebraic skills to solve problems.
* Apply combinations of mathematical skills to solve a series of related problems.
* Identify the algebraic equivalent of a stated relationship.
* Identify the proper equation or expression to solve word problems involving one and two variables.

Word Problems

The key to converting word problems into mathematical problems is attention to *reasonableness*, with the choice of operations most crucial to success. Often, individual words and phrases translate into numbers and operations symbols, and making sure that the translations are reasonable is important. Consider this word problem:

> Roberto babysat for the Yagers one evening. They paid him $5 just for coming over to their house, plus $7 for every hour of sitting. How much was he paid if he babysat for 4 hours?

"Plus" indicates addition, and "for every hour" suggests multiplication. Thus, the computational work can be set up like this: $5 + (7 \times 4)$ = Roberto's earnings. It would have been unreasonable to use a multiplication symbol in place of the addition sign. He earned $5 *plus* $7 for each of 4 hours.

Each word problem requires an individual approach, but keeping in mind the reasonableness of the computational setup should be helpful. (See more on this topic further in this review, "Solving word problems involving one and two variables.")

Solving One- and Two-Variable Equations

When attempting to solve one-variable equations, it is helpful to think of the task as that of producing a series of equivalent equations until, in the last equation, the variable has been *isolated* on one side. There are several ways to produce equivalent equations, but chiefly they are produced by performing identical operations on the two expressions making up the sides of equations. The equation $2x = 12$, for instance, can be solved by dividing both sides of the equation by 2, as follows:

$$\frac{2x}{2} = \frac{12}{2}$$

This then gives an equivalent equation of $x = 6$. Therefore, 6 is the solution to the original equation.

There are several caveats to observe when solving one-variable equations in that manner. One is that care must be taken to perform operations on *entire* expressions, and not simply on "parts" of expressions. In the example below, the last equation fails to give a solution to the original equation because, in the second step, only *part* of the expression $2x + 8$ has been divided by 2.

$$2x + 8 = 14$$
$$\frac{2x}{2} + 8 = \frac{14}{2}$$
$$x + 8 = 7$$
$$x = -1$$

Avoid dividing by zero. That operation is considered meaningless and will not provide a solution. Also, not all single-variable equations have solutions. $0x + 3 = 9$, for instance, has no real number solutions. If the variable carries an exponent, as in $x^2 = 16$, taking the square root of each side of the equation produces the solutions. (Note that *both* 4 and –4 work.)

"Solving one variable in terms of a second" simply means rewriting multivariable equations such that the desired variable is isolated on one side of the equation. For instance, the equation $x - 3y = 5$ can be rewritten as $x = 3y + 5$. The variable x has been solved in terms of the second variable y.

Solving a *system* of two-variable linear equations (such as $y = x + 6$ and $2y = 4x$) means finding the ordered pair (or pairs) of numbers that solves both equations simultaneously. Using trial and error, we can see that (6, 12) works in both of the equations above. There are also more formal methods for solving systems of two-variable equations. If we graph each equation on the coordinate plane, the point of intersection (if any) will give the solution to the system. Another method is to literally add or subtract one equation from the other, with the intention of eliminating one variable in the process, enabling us to solve for one variable, then the other. (One or both equations may first require multiplication in order to "line up" variables with opposite coefficients.) In the example that follows, the system of $y = x + 6$ and $2y = 4x$ has been solved using multiplication and addition.

$$y = x + 6$$
$$2y = 4x$$
$$-2y = -2x - 12$$
$$2y = 4x$$
$$0 = 2x - 12$$
$$x = 6$$

If $x = 6$, y must equal 12, so the solution to the system is (6, 12).

Solving Word Problems Involving One and Two Variables

One helpful approach when attempting to solve algebraic word problems is to *translate* the word problem into an equation (or, sometimes, an inequality), then solve the equation. Consider the word problem: "The Acme Taxicab Company charges riders 3 dollars just for getting into the cab, plus 2 dollars for every mile or fraction of a mile driven. What would be the fare for a 10-mile ride?" "Translating into math" we get $x = 3 + (2 \times 10)$. The equation can be read as "the unknown fare (x) is equal to 3 dollars *plus* 2 dollars for each of the 10 miles driven." Solving the equation gives 23 for x, so $23 is the solution to the word problem.

There are several common translations to keep in mind: The word *is* often suggests an equal sign; *of* may suggest multiplication, as does *product*. *Sum* refers to addition; *difference* suggests subtraction; and a *quotient* is obtained after dividing. The key when translating is to make sure that the equation accurately matches the information and relationships given in the word problem.

Understanding Operations with Algebraic Expressions

Only like (or similar) algebraic terms can be added or subtracted to produce simpler expressions. For instance, $3x^2$ and $5x^2$ can be added together to get $8x^2$, because the terms are like terms; they both have a base of x^2. We *cannot* add $8m^3$ and $6m^2$; m^3 and m^2 are unlike bases.

When multiplying exponential terms together, the constant terms are multiplied, but the exponents of terms with the same variable bases are *added* together, which is somewhat counterintuitive. For example, $5w^2$ times $2w^3$ gives $10w^5$ (*not* $10w^6$, as one might guess).

When like algebraic terms are divided, exponents are subtracted. For example,

$$\frac{7w^5}{2w^2}$$

becomes

$$\frac{7w^3}{2}$$

In algebra, we frequently need to multiply two binomials together. (*Binomials* are algebraic expressions of two terms.) The FOIL method is one way to multiply binomials. FOIL stands for "first, outer, inner, last." Multiply the first terms in the parentheses, then the "outermost" terms, followed by the "innermost terms," and finally the last terms, then add the products together. For example, to multiply ($x + 2$) and ($3x - 1$), we multiply x by $3x$ (the "firsts"), x by -1 ("outers"), 2 by $3x$ ("inners"), and 2 by -1 ("lasts"). The four products ($3x^2$, $-x$, $6x$ and -2) add up to $3x^2 + 5x - 2$. If the polynomials to be multiplied have more than two terms (*trinomials*, for instance), make sure that *each* term of the first polynomial is multiplied by *each* term of the second.

The opposite of polynomial multiplication is factoring. Factoring a polynomial means rewriting it as the product of factors (often two binomials). The trinomial $x^2 - 4x - 21$, for instance, can be factored into ($x + 3$)($x - 7$). (You can check this by "FOILing" the binomials.)

When attempting to factor polynomials, it is sometimes necessary to first "factor out" any factor that might be common to all terms. The two terms in $3x^2 - 12$, for example, both contain the factor 3. This means that the expression can be rewritten as $3(x^2 - 4)$, and then, $3(x - 2)(x + 2)$.

The task of factoring a polynomial is often aided by first setting up a pair of "empty" parentheses, like this: $2x^2 - 9x - 5 = ($ $)($ $)$. The task is then to fill in the four spaces with values which, when multiplied (FOILed), will "give back" $2x^2 - 9x - 5$.

Factoring is useful when solving some equations, especially if one side of the equation is set equal to zero. Consider $x^2 + 3x - 8 = 2$. It can be rewritten as $x^2 + 3x - 10 = 0$. This allows the left side to be factored into $(x - 2)(x + 5)$, giving equation solutions of 2 and –5.

Chapter 4

Computation Skills

Basic Number Skills

Competency 0012

Solve word problems involving integers, fractions, decimals, and units of measurement.

The following topics are examples of content that may be covered under this competency.
- Solve word problems involving integers, fractions, and decimals (including percentages).
- Solve word problems involving ratio and proportions.
- Solve word problems involving units of measurement and conversions (including scientific notation).

Fractions need to have common denominators before adding. Thus, to add, say, $\frac{1}{2}$ and $\frac{2}{3}$, change both fractions to equivalent fractions. These new equivalent fractions will have the same *value* as $\frac{1}{2}$ and $\frac{2}{3}$ and will have common (same) denominators, but will look different from the original fractions. The lowest common denominator is 6, because both of the original denominators can be changed into 6; $\frac{1}{2}$ can be written as $\frac{3}{6}$, and $\frac{2}{3}$ can be written as $\frac{4}{6}$.

After changing the "appearance" of $\frac{1}{2} + \frac{2}{3}$ to $\frac{3}{6} + \frac{4}{6}$, we can then simply add the numerators together, giving $\frac{7}{6}$, or $1\frac{1}{6}$.

When adding mixed fractions (those made up of a whole number and a fraction), add the fractions first, then—separately—the whole numbers. If the fractions add up to more than 1, add 1 to the whole number sum. For example, if after adding we have 3 and $1\frac{3}{4}$, the final sum is $4\frac{3}{4}$.

The algorithm for subtracting fractions is generally the same as that for adding. Common denominators are required. A problem, however, may be encountered when attempting to subtract mixed fractions such as $3\frac{2}{5}$ and $1\frac{4}{5}$. Note that $\frac{4}{5}$ can't be subtracted from $\frac{2}{5}$ (without involving negative numbers.) The solution is to rename $3\frac{2}{5}$ as $2\frac{7}{5}$. (This is accomplished by "borrowing" 1, or $\frac{5}{5}$, from the 3.) The new problem—still equivalent to the original—is $2\frac{7}{5}$ minus $1\frac{4}{5}$, or $1\frac{3}{5}$.

One approach to multiplying fractions is to multiply the numerators together and the denominators together, then simplify the resulting product. $\frac{2}{3} \times \frac{3}{4}$, for instance, equals $\frac{6}{12}$, or $\frac{1}{2}$. There is no need to use common denominators (as with fraction addition and subtraction.)

If the numbers to be multiplied are mixed fractions, first rewrite them as "improper" fractions, such as $\frac{14}{3}$, then use the procedure described earlier.

To divide fractions, invert the divisor (or the "second" number; the one "doing the dividing") and multiply instead. In the case of $\frac{1}{5}$ divided by $\frac{3}{8}$, change the original problem to the equivalent problem $\frac{1}{5} \times \frac{8}{3}$. Using the algorithm for multiplying fractions, we get $\frac{8}{15}$ as the quotient.

Decimal notation provides a different way of representing fractions whose denominators are powers of 10. $\frac{13}{100}$, for instance, is written as 0.13, $\frac{1}{1000}$ as 0.001, and so forth.

To add or subtract decimal numbers, arrange them vertically, aligning decimal points, then add or subtract as one would whole numbers. (A whole number can be written as a decimal numeral by placing a decimal point to its right, with as many zeros added as needed. Thus, 7 becomes 7.0, or 7.00, etc.) The decimal point then "drops down" directly into the sum or difference; its position is not shifted.

Using the traditional algorithm for multiplying decimal numbers does *not* require aligning decimal points; the numbers to be multiplied can simply be arranged vertically, with right "justification." The numbers can then be multiplied as if they were whole numbers. The number of digits to the right of the decimal point in the product should equal the total number of digits to the right of the two factors. Here is an example:

$$\begin{array}{r} 1.64 \\ \times\ 0.3 \\ \hline = 0.492 \end{array}$$

One method for dividing decimal numbers is to use the traditional whole number division algorithm, placing the decimal point properly in the answer. The number of digits to the right of the decimal point in the divisor is how far the decimal point in the quotient (the answer) should be moved to the right, with the decimal point in the dividend as our starting position. Here is an example:

$$0.3\overline{)1.44} = 4.8$$

Note that careful placement of digits when writing both the problem and the quotient helps ensure a correct answer.

The rules for performing operations on integers (whole numbers and their negative counterparts) and on fractions and decimal numbers where at least one is negative are generally the same as the rules for performing operations on non-negative numbers. The trick is to pay attention to the sign (the positive or negative value) of each answer. The rules for multiplication and division when at least one negative number is involved are the same: two positives or two negatives give a positive, whereas "mixing" a positive and a negative gives a negative ($-5 \times 3 = -15$, for instance). When at least one negative number is involved in addition and subtraction, it may be useful to think of the values as money, with "adding" being thought of as "gaining," "subtracting" being thought of as "losing," positive numbers being seen as "credits" and negative numbers, "debts." (Careful: Adding or "gaining" -8 is like *losing* 8.)

Sometimes, mathematical expressions indicate several operations. When simplifying such expressions, there is a universally agreed-upon order for "doing" each operation. First we compute any multiplication or division, left to right. Then, compute any addition or subtraction, also left to right. (If an expression contains any parentheses, all computation within the parentheses must be completed first.) Treat exponential expressions ("powers") as multiplication. Thus, the expression $3 + 7 \times 4 - 2$ equals 29. (Multiply 7 by 4 *before* doing the addition and subtraction.)

Exponential notation is a way to show repeated multiplication more simply. $2 \times 2 \times 2$, for instance, can be shown as 2^3, and is equal to 8. (Note: 2^3 does *not* mean 2×3.)

Scientific notation provides a method for showing any numbers using exponents (although it is most useful for very large and very small numbers.) A number is in scientific notation when it is shown as a number between 1 and 10 times a power of 10. Thus, the number 75,000 in scientific notation is shown as 7.5×10^4.

Other common mathematical notation symbols include the following:

$<$ means "less than"
$>$ means "greater than"
$\neq$ means "not equal to"

Graphing and Solving Equations

Competency 0013

Graph and solve algebraic equations with one and two variables.

The following topics are examples of content that may be covered under this competency.

- Graph numbers or number relationships.
- Find the value of the unknown in a given one-variable equation.
- Express one variable in terms of a second variable in two-variable equations.

Two-Dimensional Graphing

The coordinate plane is useful for graphing individual ordered pairs and relationships. The coordinate plane is divided into four quadrants by an *x*-axis (horizontal) and a *y*-axis (vertical). The upper right quadrant is quadrant I, and the others (moving counterclockwise from quadrant I) are II, III, and IV.

Ordered pairs indicate the locations of points on the plane. For instance, (−3, 4) describes a point that's three units *left* from the center of the plane (the "origin") and four units *up*, as shown below.

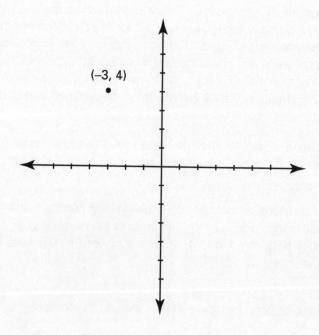

Sets of data can be paired to form many ordered pairs, which in turn can be graphed on the coordinate plane. Consider the following sets of data, which have been paired:

x	y
3	5
4	6
5	7
6	8

Considering each pairing individually, the following ordered pairs are produced: (3, 5), (4, 6), (5, 7), (6, 8). *Plotting* each pair on the coordinate plane produces the following graph:

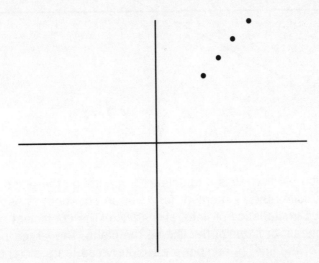

If the sets represent continuous change, the resulting graph may be a line (straight or curved in various ways). Often, relationships between sets of data can be shown as two variable equations or inequalities. Consider the following ordered pairs: (–4, –2), (–2, –1), (0, 0), (2, 1), (4, 2).

Note that the first value in each (the *x* value) is twice as big as the second (the *y* value). Assuming that the ordered pairs represent continuous change, the equation $x = 2y$ can be used to describe the relationship of the *x* values and the *y* values. It is helpful to think of the equation as stating that "*x* is always twice as big as *y*." We can show the equation on the coordinate plane by graphing at least two of the points, then connecting them as shown below.

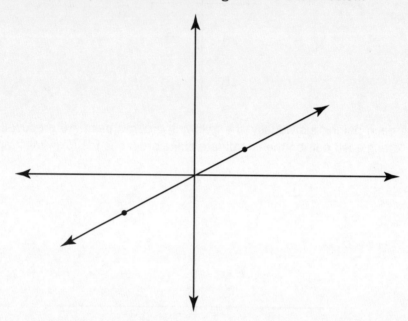

The generic equation $y = mx + b$ is a template for graphs on the plane that are straight lines. That form (sometimes called the "*y*-intercept form" of an equation) is especially useful because it tells two important characteristics of lines at a glance. The coefficient of *x* in the equation (or *m*) indicates the steepness, or *slope* of the line on the plane. The larger the absolute value of *m*, the steeper the slope of the line. (A number's absolute value is its distance from zero, giving no regard to negative signs.) Consider the two equations that follow and their accompanying graphs.

$y = 1/4x + 2$ $y = 5x - 1$

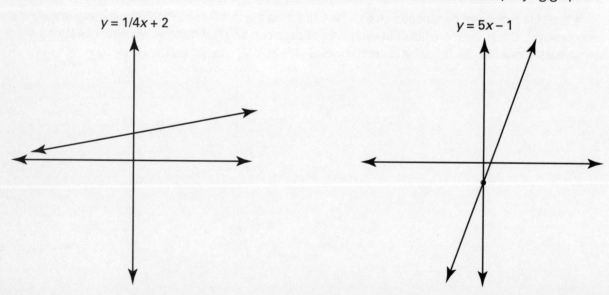

Note that the equation on the left has a small slope ($\frac{1}{4}$), so its graph is nearly horizontal. The other equation has a comparatively large slope (5), so it is steep.

If the coordinates of any two points of a straight line are known, the numerical slope of that line can easily be computed by finding the difference between the points' y values and dividing by the difference of the points' x values. For example, if (2, 5) and (4, 10) are points on a line, the slope of the line is $\frac{5}{2}$ [(5 − 10) ÷ (2 − 4)]. Note that slopes are generally shown as fractions or whole numbers, but not as mixed fractions.

The equation of a straight line in the form $y = mx + b$ tells something else about the line at a glance. The b value indicates where the line will cross or *intercept* the y (vertical) axis. Consider the graph of $y = 2x + 3$ that follows.

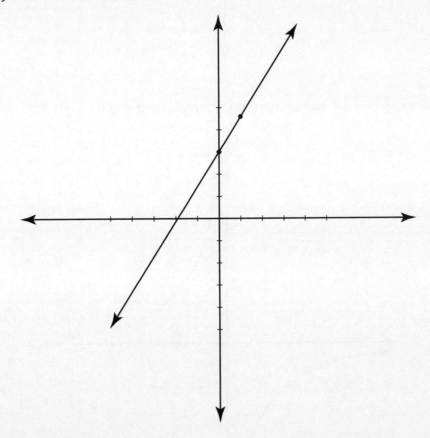

Note that the graph crosses the y-axis at a point that is 3 units above the origin. As long as the equation of a straight line is in the form $y = mx + b$, m gives the slope and b gives the y-intercept. (Note: If $b = 0$, the graph will pass through the origin. In that case, both the equation and the graph are referred to as *direct variations*.)

Other equations may produce curved graphs. For instance, $y = x^2$ produces the following graph, known as a *parabola*.

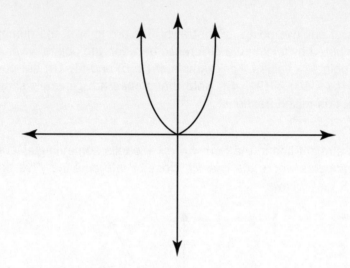

The equation $y = \frac{1}{x}$ is an *inverse variation*; it produces a graph known as a *hyperbola*, as shown below.

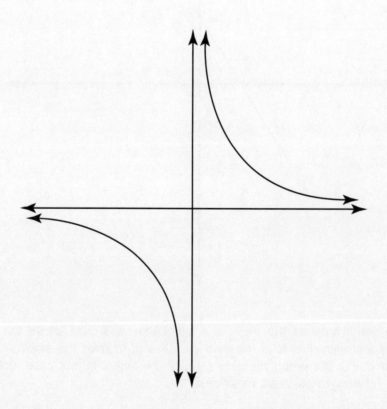

The graphs of *functions* can be shown on the coordinate plane. Such graphs always indicate a continuous (although not necessarily consistent) "movement" from left to right. Below left is the graph of a function; the graph on the right is *not* a function.

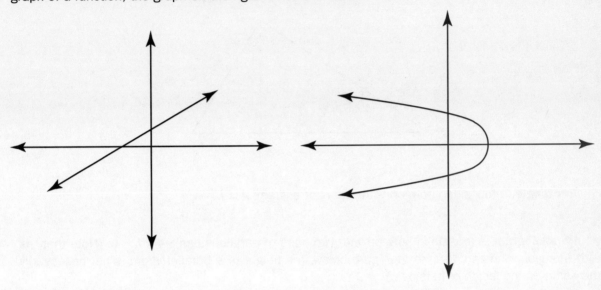

Geometry

Competency 0014

Solve problems involving geometric figures.

The following topics are examples of content that may be covered under this competency.
- Solve problems involving two-dimensional geometric figures (e.g., perimeter and area problems).
- Solve problems involving three-dimensional geometric figures (e.g., volume and surface area problems).

Solving Problems Involving Geometric Figures

The following are formulas for finding the areas of basic polygons (informally defined as closed, coplanar geometric figures with three or more straight sides). Abbreviations used are as follows: *A* stands for *area*, *l* stands for *length*, *w* stands for *width*, *h* stands for *height*, and *b* stands for *length of the base*.

Triangle (a three-sided polygon): $A = \frac{b \times h}{2}$. (Note that, as shown in the figure that follows, the height of a triangle is not necessarily the same as the length of any of its sides.)

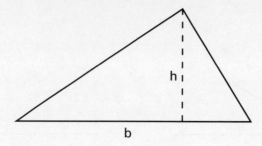

Rectangle (a four-sided polygon with four right angles): $A = l \times w$

Parallelogram (a four-sided polygon with two pairs of parallel sides): $A = l \times w$. (Note that, as with triangles, and as shown in the figure below, the height of a parallelogram is not necessarily the same as the length of its sides.)

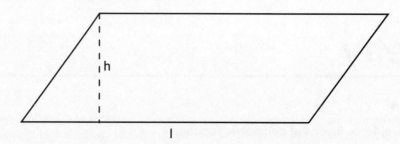

The area of a circle can be found by squaring the length of its radius, then multiplying that product by π. The formula is given as $A = \pi r^2$. (π, or pi, is the ratio of a circle's circumference to its diameter. The value of π is the same for all circles; approximately 3.14159. The approximation 3.14 is adequate for many calculations.) The approximate area of the circle shown below can be found by squaring 6 (giving 36), then multiplying 36 by 3.14, giving an area of about 113 square units.

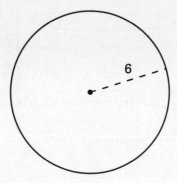

Here are several commonly used volume formulas:

The volume of a rectangular solid is equal to the product of its length, width, and height; $A = l \times w \times h$. (A rectangular solid can be thought of as a box, wherein all intersecting edges form right angles.)

A prism is a polyhedron with two congruent, parallel faces (called bases) and whose lateral (side) faces are parallelograms. The volume of a prism can be found by multiplying the area of the prism's base by its height. The volume of the triangular prism shown hereafter is 60 cubic units. (The area of the triangular base is 10 square units, and the height is 6 units.)

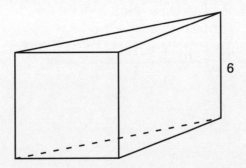

A cylinder is like a prism in that it has parallel faces, but its rounded "side" is smooth. The formula for finding the volume of a cylinder is the same as the formula for finding the volume of a prism: The area of the cylinder's base is multiplied by the height. The volume of the cylinder in the following figure is approximately 628 cubic units. $(5 \times 5 \times \pi \times 8)$.

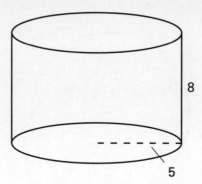

A property of all triangles is that the sum of the measures of the three angles is 180°. If, therefore, the measures of two angles are known, the third can be deduced using addition, then subtraction.

Right triangles (those with a right angle) have several special properties. A chief property is described by the Pythagorean Theorem, which states that in any right triangle with legs (shorter sides) a and b, and hypotenuse (the longest side) c, the sum of the squares of the sides will be equal to the square of the hypotenuse ($a^2 + b^2 = c^2$). Note that in the right triangle shown hereafter, $3^2 + 4^2 = 5^2$.

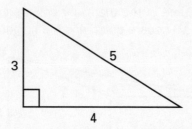

Applying Reasoning Skills

Geometric figures are *similar* if they have the exact same shapes, even if they do not have the same sizes. In transformational geometry, two figures are said to be similar if and only if a similarity transformation maps one figure onto the other. In the figure that follows, triangles A and B are similar.

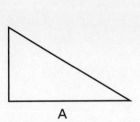
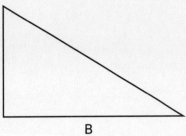

A   B

Corresponding angles of similar figures have the same measure, and the lengths of corresponding sides are proportional. In the similar triangles below, $\angle A \cong \angle D$ (meaning "angle A is congruent to angle D"), $\angle B \cong \angle E$, and $\angle C \cong \angle F$. The corresponding sides of the triangles below are proportional, meaning that:

$$\frac{AB}{DE} = \frac{BC}{EF} = \frac{CA}{FD}$$

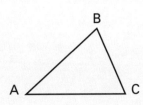
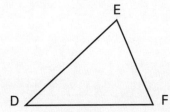

Figures are *congruent* if they have the same shape *and* size. (Congruent figures are also similar.) In the figure below, rectangles A and B are congruent.

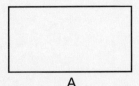
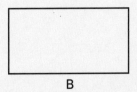

A   B

Straight lines within the same plane that have no points in common (that is, they never cross) are parallel lines. Note that the term *parallel* is used to describe the relationship between two coplanar lines that do not intersect. Lines that are not coplanar—although they never cross—are not considered to be parallel. Coplanar lines crossing at right angles (90°) are perpendicular.

Liberal Studies: Science, Art, Literature, and Social Sciences

Scientific Principles

Competency 0015

Understand and analyze major scientific principles, concepts, and theories, and apply skills, principles, and procedures associated with scientific inquiry.

The following topics are examples of content that may be covered under this competency.

- Analyze the nature of scientific thought and inquiry.
- Use an appropriate illustration or physical model to represent a scientific theory or concept.
- Relate major scientific principles, concepts, or theories to everyday phenomena.
- Apply scientific principles to assess real-world questions or problems.

What Is Science?

The modern word "science" is derived from the Latin *sciencia*, or "knowledge," and refers both to the process of gathering knowledge about the physical world and to the accumulated body of knowledge which is its result. The nature and goals of "science" can be understood in more than one way. Science is often categorized as either "pure," in which scientific knowledge is pursued as its own end, or as "applied," which designates fields such as medicine or engineering that use scientific knowledge to address human needs. Furthermore, the process through which such knowledge is achieved can be classified in two ways. Scientific practice can be divided into **experiment**, which seeks to gather first-hand information, and **theory**, or the development of models to explain these observations. The **empirical** school of thought emphasizes inductive reasoning and reliance on the senses and on individual observation and experience. It holds that scientific theories are objective and can be tested and contradicted. **Scientific realism**, on the other hand, is based on the idea that scientific claims build on one another to become progressively more accurate, and aims to discover an "ideal scientific theory" which accounts for unobservable as well as observable phenomena.

All science relies on the **scientific method** for the collection of reliable data. Although the scientific method is not a specific and uniform set of procedures, it can usefully be broken down into four broad components:

- **Characterization**, or preliminary observations and measurements

- **Hypotheses**, or theoretical explanations for these observations and measurements

- **Predictions**, or logical deductions based on the hypotheses

- **Experiments**, or strategically designed testing of all of the above

The final three steps are frequently repeated until a hypothesis that stands up to testing is achieved. If the conclusions drawn from a hypothesis are not disproved, that hypothesis becomes an accepted scientific **theory** or **law**. It is critical to note that no scientific theory or law is ever definitively proven to be true. If subsequent experimentation disproves it entirely or in part, even a long-standing theory or law must be discarded or modified. The best known recent example of this process is of course the advent of quantum mechanics when, after over two hundred years, Newtonian mechanics were found to be inaccurate for speeds approaching that of light.

Measurement is also central to the scientific method. For a hypothesis to be accepted, the results of an experiment must be **reproducible**; that is, another scientist following the same procedure should be able to duplicate them. Scientific experiments should be carefully designed and controlled, as far as possible, to yield quantitative rather than qualitative results. Thus, science relies heavily on the related discipline of **mathematics**, which scientists use as a tool to evaluate the results of their observations and to organize large quantities of data into averages, ranges, and statistical probabilities. All measurements are limited by the fundamental uncertainty of the measuring device, which necessitates the use of **significant figures**. This concept is based on the fact that calculations on measurements cannot generate results that are more precise than the measurements themselves. When scientists read the results of measurements made by others, therefore, they presume that the recorded values involve a final digit that is an estimate based on the inherent accuracy of the instrument or device.

Science can be roughly divided into three main areas: the **physical sciences**, the **earth sciences**, and the **life or biological sciences**. The physical sciences include physics, chemistry, and astronomy; the earth sciences include geology, paleontology, oceanography, and meteorology, and the life sciences include all the branches of botany, zoology, and cell or microbiology. These areas of specialization can be divided into further sub-sections. Physics, for example, has given rise to disciplines that include mechanics, thermodynamics, and optics. In addition, there are numerous scientific fields that combine the three main branches of science, such as geophysics or biochemistry.

Teaching Science

The sheer bulk and variety of scientific knowledge both provides ample opportunities for students to apply scientific principles and methods to real-world questions and phenomena, and raises questions about how to teach these skills. Models and illustrations can often help to make scientific concepts accessible by helping students to visualize a relevant system—for example, a volcano, a cell wall, or a virus. All models share some important features and limitations. In general and abstract terms, models have an information input, an information processor, and an output of expected results. It is important to emphasize the artificiality of any given model, its status as a simplified replica of the system it illustrates. For models to be effective as teaching tools, certain guiding parameters must be in place: simplifying assumptions must be acknowledged, boundary conditions or initial conditions must be identified, and the range of applicability of the model should be understood. The following are varieties of models frequently employed in the classroom:

Conceptual Models are qualitative, often schematic, models that make sense of real world systems and processes. They are used as a first step in the development of more complex models. Conceptual models should be familiar to students, as human beings are constantly, if unconsciously, employing them. Everyone receives information, processes it, and responds accordingly on a daily basis. This sort of processing of information results in a sort of mental model teachers can use deliberately to explain how things in our surrounding environment work.

Interactive Demonstrations replicate part of a system of interest and are often constructed from materials or objects familiar to students from everyday life. Interactive demonstrations are accessible physical models of systems that share key characteristics with their extant counterparts. These models often provide a link between conceptual models and models of more complex real-world systems.

Mathematical and Statistical Models involve solving equations relevant to a system or characterizing it based on statistical values such as mean, mode, or variance. Mathematical models can be further divided into *Analytical Models* and *Numerical Models*. Statistical models are useful in identifying patterns and underlying relationships between data sets.

Visual Models are models, including illustrations, charts, graphs, and diagrams, that help students "see" how a system operates. A visual model such as a graph can stand alone as a direct rendering of data, or it can be applied to one or more other types of model in order to present its output in a visually accessible format.

In practice, most models combine more than one of the above functions.

In recent decades, many science educators have become concerned that, despite access to models and to hands-on experimentation, traditional science programs emphasize memorized facts and formulas over critical thinking and application of the scientific method, thus making it difficult for students to apply scientific knowledge to the real world. They advocate programs which foster **conceptual change**, or the process of identifying students' incorrect assumptions and replacing them through experimentation, thus enabling them to construct their own models of scientific principles. Science education, according to proponents of conceptual change, should:

- *Stress relevance.* Unless students appreciate the relevance of their experiments to their everyday life, they may dismiss surprising results as applicable only to the classroom or laboratory setting.

- *Encourage students to make predictions.* Students asked to predict the results of their experiments are more willing to change their minds than those who observe passively. This aspect of science instruction is essential because it asks students to link their new and existing knowledge in order to form hypotheses.

- *Stress consistency.* Teachers should make students aware of inconsistencies in their thinking and ask them to consider how two contradictory statements could be true. Ideally, students will confront inconsistencies and change their thinking as a result.

The goal of these science programs is the development of logical, consistent thought and of an orderly view of the world which prevents the compartmentalization of knowledge.

The Development and Social Contexts of Science

Competency 0016

Understand and analyze the historical development and cultural contexts of science and technology and the impact of science on society.

The following topics are examples of content that may be covered under this competency.
- Analyze the historical development and impact of key scientific ideas and discoveries.
- Evaluate factors that have promoted or hindered developments in science and technology.
- Assess the implications of recent developments in science and technology.

The Origins of Science

The combination of theory and practice that we know as modern science is a relatively recent development which had separate beginnings in the technology of early tool-making and other crafts, and in philosophy and religion. In the early civilizations of the Tigris-Euphrates and Nile valleys, for example, artisans and craft-workers were responsible for practical advances in metallurgy, agriculture, transportation, and navigation, and priests and scribes developed written language and early mathematics for the purposes of record keeping, land division, and calendar determination.

Science in Western Antiquity

What we think of as "pure science," or scientific theory devised simply for the expansion of knowledge or understanding of the physical world, has its roots in early Greek, or Hellenic, culture and its attempts to order the world according to philosophical principles. Notable among these is the theory, which persisted into the Middle Ages and Renaissance, that the universe is composed of the four basic elements earth, air, fire, and water. Early Greece produced such scientific figures as Hippocrates of Cos (4th century BCE), who formulated the science of diagnosis based on accurate descriptions of the symptoms of various diseases, and the philosophers Plato (427–347 BCE) and Aristotle (384–322 BCE).

Early Eastern Contributions to Science

Although a great deal of Eastern thought was devoted to theological and political rather than "scientific" concerns, prevailing religious and philosophical doctrines gave rise to multiple theories of metallurgy, alchemy, and medicine. Eastern societies were also the first to adopt many advanced technologies, making several accomplishments in science parallel to early developments in the West. Important early discoveries made by Asian scientists include paper, in the 2nd century CE, block printing in the 7th, movable clay type by the 11th, and cast-metal type in Korea by the beginning of the 15th. Gunpowder was invented in the 3rd century and firearms were in use by the 13th, as was the magnetic compass during the 11th and 12th. Indian mathematicians developed a numeral system based on place value and including a zero, and important Hindu scientists flourished in the 6th and 7th centuries, making contributions to astronomy and mathematics. During the 7th and 8th centuries, Muslim scholars introduced and preserved the scientific works both of these Hindu and other Asian scholars and of the Greeks, modifying them and adding valuable commentary. This body of learning first began to be discovered by Europeans in the 11th century.

The European Renaissance and the Scientific Revolution

The commonplace description of the Middle Ages as "Dark Ages" is a misnomer. The Middle Ages saw the establishment of many of Europe's great universities, as well as the development of several important labor-saving technologies and, in the 15th century, of the printing press. Nevertheless, science, in the modern sense of the term, is a 16th or 17th century development made possible by the union of the technologically motivated craft tradition with philosophically based scientific theory. A pervasive feeling of dissatisfaction with extant modes of understanding, which dated back to the later Middle Ages and was both the product and the stimulus of events such as the Protestant Reformation and the widespread growth of literacy in Europe, also gave rise to the revolution in science embodied in the work of Copernicus, Paracelsus, Vesalius, and others. The development of practical tools of observation such as the telescope, microscope, and mechanical clock were also of course central to the rise of empiricism and the scientific method.

Another important factor in the scientific revolution was improved communication and general societal interest, made manifest in the 17th and 18th centuries, in the establishment of learned societies and academies throughout Europe. The Royal Society in England (est. 1660) and the Academy of Sciences in France (est. 1666) were two of the most important early societies, to be joined later by royal academies established at Berlin (1700) and at St. Petersburg (1724). The societies and academies provided early opportunities for the widespread dissemination and consideration of scientific methodologies and results. The best-known figure associated with the scientific societies is Sir Isaac Newton, whose work on mechanics and astronomy dominated those fields for over two centuries.

Technological Advancement and the Industrial Revolution

It was during the 18th and 19th centuries that the individual branches of science developed into the traditional forms by which they are recognized today. The major 19th-century technological impetus was the Industrial Revolution. The need to supply power to factories, mines, ships, and railroads led to the invention of the steam engine. The development of the internal combustion engine led to the growth of petroleum technology. The 19th century also saw new agricultural machinery and a drastic accompanying increase in productivity as well as the invention of the electric generator, electric motor, and numerous other electric devices central to contemporary life.

New Directions: The Rise of Modern Science

In addition to rapid technological development, the 18th and early 19th centuries were characterized by a feeling of certainty that most important scientific discoveries had been made and that remaining areas of the unknown could be addressed by resolving minor details within the existing corpus of knowledge. Subsequent discoveries in all areas of science, however, have forced scientists to reevaluate some of their most fundamental assumptions. In physics, the early 20th century explanation of atomic structure necessitated the rejection of classical notions of space, time, matter, and energy in favor of the quantum theory and the theory of relativity. Related developments, such as Werner Heisenberg's Uncertainty Principle—which states that accurate measurement of one quality, such as momentum, makes the precise measurement of another, such as position, impossible—have cast doubt on the fundamental possibility of understanding the physical world. These theories, particularly the quantum theory, have revolutionized chemistry, biology, physics, and every other scientific field.

In biology, the modern revolution began in the 19th century with the publication of Charles Darwin's theory of evolution (1859) and Gregor Mendel's theory of genetics. The development of biochemistry and the field of molecular biology have enabled such monumental results as the discovery of the structure of deoxyribonucleic acid (DNA), the molecule carrying the genetic code. In medicine, modern biology and biochemistry have made possible drugs such as penicillin and insulin, mechanical devices such as pacemakers, and procedures for implantation of artificial or donated organs.

Practical and Ethical Implications of Scientific Development

Modern science has had an immeasurable impact on everyday life. The recent proliferation of electronic computers has revolutionized not only medicine but also communication, education, and business. Also instrumental in the development of these areas has been a dramatic improvement in transportation capacity, from the advent of the automobile and the early airplane to the modern supersonic jet, and finally, the realization of space travel. Prevention or cure seems on the horizon for an unprecedented number of diseases, and science is also working toward increased control over the environment and new sources of energy.

Modern science also faces a number of challenges. Some of these are practical, such as the production and distribution of enough food and energy to meet the demands of a population which is both rapidly growing and increasingly dependent on technology and the elimination or reduction of pollutants in the environment. Science must also, however, address a myriad of political and sociological questions. Recent issues have included the proliferation of nuclear, biological, and chemical weapons, and questions regarding the use of computers and other electronic devices that may seriously infringe on individual privacy and freedom. Many recent developments in medicine and biology, such as gene manipulation, organ transplantation, and the increasing capacity to artificially sustain life, have important and complex ethical implications. Science is a self-consciously "rational" discipline, but can never really exist in cerebral isolation. Scientific research and development is, rather, in constant interaction with political and social events, developments in the arts, philosophy, and religion, and the life experience of the individual scientist.

The Fine Arts

Competency 0017

> **Understand, interpret, and compare representations from the visual and performing arts from different periods and cultures, and understand the relationship of works of art to their social and historical contexts.**
>
> The following topics are examples of content that may be covered under this competency.
> * Identify and evaluate major historical and contemporary developments and movements in the arts.
> * Interpret and compare representations of works of art from different periods and cultures in terms of form, theme, mood, or technique.
> * Analyze ways in which the content of a given work of art reflects or influences a specific social or historical context.

Visual Arts in the Western World

The earliest Western works of painting and sculpture were generally religious in nature. In Egypt and Mesopotamia, as well as Europe and the Americas, very early artists created representations of deities or other pieces with religious or ritual significance or use. Classical and Hellenic Greek art was more strictly representational, and took as its most common subject the human form: the Greeks' naturalistic rendering of the human body would influence European sculpture for centuries to come. Roman adaptations of the Greek style were less concentrated on idealizing the body than on reproducing its particularities, and ushered in the craft of portraiture.

European art during the Middle Ages, however, was almost entirely religious in subject matter and was unconcerned with realism. Medieval artists strove to express theological truths, rather than to reproduce reality, and the media they most commonly employed were part of Christian practice—stained glass, wall paintings, and statuary in cathedrals, and illuminated manuscripts of devotional texts. Late medieval, or Gothic, architecture was popularly revived in the late 18th and early 19th centuries.

The Renaissance brought a return to classical models and a renewed interest in realism, along with a broader variety of subject matter. Renaissance artwork was still generally large scale and for public consumption. The most famous example is perhaps Michelangelo's Sistine Chapel. Painting and sculpting, in the 17th and 18th century, were to become increasingly detailed and ornate, elaborate and rich in texture and—for painting—color.

The late 18th and early 19th century saw diverse reactions against this trend, producing a great number of smaller and more intimate paintings suitable for private homes and allowing the expression of emotion to take precedence over the extreme realism that characterized the preceding centuries.

Art produced during the 19th and 20th centuries took many directions, but generally, painters began to revolt against the classic codes of composition, careful execution, harmonious coloring, and heroic subject matter. Patronage by the church and state sharply declined at this time, and artists' views became more independent and subjective.

Major Movements in Western Painting and Sculpture			
Style	**Historical Period**	**Defining Aesthetic**	**Major Artists**
Gothic	12th – 16th C.	Religious themes, schematic rather than realistic composition,	Generally anonymous. Martini, Pisano
Renaissance	14th – 17th C.	Realism, interest in anatomy, perspective. Large-scale works.	Botticelli, Da Vinci, Ghirlandio, Michelangelo
Baroque/Rococo	17th – 18th C.	Less complex. Realistic, emotional, increasingly ornate.	Caravaggio, Bernini, Caracci, Boucher
Neoclassicism	mid 18th – early 19th C.	Borrows heavily from ancient Greeks. Less emotional, rigid.	Canova, Antoine, Ingres
Romanticism	late 18th – mid-19th C.	Reaction to Neoclassicism. Emotional, individual.	Constable, Turner, Blake
Impressionism	1860s – 1880s	Reproduces the subjective impression of light.	Monet, Sisley, Renoir
Post-Impressionism	1880s – 1900s	Various. Generally emotionally charged, often dystopic.	Gauguin, Cezanne, Van Gogh, Rousseau, Toulouse-Lautrec
Expressionism/ Abstract Expressionism	1910s – 1940s	Subjective. Without object, or does not represent accurately.	Kandinsky, Rothko, Pollock
Surrealism	1924 – 1950s	Fantastic visuals from subconscious. No logical composition.	Dalí, Arp, Magritte, Modigliani
Contemporary art	~1960 – present	Various. Often multi-media and political.	Quinn, Mapplethorpe, Cathal, Haring, Basquiat

Performing Arts in the Western World

Western performing arts have their beginnings in the Greek tragedies written by such playwrights as Seneca and Euripides. These performances were shaped by the large outdoor arenas in which they were performed, and the actors, all of whom were male, employed exaggerated facial expressions and costuming in order to make themselves understood by the audience. Medieval drama also tended to privilege expressiveness over realism. It took the form of mystery and morality plays in which guilds of amateurs—also all men—enacted Biblical or other religious pieces in the spirit of broad comedy, interacting freely with the audience.

Modern professional acting began in the 16th century, a period perhaps best known for the works of playwrights such as William Shakespeare and Christopher Marlowe. Although actors in the early Renaissance remained exclusively male, the period saw the beginnings of psychological realism and of efforts to sustain the illusion of naturalism. Theater in the late 17th and early 18th centuries tended to be more comedic and irreverent, and women were beginning to appear on the stage. Despite the contemporary theater's interest in naturalism, though, actors still declaimed their lines in the deliberate style that, innovations by actors such as David Garrick and Charles Macklin notwithstanding, would hold sway until the beginning of the 20th century.

The best known figure behind the shift to a more natural style of acting is Constantin Stanislavsky, whose intensely psychological Method was made famous by actors such as Marlon Brando. Contemporary performance art merges the visual and the performing arts, blending acting with film, video, sound, and static visual imagery. Although the drama of every period has commented—some times more explicitly than others—on the social and political realities of the regime which produced it, modern drama is often overtly political, addressing issues including the experience of women, minorities, and gay and lesbian artists, foreign policy, and crises such as the AIDS epidemic.

Literature

Competency 0018

> **Understand, interpret, and compare examples of literature from different periods and cultures, and understand the relationship of works of literature to their social and historical contexts.**
>
> The following topics are examples of content that may be covered under this competency.
> - Identify and evaluate major historical and contemporary developments and movements in world literature.
> - Interpret and compare works of literature from different periods and cultures in terms of form, subject, theme, mood, or technique.
> - Analyze ways in which the content of a given work of literature reflects or influences a specific social or historical context.

While it is impossible to be an expert in all areas of literature, one would do well to have at least a passing familiarity with the works of the following authors. Keep in mind that this list is not meant in any way to be exhaustive or comprehensive; rather, it is meant to serve as a catalyst to begin thinking about literature in its historical context.

Important Authors

Edward Abbey	F. Scott Fitzgerald	George Orwell
Chinua Achebe	Gustave Flaubert	Ovid
Richard Adams	Robert Frost	Walker Percy
Edward Albee	Gabriel García Márquez	Sylvia Plath
Louisa May Alcott	William Gass	Plato
Sherman Alexie	Nikolai Gogol	Edgar Allan Poe
Nelson Algren	Gunter Grass	Ezra Pound
Maya Angelou	Graham Greene	Richard Powers
Aristophanes	Thomas Hardy	Marcel Proust
Jane Austen	Nathaniel Hawthorne	Alexander Pushkin
Paul Auster	Joseph Heller	Thomas Pynchon
James Baldwin	Ernest Hemingway	Ishmael Reed
Amiri Baraka (LeRoi Jones)	Herman Hesse	John (Jack) Reed
Donald Barthleme	Abbie Hoffman	Carter Revard
Baudelaire	Homer	Adrienne Rich
Samuel Beckett	Nick Hornby	Philip Roth
Saul Bellow	Langston Hughes	Arundati Roy
Ray Bradbury	Victor Hugo	Salman Rushdie
Bertolt Brecht	Zora Neale Hurston	J.D. Salinger
Joseph Bruchac	Aldous Huxley	David Sedaris
Jorge Luis Borges	Henrik Ibsen	William Shakespeare
Charlotte and Emily Bronte	John Irving	George Bernard Shaw
Pearl S. Buck	Henry James	Mary Shelley
Charles Bukowski	Stephen Graham Jones	Sam Sheppard
William S. Burroughs	James Joyce	Leslie Marmon Silko
Albert Camus	Franz Kafka	Upton Sinclair
Truman Capote	John Keats	Susan Sontag
Lewis Carroll	Jack Kerouac	Gertrude Stein
Raymond Carver	Ken Kesey	John Steinbeck
Willa Cather	Jamaica Kincaid	Wallace Stevens
Louis-Ferdinand Celine	Maxine Hong Kingston	Robert Louis Stevenson

Miguel de Cervantes

Paddy Chayefsky

Raymond Chandler

Geoffrey Chaucer

Anton Chekhov

Sandra Cisneros

J.M. Coetzee

Joseph Conrad

James Fenimore Cooper

Quentin Crisp

e.e.cummings

Dante Alighieri

Daniel Defoe

Don DeLillo

Charles Dickens

Emily Dickinson

Joan Didion

Isak Dinesen

Stephen Dixon

John Dos Passos

Fyodor Dostoevsky

Frederick Douglass

W.E.B. DuBois

Alexander Dumas

Umberto Eco

Dave Eggers

George Eliot

T.S. Eliot

Ralph Ellison

Ralph Waldo Emerson

Louise Erdrich

William Faulkner

Lawrence Ferlinghetti

Rudyard Kipling

Milan Kundera

Jerzy Kosinsky

Nella Larsen

D.H. Lawrence

Harper Lee

Ursula K. LeGuin

Sinclair Lewis

Jack London

Federico Garcia Lorca

Norman Mailer

Thomas Mann

William Maxwell

D'Arcy McNickle

Herman Melville

Arthur Miller

Henry Miller

N. Scott Momaday

Irvin Morris

Toni Morrison

Alice Munro

Robert Musil

Vladimir Nabokov

Howard Nemerov

Pablo Neruda

Frederick Nietzsche

Frank Norris

Joyce Carol Oates

Flannery O'Connor

Clifford Odets

Kole Omotoso

Ayn Rand

Bram Stoker

Jonathan Swift

Luci Tapahonso

Dylan Thomas

Hunter S. Thompson

Henry David Thoreau

Laura Tohe

Leo Tolstoy

John Kennedy Toole

Dalton Trumbo

Mark Twain

John Updike

Edgardo Vega Yunque

Jules Verne

Gore Vidal

Voltaire

Kurt Vonnegut, Jr.

David Foster Wallace

H.G. Wells

Nathaniel West

Edith Wharton

Walt Whitman

Oscar Wilde

Tennessee Williams

William Carlos Williams

Sloan Wilson

Virginia Woolf

Richard Wright

Howard Zinn

Emile Zola

Some Important Literary Movements

Victorian	British Realism
American Colonial Literature	Post-Modern Meta-Fiction
Harlem Renaissance	German Expressionism
The Beat Poets	Existentialism
Southern Gothic	Transcendentalism

History and Its Influences

Competency 0019

Understand and analyze the major political, social, economic, scientific, and cultural developments that shaped the course of history.

The following topics are examples of content that may be covered under this competency.
- Demonstrate an understanding of the principal characteristics and important cultural values of the major civilizations of Asia, Africa, Europe, and the Americas.
- Evaluate the influence of varied ideas, movements, and historical developments on Western religious, artistic, scientific, and political ideas and beliefs (e.g., the Renaissance, the Reformation, the French Revolution).
- Analyze the major causes of varied historical developments (e.g., the Industrial Revolution, Colonialism) and evaluate their impact on the politics and culture of the modern world.
- Demonstrate knowledge of the major political movements of the twentieth century and analyze their influence on contemporary societies.
- Demonstrate an understanding of significant individuals, movements, ideas, and conflicts that have shaped U.S. history and culture (e.g., the Civil War, the New Deal).

World History

From earliest times, humans lived in hunter-gatherer societies, often nomadic and heavily dependent on local natural resources such as edible plants and game animals. Over time, other forms of social organization have developed, such as semi-nomadic livestock herding and subsistence farming, village-based subsistence farming, city-states, kingdoms, and empires. Societies have been classified according to their level of technological development based on whether their tools were made of stone, bronze, iron, or more advanced materials. This has led to the designations Stone Age, Bronze Age, Iron Age, etc.

These designations have also applied to historical periods in Western civilization based on the level of technology in use at the time. During these periods, civilizations arose in the ancient Middle East to which modern Western civilization can trace its roots. These civilizations include Sumeria, Israel, Egypt, Assyria, Babylonia, and Medo-Persia. In these empires, writing systems and codes of laws were developed that represent the earliest origins of modern Western writing systems and law codes.

Of pivotal importance in Western history is the rise of the ancient Greek civilization, beginning with the conquest by Alexander the Great in the 4th century B.C.E. of much of the former territory of the previous Middle Eastern empires. This led to the spread of the Greek culture and language throughout the region. The presence of many words with Greek roots in modern European languages, including English, testifies to the lasting impact of ancient Greek civilization. Even after the fall of the political structures founded by Alexander the Great, ancient Greek learning in the arts, the sciences, philosophy, and political thought formed part of the basis of Western learning for centuries to come.

The civilization of Rome was strongly influenced by ancient Greece, but in time achieved greater dominance in the Middle East and the Mediterranean region. By conquering the Greek dynasty ruling over Egypt in 31 B.C.E., Rome became the undisputed regional power and in time went on to conquer much of the known world. Rome was the first empire to extend the ancient Middle Eastern and Greek cultures northward into Europe. In the first and second centuries C.E., the period known as *Pax Romana* (Roman Peace) saw the development of an extensive system of roads, as well as a postal system, that facilitated transportation and thus favored the expansion of trade. This was also favored by a relative absence of internal conflicts, enforced by Roman troops. The peace of this period led to a flourishing of the arts and higher learning, still heavily influenced by classical Greek models.

Beginning in the 3rd century, Rome began a long decline as the succession of emperors grew unstable and the army began to encounter problems maintaining control over outlying provinces. In the 5th century, Rome was conquered by invading Germanic tribes. Remnants of imperial power survived, however, in the Eastern Empire with its capital in Constantinople and the Roman Catholic Church. The Germanic invaders also preserved and adopted much of what was left of the Roman Empire.

Even after Rome's power was broken, its impact was still felt in its former territories in Europe. The vacuum of power resulting from Rome's fall was filled by the Church and the feudal system. In this system of social organization, the peasants, who worked the land, were ruled by nobles. Among the nobles, the less powerful swore oaths of loyalty to the more powerful, who promised them military protection in exchange for their loyal support. This system, with many variations, was the dominant system in Europe throughout the Middle Ages. The Holy Roman Empire was the foremost political organization of the feudal system in Europe.

The Middle Ages were also known as the Dark Ages because of political instability in the early centuries after Rome's fall. The sharp decrease in the spread of knowledge, widespread illiteracy and disasters such as the Black Plague of the 14th century contributed to the problems of the era. Stability was highly valued in the midst of such problems, and medieval world views emphasized finding security by accepting one's status in the great scheme of things. In time, however, the increase of political stability and the growth of trade and commerce set the stage for the early modern era of Western history.

The modern era began with the period known as the Renaissance, meaning "rebirth," beginning around 1450. In this period, an increased interest in classical Roman and Greek learning led to advances in the arts. The growth of commerce, banking, and industry in this period favored the spread of knowledge among the rising middle class. Around the time of the Renaissance, the Reformation also challenged the dominance of the Roman Catholic Church and led to the development of Protestantism, which more closely reflected the values of Northern European cultures and the middle class. The interest in discovering new knowledge, and the attitude of challenging traditional views, have continued until today. At this time England, Spain, and Portugal also began exploring the globe and founding overseas colonies.

The renewed interest in classical learning of the Renaissance spurred a great increase of scientific knowledge in the 17th century, which further challenged traditional views of humanity, earth, and the universe. This period was also marked by political change as the feudal system slowly gave way to the development of monarchies in Western Europe. In this form of government, power was centralized in the hands of the king rather than shared among the nobles. Advances continued in the fields of science, politics, education, and commerce; these advances further removed Europe from its medieval past and favored the growth of the middle class.

The 18th century saw the development of such ideals as rationality, reason, logic, and the application of scientific knowledge for the good of society. This period, known as the Enlightenment, further challenged medieval ideals of stability and order by championing progress and planned change. The growing pressures for progress caused strained relations between the ruling class and the middle class; the conflict eventually exploded in the French Revolution of 1792. This event highlighted the need for the rule of law in order to restrain the excesses of nobles and monarchs, and favored the development of representative forms of government.

Meanwhile, the Industrial Revolution and colonialism were transforming the face of Europe and many other regions of the world. In the 19th century, the pressures for progress unleashed in the Enlightenment found expression in the unprecedented growth of industry and technology, and Western civilization expanded its power throughout the rest of the world. While Spain and Portugal were losing their colonies in the Americas, England, France, the Netherlands, and Germany expanded into Africa, Asia, and the Pacific, including areas that had never been colonized by Western nations before. The colonies were intended to serve as sources of cheap raw materials for Western industry, and markets for the manufactured goods it produced.

Patterns of Historical Development in Recent Times

The competition for the resources from overseas colonies was one of the major reasons for World War I, which, despite its name, was mainly a European war. Sparked by the assassination of the heir to the throne of Austria-Hungary, it soon claimed the lives of many more soldiers than any previous war. In addition, in countries such as Great Britain and Germany, the scale of the war meant for the first time that people from all walks of life—not just professional soldiers—became casualties of the war. In France, about half the men of an entire generation were killed, and in one battle (the battle of Sommes) the British suffered over 60,000 casualties on the first day alone.

Germany, the major instigator of World War I, fell far short in its attempt to expand its empire. At the end of World War I, the few colonies that Germany controlled fell into the hands of Great Britain and France, and Germany was a much poorer country than it had been before losing the war. Even though most of the world, especially Europe, was horrified over the carnage of World War I, Germany turned to a dictator who promised to restore the country's military might less than 20 years after the end of the first war. Adolf Hitler eventually failed in that mission, but he did temporarily make Germany a feared military power, killing 12 million people in concentration camps, including 6 million Jews, and 20 million Soviets while trying to conquer Europe. During World War II, which began in 1939 when Hitler invaded Poland, Germany was joined by Japan and Italy to form the Axis, which fought against the Allies—mainly Great Britain, the United States, and the Soviet Union. (France, perhaps remembering the dead of World War I, surrendered to Germany early in the war.) Although Great Britain was supposedly among the winners of the war, it expended so many resources in winning that it was no longer the dominant power in the world.

The Soviet Union was formed from Russia and other countries under Russian rule during World War I, by way of a Communist revolution. Communism had arisen during the nineteenth century, partly in response to the Industrial Revolution and the spread of capitalism. Its main theorist, Karl Marx, had expected revolution to come in one of the more industrially advanced countries, such as Britain or his native Germany, but the unpopularity of World War I helped create a power vacuum in Russia, where there had been plenty of misery among the poor along with relatively organized protest against the rich. The Communist Party under Vladimir Lenin took advantage of this to create a promised "worker's paradise." The Soviet Union was, however, beset by many problems from the beginning, and the Communist system was not well equipped to handle them. After Lenin's death in 1927, Josef Stalin took over the political machinery, and through disastrous policies and legal executions, Stalin was responsible for a tremendous amount of death and suffering. After Hitler invaded Poland in 1939, Stalin signed a non-aggression treaty with Germany, but Hitler nevertheless invaded the Soviet Union soon thereafter. The Soviets suffered far greater devastation than any other country during World War II, but they persevered and eventually drove the German armies all the way back to Germany and became one of the two main beneficiaries of the war.

Almost immediately after World War II, the Cold War began. The British Empire began to crumble. Its most important colony, India, broke away in 1948 under the famously nonviolent leadership of Mohandas Gandhi, and it was unable to prevent the establishment of the Jewish state of Israel in formerly British Palestine in the same year. Most of Britain's African colonies became independent in the 1950s and 1960s. In the meantime, Europe was divided by a figurative Iron Curtain between U.S.-dominated Western Europe and Soviet-dominated Eastern Europe.

In most of the rest of the world—what came to be known as the Third World—the two Cold War antagonists used both military might and peacefully persuasive means to gather as many countries as possible into their sphere. China, in which a Communist revolution under Mao Ze-Dong succeeded following the great devastation of Japanese occupation during World War II, was solidly in the Soviet camp for many years but was also rather independent during much of the Cold War. Japan, though not allowed to have a military as a condition of its defeat in World War II, became a U.S. ally and a dominant Asian economic power. The United States and the Soviet Union waged war through their allies in Korea (each side got half the country) and Vietnam (the Soviets got the whole country, but the United States succeeded in stopping the expansion of Soviet influence beyond Southeast Asia). The Cold War came to an end in 1989, when the Soviet Union essentially surrendered. It had never been a war between equals; the United States had emerged much stronger than had its rival, but the Soviet Union was able to keep up the appearance of equality by mimicking the U.S. development of weapon systems centered around nuclear devices. Even in that arena, however, the United States eventually wore down the Soviet Union, and the post–Cold War government soon gave independence to most of the non-Russian countries under its control and withdrew its troops from Eastern Europe.

The end of the Cold War did not, however, bring peace to the world. In the formerly Soviet-dominated state of Yugoslavia, long-buried ethnic rivalries (of which most Yugoslav citizens were barely aware) led to civil war, genocide, and an eventual split into three countries. In Africa, many of the countries that France and Britain had set up during the Colonial Period started to break apart along old tribal lines, occasionally leading to terrible bloodbaths, such as the Rwandan slaughter of the Tutsis. Although the South African revolution, led by Nelson Mandela, was a relatively peaceful victory for the people of that country, most of Africa is still subject to poverty, disease, and war. In the Middle East, the presence of Israel, along with the failure of the governments of the mostly Muslim countries of the region to defeat Israel or establish wealth for most of their citizens, has led to a spread of fundamentalist Islam. These extremist groups have wreaked much havoc in the world, most notably in the attacks on the World Trade Center and the Pentagon in 2001. Although extreme wings of all the major religions have dealt death and destruction throughout history, the fundamentalist Muslim extremists are perhaps the most feared threat to peace in the early twenty-first century.

Critical Thinking
Skills: Writing

SUBAREA VI—CRITICAL THINKING SKILLS: WRITING

Competency 0021

Prepare an organized, developed composition in edited English in response to instructions regarding content, purpose, and audience.

The following topics are examples of content that may be covered under this competency.

- Demonstrate the ability to prepare a unified and focused piece of writing on a given topic using language and style appropriate to a specified audience, purpose, and occasion.
- Demonstrate the ability to take a position on a contemporary social or political issue and defend that position with reasoned arguments and supporting examples.
- Demonstrate the ability to use effective sentence structure and apply the standards of edited English.
- Demonstrate the ability to spell, capitalize, and punctuate according to the standards of edited English.

This portion of the OGET contains a writing assignment. The written assignment asks test-takers to compose a composition, or written response, on a given subject. You will be evaluated on your ability to communicate the written message to a specified audience. The compositions are graded on the following criteria: appropriateness (how the writer uses language and style in relation to the given audience and purpose), unity and focus (the clarity of the main idea), development (supporting details are specific and clearly understood), organization (logical sequence of thoughts and ideas, and overall clarity of the work), sentence structure, usage, and mechanical conventions (the extent to which the response has no errors in usage, spelling, capitalization, punctuation, and the precision of word choice). The responses are graded on a scale from "4" to "U," or "Unscorable," or "B", "Blank."

In an essay earning a score of 4, ideas are presented clearly, arguments are well organized, and there is extensive and specific supporting detail. The writer communicates through effective sentence structure and uses proper spelling, grammar, and punctuation.

In an essay scoring 3, ideas are well communicated, but supporting details might not be as precise or extensive as in a paper scoring 4. The ideas might be incomplete or generally ineffective. Minor errors in areas such as punctuation, spelling, word choice, or general usage are present.

A score of 2 is given to essays that do not support the main idea with specific details, and in which the overall organization of the work is unclear. The purpose of the essay might need to be inferred because it is vaguely stated. Errors are found in word choice, usage, sentence structure, spelling, and punctuation.

The response score 1 would be given to an essay that does not communicate the overall message and is lacking logical sequence of ideas. Often the main idea is not clearly stated, and supporting details are confusing. Common errors include incorrect use of language and sentence structure. Spelling and punctuation errors are found throughout the response.

A response given a U is deemed unscorable. A U score would be given if the essay is not on the given topic, is illegible, too short, or not written in English.

A response given a B is self-explanatory (i.e., a blank sheet that contains no answer).

Sample essays from different scoring levels appear at the end of the Practice Test, accompanied by critical commentary.

Carefully read the assignment before you begin to write. Think about your ideas and what you would like to communicate to the reader. You may wish to make an outline for the topic to help organize your thoughts, but be sure to write the final draft of your response in the test booklet. Your score will be based on what is written in the response booklet. When you have finished writing, be sure to review your work and make any changes you believe would enhance your score.

This review will guide you through a step-by-step process of how to write an essay, from writing strategies to budgeting time during the exam. Even if you feel that you are a good writer, you should still study this review, as it will help you become familiar with essay writing. The strategies included are provided to help you write an essay that is to the point, easily understood, properly structured, well supported, and correct according to the rules of grammar. You will not be expected to write a best-selling book in order to pass this test. Remember, the more you practice the strategies provided in this review, the easier it will be for you to write a good essay.

Strategies for the Essay

To give yourself the best chance of writing a good essay, you should follow these steps.

Before the test, this is your plan:

Step 1:   Study the following review to enhance your ability to write an essay. Remember, the sharper your skills, the more likely you are to receive a passing grade on your writing sample.

Step 2:   Practice writing an essay. The best way to do this is to complete the Practice Test.

Step 3:   Learn and understand the directions, so that you don't waste valuable time reading them on the test day. This will allow you to quickly review them before writing your essay.

Step 4:   Develop your essay from the notes you have made. Present your position clearly and logically, making sure to provide adequate examples and/or support. Write your draft on scratch paper.

Step 5:   Proofread your essay! Check every word for errors in spelling. Be sure that your sentences are concise and grammatically correct. Make any necessary revisions.

Step 6:   Copy the final version of your essay into the response booklet.

Additional Tips

- Be sure that you have not strayed from your topic or introduced points that you have not explained.

- Vary your types of sentences so that your essay flows smoothly and is easy to read.

- Use vocabulary that suits your audience. Make sure not to insult your audience by using simple vocabulary, or by explaining things they already know. Likewise, do not alienate your audience by using complicated jargon, or by assuming that they are already familiar with the subject on which you are writing.

Use vocabulary that suits your audience.

Fast Facts

Recognizing Effective Writing

Why Essays Exist

People write essays for purposes other than testing. Some of our best thinkers have written essays that we continue to read from generation to generation. Essays offer the reader a logical, coherent, and imaginative written composition showing the nature or consequences of a single controlling idea when considered from the writer's unique point of view. Writers use essays to communicate their opinion or position on a topic to readers who cannot be present during their live conversation. Writers use essays to help readers understand or learn about something that readers should or may want to know or do. Essays always express more or less directly the author's opinion, belief, position, or knowledge (backed by evidence) about the idea or object in question.

Organization and Purposeful Development

For this test you will need to recognize and generate the elements of an excellent essay. In essence, you will be taking the principles covered in this review and utilizing them to create your own original essay. With that in mind, read carefully the standards and explanations below to prepare you for what to look for in your own essay response.

Essay Writing

In academic writing, two purposes dominate essays:

1.   Persuasion through argumentation using one, some, or all of the logical patterns described here.

2.   Informing and educating through analysis and using one, some, or all of the logical patterns described here.

All of an essay's organizational strategies may be used to argue in writing. The author offers reasons and/or evidence so an audience will be inclined to believe the position that the author presents about the idea under discussion. Writers use seven basic strategies to organize information and ideas in essays to help prove their point (thesis). All of these strategies might be useful in arguing for an idea and persuading a reader to see the issue the writer's way. Your job is to use strategies that are appropriate to demonstrate your thesis. For example, you may wish to use comparison and contrast to demonstrate that one thing or idea is better or worse than another.

The following seven steps can be used to prove a thesis.

Seven Steps to Prove a Thesis

1. Show how a *process* or procedure does or should work, step by step, in time.

2. *Compare or contrast* two or more things or ideas to show important differences or similarities.

3. *Identify a problem* and then explain how to solve it.

4. *Analyze* into its components, or *classify* by its types or categories an idea or thing to show how it is put together, how it works, or how it is designed.

5. *Explain* why something happens to produce a particular result or set of results.

6. *Describe* the particular individual characteristics, beauty and features of a place, person(s), time, or idea.

7. *Define* what a thing is or what an idea means.

Depending upon the purpose of the essay, one pattern tends to dominate the discussion question. (For example, the writer might use *description* and *explanation* to define the varied meanings of "love.")

During this test you will be called upon to exercise control over your writing by using the writing process and by knowing the pitfalls of weak writing and correcting them. Using the steps outlined below, compose your essay in the order suggested and note the elements and qualities to correct during each stage of the process of composing your essay test response. Make any corrections you need during the appropriate stage of the writing process; to correct errors at the wrong stage may waste time and interfere with your producing the best essay response.

Composing Your Essay: Using the Writing Process

Some people (erroneously) think that writers just sit down and churn out a wonderful essay or poem in one sitting in a flash of genius and inspiration. This is not true. Writers use the writing process from start to finish to help them to write a clear document. If you do not reflect on your composition in stages and make changes as you develop it, you will not see all the problems or errors in it. Don't try to write an essay just once and leave the room. Stay and look through it. Reflect upon it using the writing process.

The writing process has five steps: (1) Prewriting, or planning time; (2) The rough draft; (3) Organizing and revising the ideas (not the words or sentences themselves); (4) Polishing, or editing (making sure sentences themselves are sentences, that the words you use are the right words, and that the spelling and punctuation are correct); and (5) Proofreading, to make sure no mistakes are left.

Using this process does not mean that you have to write five drafts. Write one draft (stages 1 and 2), leaving space for corrections (e.g., writing on every other line) and then working on the existing draft through the rest of the stages (3 through 5). If time allows, you may want to do the whole process on scrap paper and then copy the finished product onto the allotted test paper. But if you do copy it, make sure you proofread your copy to see whether, while transcribing it, you left anything out or said a word twice or made any other errors.

Writing Your Essay

Prewriting/Planning Time

Read the essay question and decide on your purpose. Do you want to persuade your reader? Would you rather explain something?

Sample: "Television is bad for people."

Do you agree or disagree with this statement? Decide. Take a stand. Don't be noncommittal. Write down the statement of your position.

Sample: "I agree that television is bad for people."

or

"Television is an excellent learning tool and is good for most people."

This is your thesis.

Consider Your Audience

The writer's responsibility is to write clearly, honestly, and cleanly for the reader's sake. Essays would be pointless without an audience. Why write an essay if no one wants or needs to read it? Why add evidence, organize your ideas, or correct bad grammar? The reason to do any of these things is that someone out there needs to understand what you mean to say. What would the audience need to know in order to believe you or to come over to your position? Imagine someone you know (visualize her or him) listening to you declare your position or opinion and then saying, "Oh yeah? Prove it!"

Fast Facts

The writer's responsibility is to write clearly, honestly, and cleanly for the reader's sake.

In writing your essay, make sure to answer the following questions: What evidence do you need to prove your idea to this skeptic? What would she disagree with you about? What does she share with you as common knowledge? What does she need to be told by you?

Control Your Point of View

We may write essays from one of three points of view, depending upon the essay's audience. The points of view below are discussed from informal to formal.

1. Subjective/Personal Point of View:
   "I think/believe/feel cars are more trouble than they are worth."

2. Second-Person:
   "If you own a car, you soon find out that it is more trouble than it is worth."

3. Third-Person Point of View (focuses on the idea, not what "I" think of it):
   "Cars are more trouble than they are worth."

For now, stick with one or another; don't switch your "point of view" in the middle. Any one is acceptable.

Consider Your Support

Next, during prewriting, jot down a few phrases that show ideas and examples that support your point of view. Do this quickly on a separate piece of paper for about five minutes. Don't try to outline, simply list things that you think might be important to discuss. After you have listed several, pick at least three to five things you want or need to discuss, and number them in the order of importance that is relevant to proving your point.

Write Your Rough Draft

Spend about ten to twenty minutes writing your rough draft. Looking over your prewriting list, write down what you think is useful to prove your point in the order you think best to convince the reader. Be sure to use real evidence from your life experience or knowledge to support what you say. You do not have to draw evidence from books; your own life is equally appropriate.

For example, don't write, "Cars are more trouble to fix than bicycles," and then fail to show evidence for your idea. Give examples of what you mean: "For example, my father's Buick needs 200 parts to make one brake work, but my bicycle only has four pieces that make up the brakes, and I can replace those myself." Write naturally and quickly. Don't worry too much at this point about paragraphing, spelling, or punctuation—just write down what you think or want to say in the order determined on your list.

Transitions

To help the reader follow the flow of your ideas and to help unify the essay, use transitions to show the connections among your ideas. You may use transitions at the beginnings of paragraphs, or you may use them to show the connections among ideas within a single paragraph.

Here are some typical transitional words and phrases that you should use when writing your essay.

To link similar ideas, use the words:

again	equally important	in addition	of course
also	for example	in like manner	similarly
and	for instance	likewise	too
another	further	moreover	
besides	furthermore	or	

To link dissimilar or contradictory ideas, use words such as:

although	and yet	as if	but
conversely	even if	however	in spite of
instead	nevertheless	on the contrary	on the other hand
otherwise	provided that	still	yet

To indicate cause, purpose, or result, use:

as	consequently	hence	then
as a result	for	since	therefore
because	for this reason	so	thus

To indicate time or position, use words like:

above	at the present time	first	second
across	before	here	thereafter
afterward	beyond	meanwhile	thereupon
around	eventually	next	
at once	finally	presently	

To indicate an example or summary, use phrases such as:

as a result	in any case	in conclusion	in short
as I have said	in any event	in fact	on the whole
for example	in brief	in other words	to sum up
for instance			

Providing Evidence in Your Essay

You may employ any one of the seven steps previously listed to prove any thesis that you maintain is true. You may also call on evidence from one or all of the four following kinds of evidence to support the thesis of your essay. Identify which kind(s) of evidence you can use to prove the points of your essay. In test situations, most essayists use anecdotal evidence or analogy to explain, describe, or prove a thesis. But if you know salient facts or statistics, don't hesitate to call upon them.

1. **Hard data** (facts, statistics, scientific evidence, research)—documented evidence that has been verified to be true.

2. **Anecdotal evidence**—stories from the writer's own experience and knowledge that illustrate a particular point or idea.

3. **Expert opinions**—assertions or conclusions, usually by authorities, about the matter under discussion.

4. **Analogies**—show a resemblance between one phenomenon and another.

Organizing and Reviewing the Paragraphs

The unit of work for revising is the paragraph. After you have written what you wanted to say based on your prewriting list, spend about twenty minutes revising your draft by looking to see whether you need to indent for paragraphs anywhere. If you do, make a proofreader's mark to indicate to the reader that you think a paragraph should start here. Check to see whether you want to add anything that would make your point of view more convincing. Be sure to supply useful transitions to keep up the flow and maintain the focus of your ideas. If you don't have room on the paper, or if your new paragraph shows up out of order, add that paragraph and indicate with a number or some other mark where you want it to go. Check to make sure that you gave examples or illustrations for your statements. In the examples below, two paragraphs are offered: one without concrete evidence and one with evidence for its idea. Study each. Note the topic sentence (T) and how that sentence is or is not supported with evidence.

Paragraphing with No Evidence

Television is bad for people. Programs on television are often stupid and depict crimes that people later copy. Television takes time away from loved ones, and it often becomes addictive. So, television is bad for people because it is no good.

In this example, the author has not given any concrete evidence for any of the good ideas presented. He just declares them to be so. Any one of the sentences above might make a good opening sentence for a whole paragraph. Take the second sentence, for example:

Watching television takes time away from other things. For example, all those hours people spend sitting in front of the tube, they could be working on building a chair or fixing the roof. (*Second piece of evidence*) Maybe the laundry needs to be done, but because people watch television, they may end up not having time to do it. Then Monday comes around again and they have no socks to wear to work—all because they couldn't stand to miss that episode of "Everybody Loves Raymond." (*Third piece of evidence*) Someone could be writing a letter to a friend in Boston who hasn't been heard from or written to for months. (*Fourth piece of evidence*) Or maybe someone misses the opportunity to take in a beautiful day in the park because she had to see "General Hospital." They'll repeat "General Hospital," but this beautiful day only comes around once.

Watching television definitely keeps people from getting things done.

The primary evidence the author uses here is that of probable illustrations taken from life experience that is largely anecdotal. *Always* supply evidence. Three examples or illustrations of your idea per paragraph is a useful number. Don't go on and on about a single point. You don't have time. In order for a typical test essay to be fully developed, it should have about five paragraphs. They ought to be organized in the following manner:

Introduction: A paragraph that shows your point of view (thesis) about an issue and introduces your position with three general ideas that support your thesis.

Development: Three middle paragraphs that prove your position from different angles, using evidence from real life and knowledge. Each supporting paragraph in the middle should in turn support each of the three ideas you started out with in the introductory or thesis paragraph.

Conclusion: The last paragraph, which sums up your position and adds one final reminder of what the issue was, perhaps points to a solution:

So, television takes away from the quality of life and is therefore bad for human beings. We should be watching the sun, the sky, the birds, and each other, not the "boob tube."

Write a paragraph using this sentence as your focus: "Television takes valuable time away from our loved ones."

Check for Logic

Make sure that you present your argument in a logical manner. If you have not, you may not have proven your point. Your conclusion must follow from a logical set of premises, such as:

- Either/Or—The writer assumes that only two opposing possibilities may be attained: "Either _____, or this _____."

- Oversimplification—The writer simplifies the subject: "The rich only want one thing."

- Begging the question—The writer assumes she has proven something (often counterintuitive) that may need to be proven to the reader: "The death penalty actually increases, rather than deters, violent crime."

- Ignoring the issue—The writer argues against the truth of an issue due to its conclusion: "John is a good boy and, therefore, did not rob the store."

- Arguing against a person, not an idea—The writer argues that somebody's idea has no merit because he is immoral or personally stupid: "Eric will fail out of school because he is not doing well in gym class."

- Non Sequitur—The writer leaps to the wrong conclusion: "Jake is from Canada; he must play hockey."

- Drawing the wrong conclusion from a sequence—The author attributes the outcome to the wrong reasons: "Betty married at a young age to an older man and now has three children and is therefore a housewife."

Polishing and Editing Your Essay

If the unit of work for revising is the paragraph, the unit of work for editing is the sentence. Check your paper for mistakes in editing. To help you in this task, use the following checklist.

Polishing Checklist

- Are all your sentences *really* sentences, or have you written some fragments or run-on sentences?

- Are you using vocabulary correctly?

- Have you used a word that seems colloquial or too informal?

- Did you leave out punctuation anywhere? Did you capitalize, or not capitalize, correctly? Did you check for commas, periods, and quotation marks?

Proofreading

In the last three to five minutes, read your paper word for word, first forward and then backward, reading from the end to the beginning. Doing so can help you find errors that you may have missed by having read forward only.

OGET

Oklahoma General Education Test

Practice Test

TEST DIRECTIONS

A sample of the general directions for the OGET is shown in the box below. You may want to familiarize yourself with the directions, as similar versions will be used for the actual examination.

You should have in front of you:

(1) a test booklet for the test for which you registered (check the field name on the front cover);

(2) an answer document (be sure you have signed your answer document and filled in the required information on pages 1 and 3); and

(3) a No. 2 lead pencil.

IF YOU DO NOT HAVE ALL OF THESE MATERIALS, PLEASE INFORM THE TEST ADMINISTRATOR. REMOVE ALL OTHER MATERIALS FROM YOUR DESK.

GENERAL DIRECTIONS

This test booklet contains two sections: a selected-response section and a writing assignment. You may complete the sections in the order you choose, but it is suggested that you complete the selected-response section of the test first. The directions for each section appear immediately before that section.

Each selected-response question in this booklet has four answer choices. Read each question carefully and choose the ONE best answer. Record your answer on the answer sheet in the space that corresponds to the question number. Completely fill in the space having the same letter as the answer you have chosen. *Use only a No. 2 lead pencil.*

Sample Question:

1.   Which of these cities is farthest north?

    A.   Oklahoma City

    B.   Muskogee

    C.   Tulsa

    D.   Lawton

The correct answer to this question is C. You would indicate that on the answer sheet as follows:

1.   Ⓐ Ⓑ ● Ⓓ

For the writing assignment, you will be asked to prepare a written response to a writing assignment. Record your written response on pages 3 to 6 of the answer document. You may use **ONLY** one answer document. You may either print or write, as long as your handwriting is legible. You must use a pencil. Make sure that you have time to plan, write, review, and revise what you have written.

You should answer all questions. Even if you are unsure of an answer, it is better to guess than not to answer a question at all. You may use the margins of the test booklet for scratch paper, but all of your answers, including your response to the writing assignment, must be recorded in your answer document. Answers that are written in the test booklet will **NOT** be scored.

The words "End of Section" indicate you have completed a section. After you have completed one section, you may go on to the other section. You may go back and review your answers and your written response to the writing assignment, but be sure you have answered all selected-response questions, completed the writing assignment, and rechecked all the information in your answer document, particularly your identification information on pages 1 and 3, before you raise your hand for dismissal. Your test materials must be returned to a test administrator when you finish the test.

FOR TEST SECURITY REASONS, YOU MAY NOT TAKE NOTES OR REMOVE ANY OF THE TEST MATERIALS FROM THE ROOM.

This session will last four hours. You may work at your own pace on the different sections of the test. If you have any questions, please ask them now before you begin the test.

STOP

DO NOT GO ON UNTIL YOU ARE TOLD TO DO SO.

Answer Sheet

1. Ⓐ Ⓑ Ⓒ Ⓓ	26. Ⓐ Ⓑ Ⓒ Ⓓ	51. Ⓐ Ⓑ Ⓒ Ⓓ	76. Ⓐ Ⓑ Ⓒ Ⓓ
2. Ⓐ Ⓑ Ⓒ Ⓓ	27. Ⓐ Ⓑ Ⓒ Ⓓ	52. Ⓐ Ⓑ Ⓒ Ⓓ	77. Ⓐ Ⓑ Ⓒ Ⓓ
3. Ⓐ Ⓑ Ⓒ Ⓓ	28. Ⓐ Ⓑ Ⓒ Ⓓ	53. Ⓐ Ⓑ Ⓒ Ⓓ	78. Ⓐ Ⓑ Ⓒ Ⓓ
4. Ⓐ Ⓑ Ⓒ Ⓓ	29. Ⓐ Ⓑ Ⓒ Ⓓ	54. Ⓐ Ⓑ Ⓒ Ⓓ	79. Ⓐ Ⓑ Ⓒ Ⓓ
5. Ⓐ Ⓑ Ⓒ Ⓓ	30. Ⓐ Ⓑ Ⓒ Ⓓ	55. Ⓐ Ⓑ Ⓒ Ⓓ	80. Ⓐ Ⓑ Ⓒ Ⓓ
6. Ⓐ Ⓑ Ⓒ Ⓓ	31. Ⓐ Ⓑ Ⓒ Ⓓ	56. Ⓐ Ⓑ Ⓒ Ⓓ	81. Ⓐ Ⓑ Ⓒ Ⓓ
7. Ⓐ Ⓑ Ⓒ Ⓓ	32. Ⓐ Ⓑ Ⓒ Ⓓ	57. Ⓐ Ⓑ Ⓒ Ⓓ	82. Ⓐ Ⓑ Ⓒ Ⓓ
8. Ⓐ Ⓑ Ⓒ Ⓓ	33. Ⓐ Ⓑ Ⓒ Ⓓ	58. Ⓐ Ⓑ Ⓒ Ⓓ	83. Ⓐ Ⓑ Ⓒ Ⓓ
9. Ⓐ Ⓑ Ⓒ Ⓓ	34. Ⓐ Ⓑ Ⓒ Ⓓ	59. Ⓐ Ⓑ Ⓒ Ⓓ	84. Ⓐ Ⓑ Ⓒ Ⓓ
10. Ⓐ Ⓑ Ⓒ Ⓓ	35. Ⓐ Ⓑ Ⓒ Ⓓ	60. Ⓐ Ⓑ Ⓒ Ⓓ	85. Ⓐ Ⓑ Ⓒ Ⓓ
11. Ⓐ Ⓑ Ⓒ Ⓓ	36. Ⓐ Ⓑ Ⓒ Ⓓ	61. Ⓐ Ⓑ Ⓒ Ⓓ	86. Ⓐ Ⓑ Ⓒ Ⓓ
12. Ⓐ Ⓑ Ⓒ Ⓓ	37. Ⓐ Ⓑ Ⓒ Ⓓ	62. Ⓐ Ⓑ Ⓒ Ⓓ	87. Ⓐ Ⓑ Ⓒ Ⓓ
13. Ⓐ Ⓑ Ⓒ Ⓓ	38. Ⓐ Ⓑ Ⓒ Ⓓ	63. Ⓐ Ⓑ Ⓒ Ⓓ	88. Ⓐ Ⓑ Ⓒ Ⓓ
14. Ⓐ Ⓑ Ⓒ Ⓓ	39. Ⓐ Ⓑ Ⓒ Ⓓ	64. Ⓐ Ⓑ Ⓒ Ⓓ	89. Ⓐ Ⓑ Ⓒ Ⓓ
15. Ⓐ Ⓑ Ⓒ Ⓓ	40. Ⓐ Ⓑ Ⓒ Ⓓ	65. Ⓐ Ⓑ Ⓒ Ⓓ	90. Ⓐ Ⓑ Ⓒ Ⓓ
16. Ⓐ Ⓑ Ⓒ Ⓓ	41. Ⓐ Ⓑ Ⓒ Ⓓ	66. Ⓐ Ⓑ Ⓒ Ⓓ	91. Ⓐ Ⓑ Ⓒ Ⓓ
17. Ⓐ Ⓑ Ⓒ Ⓓ	42. Ⓐ Ⓑ Ⓒ Ⓓ	67. Ⓐ Ⓑ Ⓒ Ⓓ	92. Ⓐ Ⓑ Ⓒ Ⓓ
18. Ⓐ Ⓑ Ⓒ Ⓓ	43. Ⓐ Ⓑ Ⓒ Ⓓ	68. Ⓐ Ⓑ Ⓒ Ⓓ	93. Ⓐ Ⓑ Ⓒ Ⓓ
19. Ⓐ Ⓑ Ⓒ Ⓓ	44. Ⓐ Ⓑ Ⓒ Ⓓ	69. Ⓐ Ⓑ Ⓒ Ⓓ	94. Ⓐ Ⓑ Ⓒ Ⓓ
20. Ⓐ Ⓑ Ⓒ Ⓓ	45. Ⓐ Ⓑ Ⓒ Ⓓ	70. Ⓐ Ⓑ Ⓒ Ⓓ	95. Ⓐ Ⓑ Ⓒ Ⓓ
21. Ⓐ Ⓑ Ⓒ Ⓓ	46. Ⓐ Ⓑ Ⓒ Ⓓ	71. Ⓐ Ⓑ Ⓒ Ⓓ	96. Ⓐ Ⓑ Ⓒ Ⓓ
22. Ⓐ Ⓑ Ⓒ Ⓓ	47. Ⓐ Ⓑ Ⓒ Ⓓ	72. Ⓐ Ⓑ Ⓒ Ⓓ	97. Ⓐ Ⓑ Ⓒ Ⓓ
23. Ⓐ Ⓑ Ⓒ Ⓓ	48. Ⓐ Ⓑ Ⓒ Ⓓ	73. Ⓐ Ⓑ Ⓒ Ⓓ	98. Ⓐ Ⓑ Ⓒ Ⓓ
24. Ⓐ Ⓑ Ⓒ Ⓓ	49. Ⓐ Ⓑ Ⓒ Ⓓ	74. Ⓐ Ⓑ Ⓒ Ⓓ	99. Ⓐ Ⓑ Ⓒ Ⓓ
25. Ⓐ Ⓑ Ⓒ Ⓓ	50. Ⓐ Ⓑ Ⓒ Ⓓ	75. Ⓐ Ⓑ Ⓒ Ⓓ	100. Ⓐ Ⓑ Ⓒ Ⓓ

Practice Test

WATER

The most important source of sediment is earth and rock material carried to the sea by rivers and streams; glaciers and winds may also have transported the same materials. Other sources are volcanic ash and lava, shells and skeletons of organisms, chemical precipitates formed in seawater, and particles from outer space.

Water is a most unusual substance because it exists on the surface of the Earth in its three physical states: ice, water, and water vapor. There are many substances that exist in a solid and liquid or gaseous state at temperatures normally found at the Earth's surface, but there are fewer substances that occur in all three states.

Water is odorless, tasteless, and colorless. It is a substance known to exist in a natural state as a solid, liquid, or gas on the surface of the Earth. It is a universal solvent. Water does not corrode, rust, burn, or separate into its components easily. It is chemically indestructible. It can corrode almost any metal and erode the most solid rock. A unique property of water is that, when frozen in its solid state, it expands and floats on water. Water has a freezing point of 0°C and a boiling point of 100°C. Water has the capacity to absorb great quantities of heat with relatively little increase in temperature. When *distilled*, water is a poor conductor of electricity but when salt is added, it is a good conductor of electricity.

Sunlight is the source of energy for temperature change, evaporation, and currents for water movement through the atmosphere. Sunlight controls the rate of photosynthesis for all marine plants, which are directly or indirectly the source of food for all marine animals. Migration, breeding, and other behaviors of marine animals are affected by light.

Water, as the ocean or sea, is blue because of the molecular scattering of the sunlight. Blue light, being of short wavelength, is scattered more effectively than light of longer wavelengths. Variations in color may be caused by particles suspended in the water, water depth, cloud cover, temperature, and other variable factors. Heavy concentrations of dissolved materials cause a yellowish hue, while algae will cause the water to look green. Heavy populations of plant and animal materials will cause the water to look brown.

1. Which of the following lists of topics best organizes the information in the selection?

   A. I.   Water as vapor
       II.   Water as ice
       III. Water as solid

   B. I.   Properties of seawater
       II.   Freezing and boiling points of water
       III. Photosynthesis
       IV.   Oceans and seas

   C. I.   Water as substance
       II.   Water's corrosion
       III. Water and plants
       IV.   Water and algae coloration

   D. I.   Water's physical states
       II.   Properties of water
       III. Effects of the sun on water
       IV.   Reasons for color variation in water

2. According to the passage, what is the most unique property of water?

   A. Water is odorless, tasteless, and colorless.

   B. Water exists on the surface of the Earth in three physical states.

   C. Water is chemically indestructible.

   D. Water is a poor conductor of electricity.

3. Which of the following best defines the word *distilled* as it is used in the last sentence of the third paragraph?

   A. Free of salt content

   B. Free of electrical energy

   C. Dehydrated

   D. Containing wine

4. The writer's main purpose in this selection is to

   A. explain the colors of water.

   B. examine the effects of the sun on water.

   C. define the properties of water.

   D. describe the three physical states of all liquids.

5. The writer of this selection would most likely agree with which of the following statements?

    A. The properties of water are found in most other liquids on this planet.

    B. Water should not be consumed in its most natural state.

    C. Water might be used to serve many different functions.

    D. Water is too unpredictable for most scientists.

Read the passage below; then answer the five questions that follow.

---

¹DeMarco was asked if he had read any of the books that were on display in Mrs. W's classroom. ²He answered that he had read none of them yet, although he usually keeps one or more in his desk.

³Nevertheless, the researcher did see him respond positively to the first classroom reading experience of the year. ⁴Mrs. W was reading Louis Sachar's *Sideways Stories from Wayside School* while the children, each of whom had a copy of the book, were silently reading along. ⁵Like nearly all of the class, DeMarco was laughing in all the right places. ⁶The researcher has since noticed that he grasps and comprehends just about anything well when it is read by a competent reader, whether a teacher or an advanced fellow student.

⁷_____ ⁸The class writes almost daily in a "Small Moments Journal," in which they are to record, in a few sentences and perhaps a picture, memorable events in their lives. ⁹Mrs. W has spent considerable time prompting the students to write down topics, with the result that some students have well over 100 topics listed so far. ¹⁰DeMarco, through the last day he was observed, had seven. ¹¹He had written only two entries in his journal, both about a visit two years ago to his relatives in Mississippi. ¹²Like many of his classmate's accounts of their comings and goings, his writing lacks detail and personality, but most others have written appreciably more. ¹³Asked follow-up questions about the events he has written about, his answers were evasive.

6. Which of the following sentences, used in place of the blank labeled sentence 7, would best make a transition to the new paragraph?

    A. Another topic of interest of the study was DeMarco's writing ability.

    B. Moreover, DeMarco's writing shows no enthusiasm.

    C. DeMarco's writing, however, shows no spark at all.

    D. Consequently, it is advisable that we look at DeMarco's writing.

7. Which of the numbered sentences should be revised to reduce unnecessary repetition?

    A. sentence 3

    B. sentence 5

    C. sentence 6

    D. sentence 8

8. Which of the numbered sentences should be revised to correct an error in sentence structure?

    A. sentence 2

    B. sentence 9

    C. sentence 10

    D. sentence 13

9. Which of the following changes is needed in the passage?

    A. Sentence 4: Change *Sideways Stories from Wayside School* to "Sideways Stories from Wayside School"

    B. Sentence 11: Change "had" to "has"

    C. Sentence 11: Change "journal" to "Journal"

    D. Sentence 12: Change "classmate's" to "classmates'"

10. Which of the underlined words or phrases in the third paragraph should be replaced by more precise or appropriate words?

    A. record

    B. considerable

    C. comings and goings

    D. appreciably

11. The distance from Tami's house to Ken's house is 3 miles. The distance from Ken's house to The Soda Depot is 2 miles. Which of the following statements are true?

      I. The greatest possible distance between Tami's house and The Soda Depot is five miles.

     II. The greatest possible distance between Tami's house and The Soda Depot is six miles.

   III. The shortest possible distance between Tami's house and The Soda Depot is one mile.

   IV. The shortest possible distance between Tami's house and The Soda Depot is two miles.

A. I and III only

B. I and IV only

C. II and III only

D. II and IV only

12. Use the figure to answer the question that follows.

```
75 MPH
MAXIMUM

40 MPH
MINIMUM
```

Which inequality describes the allowable speeds indicated by the speed limit sign?

A. $75 \leq x \leq 40$

B. $75 < x > 40$

C. $40 \leq x \leq 75$

D. $40 < x > 75$

13. Which types of graphs or charts would be appropriate for displaying the following information?

Favorite lunch foods of 40 surveyed 6th graders

Pizza	18
Chicken Nuggets	12
Macaroni and Cheese	4
Tacos	4
Hamburgers	2

    I. bar graph
   II. circle (pie) chart
  III. scatter plot
  IV. broken-line graph

A. I and II only

B. III and IV only

C. I and III only

D. II and IV only

14. Which one of the following statements is most true regarding the materials of visual art?

A. Industrial innovations in art-making materials have improved art in the past 150 years.

B. The use of uncommon materials in art making has improved art in the past 150 years.

C. The use of unusual materials in art making has changed the standards by which we view art.

D. Industrial innovations in art-making materials have had little influence on visual art.

Read the passage below; then answer the four questions that follow.

The issue of adult literacy has finally received recognition as a major social problem. Unfortunately, the issue is usually presented in the media as a "women's interest issue." Numerous governors' wives and even Laura Bush have publicly expressed concern about literacy. As well-meaning as the politicians' wives may be, it is more important that the politicians themselves recognize the seriousness of the problem and support increased funding for literacy programs.

Literacy education programs need to be directed at two different groups of people with very different needs. The first group is composed of people who have very limited reading and writing skills. These people are complete illiterates. A second group is composed of people who can read and write but whose skills are not sufficient to meet their needs. This second group is called *functionally illiterate*. Successful literacy programs must meet the needs of both groups.

Instructors in literacy programs have three main responsibilities. First, the educational needs of the illiterates and functional illiterates must be met. Second, the instructors must approach the participants in the program with empathy, not sympathy. Third, all participants must experience success in the program and must perceive their efforts as worthwhile.

15. What is the difference between illiteracy and functional illiteracy?

    A. There is no difference.

    B. A functional illiterate is enrolled in a literacy education program but an illiterate is not.

    C. An illiterate cannot read or write, a functional illiterate can read and write but not at a very high skill level.

    D. There are more illiterates than functional illiterates in the United States today.

16. What does "women's interest issue" mean in the passage?

    A. The issue is only interesting to women.

    B. Many politicians' wives have expressed concern over the issue.

    C. Women illiterates outnumber male illiterates.

    D. Politicians interested in illiteracy often have their wives give speeches on the topic.

17. According to the passage, which of the following is NOT a characteristic of successful literacy programs?

    A. Participants should receive free transportation.

    B. Participants should experience success in the program.

    C. Instructors must have empathy, not sympathy.

    D. Programs must meet the educational needs of illiterates.

18. What is the author's opinion of the funding for literacy programs?

    A. Too much

    B. Too little

    C. About right

    D. Too much for illiterates and not enough for functional illiterates

SOURCES OF IMMIGRATION, 1820–1840

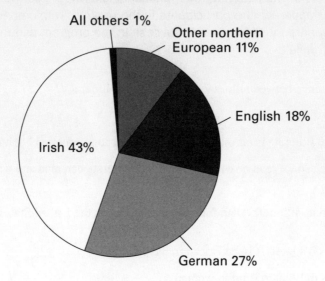

All others 1%

Other northern
European 11%

English 18%

Irish 43%

German 27%

19. According to the graph, from 1820 to 1840

    A. there were more Irish immigrants than all other nationalities combined.

    B. the combined number of immigrants from England and Germany exceeded those from Ireland.

    C. one percent of American immigrants were from Italy.

    D. there were an equal number of English and German immigrants.

20. A hot-air balloon rises when propane burners in the basket are used to heat the air inside the balloon.
     Which of the following statements correctly identifies the explanation for this phenomenon?

    A. Heated gas molecules move faster inside the balloon, their force striking the inside causes the
        balloon to rise.

    B. Hot gas molecules are themselves larger than cool gas molecules, resulting in the expansion of
        the gas.

    C. The amount of empty space between gas molecules increases as the temperature of the gas in-
        creases, resulting in the expansion of the gas.

    D. The combustion of propane releases product gases that are lighter than air which are trapped in
        the balloon causing it to rise.

21. A marble and a feather are both released at the same time inside a tube that is held at very low pressure (a near vacuum). Which of the following correctly links the observation to explanation?

   A. The marble falls faster because it is heavier.

   B. The marble falls faster because it has less air resistance.

   C. Both fall at the same rate because there is no air resistance in a vacuum.

   D. Both fall at the same rate because the forces of gravity are different in a vacuum.

Read the passage below; then answer the five questions that follow.

[1]The Tuskegee Experiment's true nature had to be hidden from the subjects to ensure their cooperation. [2]The sharecroppers' grossly disadvantaged lot in life made them easy to manipulate. [3]Pleased at the prospect of free medical care—almost none of them had ever seen a doctor before—these unsophisticated and trusting men became the dupes in what James Jones, author of the excellent history on the subject, *Bad Blood,* identified as "the longest nontherapeutic experiment on human beings in medical history".

[4]The study was meant to discover how syphilis <u>effected</u> African Americans as opposed to whites—the theory being that whites experienced more neurological complications from syphilis <u>whereas</u> African Americans were more <u>susceptible</u> to cardiovascular damage. [5]_____ [6]Although the scientists touted the study as one of great scientific merit, from the <u>outset</u> its actual benefits were hazy. [7]It took almost forty years before someone involved in the study took a hard and honest look at the end results, he reported that "nothing learned will prevent, find, or cure a single case of infectious syphilis or bring us closer to our basic mission of controlling venereal disease in the United States." [8]When the media learns of the experiment in 1972, the CBS news anchor Harry Reasoner called it a project that "used human beings as laboratory animals in a long and inefficient study of how long it takes syphilis to kill someone."

22. Which of the following sentences, used in place of the blank labeled sentence 5, would be most consistent with the writer's purpose and intended audience?

   A. If the theory had been proven, much would have changed in the clinical treatment of syphilis.

   B. How this knowledge would have changed the clinical treatment of syphilis is uncertain.

   C. On the other hand, neurological complications were much more important to the scientists.

   D. We will never know what the racist scientists of the 1920s were thinking when they devised this theory.

23. Which of the underlined words or phrases in the second paragraph should be replaced by more precise or appropriate words?

    A. effected

    B. whereas

    C. susceptible

    D. outset

24. Which of the numbered sentences should be revised to correct a nonstandard use of a comma?

    A. sentence 2

    B. sentence 3

    C. sentence 7

    D. sentence 8

25. Which of the following changes is needed in the first paragraph?

    A. Sentence 1: Change "Experiment's" to "Experiments"

    B. Sentence 3: Change "had" to "has"

    C. Sentence 2: Change "easy to manipulate" to "easily manipulated"

    D. Sentence 3: Move the period at the end inside the quotation mark

26. Which of the numbered sentences contains nonstandard use of a verb form?

    A. sentence 2

    B. sentence 3

    C. sentence 6

    D. sentence 8

27. Each month the teacher kept track of the number of books as well as the genre of the books the students read during free-reading time in school. Here is the graph constructed from the data from September and May of the same year. This teacher completed a unit on fairy tales in April. What conclusions could be reached?

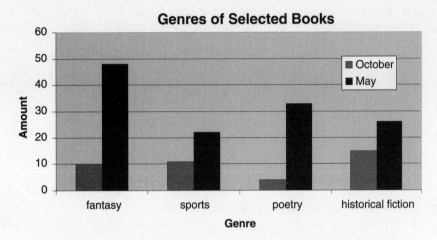

I. These children are reading more titles during free reading time.
II. Completing a fairy tale unit created interest in the fantasy genre.
III. These children need to complete more worksheets.
IV. These children are participating in an Accelerated Reader Program.

A. I, II, and III

B. All of the above

C. None of the above

D. I and II

28. Use the figure to answer the question that follows.

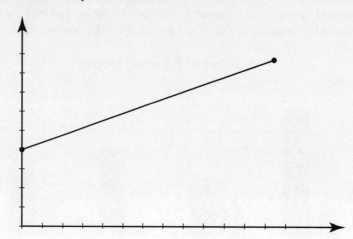

Which of the following situations might the graph illustrate?

    I.   The varying speed of an experienced runner over the course of a 26-mile race.

    II.   The number of households a census taker still has to visit over the course of a week.

    III.   The value of a savings account over time, assuming steady growth.

    IV.   The changing height of a sunflower over several months.

A.   I and II only

B.   III and IV only

C.   II, III, and IV only

D.   I, III, and IV only

29. The following graph shows the distribution of test scores in Ms. Alvarez's class.

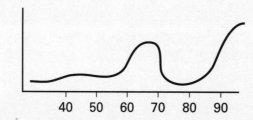

Which of the following statements do you know to be true?

    I.   The majority of students scored higher than 60.

    II.   The test was a fair measure of ability.

    III.   The mean score is probably higher than the median.

    IV.   The test divided the class into distinct groups.

A.   I and II only

B.   I and IV only

C.   I, III, and IV only

D.   IV only

30. What is the solution to this equation?

    $\frac{x}{3} - 9 = 15$

    A. 18

    B. 8

    C. 36

    D. 72

31. What are the solutions of this equation?

    $3x^2 - 11 = 1$

    A. 2 and –2

    B. 3 and –3

    C. 4 and –4

    D. 1 and –1

32. The atmospheres of the Moon and other planets were studied using telescopes and spectrophoto-meters long before the deployment of interplanetary space probes. In these studies, scientists studied the spectral patterns of sunlight that passed through the atmosphere of distant objects to learn what elements make up those atmospheres. Which of the following explains the source of the black-line spectral patterns?

    A. When an element is excited, it gives off light in a characteristic spectral pattern.

    B. When light strikes an object, some wavelengths of light are absorbed by the surface and others are reflected to give the object its color.

    C. When light passes through a gas, light is absorbed at wavelengths characteristic of the elements in the gas.

    D. The black lines are the spectra of ultraviolet light, which is called black light because it cannot be seen with human eyes.

33. We may be told to "gargle with saltwater" when we suffer from a sore throat. Which of the following phenomena would be used to explain this advice?

    A. lowering of vapor pressure

    B. increasing osmotic pressure

    C. increasing boiling point

    D. decreasing freezing point

34. In announcing the Emancipation Proclamation, Lincoln's immediate purpose was to

    A. free black slaves in all of the slave states.

    B. free black slaves in only the border slave states that had remained loyal to the Union.

    C. let the Southern states know that whether or not they chose to secede from the Union, slavery would not be tolerated by his administration once he took office.

    D. rally Northern morale by giving the war a higher moral purpose than just preserving the Union.

Read the passage below; then answer the four questions that follow.

Language not only expresses an individual's ideology, it also sets perimeters while it persuades and influences the discourse in the community that hears and interprets its meaning. Therefore, the language of failure should not be present in the learning environment (i.e., the classroom) because it will have a prohibitive impact on the students' desire to learn as well as a negative influence on the students' self-esteem. The *Oxford English Dictionary* defines *failure* as a fault, a shortcoming, a lack of success, a person who turns out unsuccessfully, becoming insolvent, etc. We as educators might well ask ourselves if this is the sort of doctrine that we want to permeate our classrooms. Perhaps our own University axiom, *mens agitat molem* (the mind can move mountains), will help us discover if, indeed, the concepts of failure are really the types of influences we wish to introduce to impressionable new students. Is the mind capable of moving a mountain when it is already convinced it cannot? One must remain aware that individuals acquire knowledge at independent rates of speed. Certainly no one would suggest that one infant "failed" the art of learning to walk because she acquired the skill two months behind her infant counterpart. Would anyone suggest that infant number one *failed* walking? Of course not. What would a mentor project to either toddler were he to suggest that a slower acquisition of walking skills implied failure? Yet we as educators feel the need to suggest student A failed due to the slower procurement of abstract concepts then student B. It is absolutely essential to shift the learning focus from failure to success.

35. Which of the following statements best conveys the meaning of the passage?

    A. Learning is something that happens at different speeds and is, therefore, natural.

    B. Instructors need to be sensitive to students' individual needs.

    C. Instructors need to shift the educational focus from failure to success in learning environments.

    D. Failure is a potential hazard in the classroom and should be avoided at all costs.

36. As stated in the context of the passage, what does University axiom mean?

    A. University Latin

    B. University motto

    C. University rhetoric

    D. University sophomore

37. According to the passage, what will have a negative effect on student self-esteem?

    A. The rhetoric of diction

    B. The slower procurement of abstract concepts

    C. The learning focus from failure to success

    D. The language of failure

38. According to the passage, what does language do besides aid individual expression?

    A. It establishes individual thought and tells of individual philosophies.

    B. It paints visual images and articulates individual declaration.

    C. It suggests individual axioms and community philosophy.

    D. It persuades and influences the discourse in the community that hears and interprets its meaning.

39. Solve for y.

    $\frac{y}{3} - \frac{x}{2} = 4$

    A. $y = \frac{x}{2} + 12$

    B. $y = \frac{3x}{2} + 12$

    C. $y = \frac{3x}{2} - 12$

    D. $y = -\frac{3x}{2} - 12$

40. Translate this problem into a one-variable equation, then solve the equation.

    "There are ten vehicles parked in a parking lot. Each is either a car with four tires or a motorcycle with two tires. (Do not count any spare tires.) There are 26 wheels in the lot. How many cars are there in the lot?"

    A. 8

    B. 6

    C. 5

    D. 3

41. Which equation could be used to solve the following problem?

    "Three consecutive odd numbers add up to 117. What are they?"

    A. $x + (x + 2) + (x + 4) = 117$

    B. $1x + 3x + 5x = 117$

    C. $x + x + x = 117$

    D. $x + (x + 1) + (x + 3) = 117$

42. Which equation could be used to solve the following problem?

    "Here is how the Acme Taxicab Company computes fares for riders: People are charged three dollars for just getting into the cab, then they are charged two dollars more for every mile or fraction of a mile of the ride. What would be the fare for a ride of 10.2 miles?"

    A. $3 \times (2 \times 10.2) = y$

    B. $3 + (2 + 11) = y$

    C. $3 \times (2 + 10.2) = y$

    D. $3 + (2 \times 11) = y$

43. The characteristics of fascism include all of the following EXCEPT:

    A. democracy.

    B. totalitarianism.

    C. romanticism.

    D. militarism.

44. The industrial economy of the nineteenth century was based upon all of the following EXCEPT:

    A. the availability of raw materials.

    B. an equitable distribution of profits among those involved in production.

    C. the availability of capital.

    D   a distribution system to market finished products.

45. The term "Trail of Tears" refers to

    A. the Mormon migration from Nauvoo, Illinois, to what is now Utah.

    B. the forced migration of the Cherokee tribe from the southern Appalachians to what is now Oklahoma.

    C. the westward migration along the Oregon Trail.

    D. the migration into Kentucky along the Wilderness Road.

46. Thomas Paine's pamphlet *Common Sense* was significant in that it

    A. emotionally aroused thousands of colonists to the abuses of British rule, the oppressiveness of the monarchy, and the advantages of colonial independence.

    B. rallied American spirit during the bleak winter of 1776, when it appeared that Washington's forces, freezing and starving at Valley Forge, had no hope of surviving the winter, much less defeating the British.

    C. called for a strong central government to rule the newly independent American states and foresaw the difficulties inherent within the Articles of Confederation.

    D. asserted to its British readers that they could not beat the American colonists militarily unless they could isolate New England from the rest of the American colonies.

Read the passage below; then answer the six questions that follow.

[1]Before the Europeans arrived, animism and spirit worship was the hallmark of Timorese belief in a superior force. [2]The great Hindu, Buddhist, and Islamic kingdoms that dominated South and Southeast Asia had not taken root in Timor. [3]The island's geographic location, which was far from the major ports of Asia, and its subsequent lack of commercial activity, placed it off the beaten track for traders and proselytizers. [4]The exceptions being sandalwood and later slave trade.

[5]All that changed with the arrival of the Europeans. [6]By the late 1500s Dominican friars from Portugal had established a mission on Timor, _____ they made only modest headway in converting the Timorese to Christianity. [7]Although the Portuguese were in Timor for centuries they had little positive influence on Timorese culture until after World War II. [8]For years the local people consistently resisted Portugal's attempts to take control of their island, and some of the Dominican missionaries who were posted there supported them in this effort. [9]It was not until Portugal considered granting East Timor its independence that Catholicism began to be accepted among the people, and _____ it was not until the Indonesian invasion in 1975 that large numbers of Timorese embraced the Catholic faith. [10]Indonesian law requires citizens to have a religious affiliation. [11]The Catholic Church was the only organization that the Indonesian government in Timor allowed relative freedom.

[12]Timorese also found the Church a source of support during the guerrilla war against the Indonesians. [13]Timorese fled to the highlands to escape Indonesian rule, and their families were often relocated in camps far from their villages to prevent them from lending assistance to the guerrillas. [14]The Church saw the abject misery of the people and provided support and comfort. [15]Membership in the Catholic Church grew dramatically from 1975 to 1999 as the Timorese people came to rely on it to protect them and to help them locate missing family members. [16]Today 90% of East Timor's population is Catholic, although many Timorese Catholics include some aspects of animism in their beliefs.

47. Read the following sentence:
"The priests and nuns of the church provided health and education to the Timorese during that chaotic period."
In which of the following locations in the third paragraph should this sentence be placed?

    A.   Before sentence 13

    B.   Before sentence 14

    C.   Before sentence 15

    D.   Before sentence 16

48. The method of organization for the second and third paragraphs, respectively, is

    A.   chronological order; problem and solution

    B.   chronological order; cause and effect

    C.   order of importance; chronological order

    D.   comparison and contrast; cause and effect

49. Which of the numbered sentences should be revised to correct a nonstandard sentence structure?

    A.   sentence 2

    B.   sentence 4

    C.   sentence 7

    D.   sentence 8

50. Which of the following changes is needed in the second paragraph?

    A.   Sentence 7: Insert comma after "centuries"

    B.   Sentence 8: Change "who" after "missionaries" to "whom"

    C.   Sentence 9: Change "its" to "their"

    D.   Sentence 11: Capitalize "government"

51. Which words or phrases would, if inserted *in order* into the blanks in the second paragraph, help the reader understand the logical sequence of the writer's ideas?

    A.   however; therefore

    B.   and so; in those circumstances

    C.   however; even then

    D.   but; even then

52. Which of the numbered sentences should be revised to correct a nonstandard verb form?

    A.   sentence 1

    B.   sentence 3

    C.   sentence 10

    D.   sentence 16

53. In the figure below, what is the perimeter of square *ABCD* if diagonal *AC* = 8?

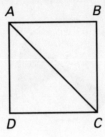

    A.   32

    B.   64

    C. $4\sqrt{2}$

    D. $16\sqrt{2}$

54. Three small circles, all the same size, lie inside a large circle as shown below. The diameter *AB* of the large circle passes through the centers of the three small circles. If each of the smaller circles has area 9π, what is the circumference of the large circle?

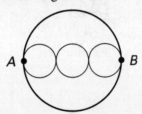

    A.   9

    B.   18

    C. 18π

    D. 27π

55. If $2x^2 + 5x - 3 = 0$ and $x > 0$, then what is the value of x?

   A. $-\frac{1}{2}$

   B. $\frac{1}{2}$

   C. 1

   D. $\frac{3}{2}$

56. The center of the following circle is the point O. What percentage of the circle is shaded if the measure of arc AB is 65° and the measure of arc CD is 21.4°?

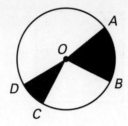

   A. 86.4%

   B. 24%

   C. 43.6%

   D. 27.4%

57. According to the chart, in what year was the total sales of Brand X televisions the greatest?

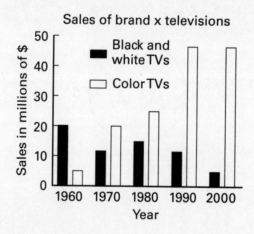

   A. 1960

   B. 1970

   C. 1980

   D. 1990

58. Dance can be a mirror of culture. Which of the following is not an illustration of this statement?

    A.   Women in the Cook Islands dance with their feet together and sway while the men take a wide stance and flap their knees.

    B.   Movement basics include body, space, time, and relationship.

    C.   In Africa, the birth of a child is an occasion for a dance that asks for divine blessings.

    D.   The court dancers of Bali study for many years to achieve the balance, beauty, and serenity of their dance.

59. Which of the following best explains why the boiling point of water is reduced and cooking times are increased at high altitudes?

    A.   At high altitudes there is greater atmospheric pressure than at sea level.

    B.   At high altitudes there is less oxygen than at sea level.

    C.   At high altitudes the vapor pressure of water is reduced because of the reduced atmospheric pressure.

    D.   At high altitudes water boils at a lower temperature because of the reduced atmospheric pressure.

Read the passage below; then answer the three questions that follow.

The teaching apprentice initiated the discussion in a clear and well-prepared manner. To _____ the lecture topic, the teaching apprentice utilized overhead transparencies of both lexicon and abstract representation to better _____ the theories behind various pedagogical concepts. The class culminated whereby students established enthymemes extrapolated from the class discussion. The class maintained integrity and continuity.

60. Which of these grouped words, if inserted *in order* into the passage's blank lines, would address the logical sequencing of the narrative?

    A.   refute; criticize

    B.   conflate; discern

    C.   undermine; explain

    D.   support; illustrate

61. The definition of the term "pedagogical" as used in the passage means

    A. academic.

    B. abstract.

    C. meaningless.

    D. obtuse.

62. The passage suggests that the author's classroom experience was

    A. a needless waste of time and energy.

    B. intelligible and pragmatic.

    C. haphazard and disorderly.

    D. too advanced and complicated.

63. What does it mean that multiplication and division are *inverse operations*?

    A. Multiplication is commutative, whereas division is not. For example: 4×2 gives the same product as 2×4, but $4 \div 2$ is not the same as $2 \div 4$.

    B. Whether multiplying or dividing a value by 1, the value remains the same. For example, 9×1 equals 9; $9 \div 1$ also equals 9.

    C. When performing complex calculations involving several operations, all multiplication must be completed before completing any division, such as in $8 \div 2 \times 4 + 7 - 1$.

    D. The operations "undo" each other. For example, multiplying 11 by 3 gives 33. Dividing 33 by 3 then takes you back to 11.

64. One day, 31 students were absent from Pierce Middle School. If that represents about 5.5% of the students, what is the population of the school?

    A. 177

    B. 517

    C. 564

    D. 171

65. Which of the following are equivalent to 0.5%?
    I. One-half of one percent
    II. 5%
    III. 1/200
    IV. 0.05

    A. I and III only

    B. I and IV only

    C. II and III only

    D. II and IV only

Read the passage below; then answer the two questions that follow.

America's national bird, the mighty bald eagle, is being threatened by a new menace. Once decimated by hunters and loss of habitat, this newest danger is suspected to be from the intentional poisoning by livestock ranchers. Authorities have found animal carcasses injected with restricted pesticides. These carcasses are suspected to have been placed to attract and kill predators such as the bald eagle in an effort to preserve young grazing animals. It appears that the eagle is being threatened again by the consummate predator, humans.

66. One can conclude from this passage that

    A. the pesticides used are beneficial to the environment.

    B. ranchers believe that killing the eagles will protect their ranches.

    C. ranchers must obtain licenses to use illegal pesticides.

    D. poisoning eagles is good for livestock.

67. The author's attitude is one of

    A. uncaring observation.

    B. concerned interest.

    C. uninformed acceptance.

    D. suspicion.

68. Use the figure to answer the question that follows.

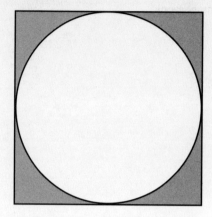

What is the approximate area of the shaded region, given that:

    a.   the radius of the circle is 6 units

    b.   the square inscribes the circle

  A.   106 square units

  B.   31 square units

  C.   77 square units

  D.   125 square units

69. How many lines of symmetry do all non-square rectangles have?

  A.   0

  B.   2

  C.   4

  D.   8

70. Use the figure to answer the question that follows.

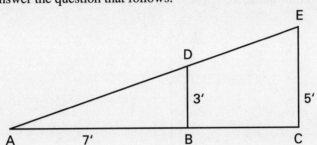

The figure above is a sketch of a ramp. Given that the two ramp supports (DB and EC) are perpendicular to the ground, and the dimensions of the various parts are as noted, what is the approximate distance from point B to point C?

A. 4.7 feet

B. 4.5 feet

C. 4.3 feet

D. 4.1 feet

71. What is the slope of a line passing through points (–2, 6) and (4, –2) on the coordinate plane?

A. $-\frac{3}{4}$

B. $\frac{3}{4}$

C. $-\frac{4}{3}$

D. $\frac{4}{3}$

72. Use the graph to answer the question.

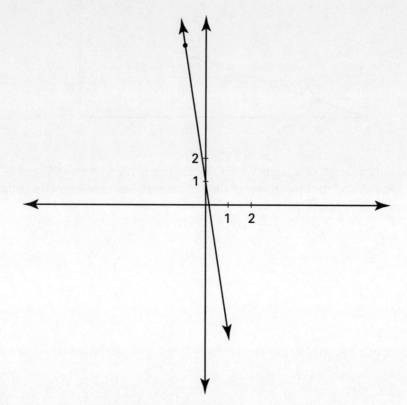

Which equation best describes the graph above?

A. $y = 0x$

B. $y = x + 0$

C. $y = -8x$

D. $y = 8x$

73. Which point represents the y-intercept of the equation $2x = 3y - 12$?

A. $(4, 0)$

B. $(0, -6)$

C. $(-6, 0)$

D. $(0, 4)$

Read the passage below; then answer the three questions that follow.

The early decades of the fifteenth century were a period in our history when English took a "great (linguistic) vowel shift" by redistributing the vowel pronunciation and configuration. Each vowel changed its sound quality, but the distinction between one vowel and the next was maintained. There was a restructuring of the sounds and patterns of communication. One has to conclude that a concurrent stress and exhilaration was also occurring within the perimeters of the literate society. Musicians, artists, poets, and authors all must have relished the new freedom and experimentation that was now possible with the new-found linguistic shifts.

74. The passage tells about

    A.   a shift in vowel pronunciation and configuration.

    B.   a fifteenth-century renaissance for musicians, artists, poets, and authors.

    C.   a new-found linguistic freedom from conventional sound and linguistic structure.

    D.   various vowel stresses and their effect on artistic expression.

75. What is the meaning of the word *linguistic* as used in the passage?

    A.   Artistic freedom

    B.   Verbal or rhetorical

    C.   Social or expressive

    D.   Vowel configuration

76. Because "each vowel changed its sound quality,"

    A.   there was a restructuring of the sounds and patterns of communication.

    B.   language could never be spoken in the same way again.

    C.   artists had to develop new means of expression.

    D.   communication went through a divergent change of status and culture.

77. Ms. Williams plans to buy carpeting for her livingroom floor. The room is a rectangle measuring 14 feet by 20 feet. She wants no carpet seams on her floor, even if that means that some carpeting will go to waste. The carpeting she wants comes in 16-foot-wide rolls. What is the minimum amount of carpeting that will have to be wasted if Ms. Williams insists upon her no-seams requirement?

A.   40 square feet

B.   60 square feet

C.   80 square feet

D.   100 square feet

78. Use the figure to answer the question that follows.

Consider this sequence of calculator keystrokes:

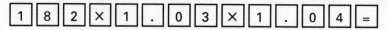

That sequence would be useful for finding which of the following values?

A.   The total distance an automobile travels if it covers 182 miles one day, but only 1.03 and 1.04 miles over the next two days.

B.   The amount of money in a savings account after the original deposit of $182 earns 3% and then 4% simple annual interest over two years.

C.   The total distance an automobile travels if it covers 182 miles one day, 103 miles the next day, and 104 miles the third day.

D.   The amount of money in a savings account after the original deposit of $182 grows by $1.03 and $1.04 in interest over two days.

79. The distribution of a high school chorus is depicted in the graph below. There is a total of 132 students in the chorus.

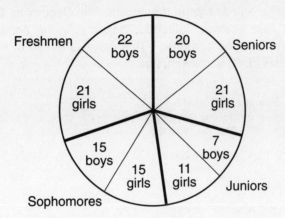

Which of the following expressions represents the percentage of freshman and sophomore girls in the chorus?

A. $\dfrac{21+15}{132} \times 100$

B. $\dfrac{21+15}{132} + 100$

C. $\dfrac{21+15}{132}$

D. $\dfrac{21+15}{100} \times 132$

Read the passage below; then answer the two questions that follow.

[1]The Dead Sea Scrolls are considered the archaeological find of the century. [2]The scrolls, about 800 different documents, are written on leather and papyrus. [3]They may be the oldest versions of the Judeo-Christian sacred texts in existence. [4]The manuscripts are believed to have been written between 200 b.c. and a.d. 50 by the Essenes, members of an ascetic Jewish sect. [5]Most of the Old Testament books (except Esther) appear in the scrolls, and some of the scrolls are multiple copies of these books written by different scribes. [6]Other scrolls are books of the Apocrypha, such as Jubilees, Tobit, and the Wisdom of Solomon, as well as hymns, prayers, prophecies, and biblical commentaries.

[7]For nearly 2,000 years this priceless cache of sacred writings lay hidden in the desert of Judah along the Dead Sea. [8]The first find was in 1947 when a Bedouin shepherd boy discovered the scrolls in a rocky cave of Qumran, ten miles from Jerusalem on the edge of the Dead Sea. [9]Shortly after, other manuscripts were uncovered nearby in different caves. [10]The larger group of scrolls was found in 1952.

11Four photographic copies of the scrolls were distributed, and these photographic copies were kept under the strict supervision of a group of 40 scholars dedicated to studying the photographs and analyzing the copies. 12In December 1990, however, the Huntington Library in San Marino, California, began granting access to anyone who wants to view and study the photographs. 13This move is hailed by those who have felt left out of the elite cadre of 40 scroll scholars.

80. Which of the following changes is needed?

    A.   Sentence 4: Change "between" to "among."

    B.   Sentence 7: Change "lay" to "have lain."

    C.   Sentence 10: Change "larger" to "largest."

    D.   Sentence 12: Change "who" to "whom."

81. Which of the following requires revision for unnecessary repetition?

    A.   Sentence 5

    B.   Sentence 7

    C.   Sentence 8

    D.   Sentence 11

82. Use the graph to answer the question that follows.

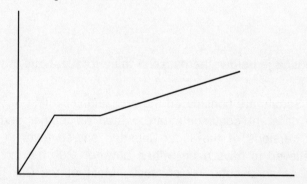

Which of the following scenarios could be represented by the graph above?

A.   Mr. Cain mowed grass at a steady rate for a while, then took a short break, and then finished the job at a steady but slower rate.

B.   Mr. Cain mowed grass at a steady rate for a while, and then mowed at a steady slower rate, then he took a break.

C.   Mr. Cain mowed grass at a variable rate for a while, then took a short break, and then finished the job at a variable rate.

D.   Mr. Cain mowed grass at a steady rate for a while, then took a short break, and then finished the job at a steady but faster pace.

83. Use the bar graph that follows to answer the question thereafter.

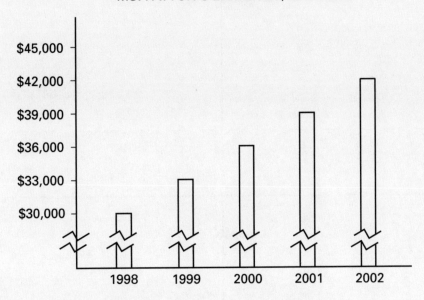

MS. PATTON'S EARNINGS, 1998–2002

Only one of the statements below is necessarily true. Which one?

A. The range of Ms. Patton's earnings for the years shown is $15,000.

B. Ms. Patton's annual pay increases were consistent over the years shown.

C. Ms. Patton earned $45,000 in 2003.

D. Ms. Patton's average income for the years shown was $38,000.

84. A line passes through points (–6,0) and (0,4) on the coordinate plane. Which of the following statements are true?

I.   The slope of the line is negative.
II. The slope of the line is positive.
III. The y-intercept of the line is –6.
IV. The y-intercept of the line is 4.

A. I and III only

B. I and IV only

C. II and III only

D. II and IV only

85. Use the graph that follows to answer the question.

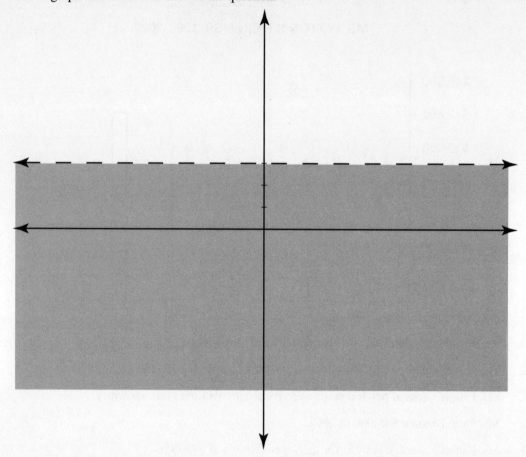

Which inequality describes the graph?

A. $y < 3$

B. $x < 3$

C. $y > 3$

D. $x > 3$

86. Use the figure to answer the question that follows.

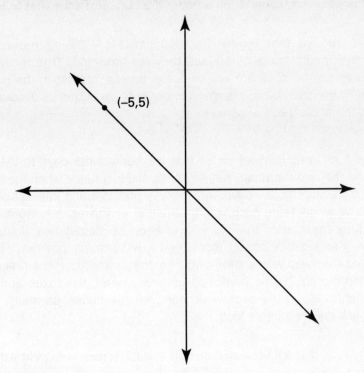

(–5,5)

Which of the following statements about the graph of a linear equation (shown) are true?
I. The graph shows an inverse variation.
II. The graph shows a direct variation.
III. The slope of the line is –1.
IV. The slope of the line is 1.

A. I and III only

B. I and IV only

C. II and III only

D. II and IV only

> **Read the passage below; then answer the two questions that follow.**

[1]Most banks require that buyers be responsible for paying hazard insurance premiums and real estate taxes on houses they are financing. [2]The reason is that if the insurance premium or taxes are not paid, the bank's interest in the property may be jeopardized. [3]Therefore, the mortgage servicer sets up a special account called an escrow account to handle these expenses.

[4]A mortgage loan is usually set up so that the homeowner pays to the bank each month an amount that will eventually pay for taxes and insurance when these expenses come due. [5]Each month's house payment, then, is principal and interest plus 1/12 of the estimated total amount due each year for interest and taxes. [6]Because the amount of taxes levied by the county may vary, and because sometimes insurance rates rise, the bank will sometimes collect more then it will actually pay out. [7]The overage is applied toward the next year's payments, so the house payment reflects a lower amount due each month. [8]If the bank has underestimated the taxes and insurance, there will be a shortage in the escrow account, so the house payments will rise in order that the bank may recoup its loss.

87. Which of the following, if added between sentences 4 and 5, is most consistent with the writer's purpose and audience?

    A. This money is put into a special account called a mortgage escrow account.

    B. Some folks resent the fact that the bank hangs on to a part of their money in an interest-free account.

    C. Most mortgage servicers do not set up an escrow account.

    D. How anybody can fail to see that banks are going out of their way to protect clients is beyond me.

88. Which of the following is needed in the second paragraph?

    A. Sentence 4: Change "set" to "sit."

    B. Sentence 6: Change "then" to "than."

    C. Sentence 7: Change "so" to "but."

    D. Sentence 8: Change "rise" to "raise."

89. Simplify the following expression.

    $\frac{2x^2}{3} + 7x + 9 + \frac{x^2}{3} - 12x + 1$

    A. $x^2 - 5x + 10$

    B. $6x^3 + 10$

    C. $6x^2 + 10$

    D. $x^4 - 5x + 10$

90. Multiply the following binomials.

    $(-2x^2 - 11)(5x^2 + 3)$

    A. $-10x^2 - 8$

    B. $-10x^2 - 14x - 8$

    C. $-10x^4 - 61x^2 - 33$

    D. $-10x^2 - 52x - 33$

91. Factor the following expression into two binomials.

    $-8x^2 + 22x - 5$

    A. $(4x - 1)(-2x + 5)$

    B. $(-4x - 1)(-2x - 5)$

    C. $(4x + 1)(-2x + 5)$

    D. $(4x + 1)(2x + 5)$

92. Use the figure below to answer the question that follows. Assume that:

Point C is the center of the circle.

Angles xyz and xcz intercept minor arc xz.

The measure of angle xyz is 40°.

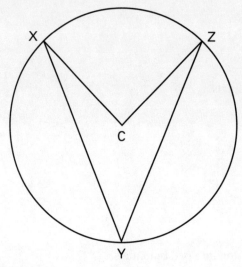

What is the measure of major arc xyz?

A.   140°

B.   280°

C.   160°

D.   320°

93. The novel *Huckleberry Finn*, by Mark Twain, has been a subject of controversy because:

A.   it contains graphic descriptions of violence considered unsuitable for young readers.

B.   it challenges contemporary attitudes toward race in America.

C.   it portrays a hostile relationship between a young boy and an escaping slave.

D.   it was thought to have influenced the outcome of the Civil War.

94. The Japanese form of poetry called haiku is known for its:

A.   brevity and concision.

B.   elaborate and flowery description.

C.   logic and directness of statement.

D.   humor and lifelike detail.

95. Which author wrote: "What's in a name? That which we call a rose/ By any other name would smell as sweet"?

    A. Christopher Marlowe

    B. Ben Johnson

    C. William Shakespeare

    D. Geoffrey Chaucer

96. Why did medieval artists not generally employ techniques such as portraiture or realistic perspective?

    A. These were advances in art which were unavailable to them.

    B. They were reacting against Classical artistic models.

    C. They used the composition of their works to express theological ideas.

    D. They considered excessive realism sacrilegious.

97. Which artistic movement saw an important revival in recent centuries?

    A. Classical

    B. Baroque

    C. Gothic

    D. A and C

98. Contemporary performance art often makes use of which media?

    A. photography

    B. film

    C. the spoken word

    D. all of the above

99. Contemporary writers of world literature such as Chinua Achebe have emphasized which of the following themes?

    A. imperialism and the impact of Western culture on traditional societies

    B. conflicts between traditional and modern ways of life

    C. the living conditions and problems of everyday life in developing nations

    D. all of the above

100. The novel *One Hundred Years of Solitude*, by Gabriel García Márquez, is characterized by:

    A.   an interweaving of exaggeration and straightforward narrative known as magic realism.

    B.   strict realism and historical accuracy.

    C.   an indifference toward politics.

    D.   a focus on the life course of a single outstanding protagonist.

Constructed-Response Question

Read the passage below on studying literature of the past, and then follow the instructions for writing your essay.

Many scholars note the decline of interest in literature written before the twentieth century. A diminishing number of students pursue studies in Classical, Medieval, and even Renaissance literature. Some observers think this trend is acceptable, since the literature of these early periods is not particularly interesting to the general public. Others say that any lessening of study about the past, and especially its artistic expression, is a negative trend.

In this essay, argue whether you feel that the trend of studying modern versus past literature is commendable or contemptible. Reflect on modern culture and the effects of literature upon it. Discuss the advantages and/or disadvantages of a course of study that excludes or minimizes the literature of earlier periods. Finally, draw upon your own exposure to and attitude toward modern and past literatures, respectively.

Practice Test Answer Sheets

Begin your essay on this page. If necessary, continue on the next page.

_____

_____

_____

_____

_____

_____

_____

_____

_____

_____

_____

_____

_____

_____

_____

Continue on the next page if necessary.

Continuation of your essay from previous page, if necessary.

OGET

Oklahoma General Education Test

Practice Test Answers

Answer Key

1.	(D)	26.	(D)	51.	(D)	76.	(A)
2.	(B)	27.	(D)	52.	(A)	77.	(A)
3.	(A)	28.	(B)	53.	(D)	78.	(B)
4.	(C)	29.	(B)	54.	(C)	79.	(A)
5.	(C)	30.	(D)	55.	(B)	80.	(C)
6.	(C)	31.	(A)	56.	(B)	81.	(D)
7.	(C)	32.	(C)	57.	(D)	82.	(A)
8.	(D)	33.	(B)	58.	(B)	83.	(B)
9.	(D)	34.	(B)	59.	(D)	84.	(D)
10.	(C)	35.	(C)	60.	(D)	85.	(A)
11.	(A)	36.	(B)	61.	(A)	86.	(C)
12.	(C)	37.	(D)	62.	(B)	87.	(A)
13.	(A)	38.	(D)	63.	(D)	88.	(B)
14.	(C)	39.	(B)	64.	(C)	89.	(A)
15.	(C)	40.	(D)	65.	(A)	90.	(C)
16.	(B)	41.	(A)	66.	(B)	91.	(A)
17.	(A)	42.	(D)	67.	(B)	92.	(B)
18.	(B)	43.	(A)	68.	(B)	93.	(B)
19.	(B)	44.	(B)	69.	(B)	94.	(A)
20.	(C)	45.	(B)	70.	(A)	95.	(C)
21.	(C)	46.	(A)	71.	(C)	96.	(C)
22.	(B)	47.	(A)	72.	(C)	97.	(D)
23.	(A)	48.	(B)	73.	(D)	98.	(D)
24.	(C)	49.	(B)	74.	(A)	99.	(D)
25.	(D)	50.	(A)	75.	(B)	100.	(A)

Detailed Explanations of Answers

1. **D**

   D is correct because its precepts are summations of each of the composition's main paragraphs. Choice A only mentions points made in the second paragraph; B and C only mention scattered points made throughout the passage, each of which does not represent a larger body of information within the passage.

2. **B**

   The second paragraph states that this is the reason that water is a most unusual substance. Choices A and C list unusual properties of water, but are not developed in the same manner as the property stated in B. Choice D is not correct under any circumstances.

3. **A**

   The sentence contrasts distilled water to that which contains salt, so A is correct. Choices B, C, and D are not implied by the sentence.

4. **C**

   The writer's didactic summary of water's properties is the only perspective found in the passage. Choices A and B are the subjects of individual paragraphs within the passage, but hardly represent the entire passage itself. An in-depth discussion of the physical states of liquids is not offered within the passage.

5. **C**

   The correct choice is C because of the many properties of water ascribed to it in the passage, each of which might serve one practical purpose or another. Choices A and D are contradicted within the passage, while B is not implied at all by the passage.

6. **C**

This sentence includes a remark about the "lack of spark" in DeMarco's writing, which makes a contrast with the previous sentence, where his potential reading competence is regarded as positive. The rest of the paragraph supports this observation. Choice B is also supported by the rest of the paragraph, but it contains no transition of contrast (moreover rather than however).

7. **C**

The best answer here is sentence 6, with its "grasps and comprehends." These two words mean exactly the same thing in this context, so one of them is unnecessary. The phrase "all of the class" in sentence 5 is somewhat wordy (it could be "the whole class"), but it is not redundant.

8. **D**

*Sentence 13 contains a **dangling modifier**. The verbal phrase at the beginning of the sentence should modify a person ("answers" cannot be asked a question), but the only choices are "his" and "answers." Thus the phrase modifies nothing and is a dangling modifier.*

9. **D**

Sentence 12 refers to journals of all classmates, so the apostrophe should follow the s. Choice A is wrong because Sideways Stories from Wayside School is a book, not a story, a fact that prospective elementary teachers should know.

10. **C**

The phrase "comings and goings" could possibly fit into this sentence, but it is slightly off, whereas the other choices have little or nothing wrong with them. One problem with "comings and goings" is its informal tone: a case study in a textbook usually does not use slangy terms like this one. In addition, the sentence refers to all the students' accounts, not just their travels.

11. **A**

Drawing a sketch with dots marking the possible locations of the two houses and The Soda Depot is a good idea. You can start with dots for the two houses, using inches for miles:

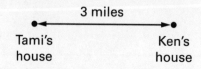

3 miles

Tami's house   Ken's house

If you then draw a dot representing The Soda Depot two miles (inches) to the right of Ken's house, as in the figure that follows, you see that the greatest possible distance between Tami's house and The Soda Depot is five miles.

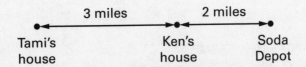

If you draw The Soda Depot dot to the left of Ken's house, as in the figure below, you see that The Soda Depot could be as close as one mile to Tami's house, but no closer. Only statements I and III, then, are true.

```
        1 miles      2 miles
      •←→•←————————→•
    Tami's  Soda        Ken's
    house   Depot       house
```

12. **C** ———————————————————————————————————————

Each combined inequality can be seen as the combination of two single inequalities. Inequality A, for instance, can be seen as the combination of the following two single inequalities:

$75 \leq x$

and

$x \leq 40.$

The meaning of a single inequality is often made clearer if you transpose the statement, placing the variable on the left. That is:

$75 \leq x$

means the same thing as

$x \geq 75.$

So, combined inequality A says that x (the speeds that vehicles may drive at) is greater than or equal to 75 mph and less than or equal to 40 mph.

You can separate combined inequalities B and D into individual inequalities in the same way:

Combined inequality B, 75 < x > 40, means the same as

$x > 75$

and

$x > 40.$

That means that drivers have to drive faster than 75 mph! That doesn't match what the sign says.

Combined inequality D, 40 < *x* > 75 means the same as

x > 40

and

x > 75.

That's the same as combined inequality B.

The correct answer is C, 40 ≤ x ≤ 75, because that combined inequality means the same as

x ≥ 40

and

x ≤ 75.

That is, vehicles can travel at or faster than 40 mph, but no faster than 75 mph.

13. **A** ——

A bar graph works well here. The height of each of five bars would be determined by the number of votes for each lunch food.

A circle or pie chart could also be used. The 18 votes for pizza give the fraction 18/40, so pizza would be assigned 45% of the area of a circle chart, or 162°. The same approach would tell us the appropriate size of each lunch food's slice of the pie chart.

A scatter plot illustrates the relationship between sets of data. A broken-line graph generally illustrates change over time. Neither is appropriate for illustrating the given data.

14. **C** ——

Choice C is the correct answer. The use of uncommon materials has dramatically changed the criteria by which one assesses visual art.

15. **C** ——

Choice C is correct because this is the definition of illiterate and functional illiterate stated in paragraph two. Choice A cannot be correct because the passage clearly distinguishes between illiterates and functional illiterates. Choice B is not correct because the definition stated is not related to participation in a program. Choice D is incorrect because the relative number of illiterates and functional illiterates is not discussed.

16. **B** ——

Choice B is correct because the passage begins by stating that many politicians' wives have expressed interest in literacy. Choice A is incorrect because the author of the passage does not suggest that only women are interested. Choice C is incorrect because the passage does not discuss the number of male or female illiterates. Choice D is incorrect because there is no discussion in the passage of politicians' wives giving speeches.

17. **A**

This question must be answered using the process of elimination. You are asked to select a statement that names a possible program component which is not characteristic of successful literacy programs. Choice A is correct because choices B, C, and D are specifically mentioned in the passage.

18. **B**

Choice B is correct because the author specifically states that politicians should support increased funding for literacy programs. Choices A and C are incorrect because the author states that funding should be increased. There is no discussion of funding for different programs, so choice D is incorrect.

19. **B**

The combined percentages of English and German immigrants equal 45 percent (Irish immigrants represent 43 percent of the graph). Choice A is incorrect because the Irish immigrants represent less than half of the graph. Choice C is incorrect because the graph nowhere implies that the "All Others" section of the graph is restricted to Italian immigrants. D is incorrect because the English and German percentages are unequal.

20. **C**

The gas molecules themselves do not expand in size when heated, but the spaces between them increases as the molecules move faster. The expanding hot air leaves the balloon body through the opening at the bottom. With less air in the balloon casing, the balloon is lighter. The combustion products of propane are carbon dioxide (molar mass 44 g/mol), which is heavier than air, and water (molar mass 18 g/mol), which is lighter.

21. **C**

The upward force of air resistance partially counteracts the force of gravity when a feather falls in air. In a vacuum, or near vacuum, this force is dramatically reduced for the feather and both objects will fall at the same rate. The effect can be modeled without a vacuum pump by comparing the falling of two papers, one crumpled to reduce air resistance and the other flat.

22. **B**

Sentence 6 begins with "Although"—used for mentioning the scientists' public statements—and refers to the "hazy" benefits derived from the study. Thus the sentence has to deal with speculation about the "uncertain" benefits. Choice D fits in with the paragraph's development fairly well, but it is not the best answer because the pejorative word "racist" would not generally be used to characterize someone in a textbook. (There is little doubt that the author considers the experiment itself to be racist, but he or she does not otherwise characterize any of the individuals involved in this passage—and should not do so without offering evidence.)

23. **A**

The word should be "affected"; see the discussion of effect and affect in Chapter 2. The other words are used in standard ways and, even though "whereas" may sound out of place, it is not as obviously wrong as "effected" and is therefore not the best answer.

24. **C**

Sentence 7 contains a comma splice. The sentence has two independent clauses, and they are not joined by a coordinating conjunction. They must therefore be separated by a semicolon, not a comma. Sentence 3, which contains several commas, is correctly punctuated (except for the period at the end), but they are all necessary to separate the two nonrestrictive phrases: (a) author of the excellent history on the subject and (b) Bad Blood.

25. **D**

By convention in American English, periods and commas are always placed inside of quotation marks.

26. **D**

The verb learn should clearly be in past tense, not present, because it concerns something that happened in 1972. Incidentally, the word "media" is technically plural, so the verb form should be "learn" rather than "learns" even if present tense were correct.

27. **D**

This teacher is doing a good thing by collecting data and displaying the data.

28. **B**

One way to approach the problem is to examine each scenario for reasonableness. Even though a runner's mile-by-mile pace in a marathon varies up and down, the runner continually increases the distance covered, and the graph will always move upward, so situation I doesn't go with the graph. The number of households a census taker has left to visit decreases with each visit, so situation II doesn't fit either.

Both situations III and IV are examples of steady growth, so both match the graph. Answer B is therefore correct.

29. **B**

Just from looking at the graph, it's clear that most of the space under the curve is past the 60 mark on the x-axis, so answer D is eliminated because it doesn't include statement I.

Statement II can't be answered by what the graph shows. It appears possible that certain questions were too hard for many in the class and that there weren't enough questions to differen-

tiate B students from C students, but perhaps the class performed exactly as it should have, given the students' ability and Ms. Alvarez's teaching. The distribution can give a teacher many clues about the test and the students and even herself, but by itself tells us nothing about the fairness of the test. Thus, answer A can be eliminated.

Statement III is also false; in left-skewed distributions such as this one, the median is higher than the mean. This is true because the mean is lowered by the lowest scores while the median is relatively unaffected by them.

Statement IV is true: one fairly large group has scored in the high 80s and 90s and another discernible group in the low to mid 60s, whereas few students fall outside these two groups. Thus, the answer has to be B.

30. **D**

Using the rules for solving one-variable equations, the original equation is transformed as follows:

$$\frac{x}{3} - 9 = 15$$

Adding 9 to each side of the equation gives

$$\frac{x}{3} = 24$$

Multiplying both sides by 3 gives

x = 72.

31. **A**

Again, using the rules for solving one-variable equations produces these transformations:

$$3x^2 - 11 = 1$$

Adding 11 to each side of the equation gives

$$3x^2 = 12$$

Dividing both sides by 3 gives

$$x^2 = 4$$

You next find the square roots of 4: 2 and –2.

The solutions can be checked by substituting them (one at a time) into the original equation to see if they work. In this case, both 2 and –2 indeed do work.

32. **C**

Black line spectra are formed when the continuous spectra of the Sun passes through the atmosphere. The elements in the atmosphere absorb wavelengths of light characteristic of their spectra (these are the same wavelengths given off when the element is excited; for example, the red color of a Neon light). By examining the line spectral gaps, scientists can deduce the elements that make up the distant atmosphere. Choice A is true, but it explains the source of a line spectrum. B is true, and it explains why a blue shirt is blue when placed under a white or blue light source. Recall that a blue shirt under a red light source will appear black because there are no blue wavelengths to be reflected. D is a partial truth; black lights do give off ultraviolet light that the human eye cannot see.

33. B

Salt is a strong electrolyte that completely dissociates in solution. When this solution is in contact with a semi-permeable membrane, like the inflamed cells in the throat, water moves across the membrane from the side with lowest solute concentration to the side of higher solute concentration. In the case of the sore throat, water from inside the inflamed cells moves out toward the higher concentration salt water and the throat cells shrink due to the loss of water. All the items listed are colligative properties that, like osmotic pressure, are a function of the number, but not the nature, of particles in solution.

34. B

Lincoln's immediate purpose in announcing the Emancipation Proclamation was to rally flagging Northern morale. Lincoln waited until after a major Union victory, at Antietam in 1862, so he couldn't be charged with making the announcement as an act of desperation. He recognized that the costs of the war had reached a point where preserving the Union would not be a powerful enough reason to motivate many Northerners to continue the war. Framing the war as a war against slavery would mobilize powerful abolitionist forces in the North and perhaps create an atmosphere of a "holy crusade" rather than one of using war to resolve a political conflict.

While the Emancipation Proclamation had the announced purpose of freeing the slaves, Lincoln himself indirectly stated that freeing the slaves was a means to a greater end, preserving the Union. In a statement released before the Emancipation Proclamation, Lincoln asserted, "If I could save the Union without freeing any slave I would do it, and if I could save it by freeing all the slaves I would do it. . . . What I do about slavery, and the colored race, I do because I believe it helps to save the Union."

35. C

The passage suggests that education is at present based primarily on failure and negative reinforcement and that, in order to create a more productive and positive learning environment, the emphasis must shift to success. While answers A and B may be correct, they are not the main ideas of the passage. D is simply a statement that is not based upon any factual evidence whatsoever. Therefore, C is the correct answer.

36. B

An axiom in this case is another word for motto. It can also mean an accepted truism or principle, which would also apply here. Answers A, C, and D are erroneous definitions; therefore, B, University motto, is the correct answer.

37. **D**

The passage states that "the language of failure . . . will have a prohibitive impact on the students' . . . self-esteem," so D is the correct answer. Answers A, B, and C do not apply in this case.

38. **D**

The first paragraph of the passage tells the reader that, in addition to personal expression, language also has the power to persuade and influence. While answers A, B, and C may indeed be attributes of language, they are not focused upon in the passage.

39. **B**

Solving for a particular variable in an equation means to isolate that variable on one side of the equation. In this case, use of the rules for transforming equations allows you to change the original equation into the desired one:

$$\frac{y}{3} - \frac{x}{2} = 4$$

Adding $\frac{x}{2}$ to each side gives

$$\frac{y}{3} = \frac{x}{2} + 4$$

Then, multiplying each side by 3 gives

$$y = \frac{3x}{2} + 12$$

40. **D**

One way to solve the problem is by writing a one-variable equation that matches the information given:

$$4x + 2(10 - x) = 26$$

The "4x" represents four tires for each car. You use x for the number of cars because you don't know how many cars there are.

(10 − x) represents the number of motorcycle tires in the lot. (If there are ten vehicles total, and x of them are cars, you subtract x from 10 to get the number of motorcycles.) Then 2(10 − x) stands for the number of motorcycle tires in the lot.

The sum of the values 4x and 2(10 − x) is 26, and that gives you your equation. Using the standard rules for solving a one-variable equation, you find that x (the number of cars in the lot) equals 3.

Another approach to the problem when given multiple answer choices is to try substituting each answer for the unknown variable in the problem to see which one makes sense.

41. **A**

The correct equation must show three consecutive odd numbers being added to give 117. Odd numbers (just like even numbers) are each two apart. Only the three values given in answer A are each two apart.

Because the numbers being sought are odd, one might be tempted to choose answer D. However, the second value in answer D (x + 1) is not two numbers apart from the first value (x); it's different by only one.

42. **D**

All riders must pay at least three dollars, so 3 will be added to something else in the correct equation. Only answers B and D meet that requirement. The additional fare of two dollars "for every mile or fraction of a mile" tells you that you will need to multiply the number of miles driven (you use 11 because of the extra fraction of a mile) by 2, leading you to answer D.

43. **A**

Democracy is the correct response because it is the antithesis of the authoritarianism of fascism. Indeed, the totalitarian, romantic, militaristic, and nationalistic characteristics were, in large part, a reaction against the perceived inadequacies of democracy.

44. **B**

The industrial economy of the nineteenth century was not based upon an equitable distribution of profits among all those who were involved in production. Marxists and other critics of capitalism condemned the creed of capitalists and the abhorrent conditions of the industrial proletariat. Raw materials, a constant labor supply, capital, and an expanding marketplace were critical elements in the development of the industrial economy.

45. **B**

The term "Trail of Tears" is used to describe the relocation of the Cherokee tribe from the southern Appalachians to what is now Oklahoma. The migration of Mormons from Nauvoo, Illinois, to the Great Salt Lake in Utah, the westward movements along the Oregon Trail, and, much earlier, the Wilderness Road, all took place and could at times be as unpleasant as the Cherokees' trek. They were, however, more voluntary than the Cherokee migration and therefore did not earn such sad titles as the "Trail of Tears."

46. **A**

Thomas Paine wrote several pamphlets before and during the American Revolution. Common Sense was the most significant because it carefully documented abuses of the British parliamentary system of government, particularly in its treatment of the American colonies. Paine portrayed a brutish monarchy interested only in itself and pointedly argued how independence would improve the colonies' long-term situation. His argument was directed at the common man, and it struck a chord unlike anything previously written in the colonies. Its publication in 1774 was perfect in reaching the public at just the moment that their questions and concerns regarding British rule were peaking. The answers provided in Paine's essays were pivotal in the subsequent behavior of many colonists who, until that time, had been unsure of what they believed regarding independence and British rule.

Answer B is incorrect. Paine wrote another essay called American Crisis *during the winter of 1776. This essay, not* Common Sense, *helped rally American spirits during that long, demoralizing winter. Answers C and D are also incorrect. Paine wrote to an American, not a British, audience. He also wrote* Common Sense *well before American independence was achieved.*

47. Ⓐ

The last phrase of the sentence—"that chaotic period"—could refer to either the guerilla war mentioned in sentence 12 or the period of relocation mentioned in sentence 13, meaning that the sentence would have to be inserted after sentence 12 or 13 (choices A or B). However, the sentence about the Church's individual members providing support cannot just sit beside a sentence about the church itself providing support: the two thoughts would have to be joined in a logical way. Thus choice B is not as good as choice A. With choice A, sentence 12 would be explained by the new sentence, and then sentence 13 would describe the circumstances under which the support was provided.

48. Ⓑ

The second paragraph proceeds from the 1500s to 1975, and the third paragraph describes the cause for the effect mentioned at the end of the second paragraph: the embrace of Catholicism by the Timorese.

49. Ⓑ

Sentence 4 is a fragment: because "being" is a verbal rather than a standard verb form, it does not act as a verb for "exceptions." (Note: Substituting "were" for "being" would fix the fragment but would not produce an effective sentence—"the exceptions" to what?) Sentence 7 does contain a punctuation error (discussed in the answer to question 50), but the question specifically asks for nonstandard "sentence structure." Be sure to read each question thoroughly.

50. Ⓐ

Sentence 7 begins with a subordinate clause, and a comma should separate that clause from the independent clause that follows, so the answer is A. The "who" in sentence 8 is correct even though it refers to "missionaries," which is the object of a preposition, because it is the subject of its own clause—"who were posted"—so B is incorrect. The "its" following East Timor in sentence 9 is correct because the pronoun refers to the country as a whole, not to all the people of the country, so C is incorrect. The word "government" in sentence 11 is not capitalized even though it occurs with the proper adjective "Indonesian," so D is incorrect.

51. **D**

Because the first blank must show a contrast with the previous thought, choice B is not possible. Because a comma rather than a semicolon precedes the first blank, "however" is not possible, either, eliminating A and C. If "however" were inserted, the sentence would have a comma splice, because "however" is not a coordinating conjunction ("but" is).

52. **A**

The first sentence has a plural subject—"animism and spirit worship"—so it should have a plural form of verb as well.

53. **D**

Let s be the length of each side of square ABCD. Since triangle ADC is a right triangle, we can use the Pythagorean Theorem to solve for s. We have $AD^2 + DC^2 = AC^2$ or $s^2 + s^2 = 8^2$. Simplifying the equation, we get: $2s^2 = 64$. Now divide both sides of the equation by two:

$$s^2 = 32 \text{ so } s = \sqrt{32} = \sqrt{16} \times \sqrt{2} = 4\sqrt{2}.$$

Therefore, the perimeter of square ABCD is

$$P = 4s = 4 \times 4\sqrt{2} = 16\sqrt{2}$$

54. **C**

Let r be the length of the radius of each of the small circles and let R be the length of the radius of the large circle. Then, R = 3r. The area of each of the small circles is $\pi r^2 = 9\pi$. Now divide both sides of the equation by π:

$r^2 = 9r = 3$. Then,

$R = 3r = 3 \times 3 = 9$.

Therefore, the circumference of the large circle is

$C = 2\pi R = 2\pi \times 9 = 18\pi$.

55. **B**

To solve the equation $2x^2 + 5x - 3 = 0$, we can factor the left side of the equation to get $(2x - 1)(x + 3) = 0$. Then use the following rule (sometimes called the Zero Product Property): If $a \times b = 0$, then either a = 0 or b = 0. Applying this to our problem gives us

$2x - 1 = 0$ or $x + 3 = 0$.

Solve these two equations:

$2x - 1 = 0 \rightarrow 2x = 1 \rightarrow \frac{1}{2}$ or $x + 3 = 0 \rightarrow x = -3$.

But x > 0, so $x = \frac{1}{2}$.

56. B

∠*AOB* and ∠*COD* are central angles, meaning that their vertices are at the center of a circle. The measure of a central angle is equal to the measure of its intercepted arc. Hence, since arc *AB* and arc *CD* are the intercepted arcs of ∠*AOB* and ∠*COD*, respectively, the measure (m) of ∠*AOB* = 65° and m∠*COD* = 21.4°. So,

m∠*AOB* + m∠*COD* = 86.4°.

Therefore, since one revolution of a circle is 360°, the shaded portion of the circle is represented by the following:

$$\frac{86.4}{360} = 0.24 = 24\%$$

57. D

First find the total sales for each year by reading the graph for the sales of (i) black and white televisions and (ii) color televisions. Then combine these numbers:

1960	$20,000,000 + $5,000,000	= $25,000,000
1970	$10,000,000 + $20,000,000	= $30,000,000
1980	$15,000,000 + $25,000,000	= $40,000,000
1990	$10,000,000 + $45,000,000	= $55,000,000
2000	$5,000,000 + $45,000,000	= $50,000,000

The greatest total sales occurred in 1990.

58. B

The statement "Movement basics include body, space, time, and relationship" is the correct answer because this describes only the dimensions of dance movement; in no way does it speak to how dance reflects the culture of which it is part.

59. D

A liquid will boil when its vapor pressure, which depends on temperature, is equal to the atmospheric pressure above the liquid. At high altitudes the atmospheric pressure is lower, thus water will boil at a lower temperature. The boiling point of water is only 100°C at 1 atmosphere pressure (760 torr). In Leadville, Colorado, elevation 10,150 feet, when the atmospheric pressure may be as low as 430 torr, the boiling point of water may be 89°C. The lower temperature increases cooking times.

60. D

A teaching apprentice would be expected to lay the foundation for her lecture and then present greater detail by way of example, or as the passage puts it, "illustration." Someone in this position, having set this task for herself, would not be prone to refuting her own lecture notes (A), attempting to cause confusion (B), or perhaps least of all, working to subvert the lecture topic she herself had elected to teach (C).

61. **A**

The definition of the term "pedagogical" is answer A, academic. The answers B, abstract; C, meaningless; and D, obtuse, are incorrect.

62. **B**

The author's classroom experience was answer B, intelligible (understandable) and pragmatic (practical or utilitarian). The passage gives credence to this by the author's use of such words as "clear and well-prepared." Answers A and C suggest the opposite of a positive experience, and there is no evidence given that the experience was too advanced or complicated (D).

63. **D**

It's true that multiplication is commutative and division isn't, but that's not relevant to them being inverse operations. Answer A doesn't address the property of being inverse.

Answer B also contains a true statement, but again, the statement is not about inverse operations.

Answer C gives a false statement. In the example shown in answer C, the order of operations tells you to compute $8 \div 2$ first, before any multiplication.

As noted in answer D, the inverseness of two operations indeed depends upon their ability to undo each other.

64. **C**

One way to arrive at the answer is to set up a proportion, with one corner labeled x:

$$\frac{31}{x} = \frac{5.5}{100}$$

To complete the proportion (and to find the answer), cross-multiply 31 and 100, giving 3100, then divide by 5.5, giving approximately 564.

65. **A**

The value 0.5 is equivalent to $\frac{5}{10}$ or $\frac{1}{2}$. That means that 0.5 percent (which is one way to read the original numeral) is the same as one-half of one percent, so answer I is correct.

One-half of one percent can't be the same as five percent, so answer II cannot be correct.

$\frac{1}{200}$ is equivalent to 0.5%. Here's why: One percent is equivalent to $\frac{1}{100}$. Half of one percent, (0.5%, as noted above) is therefore $\frac{1}{200}$, so answer III is correct. Therefore A, I and III only, is correct.

66. **B**

The ranchers believe that killing the eagles will protect their ranches. This is understood by the implication that "attract[ing] and kill[ing] predators . . . in an effort to preserve young grazing animals" will protect their ranches. Choice D is not wrong, but it is not as good a choice as B, because the passage offers no proof that the eagles do harm livestock.

67. **B**

The author's use of words such as "mighty bald eagle" and "threatened by a new menace" supports concern for the topic. For the most part, the author appears objective; thus, Choice B, concerned interest, is the correct answer.

68. **B**

First, it is helpful to view the shaded area as the area of the square minus the area of the circle. With that in mind, you simply need to find the area of each simple figure, and then subtract one from the other.

You know that the radius of the circle is 6 units in length. That tells you that the diameter of the circle is 12 units. Because the circle is inscribed in the square (meaning that the circle fits inside of the square touching in as many places as possible), you see that the sides of the square are each 12 units in length. Knowing that, you compute that the area of the square is 144 square units (12 × 12).

Using the formula for finding the area of a circle (πr^2), and using 3.14 for π, you get approximately 113 square units. (3.14 × 6 × 6). Then, you subtract 113 (the area of the circle) from 144 (the area of the square) for the answer of 31.

69. **B**

If you can fold a two-dimensional figure so that one side exactly matches or folds onto the other side, the fold line is a line of symmetry. The figure below is a non-square rectangle with its two lines of symmetry shown.

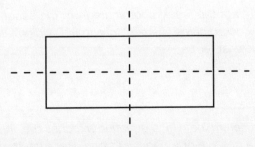

One might think that lines drawn from opposite corners are lines of symmetry, but they're not. The two halves would be the same size and shape, but wouldn't fold onto each other.

Note that the question asked about non-square rectangles. Squares (which are rectangles) have four lines of symmetry.

70. **A**

To answer the question, you must recognize that triangles ADB and AEC are similar triangles, meaning that they have the same shape. That means that the corresponding angles of the two triangles are the same, or congruent, and that corresponding sides of the two triangles are proportional. Given that, you can set up the following proportion, where x is the distance from point A to point C:

$$\frac{3}{7} = \frac{5}{x}$$

Solving the proportion by cross-multiplication, you see that the length of segment AC is about 11.7. Knowing that the length of segment AB is 7 feet, you subtract to find the length of BC (11.7 − 7 = 4.7).

71. **C**

There are several methods for finding the slope of a line if two points are known. The most straightforward method is to use the slope formula:

$$m = \frac{y_2 - y_1}{x_2 - x_1}$$

This can be read as "the slope of a line (m) is equal to the difference of the y coordinates of any two points on the line ($y_2 - y_1$) divided by the difference of the x coordinates.

($x_2 - x_1$).

For this problem, you subtract the first y coordinate from the second [(−2) − 6], giving −8. You then do the same for the x coordinates [4 − (−2)], giving 6. Dividing −8 by 6 is the same as showing the fraction $-\frac{8}{6}$ or, in lowest terms, $-\frac{4}{3}$.

72. **C**

There are several ways to determine which equation matches the line. An easy way is to decide first whether the line has a positive or a negative slope. Because the line moves from the upper left to the lower right, you would say it has a negative slope.

In a linear equation of the form y = mx + b (where y is isolated on the left side of the equation), the coefficient of x is the slope of the line. The only equation with a negative slope (−8) is response C, so that is the correct answer.

Another clue that C is correct can be found by considering the apparent slope, or steepness/shallowness of the line. The line in this problem is fairly steep, and a slope of −8 (or 8) is considered fairly steep too, suggesting that C is correct.

73. Ⓓ

The y-intercept *of a linear equation is the point at which its graph passes through, or intercepts,* the *vertical y-axis. One way to determine the y-intercept is by rewriting the equation in* y-intercept form:

$y = mx + b$

If a linear equation is in that form, b *tells you where the graph of the line intercepts the y-axis. In this case, you rewrite (or transform) the equation following these steps:*

$2x = 3y - 12$

$3y - 12 = 2x$

$3y = 2x + 12$

$y = \dfrac{2}{3}x + 4$

That final version of the equation is indeed in y-intercept form. The 4 tells you that the graph of the equation intercepts the y-axis at point (0, 4).

74. Ⓐ

The passage tells of the "great (linguistic) vowel shift" of the early fifteenth century. While the passage speaks of B, an artistic renaissance; C, new linguistic freedoms; and D, effects on artistic expression, these are all results of the shift and not the shift itself. The shift is what the passage is about. Thus, A is the correct answer.

75. Ⓑ

In this case, linguistic *refers to speaking, talking, verbiage, and/or the act of oration. A, C, and D are not acceptable definitions for the word* linguistic. *Consequently, Choice B, verbal or rhetorical, is the correct answer.*

76. Ⓐ

Answers B, C, and D are generalized answers resulting from the vowel shift. Choice A is a direct result of the shift and is quoted directly from the passage.

Therefore, A is the correct answer.

77. Ⓐ

The only way carpet from a 16-foot-wide roll will cover Ms. Williams' floor without seams is if she buys 20 feet of it. She can then trim the 16-foot width to 14 feet so that it fits her floor. Buying 20 feet of a 16-foot-wide roll means that she will have to buy 320 square feet. Her living room has an area of only 280 square feet (14 feet × 20 feet), so she'll be wasting 40 square feet (320 – 280), but no more, so A is the correct answer.

78. **B**

The keystrokes indicate multiplication, and only answer B involves multiplication. Multiplication is hidden within the concept of interest. One way to compute a new savings account balance after interest has been earned is to multiply the original balance by (1 + the rate of interest). In this case, that's first 1.03, then 1.04. The keystrokes match that multiplication.

79. **A**

In order to solve this problem we must first add the number of freshman girls to the number of sophomore girls (21 + 15). In order to find the percentage we divide this sum by the total number of students in the chorus and multiply by 100.

$$\frac{21+15}{132} \times 100 = \% \text{ of freshman and sophomore girls in chorus}$$

Answer B is incorrect; in order to find the percentage we need to multiply the fraction by 100, not divide by 100. Answers C and D are incorrect because the number of freshman and sophomore girls must be divided by the total number of students in the chorus. We then multiply by 100 to get the percent.

80. **C**

Choice C is the correct answer. The comparative degree is used for comparing two things, so "larger" should be changed to the superlative degree, "largest," because more than two caves were discovered containing scrolls. Choice A correctly uses "between" to indicate something falling between two dates; "among" is used for more than two things. In choice B, the use of "lay" is correct; the past tense is required for a condition no longer in effect. In choice D "who" is correct as the subject of the subordinate clause with the verb "wants." "Whom" is the objective case and cannot be a subject.

81. **D**

Choice D should be revised to eliminate unnecessary repetition of "photographic" and "copies." Choices A, B, and C are concise sentences.

82. **A**

The somewhat steep straight line to the left tells you that Mr. Cain worked at a steady rate for a while. The completely flat line in the middle tells you he stopped for a while—the line doesn't go up because no grass was cut then. Finally, the line continues upward (after his break) less steeply (and therefore more flatly), indicating that he was working at a slower rate.

83. **B**

Because Ms. Patton's increases were consistent ($3,000 annually), and because the directions tell you that only one statement is true, answer B must be correct. To be more confident, however, you can examine the other statements:

The range of Ms. Patton's earnings is $12,000 (the jump from $30,000 to $42,000), not $15,000, so answer A cannot be correct.

Although Ms. Patton may have earned $45,000 in 2003, you don't know that, so answer C cannot be correct.

Answer D gives the incorrect earnings average; it was $36,000, not $38,000.

84. **D**

It is helpful to make a sketch of the line on the coordinate plane. (To do that you need to know how to plot individual points.)

The line "travels" from the lower left to the upper right, meaning that it has a positive slope. Statement II is therefore true. The y-intercept of a line is the spot at which the line crosses, or intercepts, the vertical axis. In this case, that's at point (0, 4). (You can simply say that the y-intercept is 4, without mentioning the 0). Statement IV is therefore true as well.

85. **A**

Consider various random points in the shaded area: (5, –2), (–1, 2), (12, 2.5) and (–9, 1). Notice that all points in the shaded area have a y-coordinate value less than 3. The inequality that states this fact is the one in A ("y is less than 3.")

86. **C**

Inverse variations give graphs that are curves. As equations, they take the forms $xy = k$ or $y = \frac{k}{x}$. The graph shown is simpler than that, so statement I is false.

The graphs of direct variations are straight lines that pass through the point (0,0) (the origin.) As equations, they take the form $y = mx + 0$, or simply $y = mx$. The line shown is the graph of a direct variation, so statement II is true.

Because point (–5, 5) is equally distant from both the x- and y-axes, the line "cuts" quadrant II at a 45° angle. Lines that form 45° angles with the x- and y-axes (assuming the same scales on both axes) have slopes of 1 or –1. The line here travels from upper left to lower right, meaning that its slope is negative, so statement III is also true.

87. **A**

Choice A contains the transition "This money," a phrase that clearly refers to "amount" in sentence 4. Also, the repetition of "mortgage" indicates the correct flow of ideas. Choice B is too casual in using "folks," and choice D changes voice, with "me," and is also too casual in phrasing. Choice C is contradicted by information in the passage.

88. **B**

Choice B correctly changes "then," a word indicating passage of time in a narrative, to "than," a word indicating contrast. Choice A (sentence 6) correctly uses "set" in meaning that the bank's account has been set up, or arranged deliberately. Choice C incorrectly changes the transition "so," which shows cause-and-effect, to the transition word "but," which shows contrast. Sentence 8 (choice D) correctly uses "rise" to indicate something going up.

89. **A**

The key to simplifying expressions such as these is to combine only like terms. Like terms are those with identical bases. $4x^2$ and $\frac{3}{5x^2}$, for instance, have like bases. So do $9x$ and $\frac{1}{5x}$. Real numbers without attached variables are their own like terms: 4, -21, 0.12, and $\frac{5}{8}$ are all like terms. In the given expression, $\frac{2x^2}{3}$ and $\frac{x^2}{3}$ are like terms; their sum is $\frac{3x^2}{3}$, or $1x^2$, or just x^2; $-12x$ and $7x$ are like terms; they add up to $-5x$; 9 and 1 are also like terms, with a sum of 10.

Those three terms (x^2, $-5x$, and 10) are then separated by addition symbols to give the simplified version of the original expression.

90. **C**

Each *term* of each *binomial must be multiplied by* both *terms in the other binomial. That means that four products are generated:*

$(-2x^2) \times (5x^2)$ gives $-10x^4$ (and right here you see that answer C is correct).

$(-2x^2) \times (3) = -6x^2$

$(-11) \times (5x^2) = -55x^2$

$(-11) \times (3) = -33$

The two middle terms are like terms, and can be combined into $-61x^2$. The three terms (which cannot be further combined) give you the answer of $-10x^4 - 61x^2 - 33$.

91. **A**

One approach to factoring the expression is to start with a set of two empty parentheses written as follows: (__ + __) (__ + __). The task is to then fill in the four blanks with values that "multiply back" to the original expression. Educated trial and error works well here. Here's a good place to start: You know that the two blanks at the end of the parentheses must be 1 and 5, because 5 is a prime number; no other whole numbers multiply by anything to give you 5.

A bit more experimentation shows that only $(4x - 1) \times (-2x + 5)$ "multiplies back" to $-8x^2 + 22x - 5$, so A is the answer. (Be sure to pay attention to whether values are positive or negative.)

92. **B**

Angle xyz is an inscribed angle (*its vertex is on the circle*). Angle xcz is a central angle (*its vertex is at the circle's center*). When two such angles intercept (or "cut off") the same arc of the circle, there exists a specific size relationship between the two angles. The measure of the central angle will always be double the measure of the inscribed angle. In this case, that means that the measure of angle xcz must be 80°.

That means that minor arc xz also has measure 80°. Every circle (considered as an arc) has measure 360°. That means that major arc xyz has measure 280° (360 – 80), so B is correct.

93. **B**

B is correct. While the novel does contain some violent scenes, none of them are graphic enough to be considered unsuitable for young readers, so A is not correct. The relationship between Huckleberry Finn and Jim, the escaping slave, is mostly warm and trusting rather than hostile, so C is incorrect; also, the book was written after the Civil War, eliminating D. It did challenge some attitudes toward race, however, because it portrayed such close fellowship between two people of different races and showed a young white man's willingness to take risks on behalf of a black man's freedom (answer B).

94. **A**

A is correct. Haiku are by definition too short to contain much elaborate description. The haiku form does not emphasize logic or direct statements. And while some haiku are humorous and/or contain lifelike details, these qualities do not characterize all haiku poems.

95. **C**

C is correct. Those lines are spoken by Juliet in Romeo and Juliet, *by William Shakespeare.*

96. **C**

The emphasis in medieval art on theological subjects and themes was accompanied by a de-emphasis of realism.

97. **D**

During the 19th century, there was a revival of interest in Classical and Gothic styles.

98. **D**

Contemporary performance art often takes a multi-media approach, combining many different types of elements.

99. **D**

All of these themes have been emphasized in works of Chinua Achebe and Sembene Ousmane, among other writers of world literature.

100. **A**

A is correct. García Márquez is known for his use of magic realism rather than strict realism. One Hundred Years of Solitude *comments indirectly on various events of Colombian political history, and it has an extensive cast of characters, none of whom dominate the novel as the main protagonist.*

Constructed Response

WRITING SAMPLE WITH A SCORE OF 4
The Literature of the Past

The direction of modern literary scholarship points toward an alarming conclusion. The depreciation of the literary study of bygone periods is a sign of two disturbing trends. First, scholars are avoiding more difficult study in preference to what seems light or facile. Furthermore, the neglect of the literature of former eras is a denial of the contribution that past authors have made toward modern literature. This is not to suggest that all scholars who study modern literature do so because they are either intimidated by past literature or do not appreciate its value. However, the shrinking minority of past literary scholarship is a clear indication that intimidation and awe of past conventions are deterrents to many students of literature.

The dread associated with past literature reflects poorly upon our society. The attempts to simplify literature to accommodate simpler audiences has resulted in a form of literary deflation. The less society taxes its audience's minds, the less comprehensive those unexercised minds become. Information and ideas are now transmitted to the average man through the shallow medium of television programming. Modern students are evolving from this medium, and the gap separating them from the complexity of the classics is continuing to grow.

Once more, it is important to stress that this essay does not seek to diminish students of modern literature. The only demand this argument makes upon modern students is that they supplement their study with significant portions of the classics from which all subsequent literature has been derived, whether consciously or unconsciously. Failure to do so is an act akin to denying the importance of history itself. Like history, literature exists as an evolutionary process; modern literature can only have come into existence through the development of past literature.

Concerning the relative complexity of the classics to modern literature, the gap is not so great as one may think. Surely, one who glances at the works of Shakespeare or Milton without prior exposure will be daunted by them. However, a disciplined mind can overcome the comprehensive barriers erected over the past few centuries through persistence and perseverance.

Unfortunately, the ability to overcome the barriers to past literature may eventually become obsolete. The more frequently students select their courses of study through fear rather than interest, the wider the literary gap will become, until the pampered minds of all future readers will prove unequal to the task of reading the literature of our fathers. The more frequently students deny the usefulness of the literature antedating this century, the more frequently they deny their own literary heritage, the more probable it will become for modern literature's structure to crumble through lack of firm foundation.

FEATURES OF THE WRITING SAMPLE SCORING 4

Appropriateness

The paper's topic and the writer's viewpoint are both well laid out in the first paragraph. The two trends described by the author in the topic paragraph are explored in deeper detail throughout the essay. The language and style fit the writer's audience. The style is formal, but possesses a personalized voice.

Unity and Focus

The essay follows the course presented in the topic paragraph, reemphasizing major points such as the writer's reluctance to condemn all modern scholars. This emphasis is not straight repetition, but carries different viewpoints and evidence for the writer's argument. The digression on television in the second paragraph neatly rounds off the writer's overall concern for cultural consequences of historical literature's depreciation.

Development

The writer follows the suggestions of the writing assignment closely, structuring his essay around the reflections and discussions listed therein. Each paragraph bears an example to lend authority to the writer's argument.

The second paragraph uses the theory of television's vegetative influence. The third paragraph utilizes the evolutionary equality of history. The fourth paragraph evokes names that the reader can relate to in terms of comprehensive difficulty.

Organization

Many transitional conventions are utilized. "Once more . . ."; "Concerning the relative complexity . . ."; "Unfortunately . . ." The examples throughout the paragraphs have a pointed direction. The concluding paragraph completes the argument with a premonition of future calamity should its warning go unheeded.

Sentence Structure

The sentences are standardized and vary in form, although some passive constructions ("will be daunted," "the more probable it will become") might have been avoided. The repetition of "the more frequently" in the final paragraph is particularly effective and pointed.

Usage

Words are chosen to offer variety. "Past literature" is supplemented by "literary study of bygone days" and "the literature of former eras." Phrasing is consistent and standard, although the third sentence of the second paragraph ("The less society taxes . . . the less comprehensive") is slightly awkward, though the repetition does achieve some effect.

Mechanical Conventions

Spelling and punctuation are mostly standard throughout the essay. The sentences in the final paragraph might be divided and shortened, although this may diminish their effect.

WRITING SAMPLE WITH A SCORE OF 3
Modern Literature

It doesn't matter whether or not we read past literature. Past literature has been converted into what we now know as "modern literature". The elements of the past are therefore incorporated into the body of what we now have.

When we read a work of modern literature based upon the classics, such as Joyce's *Ulysses*, it doesn't matter whether or not we've read Homer's *Odyssey*. What matters is what Joyce made out of Homer's epic; not what Homer started out with.

When we see *West Side Story* in the movies, it doesn't matter whether or not we've read *Romeo and Juliet*: the end result is the same; therefore, we do not need to know the original source. I don't think it makes a difference whether or not we even recognize Tony and Maria as Romeo and Juliet. Tony and Maria are today's versions of Romeo and Juliet, and they match the culture that they are told in.

It has been said that all of the good plots have been used up by past ages, and that all we create now are variations of those plots. This statement is false. It is rather the case that these plots are universal variables that each age must interpret in its own unique way. I find it rather faseatious to study the interpretation of other cultures. We should be concerned only with our own.

Past literature is not necessary in a modern world that has reformed the mistakes of the past. Anything that hasn't carried over from the past is negligible: what was good for Shakespeare's audience may not be what we need. In conclusion, I would have to strongly conclude that the "trend of studying modern versus past literature" is commendable, and not contemptible.

FEATURES OF THE WRITING SAMPLE SCORING 3
Appropriateness

The main topic is not supplied directly within the work. Though the reader is aware of the conflict between modern and past literature, there is no sense of scholarly consensus as suggested by the writing assignment. The writer's somewhat informal style is unbalanced throughout the work by his uncertainty with his audience.

Unity and Focus

Though the writer knows the point he is trying to promote, his evidence is presented haphazardly and without a logical design. However, his rather abrupt conclusion is somewhat supported by his points.

Development

The essay does not follow a logical pattern; one premise does not meld fluidly into another. Though the premises loosely support the conclusion, they do not support each other.

Organization

Transitions are slight, if any. The repetition of "when we" opening two paragraphs is noticeable. Each point should have been further developed. The writer assumes his reader is quite familiar with *West Side Story* and its characters.

Sentence Structure

Most sentences follow standard sentence structure, although some are very irregular. The first sentence of paragraph three expresses two or three independent thoughts and should be separated accordingly. The final sentence of the fourth paragraph contains an unclear modifier: "own" should read either "own interpretation" or "own culture."

Usage

Most words are used in their proper context, and an attempt has been made to use some erudite words. "End result" is redundant; "end" should have been excluded. The declaration "this statement is false" in the fourth paragraph is not supported by logical evidence. In this case, the writer should have asserted that this was his own opinion. However, in other cases it is recommended that the writer be bold with assertions. A degree of proof is all that is required to make those assertions. "In conclusion" is redundant with "conclude" in the final sentence of the essay. Contractions such as "we've" and "don't" should be written out in their long forms.

Mechanical Conventions

Most words are spelled properly, although "faseatious" should be spelled "facetious." (The period in the second sentence of the first paragraph should lie within the quotation marks.) The comma after "commendable" in the final paragraph should be eliminated because it does not introduce a new clause.

WRITING SAMPLE WITH A SCORE OF 2 OR 1
Literature

Modern literature is no better than past literature, and vice-versa. It is interest that matters. If people aren't interested in the past, then so be it. A famous man once said "To each his own". I agree.

For example, you can see that books are getting easier and easier to understand. This is a good thing, because more knowledge may be comunicated this way. Comunication is what literature is all about: Some people comunicate with the past, and others with the present.

I communicate with the present. I'm not saying we all should. It's all up to your point of view. When a scholer chooses past over present, or vice-versa, that's his perogative. It doesn't make him better or worse than anybody else. We should all learn to accept each other's point of view.

When I read someone like Fitzgerald or Tolkien, I get a different feeling than Shakespeare. Shakespeare can inspire many people, but I just don't get that certain feeling from his plays. "The Hobbit," "The Great Gatsby," "Catcher in the Rye," and "Of Mice and Men." These are all great classics from this century. We should be proud of them. However, some people prefer "The Trojan War" and "Beowulf." Let them have it. Remember: 'To each his own."

FEATURES OF THE WRITING SAMPLE SCORING 2 OR 1
Appropriateness

The writer misconstrues the topic and writes about the relative worth of modern and past literature. The topic does not call for a judgment of period literatures; it calls for a perspective on the way in which they are studied. Her personal style is too familiarized; it is unclear to whom the essay is addressed.

Unity and Focus

The writer seems to contradict her own points at times, favoring modern literature rather than treating the subject as objectively as he had proposed. It is clear that the writer's train of thought shifted during the essay. This was covered up by ending with the catch phrase, "to each his own."

Development

The writer attempts to angle her argument in different ways by presenting such concepts as "communication" and "point of view." However, her thought processes are abrupt and underdeveloped.

Organization

There is neither direction nor logical flow in the essay. One point follows the next without any transition or connection. All three persons are used to prove his argument: the writer resorts to "I," "you," and "a famous man." There is no clear overall thesis guiding the essay.

Sentence Structure

Some sentences follow standard formation. Sentence three of the final paragraph is a fragment. The sentences are short and choppy, as are the thoughts they convey. Too many sentences are merely brief remarks on the preceding statements (e.g., "I agree," "Let them have it," etc.). These are not appropriate because they do not evoke new thought. The reference to Shakespeare in the first sentence of the final paragraph implies more than the writer intended. It should read: "than when I read Shakespeare."

Usage

Many words are repeated without any attempt to supply synonyms (e.g., "communication," "past"). Colloquial expressions are widespread and should be avoided. The *Trojan War* is evidently an improper reference to Homer's *Iliad*.

Mechanical Conventions

There are many mechanical errors. Punctuation and spelling are inconsistent. "Comunication" and "comunicate" are spelled improperly in paragraph two, while "communicate" is spelled correctly in paragraph three. "Scholer" should be spelled "scholar." "Perogative" should be spelled "prerogative." In the fourth sentence of the first paragraph, the period should lie within the quotation marks, as it does in the final sentence of the essay. The book titles in sentences three and six of the final paragraph should be underlined and not quoted.

OSAT

Oklahoma Subject Area Test
Elementary Education

Subtest 1 Review

Chapter 7

Reading

Language is an intensely complex system that allows us to create and express meaning through socially shared conventions. What is amazing about language is that children generally master their native language within their first four years of life, well before they enter the elementary school, even though their teachers (family members) generally have no special training. Once children enter elementary school, their knowledge of language continues to grow and develop through opportunities to interact with teachers and other children, as they explore the language arts skill areas.

There are four cueing systems through which we organize language, making written language possible. The first cueing system is semantics, or the meaning system of language. Children, early on, are taught that the speech stream needs to convey meaning. Likewise, text needs to be meaningful. If some words in a passage are unknown, the child will know that some words make sense in the context of the passage and other words do not. The second cue is syntax, or the structural system of language. Again, if a child gets stuck while reading, some words are semantically appropriate but can be ruled out because of syntactic constraints. The third cue, according to this view, is phonological, or letter-sound, information. The phonological cue can confirm predictions that are made based on semantics and syntax. The fourth cueing system is the pragmatic system, or the social and cultural restraints placed on the use of language, along with differences in pronunciation.

The Reading Process

SUBAREA I—READING

Competency 0001

Understand the reading process.

The following topics are examples of content that may be covered under this competency.
- Understand reading as a process of constructing meaning through dynamic interaction among the reader, the text, and the context of the reading situation.
- Understand factors that affect reading (e.g., cultural, social, linguistic, developmental, environmental).
- Understand the oral language foundation of reading and the interrelatedness of reading, writing, listening, and speaking.

Literacy can be defined as a child's ability to read and write in order to function adequately in society. A child's literacy skills begin to develop in infancy and continue to expand throughout the school years. An infant's response to a parent's singing, a toddler's ability to choose a book and ask to have it read to her, and a preschooler's interest in attempting to write his name on a birthday card are all examples of literacy development. Research has shown that early, frequent exposure to printed words, both in the real world and through being read to on a regular basis, will likely enhance a child's literacy acquisition.

As the child enters school, formal reading instruction begins. How children should be taught to read is a subject that stirs up intense feeling. Basically, it boils down to a discussion about starting points, and how to proceed with instruction. The two approaches are the skills-based approach, and the meaning-based approach.

In 1967, Jeanne Chall, a Harvard professor, was investigating successful practices in early childhood reading instruction. She wrote a book called *Learning to Read: The Great Debate*. In the book, she stated that the programs that stressed systematic phonics instruction were better at getting young children, and especially poor young children, to read. This pronouncement sparked a great deal of conversation about how small children should be taught, what they should be taught, and where instruction should begin.

Phonological Skills

Competency 0002

Understand phonological skills and strategies related to reading.

The following topics are examples of content that may be covered under this competency.

- Understand how to foster students' phonemic awareness (i.e., ability to perceive and discriminate the sounds of the English language) through rhyming, blending, and segmenting sounds in words.
- Demonstrate knowledge of instruction in letter-sound correspondences and systematic, explicit phonics.
- Understand strategies to promote students' rapid, automatic decoding through the application of phonics skills.

Phonics is a method of teaching beginners to read and pronounce words by teaching them the phonetic value of letters, letter groups, and syllables. Because English has an alphabetical writing system, an understanding of the letter-sound relationship may prove helpful to the beginning reader. However, the suggestion of this view of initial reading instruction is that these relationships should be taught in isolation, in a highly sequenced manner, followed by reading words that represent the regularities of English in print. The children are asked to read decodable texts, by sounding out words. Typically, this approach uses reading programs that offer stories with controlled vocabulary made up of letter-sound relationships and words with which children are already familiar. Thus, children might be asked to read a passage such as, "The bug is in the pan. The bug ran and ran." Writing instruction follows in the same vein; children are asked to write decodable words, and fill in the blanks with decodable words in decodable sentences in workbooks, on the assumption that, once the children progress past this initial reading instruction timeframe, meaning will follow. This type of instruction was widely used in the late 1960s and 1970s. Today, it is still being promoted. The flaw in this kind of instruction is that many English words, including the highest frequency word of all, the, are not phonetically regular. Also, comprehension of text is limited, because there is not a great deal to comprehend if the text is, for example, "The bug is in the pan. The bug ran and ran." The assumption is that textual meaning will become apparent in time. Furthermore, it must be stressed that teaching phonics is not the same as teaching reading. Also, reading and spelling require much more than just phonics; spelling strategies and word-analysis skills are equally important. Nor does asking children to memorize phonics rules ensure application of those rules, and, even if it did, the word the child is attempting to decode is frequently an exception to the stated rule. Another point: teaching children how to use phonics is different from teaching them about phonics. In summary, the skills-based approach begins reading instruction with a study of single letters, letter sounds, blends and digraphs, blends and digraph sounds, and vowels and vowel sounds in isolation in a highly sequenced manner. The children read and write decodable words, with a great emphasis on reading each word accurately, as opposed to reading to comprehend the text as a whole.

The other side of the great reading debate is the meaning-based approach to reading. This approach grew out of the work of Dr. Kenneth Goodman, who was a leader in the development of the psycholinguistic perspective, which suggests that, to derive meaning from text, readers rely more on the structure and meaning of language than on the graphic information from text. He and other researchers demonstrated that literacy development parallels language development. One of Goodman's contributions to the field was a process called miscue analysis, which begins with a child reading a selection orally, and an examiner noting variations of the oral reading from the printed text. Each variation is called a miscue and is analyzed for type of variation. Previously, preservice teachers were urged to read and reread texts with young children until the child could read every word in the text perfectly. Goodman suggested, however, that only miscues that altered meaning needed to be corrected, while other, unimportant miscues could be ignored.

Fast Facts Children are taught to ask themselves, "Does it look right? Does it sound right? Does it make sense?"

Goodman also developed a reading model that became known as the whole-language approach. It stands in sharp contrast to the emphasis on phonics that is promoted in the skills-based approach to reading. The meaning-based approach to reading emphasizes comprehension and meaning in texts. Children focus on the wholeness of words, sentences, paragraphs, and entire books, seeking meaning through context. Whole-language advocates stress the importance of children's reading high-quality children's literature and extending the meaning of the literature through conversation, projects, and writing. Instead of fill-in-the-blank workbooks, children are encouraged to write journals, letters, and lists, and to participate in writing workshops. Word-recognition skills, including phonics, are taught in the context of reading and writing, and are taught as those things relate to the text in hand. Children are taught the four cueing systems, and are taught to ask themselves, "Does it look right? Does it sound right? Does it make sense?" The children are taught that the reason people read books is to make meaning. Thus, the focus of this approach is on both comprehension and making connections. Its flaw is that it makes heavy instructional demands on the teacher. With a skilled teacher, it's a joy to watch. Today, many classrooms are places where young children enjoy learning to read and write in a balanced reading instructional program. Research into best practice strongly suggests that the teaching of reading requires solid skill instruction, including several techniques for decoding unknown words, including, but not limited to, phonics instruction embedded in interesting and engaging reading and writing experiences with whole, authentic literature-based texts to facilitate the construction of meaning. In other words, this approach to instruction combines the best skill instruction and the whole-language approach to teach both skills and meaning and to meet the reading needs of individual children.

Vocabulary Skills

Competency 0003

Understand skills and strategies related to word identification and vocabulary development.

The following topics are examples of content that may be covered under this competency.
- Apply knowledge of word identification strategies (e.g., decoding, recognizing affixes, using context clues).
- Understand ways to help students master common irregular sight words.
- Understand strategies for increasing students' vocabulary knowledge and their ability to apply vocabulary knowledge in new contexts.

Vocabulary building is a skill that needs to be worked on daily in the classroom. One of the goals of this type of instruction is to assist children in becoming skillful in rapid word recognition.

Research suggests that fluent word identification needs to be present before a child can readily comprehend text. If a child needs to painstakingly analyze many of the words in a text, the memory and attention needed for comprehension are absorbed by word analysis, and the pleasure of a good story is lost.

Vocabulary building is a skill that needs to be addressed daily in the classroom.

Fast Facts

Typically, children who are just beginning to read decode each word as they read it. Through repeated exposure to the same words, instant-recognition vocabulary grows. It is particularly important that developing readers learn to recognize those words that occur very frequently in print. A computer analysis of books in print revealed that 100 words make up approximately 50 percent of the words read. This percentage was for all books, not just children's literature. Although game-like activities and writing seem to have some impact on developing word recognition, the single best way to develop this necessary, effortless recognition is to encourage children to read, and to provide class time for reading text that is totally the child's choice. Reading and rereading rather easy text seems to be particularly effective.

In addition to working on placing some words into readily available memory, there is sound research suggesting that students can use context clues to help identify unknown words. This body of research further suggests that instruction can help improve students' use of such clues. Frequently, three kinds of context clues are discussed. First, semantic clues require a child to think about the meanings of words, and what is already known about the topic being read. For example, when reading a story about bats, good teachers help children to activate prior knowledge about bats, and to develop an expectation that the selection may contain words associated with bats, such as *swoop*, *wings*, *mammal*, and *nocturnal*. This discussion might help a child gain a sense of what might be reasonable in a sentence. The word order in a sentence might also provide clues. For example, in the sentence, "Bats can _____," the order of the words in the sentence indicates that the missing word must be a verb. Furthermore, the illustrations in the book can often help with the identification of a word. Still, context clues are often not specific enough to predict the exact word. However, when context clues are combined with other clues such as phonics and word-part clues, accurate word identification is usually possible.

Another strategy is to pay attention to letter groups, as there are many groups of letters that frequently occur within words. These clusters of letters can be specifically taught. Common prefixes, suffixes, and inflectional endings should be pointed out to students. Being able to rapidly and accurately associate sounds with a cluster of letters leads to more rapid, efficient word identification.

As young readers build an increasing store of words that they can recognize with little effort, they use the words they know to help them recognize words that are unfamiliar. For example, a child who has seen the word *bat* many times and who knows the sound associated with the consonant *r* will probably have little difficulty recognizing the word *rat*.

The best practice for helping students to gain skill in word-recognition is real reading and writing activities. As children read and reread texts of their own choice, they have many opportunities to successfully decode a word, and realize that each time the letter combination b-a-t is in the selection, it's read as *bat*. With each exposure to that word, the child reads the word more easily. A child who writes a sentence with that word as part of the sentence is developing a greater sensitivity to meaning or context clues. The child attempting to spell that word is reviewing and applying what he knows about letter–sound associations.

Reading Comprehension

Competency 0004

Understand skills and strategies involved in reading comprehension.

The following topics are examples of content that may be covered under this competency.
- Understand factors affecting reading comprehension (e.g., reading rate and fluency, prior knowledge, vocabulary knowledge).
- Demonstrate knowledge of literal, inferential, and evaluative comprehension skills.
- Identify strategies to facilitate comprehension before, during, and after reading (e.g., predicting, selfmonitoring, questioning, rereading).

Helping students read for understanding is the central goal of reading instruction. Comprehension is a complex process involving the text, the reader, the situation, and the purpose for reading. There are a number of factors that come into play as a child attempts to comprehend a passage. First, students cannot understand texts if they cannot read the words. Thus, a teacher who is interested in improving students' comprehension skills needs to teach them to decode well. In addition, children need time during the school day to read texts that are easy for them to read, and have to have time to discuss what has been read. Children need to read and reread easy texts often enough that decoding becomes rapid, easy, and accurate.

It has been noted frequently in the literature that children who comprehend well have bigger vocabularies than children who struggle with reading. In part, this is true because their knowledge of vocabulary develops through contact with new words as they read text that is rich in new words. However, it has also been suggested that simply teaching vocabulary in isolation does not automatically enhance comprehension.

Reading comprehension can be affected by prior knowledge, with many demonstrations that readers who possess rich prior knowledge about the topic of a reading often understand the reading better than classmates with less prior knowledge. Prior knowledge also affects interest. Generally, students like to read about somewhat familiar topics. This is an area in which the skill and interest of the teacher can play a significant role. An able teacher can make a previously unfamiliar topic seem familiar through pre-reading activities during which prior knowledge is activated, new prior knowledge is formed, and interest is stirred up. A good teacher will set a clear purpose for reading, and ask the students to gain an overview of the text before reading, make predictions about the upcoming text, and then read selectively based on their predictions. Best practice suggests that children should be encouraged to generate questions about ideas in text while reading. Successful teachers encourage children to construct mental images representing ideas in text, or to construct actual images from text that lends itself to such an activity. A successful teacher will help readers to process text containing new factual information through reading strategies, helping children to relate that new information to their prior knowledge. A potent mechanism for doing this is elaborative interrogation, wherein the teacher poses "why?" questions, encouraging children to question the author and check the answers through text verification. It is through conversation that children are able to compare their predictions and expectations about text content to what was read. It is through these conversations that children see the need to revise their prior knowledge when compelling new ideas that conflict with prior knowledge are encountered. As part of these ongoing conversations, teachers will become alert to students who are applying errant world knowledge as they read and will be able to encourage use of appropriate knowledge. These conversations lead children to figure out the meanings of unfamiliar vocabulary based on context clues, the opinions of others, and sometimes through the use of appropriate source materials such as glossaries, dictionaries, or an appropriate selection in another text. After reading activities, able teachers encourage children to revisit the text—to reread and make notes and paraphrase—to remember important points, interpret the text, evaluate its quality, and review important points. Children should also be encouraged to think about how ideas encountered in the text might be used in the future. As children gain competence, they enjoy showing what they know.

As a follow-up to the reading of a fictional selection, children should be encouraged to analyze the story using the story-grammar components of setting, characters, problems encountered by characters, attempts at solution to the problem, successful solution, and ending. It has been noted in the literature that even primary-level students, when asked to use comprehension strategies and monitoring, have benefited greatly from it.

As children's comprehension grows more sophisticated, they move from merely attempting to comprehend what is in the text to reading more critically. This means that they grow in understanding that any single text provides but one portrayal of the facts. With skillful instruction, children come to read not only what a text says; they also learn to attend to how that text portrays the subject matter. They recognize the various ways in which every text is the unique creation of a unique author, and they also learn to compare and contrast the treatment of the same subject matter in a number of texts. Teachers help students grow in comprehension through lessons. At first, teachers are happy if children are able to demonstrate their comprehension of what a text says by being able to engage in some after-reading activity that involves restating what was contained in the text in some authentic way. The next level is to have the children ponder what a text does: to describe an author's purpose, to recognize the elements of the text and how the text was assembled. Finally, some children can attain the skill set needed to successfully engage in text interpretation, to be able to detect and articulate tone and persuasive elements, to discuss point of view, and to recognize bias. Over time, and with good instruction, children learn to infer unstated meanings based on social conventions, shared knowledge, shared experience, or shared values. They make sense of text by recognizing implications and drawing conclusions, and they move past the point of believing the content of a selection simply because it was in print.

Fast Facts Comprehension is maximized only when readers are fluent in all the processes of skilled reading.

Another piece of the comprehension puzzle is that children need to be taught to monitor their own comprehension, and to decide when they need to exert more effort, or to apply a strategy to make sense of a text. The goal of comprehension instruction is for the children to reach a level at which the application of strategies becomes automatic.

In summary, comprehension is maximized only when readers are fluent in all the processes of skilled reading, from the decoding of words to the articulation and easy, appropriate application of the comprehension strategies used by good readers. Teachers need to teach predicting, questioning, seeking clarification, relating to background knowledge, constructing mental images, and summarizing. The teaching of comprehension strategies has to be conceived as a long-term developmental process, and the teaching of all reading strategies is more successful if they are taught and used by all of the teachers on a staff. In addition, teachers need to allow time for in-school reading, and recognize that good texts are comprehended on a deep level only through rereading and meaty discussions.

Study Skills and Strategies

Competency 0005

Understand reading instruction and study skills in the content areas.

The following topics are examples of content that may be covered under this competency.
- Apply knowledge of reading strategies to promote learning in the content areas (e.g., activating and developing prior knowledge).
- Understand strategies for reading for different purposes.
- Apply knowledge of study skills in the content areas (e.g., note-taking skills, interpretation of graphs, use of reference materials).

Students need to know how to study the information that has been presented to them in texts and other media. Graphic organizers help students to review such material, and help them see the relationships between one bit of information and another. A Venn diagram helps students see how things are alike and different. It can be used to help students see how a single topic is treated in two readings, or how two books, animals, or ecosystems are alike and different. The student labels the two overlapping circles, and lists items that are unique to each one in each respective circle. In the area in the center where there is an overlap, the student records the elements that the two items have in common.

A schematic table strips a story down to the bare bones, and helps students to see the story grammar at work:

Problem	
Who	
What	
Where	
When	
Why	
How	

↓

Attempted solution	result
Attempted solution	result

↓

End result	

Another skill students need to master is note taking. Unless you want to read passages copied directly out of an encyclopedia or other source material, take the time to actively teach note-taking techniques, and think up an authentic task that requires higher-level manipulation of the located information for the students to accomplish. First, help the children to formulate a researchable question. Next, have them highlight the words that might be used as keywords in searching for information. Then have them brainstorm in groups for other words to be used as keywords. Then ask then to list appropriate sources. Then, as they skim articles, they can fill in the chart with little chunks of information. For example:

Bats of North America						
Name	Location	Biome	Endangered?	Diet	Roost	Fact
California leaf-nosed bat	CA, AZ	desert	yes	insects	old mines, caves	
Gray bats	TN,KY, FL	forest	yes	insects	Caves near water	
Big brown bats	All states except Hawaii	varied	no	Beetles insects	Buildings, tunnels, caves, trees	Was seen flying in a snowstorm
Little brown bats	All 50 states	varied	no			Can eat 500 mosquitoes per hour

The next step here is to think up a task in which the student has to think about all the information and use it in some meaningful way.

Students also need to look closely at the structure of text in order to comprehend it. When starting a new unit of study, skillful teachers take the students on a picture, table, and graphic walk-through of the text that will be the object of study, asking questions and pointing out useful text features to the students. Most texts have titles, subtitles, headings, and key words. Where were these placed? What techniques were used to make them stand out? Figuring out the structure of a text helps readers to read more efficiently. Children can anticipate what information will be revealed in a selection when they understand textual structure. Understanding the pattern of the text helps students organize ideas. Authors have a fairly short list of organizational patterns to choose from. The following are the most common patterns:

- Chronological order—relates events in a temporal sequence from beginning to end

- Cause-and-effect relationships between described events, with the causal factors identified or implied

- Problem description, followed by solutions

- Comparisons and/or contrasts to describe ideas to readers

- Sequential materials, presented as a series of directions to be followed in a prescribed order

Genre

Competency 0006

Understand characteristic features of children's literature and strategies to promote students' literary response and analysis.

The following topics are examples of content that may be covered under this competency.
- Demonstrate knowledge of major works, authors, and genres of children's literature.
- Understand strategies to develop students' responses to literature (e.g., guided reading, reading logs, discussions about literature).
- Analyze the use of children's literature to promote respect for and appreciation of diversity.
- Understand elements of literary analysis and criticism (e.g., analyzing story elements, recognizing features of different genres, interpreting figurative language).

A genre is a particular type of literature. Classifications of genre are largely arbitrary—based on conventions that apply a basic category to an author's writing. They give the reader a general expectation of what sort of book is being picked up. Teachers today are expected to share a wide range of texts with children. Charlotte Huck, Susan Hepler, Janet Hickman, and Barbara Kiefer, in their book, *Children's Literature in the Elementary School*, define children's literature as "a book a child is reading." They go on to list picture books, traditional literature, modern fantasy, realistic fiction, historical fiction, nonfiction, biography, and poetry as genres of children's literature. Most genres can be subdivided into a variety of categories, and it is possible that genres could be mixed in a single title.

Picture books are books in which the illustrations and the text work together to communicate the story. There is a huge market for picture books, and they cover many topics. It is a very good idea to share picture books with children in a number of different formats.

Sometimes, able teachers simply read the book to the child without showing any of the pictures. The story is then discussed, and the children are asked if they would like the book to be reread, this time with the pictures being shared. Typically, this technique sparks a lively conversation about why the book with its illustrations is better than hearing the words alone.

Alternatively, teachers may take the children on a picture-walk through the book, allowing them to speculate about the story before reading it to them. Then, once the book is read, the speculations can be confirmed or reassessed.

Using picture books allows teachers to discuss the elements of higher-level comprehension without the burden of reading lengthy prose, for a picture book can be discussed with an eye on many different factors: design, color, space, media choice, cultural conventions, point of view, showing vs. telling, fairness, realism, or concerns. It is a way to raise issues in a classroom community, and it's a subtle way to affirm classroom members. Nearly any lesson worth teaching is better taught with a picture book in hand. Picture books can be very useful tools in a variety of ways: nearly any concept can be both deepened and expanded by reading the appropriate picture books.

Traditional literature comprises the stories that have their roots in the oral tradition of storytelling. This genre also includes the modern versions of these old stories. It is interesting to read and share multiple versions of old stories, and to compare and contrast each version. It is also interesting to read a number of folktales and keep track of the elements that these old stories have in common. It's also interesting to encourage children to notice where these old stories show up in their day-to-day lives. Children enjoy sharing what they notice. These old stories are woven into ads, comic books, jokes, and other selections.

Modern fantasy is a genre that presents make-believe stories that are the product of the author's imagination. The point of origin for all of these stories is the imagination of the author. Often, they are so beyond the realm of everyday life that they can't possibly be true. Extraordinary events take place within the covers of these books. Fantasy allows a child to move beyond the normal, ho-hum life in the classroom, and speculate about a life that never was, and may never be. But, maybe, just maybe, wouldn't it be grand if an owl were to swoop through an open window and drop a fat letter? What if you dumped some cereal into a bowl, and a lump dropped into the bowl with a thud, and it turned out to be a dragon's egg? What if you could step through a wardrobe and be someplace completely different? Fantasy is a genre that typically sparks rather intense discussions, and provides ample opportunities to illuminate the author's craft for the child.

Historical fiction is set in the past. This type of fiction allows children to live vicariously in times and places they do not normally experience any other way. This type of fiction often has real people and real events depicted, with fiction laced around them. Historical fiction informs the study of social studies. The textbook might say, "and then the tea was dumped in the harbor." *Johnny Tremain* vividly brings the event into focus. These books often bring the emotions of the situation into sharp relief. When reading *Pink and Say*, by Patricia Polacco, children are stunned when one of the boys is summarily hanged as he enters Andersonville. *Number the Stars*, by Lois Lowry, begins a conversation about what we would be willing to give up to save a friend.

Nonfiction books have the real world as their point of origin. These books help to expand the knowledge of children when they are studying a topic; however, these books need to be evaluated for accuracy, authenticity, and inclusion of the salient facts. It is a very good idea to include the children in this process, and, when an inaccuracy is detected, it's a good idea to encourage the child or children who spotted the flaw to write to the publisher and relate their findings. Typically, the publisher writes back, thus turning a published flaw into an authentic, empowering writing experience for a child. Again, these books can be the platform for teaching higher-level comprehension skills. Children and their teachers can discuss fact vs. theory. For example, the reintroduction of wolves into Yellowstone is a topic that exists in the real world, and reading materials on the subject are readily available. The *fact* is that wolves are carnivorous predators. The *theory* part of the investigation could be a discussion of the impact that reintroducing wolves into the Yellowstone ecosystem might have. This discussion will need to be supported with documentation. The materials read will need to be evaluated in terms of the intended audience, bias, inclusion of enough information, and text structure. These books can also be powerful in creating a community of learners, as they can be used as a means of gathering information about a topic that children are working on together as part of a cooperative learning group. Since nonfiction books are written at a variety of reading levels, all children can find a book to read, and since different titles have different information, the children end up swapping and talking about the books. It makes for some touching and powerful moments in a classroom.

Biography is a genre that deals with the lives of real people. Autobiography is a genre that deals with the life of the author. These books enliven the study of social studies because, through careful research, they often include information that transforms a name in a textbook into a person that one may like to get to know better. Did you know that George Washington had false teeth carved from the finest hippopotamus ivory? Did you know that Dolley Madison was stripping wallpaper—very expensive hand-painted silk wallpaper, no less—off the walls in the residence in the White House as British warships were moving up the Potomac River? Again, these books can provide a platform for dynamic lessons about higher-level comprehension skills, especially about bias. Consider the treatment of Helen Keller. Was any information included about how feisty and forward-thinking she was?

Poetry is a genre that is difficult to define for children, except as "not-prose." Poetry is the use of words to capture something: a sight, a feeling, or perhaps a sound. Poetry needs to be chosen carefully for a child, as poetry ought to elicit a response from the child—one that connects with the experience of the poem. All children need poetry in their lives. Poetry needs to be celebrated and enjoyed as part of the classroom experience, and a literacy-rich classroom will always include a collection of poetry to read, reread, savor, and enjoy. Some children enjoy the discipline of writing in a poetic format. Reggie Routman has published a series of slim books about teaching children to write poems on their own.

In summary, today there is an overwhelming variety of children's literature to choose from. When selecting books for use in a classroom, a teacher has a number of issues to consider. Is the book accurate? Aesthetically pleasing? Engaging? Bear in mind the idea that all children deserve to see positive images of children like themselves in the books they read, as illustrations can have a powerful influence on their perceptions of the world. Children also have a need to see positive images of children who are not like themselves, as who is or is not depicted in books can have a powerful influence on their perception of the world as well. Teachers ought to provide children with literature that depicts an affirming, multicultural view, and the selection of books available should show many different kinds of protagonists. Both boys and girls, for example, should be depicted as able.

Language Arts

The Writing Process

SUBAREA II—LANGUAGE ARTS

Competency 0007

Understand skills and strategies involved in writing for various purposes.

The following topics are examples of content that may be covered under this competency.
*   Analyze factors a writer should consider when writing for a variety of audiences and purposes (e.g., expressive, informative, persuasive), including factors related to selection of topic and mode of written expression.
*   Understand steps and procedures associated with given components of the writing process (e.g., prewriting, gathering and synthesizing information, writing a first draft, revising, proofreading).
*   Understand developmental stages of a writer, including the use of pictures and developmental spelling.
*   Compare characteristic features and requirements associated with written materials in various formats (e.g., letter, essay) and modes (e.g., narrative, descriptive, evaluative).

Since the early 1970s, Dr. Donald Graves, a professor of education at the University of New Hampshire, has been working in classrooms trying to understand why writing seems to be so difficult to master for so many children. Through conversation with many working teachers, children, their parents, university students, and working writers, and via many keen-eyed observations in classrooms, he developed an approach to writing instruction called *process writing*.

His notion was simple: let's teach children to write the way real writers write. What do writers do? Well, to begin with, they tend to write about what they want to write about. Then they may read about the subject, talk about the subject, take notes, or generally fool around with the topic before they compose. Then they may write a draft, knowing up-front that they are not done at this point. They may share the draft with others, and end up writing all over it. They may also go over every sentence, thinking about word choice, and looking for vague spots, or spots where the piece falls off the subject. They may revise the draft again, share it again, revise it again, and so on, until they are satisfied with the product. Then they publish it. Often, they receive feedback before and after the piece is published, which may lead to a new writing effort. Some writers save scraps of writing in a journal. They may save a turn of phrase, a comment overheard on a bus, a new word, good quotes, or an interesting topic.

Doesn't this sound like a process a child might find helpful? Today, it seems a bit obvious. In the 1970s, 1980s, and even into the 1990s it seemed revolutionary. However, it was well received because teachers were pleased with the way students benefited from this kind of instruction. At the same time, in many schools computers were becoming readily available to students, and many teachers were finding that writing instruction and computers were a very happy marriage. Also, there were several excellent books available about helping children to write well. Donald Graves wrote *Writing: Teachers and Children at Work* and *A Fresh Look at Writing*. Lucy Calkins wrote *The Art of Teaching Writing*, and Nancy Atwell contributed *In the Middle: Writing, Reading, and Learning with Adolescents*. All of these and others offered support for this new way to augment children's efforts toward learning to write.

Nancy Atwell was particularly skilled in describing how a literacy-rich environment ought to be established and fostered. Children need to be encouraged to read books for enjoyment, but to also look at the craft of the author. Children need to respond to reading in writing. A great deal of research supported the notion that reading informs the writing process, and that the act of writing informs the reading process.

Donald Graves advised children to think about events in their lives as a good starting point for discovering topics. He liked to talk about Patricia Polacco books. Almost all of her books are reports of real-life events, things that happened to her and her rotten red-haired brother. For example, *Meteor!* was the story of one summer's night when a meteor fell into the yard. It could be told like this: "It was hot. We were outside. A meteor fell, and almost hit us. It didn't." The difference between that account and the published story provides a starting point for a potentially rich discussion about the craft of the writer.

Lucy Calkins, in *The Art of Teaching Writing*, addresses the importance of expecting good writing from children, and then giving them ample time to write, and the needed instruction and encouragement to make it happen. She suggests that children keep a writing notebook where they can keep little scraps of writing that might find their way into a written piece some day. This suggestion also helps with classroom management during a writer's workshop. It gives children something to do instead of wandering around the room or announcing, "I'm done!" and ceasing to write.

Another part of the writing process is to share the writing with a classmate, and allow that peer to edit the piece. Able teachers provide guidance for this process, so that the students do not simply declare the work "good" or leave the classmate in tears because the draft is ruthlessly criticized. Neither end of the spectrum results in the growth of a student's writing ability.

Following an edit for content, the piece is edited for features such as punctuation, capitalization, and spelling. The use of computers has made the entire writing process much easier. Children learn to use a thesaurus, dictionary, and the functions of spelling and grammar. Revisions can be made more easily. One of the best results, however, is that the finished piece *looks* finished. Gone are the days when a child did his or her personal best, only to get the paper back with "messy" scrawled in red across it.

Another aspect of the process is celebration. Children are invited to share their work with the class. After a young author reads their piece, classmates ought to offer affirmations and suggestions. Able teachers ought to have children save each piece of paper generated in the writing process, and store them in a personal portfolio for review.

Analyzing and Revising Texts

Competency 0008

Analyze written work in relation to its stated purpose; evaluate areas in need of improvement; and revise written texts for style, clarity, and organization.

The following topics are examples of content that may be covered under this competency.
- Evaluate revision strategies for improving the effectiveness of written material in relation to a given purpose (e.g., expressive, informative, persuasive).
- Analyze given texts in terms of unity and organization, and make appropriate revisions (e.g., adding topic sentences, reordering sentences or paragraphs, using transitional words and phrases, deleting distracting details).
- Improve the clarity, precision, and effectiveness of given texts through changes in word choice.

Competency 0009

Apply knowledge of English grammar and mechanics in revising texts.

The following topics are examples of content that may be covered under this competency.
- Evaluate given texts in terms of sentence construction, and make appropriate revisions (e.g., revising run-on sentences, misplaced or dangling modifiers, lack of parallel structure).

- Revise texts for subject-verb agreement and pronoun-antecedent agreement.
- Use standard verb forms, pronouns, adverbs, adjectives, and plural and possessive forms of nouns in context.
- Make appropriate revisions involving punctuation and capitalization in a given text.

The test questions for this subarea of the OSAT are very much like the Communications Skills questions on the OGET. To prepare for these questions on the OSAT, you should look at and thoroughly review Chapter 2, pages 33–78, and Chapter 6, pages 125–136, and you should study the information below concerning expository and persuasive essays.

The Expository Essay

An expository essay can encompass a variety of subjects. It may tell how to make or do something, or it may explore an idea. Expository writing conveys information to the reader in such a way as to bring about understanding; its subject may be a process or procedure, or perhaps the writer's ideas about a concept. Here are some samples of topics that you may be asked to write about in an expository essay:

- The ideal vacation

- The qualities of a good friend

- How to plan a lesson or create a syllabus (*Note*: Expository essays could be about "how to" do just about anything, but on the OSAT, you will not be asked how to do something unless you could reasonably be expected to know how to do it—for example, you would not be asked how to bake a cake.)

- Similarities and differences between the younger generation and your own (essays like this are called "comparison-and-contrast essays")

- Characteristics of types of people you have met in school (essays like this are called "classifying essays")

- The reasons that you have decided to become a teacher (essays like this are called "cause-and-effect essays")

The structure of your expository essay will depend somewhat on the topic you are given, but the usual five-paragraph structure is a good starting point.

- Your first paragraph should begin with an attention grabber. For example, the essay about the ideal vacation might start with a sentence or two about something wonderful (or terrible) that you have done on a previous vacation, and the essay about the good friend could start with a very short anecdote about something a friend has done for you. The how-to-plan-a-lesson essay could begin with a humorous story of an unplanned lesson.

- Your first paragraph should end with a thesis statement. Creativity will be rewarded in the opening of the essay, and possibly in the conclusion, but in the thesis statement on a standardized-test essay, it is best to state your thesis as clearly as you can. Because you will be using the five-paragraph structure, try to make your thesis include three major points (for your three body paragraphs). For example, the essay on an ideal friend could include a paragraph on three different friends you've had and the traits of each, or it could focus on three different traits.

  - *This essay will discuss openness and honesty as I have experienced them in my friendships with Amanda, Tom, and Bill.*

  - *The crucial traits of an ideal friend are openness, honesty, and wit, and I shall discuss their value as I have experienced them—or their lack—in my real friendships.*

- Note, from the examples just given, that your thesis will determine the structure of your three body paragraphs. In an expository essay, your body paragraphs are not necessarily carrying an argument, as they are in a persuasive essay. You may arrange the paragraphs in any way that is convenient; just make sure that you include logical transitions between and within the paragraphs. For example, the second thesis statement above would be in an essay that had a paragraph each about openness, honesty, and wit, but you could skip back and forth between friendships in order to illustrate each of the qualities.

- The first part of the conclusion (fifth paragraph) should briefly recap the thesis and body paragraphs. The second part should include a statement that reinforces your position in a meaningful and memorable way. Creativity here will earn you some credit in the grading, but this is probably the least important part of the essay. If you can't think of something clever, don't waste much time trying to do so; the extra time is better spent revising your first four paragraphs.

The Persuasive Essay

The persuasive essay is meant to move its reader to take an action or to form or change an opinion. There are three main reasons it is included on the OSAT:

- It requires thinking skills such as analysis, synthesis, and evaluation.

- It requires writers to take a stand from among two or more alternatives.

- Persuasive writing is a skill that you will have to both teach and use in your professional life.

Because all the persuasive prompts you will receive on a test (and most persuasive writing situations you will encounter in life) ask you to choose a stand from two or more reasonable alternatives, you will have to demonstrate that you understand why the other alternatives are reasonable. More important, though, you will have to make clear that you believe your stand on the issue is better, and you need to present your supporting evidence in such a way that it might convince a reasonable person who believed an alternative stand was preferable.

Persuasive prompts on the OSAT will likely ask you to write for a general audience of educated adults, but it might also ask you to write to an audience of parents or to your principal or school board. Here are some samples of topics that you may be asked to write about in a persuasive essay:

- The effects of television on students' grades—good, bad, negligible?

- Is affirmative action appropriate in hiring and promoting teachers?

- Should national elections take place on a weekend day rather than a Tuesday?

- Should states require students to pass standardized tests in order to begin high school?

- Should high-school athletes be subjected to involuntary drug testing?

- Should students and teachers (i.e., not janitors) be responsible for keeping their school clean?

Note that you may not have a particular opinion about some of these matters. Indeed, you may not know much about the topic; the prompt will, however, typically give you enough information to help you write a good five-paragraph essay.

The structure of your persuasive essay will depend somewhat on the topic you are given, but the usual five-paragraph structure is a good starting point.

- Your first paragraph should begin with an attention grabber. One good strategy is to imagine a world in which the point of view you are against has prevailed. For example, if you take a position for affirmative action in hiring and promoting teachers, you might ask your reader to imagine a school system in which many students would go through high school without ever seeing a principal who looks like them. If you take the other side, you might ask the reader to compare two school systems, one of which had teachers who had scored an average of 20 points higher on their certification tests.

- Your first paragraph should end with a thesis statement. Creativity will be rewarded in the opening of the essay, and possibly in the conclusion, but in the thesis statement on a standardized-test essay, it is best to state your thesis as clearly as you can, especially in the persuasive essay. Because you will be using the five-paragraph structure, try to make your thesis include three major points (for your three body paragraphs). In addition, you want your thesis to state your position very clearly. If you include your summary of the other side's arguments in your thesis statement, you should always do so in a subordinate clause. For example, the thesis of the essay on involuntary drug testing might look like this:

  - *Although involuntary drug testing would be a violation of civil rights if participation in athletics were involuntary, such testing would restore integrity to athletic contests, increase student attendance, and help to protect athletes' health.*

  - *Even though participation in athletics is "voluntary," students should not be given an either-or choice between nonparticipation on the one hand and the loss of privacy and the restriction of their civil rights on the other.*

- Note, from the examples just given, that your thesis will determine the structure of your three body paragraphs. In a persuasive essay, your body paragraphs will carry your argument; you will succeed not on the basis of your eloquence in the introductory and concluding paragraphs, but on how well you organize and state facts that support your argument. It is often best to use your most convincing reason in the final body paragraph. For example, the first thesis statement above would introduce an essay that had a paragraph about doubt that currently exists about whether high-school athletes' skill is based on ability or drugs. The next paragraph would be about the good things that would happen if that doubt were resolved. The final paragraph would then switch to your most important point: that performance-enhancing drugs are bad for athletes' health. As an exercise, can you think of a structure for the three body paragraphs of the essay with the second example above as a thesis statement?

- The first part of the conclusion (fifth paragraph) should briefly recap the thesis and body paragraphs (i.e., your argument). The second part should include a statement that reinforces your position in a meaningful and memorable way. Creativity here will earn you some credit in the grading, but this is probably the least important part of the essay. If you can't think of something clever, don't waste much time trying to do so; the extra time is better spent revising your first four paragraphs.

The Listening Process

Competency 0010

Understand skills and strategies involved in listening for various purposes.

The following topics are examples of content that may be covered under this competency.
- Compare listening strategies in terms of their appropriateness for given contexts and purposes (e.g., acquiring information, appreciating literature read aloud, interpreting and evaluating information).
- Analyze barriers to effective listening and strategies for active listening.
- Apply knowledge of factors affecting the ability to listen effectively and construct meaning from oral messages in various listening situations (e.g., ability to recognize nonverbal cues, to use prior knowledge, to distinguish fact from opinion, to recognize transitions, to identify faulty reasoning).

Language is an intensely complex system for creating meaning through socially shared conventions. Very young children begin to learn language by listening and responding to the people in their lives. This early listening provides a foundation for acquisition of language. Babies are active listeners. Long before they can respond in speech per se, they encourage the person talking to them to continue by waving their arms, smiling, or wriggling, for example. On the other hand, they are also capable of clear communication when they have had enough by dropping eye contact or turning away, among other examples of body language.

Although listening is used extensively in communication, it does not receive much attention at school. Studies suggest that teachers assume that listening develops naturally. One study from 1986 suggests that teachers are not apt to get much training on teaching listening; the survey of 15 textbooks used in teacher education programs revealed that out of a total of 3,704 pages of text, only 82 pages mentioned listening.

While there is no well-defined model of listening to guide instruction, there are some suggestions. Some theorists link listening skills to reading skills. They feel that reading and listening make use of similar language comprehension processes. Listening and reading both require the use of skills in phonology, syntax, semantics, and knowledge of text structure, and seem to be controlled by the same set of cognitive processes.

However, there is an additional factor in play in listening: the recipient of the oral message can elect to listen passively, or listen actively, with active listening being the desired goal. A number of studies suggest that the teaching of listening can be efficiently taught by engaging in the kinds of activities that have been successful in developing reading, writing, and speaking proficiencies and skills such as setting a purpose for listening, giving directions, asking questions about the selection heard, and encouraging children to forge links between the new information that was just heard and the knowledge already in place. In addition, children need to be coached in the use of appropriate volume and speed when they speak, and in learning how to participate in discussions and follow the rules of polite conversation, such as staying on a topic and taking turns.

The Speaking Process

Competency 0011

Understand skills and strategies involved in speaking for various purposes.

The following topics are examples of content that may be covered under this competency.
- Analyze ways in which features of oral language (e.g., choice of language, rate, pitch, tone, volume) and nonverbal cues (e.g., body language, visual aids) affect communication in given situations.
- Evaluate various methods of organizing and presenting thoughts, feelings, ideas, and information for different audiences and purposes (e.g., giving instructions, participating in group discussions, persuading an audience, entertaining).
- Recognize factors affecting oral communication and nonverbal cues in different situations. Apply knowledge of language conventions appropriate to a variety of social situations (e.g., informal conversations, job interviews).

When preparing a speech, children should know the same thing that teachers know about their audience: it is better to have an audience that is actively listening than one that is listening passively. Children should be coached to do the following in order to make them more effective public speakers:

- Speak in a loud voice, but do not shout.

- Speak slowly and pronounce words clearly.

- Pay attention to time—and know your audience's attention span.

- Maintain good eye contact with your audience.

- Use gestures to engage your audience.

- Do not read your speech directly off note cards.

- If you use note cards, keep them down, away from your face.

- Decide which points should be emphasized by changing the tone of your voice (called *intonation*).

- Be prepared to answer any questions that your audience might have.

The use of visual aids is also important. Most schools now have PowerPoint or similar programs for their students to use, and students should probably be giving at least one such presentation a year beginning in the fourth or fifth grade. There is still a place for hand-made visual aids in school, however—certainly for younger children and even for older ones, who should have to manufacture two or three a year (perhaps in groups) so that they do not limit their ingenuity to the prepackaged visuals of a computer program.

In addition, students should learn that the preparation of a speech is very much like writing, with its prewriting, writing, and revising stages preceding the presentation. (The prewriting stage includes audience analysis, which is perhaps even more important in speaking than in writing.) It is a good idea to assess each of these stages through conferences, especially for children who are giving their first speech or are especially nervous about public speaking.

Social Studies

The Social Studies section of the OSAT Subtest 1 includes six test objectives. These objectives represent a broad range of integrated social sciences concepts from the content areas of history, geography, political science, and economics. Embedded within each broad objective are a number of essential social sciences concepts. A thorough understanding of each objective requires deep knowledge of the embedded concepts coupled with the ability to analyze and apply those concepts in a comparative analysis of Oklahoma, U.S., and world contemporary and historic society. For each objective an explanation of the embedded concepts is provided.

When preparing for the social studies portion of the elementary test, you should review the embedded concepts enumerated within each objective. Once you think you have a thorough understanding of each concept you should determine whether or not you can apply your understanding within the context of Oklahoma, U.S., and world contemporary and historic contexts.

SUBAREA III—SOCIAL STUDIES

Competency 0012

Understand major ideas, eras, themes, developments, and turning points in the history of Oklahoma, the United States, and the world; and analyze their significance from multiple perspectives.

The following topics are examples of content that may be covered under this competency.
*   Analyze the societal effects of major developments in world history (e.g., the agricultural revolution, the scientific revolution, the industrial revolution, the information revolution).
*   Understand the principal political, social, economic, and geographic characteristics of ancient civilizations and the connections and interactions among these civilizations.
*   Understand the history of interactions among American Indian peoples and European Americans in Oklahoma and the western United States.
*   Analyze the roles and contributions of individuals and groups to U.S. social, political, economic, cultural, and religious life, including historically underrepresented groups.

Competency 0013

Understand geographic concepts and phenomena, and analyze the interrelationships of geography, society, and culture in the development of Oklahoma, the United States, and the world.

The following topics are examples of content that may be covered under this competency.
*   Demonstrate an understanding of how the five themes of geography—location, place, relationships within places, movement, and regions—can be used to analyze geographic phenomena and human cultures.
*   Recognize the physical characteristics of the earth's surface, and analyze the continual reshaping of the surface by physical processes.
*   Analyze the development and interaction of social, political, cultural, and religious systems in different regions of Oklahoma, the United States, and the world.
*   Analyze the impact of human activity on the physical environment (e.g., industrial development, population growth, deforestation).

Competency 0014

Understand concepts and phenomena related to human development and interactions (including anthropological, psychological, and sociological concepts).

The following topics are examples of content that may be covered under this competency.
*   Evaluate factors that contribute to the development of personal identity (e.g., family, group affiliations, socialization processes).
*   Analyze the roles and functions of social groups and institutions in the United States (e.g., ethnic groups, schools, religions) and their influence on individual and group interactions.

- Analyze why individuals and groups hold different or competing points of view on issues, events, and historical developments.
- Understand the processes of social and cultural change.

Competency 0015

Understand economic and political principles, concepts, and systems; and relate this knowledge to historical and contemporary developments in Oklahoma, the United States, and the world.

The following topics are examples of content that may be covered under this competency.
- Analyze the basic structure, fundamental ideas, accomplishments, and problems of the U.S. economic system.
- Analyze values, principles, concepts, and key features of American constitutional democracy (e.g., individual freedom, separation of powers, due process).
- Compare different perspectives regarding economic and political issues and policies in Oklahoma and the United States (e.g., in relation to taxing and spending decisions).
- Analyze relationships between the United States and other nations (e.g., in the development of democratic principles and human rights).

Competency 0016

Understand the roles, rights, and responsibilities of citizenship in the United States and the skills, knowledge, and attitudes necessary for successful participation in civic life.

The following topics are examples of content that may be covered under this competency.
- Analyze the personal and political rights guaranteed in the Declaration of Independence, the U.S. Constitution, the constitution of the state of Oklahoma, and major civil rights legislation.
- Demonstrate an understanding of the U.S. election process and the roles of political parties, pressure groups, and special interests in the U.S. political system.
- Analyze the ways in which citizens participate in and influence the political process in the United States (e.g., the role of public opinion and citizen action in shaping public policy).
- Analyze the factors that affect attitudes toward civic life and that have expanded or limited the role of the individual in U.S. political life during the twentieth century (e.g., female suffrage, discriminatory laws, the growth of presidential primaries, the role of the media in political elections).

Competency 0017

> **Understand and apply skills related to social studies, including gathering, organizing, mapping, evaluating, interpreting, and displaying information.**
>
> The following topics are examples of content that may be covered under this competency.
> - Evaluate the appropriateness of various resources for meeting specified information needs (e.g., atlas, database, surveys, polls, the Internet).
> - Interpret information presented in one or more graphic representations (e.g., graph, table, map), and translate written or graphic information from one form to the other.
> - Summarize the purpose or point of view of a historical text.

History

Developing historical perspective includes knowledge of events, ideas, and people from the past. That knowledge encompasses an understanding of the diversity of race, ethnicity, social and economic status, gender, region, politics, and religion within history. Historic understanding includes the use of historical reasoning, resulting in a thorough exploration of cause-effect relationships to reach defensible historical interpretations through inquiry.

Significant knowledge of events, ideas, and people from the past results from careful analysis of cause and effect relationships in the following chronological eras: beginnings of civilization to 1620; colonization and settlement (1585–1763); revolution and the new nation (1754–1815); expansion and reform (1801–1861); Civil War and Reconstruction (1850–1877); the development of the industrial United States (1870–1900); the emergence of modern America (1890–1930); the Great Depression and World War II (1929–1945); postwar United States (1945–1970); and contemporary United States (1968–present).

Significant knowledge of historical events, ideas, and people from Oklahoma's past would result from careful analysis of cause and effect relationships in the chronological eras listed above for the United States. Included in this knowledge is an understanding of the evolution of political ideas, institutions, and practices in Oklahoma and the influence of technology, agriculture, urbanization, industry, and labor on the development of the Oklahoma economy. For example, pressure brought by European-American settlers on eastern land held by Native nations led to their forced migration to what is now Oklahoma, the most notable example being the Trail of Tears of 1838–1839. It is also necessary to understand the importance of family and local history.

This objective also involves the ability to analyze and interpret the past. Analysis and interpretation result from an understanding that history is logically constructed based upon conclusions resulting from careful analysis of documents, eyewitness accounts, letters, diaries, artifacts, photos, historical sites, and other primary and secondary sources.

Geography

Understanding major geographic concepts involves comprehending both physical features of geography and the cultural aspects of geography. This would include knowledge of the five fundamental themes of geography, comprehension of the relationships within and between places, understanding interdependence within the local, natural, and global communities, and familiarity with global issues and events.

The five themes of geography are: place; human-environmental interaction; location; movement and connections; and regions, patterns, and processes. An understanding of these themes would include the ability to use them to analyze regions within Oklahoma, the United States, and the world to gain a perspective about interrelationships among those regions. The use of the five themes should also result in the ability to compare regions.

An understanding of the theme of location requires knowledge of both absolute and relative location. Absolute location is determined by longitude and latitude. Relative location deals with the interactions that occur between and among places. Relative location involves the interconnectedness among people because of land, water, and technology. For example, knowledge of the history of Oklahoma City includes an understanding of how its location near several important oil fields has contributed to its economic development and vitality.

An understanding of the theme of human-environmental interaction involves consideration of how people rely on the environment, how we alter it, and how the environment may limit what people are able to do. For example, knowledge of how the Oklahoma Territory came to be settled by European-Americans in 1889 includes an understanding of the role of cattle ranching in Oklahoma's history.

An understanding of the theme of location, movement, and connections involves identifying how people are connected through different forms of transportation and communication networks and how those networks have changed over time. This would include identifying channels of the movement of people, goods, and information. For example, the Chisholm Trail used in the Texas cattle drives led to the development of railway and road transportation routes.

An understanding of the theme of regions, patterns, and processes includes identifying climatic, economic, political, and cultural patterns within regions. Understanding why these patterns were created includes understanding how climatic systems, communication networks, international trade, political systems, and population changes contributed to a region's development. An understanding of regions enables a social scientist to study their uniqueness and relationship to other regions.

Understanding global issues and events includes comprehending the interconnectedness of peoples throughout the world. For example, knowledge of the relationship between world oil consumption and oil production would result in an understanding of the impact that increased demand for oil in China would have on the price of a barrel of oil, which in turn could affect the decisions of consumers of new vehicles in the United States.

Economic and Political Principles

An understanding of economics involves exploring the implications of scarcity (the concept that wants are unlimited while resources are limited). Exploration of scarcity involves an understanding of economic principles spanning from personal finance to international trade. Economic understanding is rooted in exploring principles of choice, opportunity costs, incentives, trade, and economic systems. (For a definition of each of the economic principles see the Handy Dandy Guide [HDG] developed by the National Council on Economic Education in 1989. For brief definitions based upon this guide see the Web site *http://ecedweb.unomaha.edu/lessons/handydandy.htm*). This exploration includes analysis of how those principles operate within the economic choices of individuals, households, businesses, and governments.

In addition, economic understanding includes knowledge of the role that price, competition, profit, inflation, economic institutions, money, and interest rates play within a market system. A complete understanding of markets includes knowledge of the role of government within an economic system, including how monetary and fiscal policy impacts the market. (These economic concepts are based upon the *National Content Standards in Economics* published by the National Council on Economic Education. A brief overview and complete list of standards can be found at *http://ncee.net/ea/standards/*).

An understanding of various political systems involves the ability to compare different political systems, their ideologies, structures, institutions, processes, and political cultures. This requires knowledge of alternative ways of organizing constitutional governments from systems of shared power to parliamentarian systems. Systems of shared power include federal systems, where sovereign states delegate powers to a central government; a federal system, where a national government shares power with state and local governments; and Unitarian systems where all power is concentrated in a centralized government.

Understanding local and state governments results from knowledge of the role of federal and state constitutions in defining the power and scope of state and local government. That knowledge should include comprehension of reserved and concurrent powers. Furthermore, an understanding of state and local government results from knowledge of the organization and responsibilities of such governments.

Understanding of the role of law in a democratic society results from a knowledge of the nature of civil, criminal, and constitutional law and how the organization of the judicial system serves to interpret and apply such laws. Essential judicial principles to know include comprehension of rights, such as the right of due process, the right to a fair and speedy trial, and the right to a hearing before a jury of one's peers. Additional judicial principles include an understanding of the protections granted in the Constitution, which include protection from self-incrimination and unlawful searches and seizures.

Understanding global interdependence begins with recognition that world regions include economic, political, historical, ecological, linguistic, and cultural regions. This understanding should include knowledge of military and economic alliances such as NATO, the G8 members, or cartels such as OPEC, and how their existence affects political and economic policies within regions. Knowledge of world regions and alliances leads to identification of issues that affect people in these areas. Common issues that affect people around the world include food production, human rights, resource use, prejudice, poverty, and trade.

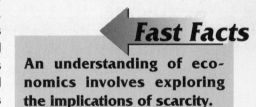

Fast Facts

An understanding of economics involves exploring the implications of scarcity.

A true sense of global interdependence results from an understanding of the relationship between local decisions and global issues. For example, how do individual or community actions regarding waste disposal or recycling affect worldwide resource availability? Or how do fuel emissions standards affect air pollution or how fuel standards affect oil supply and gas prices?

Government and the Responsibilities of Citizens

The social sciences portion of the Elementary Education test requires comprehension of the ideals of American democracy, including a core set of values expressed in America's essential founding documents, the Declaration of Independence, the Articles of Confederation, the U.S Constitution, and the Bill of Rights. Those values include life, liberty, pursuit of happiness, common good, justice, equality, truth, diversity, popular sovereignty, and patriotism.

Furthermore, the ideals of American democracy include the following essential Constitutional principles: the rule of law, separation of powers, representative government, checks and balances, individual rights, freedom of religion, federalism, limited government, and civilian control of the military. Essential democratic principles include those principles fundamental to the American judicial system: the right to due process of law, the right to a fair and speedy trial, protection from unlawful search and seizure, and the right to decline to self-incriminate.

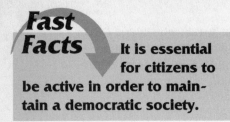

Fast Facts It is essential for citizens to be active in order to maintain a democratic society.

Comprehension of the rights and responsibilities of citizens of the United States involves understanding that it is essential for citizens to be active in order to maintain a democratic society. This activity includes participation in voting, providing service to communities, and regulating oneself in accordance with the law.

Diversity

Understanding the role of cultural diversity in shaping Oklahoma, the United States, and the world begins with knowledge of the commonalities and differences among such groups as African-Americans, Asian-Americans, Hispanic-Americans, and Native Americans. Commonalities and differences can be found when analyzing the role of language, education, religion, culture, and struggles for equality within and among groups. Understanding the role of cultural diversity in shaping Oklahoma, the United States, and the world should include an understanding of the struggles various groups undertake to gain equality and recognition within society.

A historical perspective of the role of cultural diversity in shaping the development of Oklahoma and the United States begins by gaining a sense of the types of people who came to Colonial America and their reasons for coming. This understanding can help one gain an appreciation for the diverse peoples that eventually won their independence from Great Britain. Following those people from the east during the various migrations westward can explain how various groups of people settled what today is the American West. Studies of Old Immigration (1830–1850) and New Immigration (1900–1920) further complete the picture of the settling of America that encouraged diverse peoples to come here. Within this historical understanding one should be able to identify examples of how immigrants sought to assimilate themselves into American culture, contributions of immigrant groups to American culture, and ways that immigrants have been exploited.

Diverse cultural groups have shaped world history. Diversity has both positive and negative results—from contributing to disputes over territories, creating alliances that eventually lead to world and regional conflicts, outsourcing of jobs, and relocation of companies from the United States to foreign countries, to more positive examples such as the economic specialization that enhances choice and the modern globalization that results in economic interdependence. The impact of cultural diversity on world history can be explored by careful analysis of the following events, among others: the origin and spread of Christianity and Islam; colonialism and exploration; the beginning of World War I; and contemporary conflict in the Middle East.

Locating, Organizing, and Interpreting Social Sciences Information

The ability to understand and apply skills and procedures related to the study of social sciences involves knowledge of the use of systematic inquiry. Inquiry is essential for use in examining single social sciences topics or integrated social sciences. Being able to engage in inquiry involves the ability to acquire information from a variety of resources, and organize that information, which leads to the interpretation of that information. Inquiry involves the ability to design and conduct investigations, which in turn leads to the identification and analysis of social sciences issues.

In addition, this understanding includes knowledge about and the use of the various resources used in systematic social science inquiry. Those resources include primary and secondary sources, encyclopedias, almanacs, atlases, government documents, artifacts, and oral histories.

Constructed Response

Chapter 10

In the final part of OSAT Subtest 1 you will be asked to write a constructed response. Unlike the constructed response in the OGET, knowledge of standard English is *not* a critical part of your score. Instead, the constructed-response item is written to assess your understanding in Subarea I, Reading, which consists of the following competencies:

- Understand the reading process.

- Understand phonological skills and strategies related to reading.

- Understand skills and strategies related to word identification and vocabulary development.

- Understand skills and strategies involved in reading comprehension.

- Understand reading instruction and study skills in the content areas.

- Understand characteristic features of children's literature and strategies to promote students' literary response and analysis.

The Assignment

You will typically be given a problem situation from an educational setting and asked what you would do to solve the problem. The four criteria by which you will be graded are

- Purpose—the extent to which your response fulfills the purpose of the assignment

- Subject matter knowledge—the accuracy and appropriateness with which you apply your knowledge of the subject

- Support—the quality and relevance of your supporting details

- Rationale—the soundness of your arguments and the degree of understanding you demonstrate

Of these four criteria, the most important is "support": you cannot get high scores in either "subject matter knowledge" or "rationale" unless you use the information you are given to marshal examples that will support whatever your argument is.

Here is a sample assignment. Read it through carefully.

Hiru is a fifth grader. His teacher has analyzed his performance on a fifth-grade-level passage that he has read aloud to her. She did this by keeping a running record of his miscues while reading. His accuracy rate was 88%, which is usually considered to be just below a student's instructional level (90%). He read the passage with expression (usually correctly inflected) and enthusiasm. Hiru was able to talk about the passage, but not always accurately, and he was able to make some simple predictions about what might happen next.

He did not self-correct on any of the words he misread. Here is a list of the words he substituted for:

Text	Student
shall	will
tired	tie-red
lie	lay
scratch	scrap
stretched	streaked
radiator	radio
returned	retired

In addition, the teacher had to tell him the word "admonition," and he omitted a "now" and an "and."

Using your knowledge of how to teach word identification and fluency, write a response in which you

- Analyze Hiru's pattern(s) of miscues and his overall reading fluency

- Cite specific examples to back up your analysis

- Describe at least two different types of activities that might improve Hiru's reading fluency

- Explain why these types of activities might work

Preparing to Write

Writing Process for the Constructed Response
• Prewriting
o Jot notes, make diagrams
o Outline
o Reread questions
o Adjust outline to questions if necessary
• Writing
• Revising
o Did you answer the questions?
o Do you have support for all the assertions you make?
o Is your writing clear?
o Is your writing free of grammatical/spelling mistakes?

For this constructed response, it is not necessary to frame your answer with a strong, creative opening and closing; the best strategy here is simply to begin your **prewriting** stage by jotting down notes.

Because the questions in this type of constructed response will typically be rather specific, you should begin by writing down anything that will help you answer each question—in order, if possible. For instance, the first thing you will want to do with this assignment is to organize the facts you need in order to *analyze* the pattern of misreadings. You can use the table that is already provided for you; you might add columns that are headed by "Similar Meaning," "Graphophonically Similar," and "Syntactically Acceptable" and put checkmarks in the table cells that apply. You would have checkmarks under Similar Meaning for the first and third words, and checkmarks under Graphophonically Similar for all but the first word. You would also have checkmarks under Syntactically Acceptable for four of the seven words. (That is, the substitution is the same part of speech as the actual word in the text.) At this point, you're well on the way to answering the first two questions.

Now you want to turn your prewriting attention to what types of activities will help this fifth grader improve his reading and why. His problem seems to be word recognition rather than syntactic comprehension. In addition, he seems to have mastered phonics, at least at the beginnings of words. Thus, he could be given lessons or mini-lessons, either by the teacher or by a peer, on basic word-identification strategies: phonic analysis (beyond the initial sounds), analogies (i.e., making associations with known words), syllabic analysis, and morphemic analysis (i.e., study of roots). Hiru needs to learn to recognize words that an average fifth grader knows so that he can read at grade level or above, so you should choose two strategies/activities that you are most familiar with in order to do that.

Now you are ready to outline. Outlining should not take much time, because the assignment makes a rough outline for you. You do have some choices, though, for example, you could combine the first two questions so that you can present one element of your analysis, along with your reasoning, followed by another element and your reasoning, and so on, rather than simply making an analysis and then going back to your reasons. With this assignment, it is probably better to present your reasons along with each analytic statement. You could use the same kind of organization with questions three and four: for instance, a paragraph on teaching syllabic analysis and a paragraph on giving Hiru extra morphemic analysis work. Thus, your outline might look something like this:

I. Analysis and reasoning

A. Good overall comprehension—answers questions and reads with enthusiasm, and most errors are nevertheless syntactically correct

B. Will be at frustration level with fifth-grade texts—too many words he doesn't know

C. Needs to improve word recognition—although he has a rough understanding of phonics, his ability to recognize words is below grade level

II. Strategies

A. Lessons on syllabic analysis—miscues show Hiru needs to look beyond initial sounds

B. Lessons on morphemic analysis—returned–retired pair and scratch–scrap pair have different roots

Conclusion: Hiru needs to learn to recognize words that an average fifth grader knows in order to make use of his ability at comprehension so that he can read at grade level or above, so you should choose two strategies/activities that you are most familiar with in order to do that.

This outline will give you a good start. Now is the time for **writing**: get the ideas down as clearly and as coherently as you can. In your **revising** stage, you should look at what you've written, making sure that you have indeed answered the questions clearly, that you have good examples for everything you wrote, and (even though standard English is not one of the grading criteria), your writing is free of spelling and grammatical errors.

Scoring the Constructed Response

All responses to OSAT constructed-response assignments are scored using scales that describe varying levels of performance. These scales were approved by committees of Oklahoma educators.

Each response is scored by multiple scorers according to standardized procedures during scoring sessions held immediately after each administration of the test. Scorers with relevant professional backgrounds are oriented to these procedures before the scoring session and are carefully monitored during the scoring sessions.

A constructed-response assignment response is designated unscorable if it is blank, not on the assigned topic, illegible or unintelligible, not in the appropriate language, or of insufficient length to score. *If you do not provide a scorable response for each constructed-response assignment on your test, you cannot pass the test regardless of your scores on the other sections of the test.*

Sample Performance Characteristics for Constructed-Response Assignments	
PURPOSE	The extent to which the response achieves the purpose of the assignment
SUBJECT MATTER KNOWLEDGE	Accuracy and appropriateness in the application of subject matter knowledge
SUPPORT	Quality and relevance of supporting details
RATIONALE	Soundness of argument and degree of understanding of the subject matter

Scoring Scale for Constructed-Response Assignments
"4"—The response reflects a thorough knowledge and understanding of the subject matter.
• The purpose of the assignment is fully achieved.
• There is a substantial, accurate, and appropriate application of subject matter knowledge.
• The supporting evidence is sound; there are high-quality, relevant examples.
• The response reflects an ably reasoned, comprehensive understanding of the topic.
"3"—The response reflects a general knowledge and understanding of the subject matter.
• The purpose of the assignment is largely achieved.
• There is a generally accurate and appropriate application of subject matter knowledge.
• The supporting evidence generally supports the discussion; there are some relevant examples.
• The response reflects a general understanding of the topic.
"2"—The response reflects a partial knowledge and understanding of the subject matter.
• The purpose of the assignment is partially achieved.
• There is a limited, possibly inaccurate or inappropriate application of subject matter knowledge.
• The supporting evidence is limited; there are few relevant examples.
• The response reflects a limited, poorly reasoned understanding of the topic.
"1"—The response reflects little or no knowledge and understanding of the subject matter.
• The purpose of the assignment is not achieved.
• There is little or no appropriate or accurate application of subject matter knowledge.
• The supporting evidence, if present, is weak; there are few or no relevant examples.
• The response reflects little or no reasoning about or understanding of the topic.
"U"—The response is unscorable because it is illegible, not written to the assigned topic, written in a language other than English, or of insufficient length to score.
"B"—There is no response to the assignment.

OSAT

**Oklahoma Subject Area Test
Elementary Education**

Practice Subtest 1

SUBTEST DIRECTIONS

A sample of the general directions for the OSAT is shown in the box below. You may want to familiarize yourself with the directions, as similar versions will be used for the actual examination.

You should have in front of you:

(1) a test booklet for the test for which you registered (check the field name on the front cover);

(2) an answer document (be sure you have signed your answer document and filled in the required information on pages 1 and 3); and

(3) a No. 2 lead pencil.

IF YOU DO NOT HAVE ALL OF THESE MATERIALS, PLEASE INFORM THE TEST ADMINISTRATOR. REMOVE ALL OTHER MATERIALS FROM YOUR DESK.

GENERAL DIRECTIONS

This test booklet contains two sections: a selected-response section and a writing assignment. You may complete the sections in the order you choose, but it is suggested that you complete the selected-response section of the test first. The directions for each section appear immediately before that section.

Each selected-response question in this booklet has four answer choices. Read each question carefully and choose the ONE best answer. Record your answer on the answer sheet in the space that corresponds to the question number. Completely fill in the space having the same letter as the answer you have chosen. *Use only a No. 2 lead pencil.*

Sample Question:

1. Which of these cities is farthest north?

    A. Oklahoma City

    B. Muskogee

    C. Tulsa

    D. Lawton

The correct answer to this question is C. You would indicate that on the answer sheet as follows:

1. Ⓐ Ⓑ ● Ⓓ

For the writing assignment, you will be asked to prepare a written response to a writing assignment. Record your written response on pages 3 to 6 of the answer document. You may use **ONLY** one answer document. You may either print or write, as long as your handwriting is legible. You must use a pencil. Make sure that you have time to plan, write, review, and revise what you have written.

You should answer all questions. Even if you are unsure of an answer, it is better to guess than not to answer a question at all. You may use the margins of the test booklet for scratch paper, but all of your answers, including your response to the writing assignment, must be recorded in your answer document. Answers that are written in the test booklet will **NOT** be scored.

The words "End of Section" indicate you have completed a section. After you have completed one section, you may go on to the other section. You may go back and review your answers and your written response to the writing assignment, but be sure you have answered all selected-response questions, completed the writing assignment, and rechecked all the information in your answer document, particularly your identification information on pages 1 and 3, before you raise your hand for dismissal. Your test materials must be returned to a test administrator when you finish the test.

FOR TEST SECURITY REASONS, YOU MAY NOT TAKE NOTES OR REMOVE ANY OF THE TEST MATERIALS FROM THE ROOM.

This session will last four hours. You may work at your own pace on the different sections of the test. If you have any questions, please ask them now before you begin the test.

STOP

DO NOT GO ON UNTIL YOU ARE TOLD TO DO SO.

Answer Sheet

1. Ⓐ Ⓑ Ⓒ Ⓓ
2. Ⓐ Ⓑ Ⓒ Ⓓ
3. Ⓐ Ⓑ Ⓒ Ⓓ
4. Ⓐ Ⓑ Ⓒ Ⓓ
5. Ⓐ Ⓑ Ⓒ Ⓓ
6. Ⓐ Ⓑ Ⓒ Ⓓ
7. Ⓐ Ⓑ Ⓒ Ⓓ
8. Ⓐ Ⓑ Ⓒ Ⓓ
9. Ⓐ Ⓑ Ⓒ Ⓓ
10. Ⓐ Ⓑ Ⓒ Ⓓ

11. Ⓐ Ⓑ Ⓒ Ⓓ
12. Ⓐ Ⓑ Ⓒ Ⓓ
13. Ⓐ Ⓑ Ⓒ Ⓓ
14. Ⓐ Ⓑ Ⓒ Ⓓ
15. Ⓐ Ⓑ Ⓒ Ⓓ
16. Ⓐ Ⓑ Ⓒ Ⓓ
17. Ⓐ Ⓑ Ⓒ Ⓓ
18. Ⓐ Ⓑ Ⓒ Ⓓ
19. Ⓐ Ⓑ Ⓒ Ⓓ
20. Ⓐ Ⓑ Ⓒ Ⓓ

21. Ⓐ Ⓑ Ⓒ Ⓓ
22. Ⓐ Ⓑ Ⓒ Ⓓ
23. Ⓐ Ⓑ Ⓒ Ⓓ
24. Ⓐ Ⓑ Ⓒ Ⓓ
25. Ⓐ Ⓑ Ⓒ Ⓓ
26. Ⓐ Ⓑ Ⓒ Ⓓ
27. Ⓐ Ⓑ Ⓒ Ⓓ
28. Ⓐ Ⓑ Ⓒ Ⓓ
29. Ⓐ Ⓑ Ⓒ Ⓓ
30. Ⓐ Ⓑ Ⓒ Ⓓ

31. Ⓐ Ⓑ Ⓒ Ⓓ
32. Ⓐ Ⓑ Ⓒ Ⓓ
33. Ⓐ Ⓑ Ⓒ Ⓓ
34. Ⓐ Ⓑ Ⓒ Ⓓ
35. Ⓐ Ⓑ Ⓒ Ⓓ
36. Ⓐ Ⓑ Ⓒ Ⓓ
37. Ⓐ Ⓑ Ⓒ Ⓓ
38. Ⓐ Ⓑ Ⓒ Ⓓ
39. Ⓐ Ⓑ Ⓒ Ⓓ
40. Ⓐ Ⓑ Ⓒ Ⓓ

Practice Subtest 1

DIRECTIONS: Choose the word that best fills the blank.

1. When reading, the semantic cueing system refers to _____.

    A.   the meaning system of language

    B.   the structural system of language

    C.   the letter-sound relationships in written language

    D.   the social and cultural aspects of language

2. When reading, the syntactical cueing system refers to _____.

    A.   the meaning system of language

    B.   the structural system of language

    C.   the letter-sound relationships in written language

    D.   the social and cultural aspects of language

3. When reading, the phonological cueing system refers to_____.

    A.   the meaning system of language

    B.   the structural system of language

    C.   the letter-sound relationships in written language

    D.   the social and cultural aspects of language

4. When reading, the pragmatic cueing system refers to _____.

    A.   the meaning system of language

    B.   the structural system of language

    C.   the letter-sound relationships in written language

    D.   the social and cultural aspects of language

5. Listening is a process students use to extract meaning out of oral speech. Activities teachers can engage in to assist students in becoming more effective listeners include:

      I. clearly setting a purpose for listening.
      II. allowing children to relax by chewing gum during listening.
      III. asking questions about the selection.
      IV. encouraging students to forge links between the new information and knowledge already in place.

    A. I and II

    B. II, III, and IV

    C. I, III, and IV

    D. All of the above

6. Which of the following describes best practice in writing instruction?

    A. Instruct students in writing, and give them time to write.

    B. Have students complete worksheets about writing.

    C. Have students copy famous speeches.

    D. Have the children create a mural of a story so far, and label all of the characters.

7. Which of the following descriptions best describes the western, Pacific region of Canada comprising British Columbia and the Yukon?

    A. The area contains many uninhabitable areas, including a mix of arid desert-like terrain and rugged mountain ranges that hinder rail and car transportation, resulting in minimal population settlement.

    B. The area contains arid deserts and vast grasslands that are ideal for cattle farming and oil production.

    C. The area contains the vast majority of Canada's natural resources and the majority of Canada's population.

    D. The area contains fifty percent of Canada's population, resulting in seventy percent of Canada's manufacturing.

DIRECTIONS: Read the following passage and answer the question that follows.

The Police believed that Dollree Mapp was hiding a person suspected in a crime. The police went to her home in Cleveland, Ohio, knocked, and requested entry. Mapp refused. After more officers arrived on the scene, police forced their way into Mapp's house. During the police search of the house they found pornographic books, pictures, and photographs. They arrested Mapp and charged her with violating an Ohio law against possession of pornographic materials. Mapp and her attorney appealed the case to the Supreme Court of Ohio. The Ohio Supreme Court ruled in favor of the police. Mapp's case was then appealed to the Supreme Court of the United States. Mapp and her attorney asked the Supreme Court to determine whether or not evidence obtained through a search that violated the Fourth Amendment was admissible in state courts. The U.S. Supreme Court, in the case *Mapp v. Ohio*, ruled that evidence obtained in a search that violates the Fourth Amendment is not admissible. The majority opinion states, "Our decision, founded on reason and truth, gives to the individual no more than that which the Constitution guarantees him, to the police officer no less than that to which honest law enforcement is entitled, and, to the courts, that judicial integrity so necessary in the true administration of justice."

8.   The excerpt above best illustrates which of the following features of judicial proceedings in the United States?

   A.   due process of law

   B.   a fair and speedy trial

   C.   judicial review

   D.   the exclusionary rule

DIRECTIONS: Read the story, and then respond to the five questions that follow.

BESSIE

I began my days as a cow. Well, a calf, to be more precise. I was born to the world a soft tawny color, with liquid brown eyes and soft, floppy ears that begged to be touched. My days were simple. I spent all my time in the company of other bovine females, most especially my mother. She was a prized breeder, my mother; as a result it was my misfortune to be weaned earlier than most other calves.

Only hours after my weaning, a miraculous event changed the course of my life. Princess Georgette happened to be riding by on her shaggy little pony, alongside her nanny, when she heard my lows of despair and turned.

"Whatever could be making that pitiful noise?" she asked aloud.

One of the farmers called out to her, "'Tis only a wee calf, Highness. She'll not be at it long, I assure you."

"I shall see the creature at once," she ordered, pulling her pony up against the rail and dismounting.

At this point, I had moved hopefully toward the commotion, and, as I inched my tender nose out of the barn to investigate, I came face-to-face with the oddest-looking creature I had seen so far in my somewhat short existence. She had outrageous red curls rioting all over her head, and tumbling down over her shoulders. The thing I noticed most, though, was her hopelessly freckled nose, which, at that moment, was uncomfortably close to my own. So close, in fact, that I decided to remedy my discomfort, and did so by lowing rather loudly in her petulant little face. To my astonishment, she giggled with delight at my rudeness, and reached out to stroke my furry forehead. I found myself nuzzling up to her small chest. "Oh Nan, I must have it. Such a funny furry thing must be kept in my garden where I might entertain myself endlessly with it."

So that is how I became a member of the royal household.

My days fell into an odd sort of routine. I spent my mornings cropping on the lawns and shrubs until Georgette would appear, luring me into the hedge ways with a handful of cresses nipped from the kitchen. As soon as I got close enough and started to nibble, she would shriek, and startle me into a canter, at which she would chase me into the hedges until I was so thoroughly lost, I would have to low helplessly until Georgette found me.

Tragically, calves do not stay calves forever. As the seasons passed, her interest in our games began to wane. The gardeners had, at this time, gotten very tired of working around me as I lumbered through the hedges. They communicated up through the chain of command, straight to the king himself, their wish to be rid of me. He dismissed the problem with an order to have me put down.

Georgette pouted at this and stamped her foot, but her father would not budge an inch. "Now, don't get missish with me, Georgette. I've given the order, and I'll see it done as I've dictated whether you like it or not."

Georgette, during this speech, had become thoughtful. After a long pause, she proposed: "Well, if I must see my Bessie put down as you've said, mightn't I get a handbag and boots out of her at least?"

"Very well," sighed her father.

For my part, it was a stroke of luck that this conversation had taken place just on the other side of the hedge where I had been, only moments before, contently munching on the last bit of clover to be found this season. Naturally, I took exception to being discussed in such a candid manner. In fact, I could not believe my furry, floppy ears. I felt myself slipping into a sort of self-pity, and walked away. When I passed the westernmost gate, it occurred to me that I might not have to face my doom. This door, that was normally latched and guarded, stood open. I was out that gate and on the lane nearby in an instant.

I wandered aimlessly for hours, when I abruptly came upon a little clearing. A stream ran through it, past the coziest of tiny cottages. I trotted straight over to the stream and began drinking in long draughts. After several moments of such behavior, I became aware of another presence nearby. It was a small, old man, leaning toward me in a strange sort of furry robe, and balancing himself on the most incredibly gnarled staff, and holding a silver bucket that steamed and hissed, yet smelled overwhelmingly delicious.

"Hello," he said in a pleasant tone. "I'm happy you have finally arrived. I read it in *The Book.* Would you care to drink from my bucket?" he asked. . . .

9. This is the beginning of a story. To what genre does it belong?

   A. poetry

   B. historical fiction

   C. nonfiction

   D. fantasy

10. What is likely to happen next?

   A. Bessie will go to a barn.

   B. Bessie will catch frogs.

   C. Bessie will run away.

   D. Bessie will drink the potion and turn into a brown-eyed girl.

11. How did you know what might happen next?

   A. The nanny never wanted the princess to have a pet cow.

   B. Magical things often happen in stories that begin with a princess.

   C. I read about dysfunctional families often.

   D. The princess will have a new handbag and boots.

12. How should this sort of story be introduced to children?

   A. Complete a K-W-L to activate prior knowledge about fairy tales.

   B. Ask the children to look up vocabulary words in a dictionary.

   C. Read the children a nonfiction book about dairy farming.

   D. Show a video about talking to strangers.

13. If you were going to ask the children to finish this story as a writing activity, what would you do next?

   A. Have them complete a worksheet about the vocabulary words.

   B. Ask them to diagram the first sentence.

   C. Ask them to form small groups, and talk about what might happen next.

   D. Have them complete a Venn diagram about Bessie and a real cow.

Read the passage below, written in the style of a newspaper editorial; then answer the four questions that follow.

[1]The zoning regulations of Westown have long been a thorn in the side of local real estate developers. [2]The authors of those regulations apparently believed that their regulations would be appropriate in perpetuity, because they _____ to amend. [3]The result is a growing area of blight bounded on the north by Bradley Avenue and on the east by Randolph Street.

[4]This coming Wednesday the Westown's city council has a chance to bring its zoning practices into the twenty-first century. [5]The decisive votes will come from Council members Putman, Beckett, and Reis. [6]The votes of Putman and Beckett in particular will be of interest to their constituents, because the residents of their wards would stand to gain a great deal from rezoning. [7]The proposed changes would bring the Fourth Ward some much-needed commerce in the currently run-down Randolph-MacKenzie area and would help _____ the Fifth Ward's steady population loss. [8]Although each of these self-styled "progressives" have displayed reluctance to vote for anything that would spur development in the recent past, both have strong opposition in the upcoming election and would do well to consider how their votes on this issue will impact the results of that election.

14. Which of the following changes is needed in the passage above?

    A. Sentence 1: Change "have" to "has"

    B. Sentence 4: Change "Westown's" to "Westown"

    C. Sentence 8: Change the comma after "past" to a semicolon

    D. Sentence 8: Change "how" to "that"

15. Which of the following words would be the best to insert into the blank in sentence 7?

    A. alleviate

    B. accelerate

    C. excoriate

    D. exonerate

16. Which of the numbered sentences should be revised to correct an error in verb form?

    A. sentence 3

    B. sentence 5

    C. sentence 6

    D. sentence 8

17. Which of the following phrases, inserted into the blank in sentence 2, would make sense and would be free of errors?

    A   made the regulations very easy

    B. ensured that the provisions would be difficult

    C. made them almost impossible

    D. said the zoning ordinances will be hard

18. Which of the following statements are true about economic activity in Oklahoma?

    I.   State government, the military, and the manufacturing industry are among Oklahoma's major employers.
    II. Oklahoma's livestock industry is less profitable than its cotton and wheat crops.
    III. The petroleum, natural gas, and livestock industries in Oklahoma have contributed directly to the state's manufacturing industry.
    IV. Tulsa and Oklahoma City are minor regional players in the natural gas and petroleum industry.

    A. I and II only

    B. I and III only

    C. II and III only

    D. II and IV only

19. Which of the following statements best defines the role of the World Trade Organization (WTO)?

    A. It resolves trade disputes and attempts to formulate policy to open world markets to free trade through monetary policy and regulation of corruption.

    B. It is an advocate for human rights and democracy by regulating child labor and providing economic aid to poor countries.

    C. It establishes alliances to regulate disputes and polices ethnic intimidation.

    D. It regulates trade within the United States in order to eliminate monopolistic trade practices.

20. The drought of the 1930s that spanned from Texas to North Dakota was caused by

    I.   overgrazing and overuse of farmland.
    II. natural phenomena, such as below-average rainfall and wind erosion.
    III. environmental factors, such as changes in the jet stream.
    IV. the lack of government subsidies for new irrigation technology.

    A. I and II only

    B. II and III only

    C. I and III only

    D. II and IV only

> **Read the passage below; then answer the two questions that follow.**

[1]Actually, the term "Native American" is incorrect. [2]Indians migrated to this continent from other areas, just earlier than Europeans did. [3]The ancestors of the Anasazi—Indians of the four-state area of Colorado, New Mexico, Utah, and Arizona—probably crossed from Asia into Alaska. [4]About 25,000 years ago, while the continental land bridge still existed. [5]This land bridge arched across the Bering Strait in the last Ice Age. [6]About 500 CE the ancestors of the Anasazi moved onto the Mesa Verde, a high plateau in the desert country of Colorado. [7]The Wetherills, five brothers who ranched in the area, are generally given credit for the first exploration of the ruins in the 1870s and 1880s. [8]There were some 50,000 Anasazi thriving in the four-corners area by the 1200s CE. [9]At their zenith, 700 to 1300 CE, the Anasazi had established widespread communities and built thousands of sophisticated structures—cliff dwellings, pueblos, and kivas. [10]They even engaged in trade with Indians in surrounding regions by exporting pottery and other goods.

21. Which of the following is a nonstandard sentence?

    A. sentence 1

    B. sentence 2

    C. sentence 4

    D. sentence 5

22. Which of the following draws attention away from the main idea of the paragraph?

    A. sentence 3

    B. sentence 4

    C. sentence 7

    D. sentence 8

23. Which line on the chart best matches the resources with the historical question that is being asked?

Line	Historical Research Question	Source of Information
1	How many people were living in Boston, MA, during the time of the American Revolution?	Historical atlas
2	What role did Fort Mackinac fulfill during the American Revolution?	Encyclopedia article
3	How did the average temperatures and snowfall during the winter of 1775–1776 compare with previous winters?	Historical almanac
4	When was the first U.S. treaty signed and what were the terms of the treaty?	Diary of a participant

A. line 1

B. line 2

C. line 3

D. line 4

DIRECTIONS: Use the passages below, adapted from Herodotus's *Histories*, to answer the two questions that follow.

Passage A: I think, too, that those Egyptians who dwell below the lake of Moiris and especially in that region which is called the Delta, if that land continues to grow in height according to this proportion and to increase similarly in extent, will suffer for all remaining time, from the Nile not overflowing their land, that same thing which they themselves said that the Hellenes would at some time suffer: for hearing that the whole land of the Hellenes has rain and is not watered by rivers as theirs is, they said that the Hellenes would at some time be disappointed of a great hope and would suffer the ills of famine. This saying means that if the god shall not send them rain, but shall allow drought to prevail for a long time, the Hellenes will be destroyed by hunger; for they have in fact no other supply of water to save them except from Zeus alone. This has been rightly said by the Egyptians with reference to the Hellenes: but now let me tell how matters are with the Egyptians themselves in their turn.

Passage B: If, in accordance with what I before said, their land below Memphis (for this is that which is increasing) shall continue to increase in height according to the same proportion as in the past time, assuredly those Egyptians who dwell here will suffer famine, if their land shall not have rain nor the river be able to go over their fields. It is certain however that now they gather in fruit from the earth with less labour than any other men and also with less than the other Egyptians; for they have no labour in breaking up furrows with a plough nor in hoeing nor in any other of those labours which other men have about a crop; but when the river has come up of itself and watered their fields and after watering has left them again, then each man sows his own field and turns into it swine, and when he has trodden the seed into the ground by means of the swine, after that he waits for the harvest, and when he has threshed the corn by means of the swine, then he gathers it in.

24. Which of the following best states the main issues being discussed in the above passages?

    A. Ancient Egyptians were so dependent upon the Nile River that one's location determined one's prosperity.

    B. The Nile River was so important to the prosperity of ancient Egyptians that it determined where many Egyptians settled.

    C. Egyptians who depend upon the Nile River for irrigation will not suffer from famine as those who depend upon rain.

    D. Egyptians settling in the Delta were dependent upon religion because irrigation from rain was more unpredictable than the Nile.

25. Herodotus, in passage A, could best support assertions made in the passage by presenting which of the following types of evidence?

    A. Data showing the productivity of Egyptian farmers in both the Delta and Memphis regions.

    B. Data showing the average rainfall in the Delta as compared to average rainfall in Memphis.

    C. Data showing the cycle of flooding along the Nile as compared to the cycles of rainfall in the Delta.

    D. Data showing the wealth of Egyptians in the Delta as compared to the wealth of Egyptians in Memphis.

26. Which of the following would be considered a primary source in researching the factors that influenced U.S. involvement in the Korean War?

    I. The personal correspondence of a military man stationed with the 5th Regimental Combat Team (RCT) in Korea.
    II. A biography of Harry S. Truman by David McCullough, published in 1993.
    III. A journal article about the beginning of the Korean War by a noted scholar.
    IV. An interview with Secretary of Defense George Marshall.

    A. I and II only

    B. II and IV only

    C. II and III only

    D. I and IV only

27. Which of the following was *not* a major Native American tribe that resided in Oklahoma before the 1800s?

    A. the Chickasaw

    B. the Osage

    C. the Quapay

    D. the Mound Builders

Read the passage below; then answer the three questions that follow.

[1]We've grown accustomed to seeing this working woman hanging from the subway strap during commuting hours. [2]We may refer disparagingly to her tailored suit and little tie, but we no longer visualize her in a house dress with her hair uncombed. [3]The woman who leaves her children to go to work in the morning is no longer a pariah in her community or her family. [4]Her paycheck is more than pin money; it buys essential family staples and often supports the entire family. [5]But she is not the only beneficiary of the increasing presence of women in the workplace.

[6]The situation for men has also changed as a result of women's massive entry into the work force for the better. [7]Men who would once have felt unrelenting pressure to remain with one firm and climb the career ladder are often freed up by a second income to change careers in midlife. [8]They enjoy greatest intimacy and involvement with their children.

[9]The benefits for business are also readily apparent. [10]No senior manager in the country would deny that the huge generation of women who entered management seven or eight years ago has functioned superbly, often outperforming men.

[11]Yet the prevailing message from the media on the subject of women and business is one filled with pessimism. [12]We hear about women leaving their employers in the lurch when they go on maternity leave. [13]Or we hear the flip side, that women are overly committed to their careers and neglectful of their families. [14]And in fact, it is true that problems arising from women's new work force role do exist, side by side with the benefits.

[15]The problems hurt business as well as individuals and their families, affordable quality childcare, for one example, is still a distant dream. [16]Some women are distracted at work, and men who would have felt secure about their children when their wives were home are also anxious and distracted. [17]Distraction also impedes the productivity of some high-achieving women with the birth of their first child and causes some to depart with the birth of their second.

28. Which of the following sentences displays a nonstandard placement of a modifying phrase?

    A. sentence 1

    B. sentence 3

    C. sentence 6

    D. sentence 7

29. Which of the following sentences displays a nonstandard use of a comparative form?

    A. sentence 4

    B. sentence 8

    C. sentence 10

    D. sentence 13

30. Which of the following sentences is a nonstandard sentence?

    A. sentence 14

    B. sentence 15

    C. sentence 16

    D. sentence 17

31. Which of the following best describes a major difference between a state government and the federal government?

    A. State governments have more responsibility for public education than the federal government.

    B. State governments are more dependent upon the personal income tax for revenue than the federal government.

    C. State governments are more dependent upon the system of checks and balances than the federal government.

    D. State governments are subject to term limits, where as federal government representatives serve unlimited terms.

32. Which of the following were major causes of the Great Depression?
    I. Hoarding money greatly reduced the money supply, resulting in higher prices on consumer goods.
    II. The gold standard limited the amount of money in supply, reducing money circulation, and causing a drop in prices and wages.
    III. Smoot-Hawley Tariff increased tariffs, which resulted in increased prices for consumer goods.
    IV. The stock market crash reduced the value of companies, causing them to raise prices of consumer goods.

    A. I and II only

    B. II and III only

    C. III and IV only

    D. I, II, and III

33. Before reading a story about a veterinary hospital to his first-grade class, Mr. Drake constructs a semantic map of related words and terms using the students' input. What is his main intention for doing this?

    A.   To demonstrate a meaningful relationship between the concepts of the story and the prior knowledge of the students

    B.   To serve as a visual means of learning

    C.   To determine the level of understanding the students will have at the conclusion of the topic being covered

    D.   To model proper writing using whole words

34. If a teacher is interested in improving the comprehension skills of students, that teacher should
    I.   teach students to decode well.
    II. allow time during the day to read and reread selections.
    III. discuss the selections after reading to clarify meaning and make connections.
    IV. tell jokes.

    A.   I and II only

    B.   I, II, and IV

    C.   I, II, and III

    D.   All of the above

Read the passage below; then answer the three questions that follow.

[1]In the past 30 years, television has become a very popular pastime for almost everyone. [2]From the time the mother places the baby in her jumpseat in front of the television until the time the senior citizen in the retirement home watched Vanna White turn the letters on "Wheel of Fortune," Americans spend endless hours in front of the "boob tube." [3]How did we get to be this way?

[4]When my mother was a little girl, what did children do to entertain themselves? [5]They played. [6]Their games usually involved social interaction with other children as well as imaginatively creating entertainment for themselves. [7]They also developed hobbies like woodworking and sewing. [8]Today, few children really know how to play with each other or entertain themselves. [9]Instead, they sit in front of the television, glued to cartoons that are senseless and often violent. [10]Even if they watch educational programs like "Sesame Street," they don't really have to do anything but watch and listen to what the answer to the question is.

[11]Teenagers, also, use television as a way of avoiding doing things that will be helping them mature. [12]How many kids does much homework anymore? [13]Why not? [14]Because they work part-time jobs and come home from work tired and relax in front of the television.

35. Which of the following sentences uses a nonstandard verb form?

    A. sentence 4

    B. sentence 7

    C. sentence 8

    D. sentence 12

36. Which of the following sentences in the passage is nonstandard?

    A. sentence 2

    B. sentence 7

    C. sentence 10

    D. sentence 14

37. Which of the following changes is needed in the first two paragraphs?

    A. Sentence 1: Change "has become" to "is."

    B. Sentence 2: Change "watched" to "watches."

    C. Sentence 4: Change "When" to "Being that."

    D. Sentence 9: Change "sit" to "sat."

38. The Silk Road did not connect to which of the following countries?

    A. China

    B. Greece

    C. Iran

    D. India

39. When a member of the House of Representatives helps a citizen from his or her district receive federal aid to which that citizen is entitled, the representative's action is referred to as

    A. casework.

    B. pork barrel legislation.

    C. lobbying.

    D. logrolling.

40. Why should children be encouraged to figure out the structure and the features of the text they are attempting to comprehend and remember?

      I. It helps the students to understand the way the author organized the material to be presented.

      II. It helps the students to really look at the features of the text.

      III. Talking about the structure of the text provides an opportunity for the teacher to point out the most salient features to the students.

      IV. The discussions may help the child make connections between the new material in the chapter and what is already known about the topic.

A. I and III

B. II and IV

C. I and IV

D. All of the above

Constructed Response

Use the information below to complete the exercise that follows.

Mrs. Whalen, a fifth-grade teacher, is assessing Demetrius, a new student to the school, for reading fluency and comprehension. She has him read the following passage aloud.

My name is Jake. That's my first name, obviously. I can't tell you my last name. It would be too dangerous. The controllers are everywhere. Everywhere. And if they knew my full name, they could find me and my friends, and then . . . well, let's just say I don't want them to find me. What they do to people who resist them is too horrible to think about.

I won't even tell you where I live. You'll just have to trust me that it is a real place, a real town. It may even be *your* town.

I'm writing this all down so that more people will learn the truth. Maybe then, somehow, the human race can survive until the Algonites return and rescue us, as they promised they would.

Maybe.

My life used to be normal. Normal, that is, until one Friday night at the mall. I was there with Marco, my best friend. We were playing video games and hanging out at this cool store that sells comic books and stuff. The usual.

Demetrius has trouble pronouncing nearly every word longer than two syllables: "obviously," "controllers," and "Algonites," for example. He also needs help in pronouncing the word "resist." He reads with some expression and fairly quickly, except for the words he stumbles over. When questioned about the content of the passage, he answers as follows:

Mrs. Whalen: Can you tell me something about what you were just reading?

Demetrius: There's a guy who likes video games. I think his name is Jake.

Mrs. Whalen: What can you tell me about Jake?

Demetrius: Well, he's scared. He's in trouble.

Mrs. Whalen: How do you know he's in trouble?

Demetrius: He can't give out his last name.

Mrs. Whalen: Do you have any idea what he's afraid of?

Demetrius: Not really—they're An-guh-...

Mrs. Whalen: The Algonites?

Demetrius: Yeah, them. I guess they're after the whole world.

Based on your knowledge of reading comprehension, write a response that:

•   identifies two comprehension needs demonstrated by this student;

•   provides evidence for the needs you identify;

•   suggests two different instructional strategies to address the needs you identify; and

•   explains why these strategies might be effective.

Practice Test Answer Sheets

Begin your essay on this page. If necessary, continue on the next page.

Continue on the next page if necessary.

279

Continuation of your essay from previous page, if necessary.

OSAT

**Oklahoma Subject Area Test
Elementary Education**

Answers:
Practice Subtest 1

Answer Key

1.	(A)	11.	(B)	21.	(C)	31.	(A)
2.	(B)	12.	(A)	22.	(C)	32.	(B)
3.	(C)	13.	(C)	23.	(C)	33.	(A)
4.	(D)	14.	(B)	24.	(C)	34.	(C)
5.	(C)	15.	(A)	25.	(D)	35.	(D)
6.	(A)	16.	(D)	26.	(D)	36.	(D)
7.	(A)	17.	(B)	27.	(A)	37.	(B)
8.	(D)	18.	(B)	28.	(C)	38.	(B)
9.	(D)	19.	(A)	29.	(B)	39.	(A)
10.	(D)	20.	(A)	30.	(B)	40.	(D)

Practice Subtest

Detailed Explanations of Answers

1. **A**

   Semantic cueing involves using the meaning of the text and the context to figure out an unknown word. The genre of the selection, the illustrations, the reader's knowledge of the topic of the selection, and the context of the written words can provide semantic cues as the reader tries to unlock an unknown word.

2. **B**

   Syntactic cueing involves using the reader's grammatical knowledge of spoken and written language to figure out the significance of an unknown word in a text.

3. **C**

   Phonological cueing involves using the knowledge of matching written symbols with their sounds. This cueing strategy has limitations: it can be used effectively only for words where the letter patterns are known by the reader. The reader must also know how to analyze an unknown word.

4. **D**

   The pragmatic cueing system involves using the understanding that people use language differently in different contexts. This knowledge may help a reader to correctly interpret a text.

5. **C**

Clearly setting a purpose for listening, asking questions about the selection, and encouraging students to forge links between the new information and knowledge already in place are all supported by research as effective strategies.

6. **A**

There is a direct relationship between what is taught in school and what is learned in school. Also, if you want children to improve in writing, they need time to write.

7. **A**

The western or Pacific Coast of Canada is known as the Cordillera region. It receives an exceptional amount of rain and includes some of the tallest and oldest trees in Canada, similar to northern California. The area is full of rugged mountains with high plateaus and desert-like areas. For more information on Canada's regions visit http://www.members.shaw.ca/kcic1/geographic.html.

8. **D**

Due process is the legal concept that every citizen is entitled to equal treatment under the law. The excerpt illustrates one aspect of due process, the exclusionary rule. The exclusionary rule is applied when evidence is seized in violation of due process. So the most correct answer is D, the exclusionary rule.

9. **D**

Many of the classic stories for children exist in the realm of fantasy because of the timeless quality of such tales. Fantasy allows children to explore places and events that have never taken place, and will never take place, yet somehow contain messages that we can discuss, savor, and learn from. Faith Ringgold, an author of books for children, has stated, "One of the things you can do so well with children is to blend fantasy and reality. Kids are ready for it; they don't have to have everything lined up and real. It's not that they don't know it's not real, they just don't care."

10. **D**

Most books that begin with a princess have similar outcomes.

11. **B**

Stories that begin with an issue and a princess in place normally contain many magical events. Please consider some of the following titles: The Paper Bag Princess *by Robert Munsch;* The Frog Prince, Continued *by Jon Scieszka;* Princess Furball *by Charlotte Huck; and* Sleeping Ugly *by Jane Yolen.*

12. **A**

A K-W-L isn't just for content area lessons. Some children come to think of fairy tales as "babyish" or "girlish." This kind of discussion, laced with little chunks of stories being read aloud, helps children to recognize how delightful and charming this genre can be. It also helps them to figure out the rules of the genre, which improves their reading and writing.

13. **C**

This is the next step in the writing process.

14. **B**

The presence of "the" before "Westown's" means that the reference is to the council, not to a council belonging to Westown. The sentences in the other choices are all currently correct, and changing them would make them nonstandard.

15. **A**

The editorial is suggesting that the population loss is a bad thing and that proposed changes would be a good thing. Thus, population loss is something the author wants stopped, or at least lessened, so alleviate, which means to lessen, is the only possible choice.

16. **D**

The subject of the first clause is "each," which is singular, so the verb should be "has."

17. **B**

Choice A is wrong because it makes no sense within the sentence; the zoning regulations cannot be easy to change. Choice C makes sense, but its use of "them" is ambiguous—does it refer to the authors or the regulations? Choice D is wrong because, if the authors said the regulations would be hard to change, the word apparently earlier in the sentence would make no sense. Thus Choice B is the best answer.

18. **B**

I and III are correct. Among the major employers in Oklahoma are the Oklahoma state government, the U.S. Air Force, and General Motors. Also, Oklahoma's food processing plants, rubber and plastic manufacturing and other heavy industry are directly related to the livestock, petroleum, and natural gas industries in the state. II is incorrect because Oklahoma's livestock industry is more profitable, not less, than agriculture. IV is incorrect because Tulsa and Oklahoma City are among the great natural gas and petroleum centers of the world.

19. **A**

The main purpose of the WTO is to open world markets to all countries to promote economic development and to regulate the economic affairs between member states.

20. **A**

Overgrazing, overuse of farmland, and a lack of rainfall caused the drought of the 1930s.

21. **C**

Choice C is a prepositional phrase, "About 25,000 years ago," which is followed by a subordinate clause. This part should be linked to the previous sentence as it is integral to the migration of the Anasazi. Choices A, B, and D are all complete sentences.

22. **C**

Choice C has to do with the later history of the Mesa Verde area, after the Anasazi had abandoned it. Because this is so far removed chronologically, sentence 7 should be deleted or further developed in a second paragraph. Choices A and B discuss the very early history of the Indians. Choice D follows the chronological time order from 500 CE and leads into a discussion of the height of the Anasazi civilization.

23. **C**

Historical almanacs contain yearly data of certain events, including the time at sunrise and sunset along with weather-related data and statistics, so C is correct. Historical atlases contain a collection of historical maps. These maps may or may not include population data, so A is incorrect. Historical population data may best be found in government publications on the census. An encyclopedia article would contain a factual summary of the colonial period and the American Revolution, but may not include an analysis of the role of Fort Mackinac during the American Revolution, as encyclopedias attempt to give overviews rather than interpretations or analysis, so B is incorrect. A secondary source on Michigan during the colonial period may better address this question. Information on when the first treaty was signed and the terms of the treaty would most likely appear in a history book or government publication; a participant's diary may not be as accurate.

24. **C**

The Nile River's flooding was more predictable than rainfall in Greece (home of the "Hellenes") was.

25. **D**

Productivity directly measures the prosperity and viability of farming in an area.

26. **D**

Both the personal correspondence of a military man stationed with the 5th RCT in Korea and an interview with Secretary of Defense George Marshall are primary sources, as they involve correspondence or testimony from individuals who were actually involved with the Korean War.

27. **A**

The Osage and Quapay inhabited the region now known as Oklahoma in the 18th century. The Mound Builders had also occupied a small area long before the 1800s. The Chickasaw came to the region in the 19th century, so A is correct.

28. **C**

It is not the work force that is "for the better," but the situation for men. This is also supported by the rest of the evidence offered in the paragraph. The other sentences have their modifying phrases directly related to the idea they qualify.

29. **B**

The writer is comparing before and after the appearance of women in management; only two things—therefore the comparative form, not the superlative, is correct: "greater." A, B, and D are all incorrect responses; they have no comparative adjectives, just adverbs used as qualifiers, e.g., "overly." These are used in a standard way.

30. **B**

Sentence 15 is a run-on sentence, incorrectly punctuated with a comma after "families" instead of a semicolon (i.e., it's a comma splice). The rest of the choices are all standard sentences.

31. **A**

The responsibility for public education belongs to the state governments. The federal government has often passed legislation to regulate and provide funds for public education, but the main responsibility for establishing and regulating education resides with the state governments.

32. **B**

A limited money supply and rising prices were major causes of the Great Depression. The money supply was most affected by the Gold Standard and the Smoot-Hawley Tariff further affected consumer prices.

33. **A**

By mapping out previous knowledge, information already known can be transferred to support new information. Although words on the board are visual (B), this is not the underlying motive. Semantic mapping done at the beginning of a story tests how much knowledge the students have about the topic at the outset, not the conclusion (C). This mapping process does model proper use of words (D), but doing so is not the main intent of the exercise.

34. **C**

Teaching effective comprehension is a process that takes time and practice. It seems obvious that a student cannot comprehend a text if the text cannot be decoded. It also seems obvious that, if you want students to get better at reading, they need time to read. Students also need input, usually in the form of conversation, to make connections between what is read and what is already known.

35. **D**

Sentence 12 has an incorrect agreement between "kids" and "does," so D is the answer. Kids [they] do [something] is correct. All the other sentences use standard English syntax.

36. **D**

The sentence is a rhetorical clause that begins with a subordinating conjunction, "because." Consequently, it cannot stand alone as a complete standard sentence. The other choices are standard.

37. **B**

Although time is passing in sentence 2, the verb tense regarding infancy and old age should be the same in this sentence. Thus, the present tense of the first clause should be matched by present tense in the second ("watches"), so B is correct.

38. **B**

The Silk Road was a transcontinental trade route that branched out over a vast area, including A, western China; C, northern Iran; D, northern India; and eventually the Sahara.

39. **A**

A is the best answer, since the term "casework" is used by political scientists to describe the activities of congressmen on behalf of individual constituents. These activities might include helping an elderly person secure social security benefits, or helping a veteran obtain medical services. Most casework is actually done by congressional staff and may take as much as a third of the staff's time. Congressmen supply this type of assistance for the good public relations it provides. Answer B fails because pork barrel legislation is rarely if ever intended to help individual citizens. Pork barrel legislation authorizes federal spending for special projects, such as airports, roads, or dams, in the home state or district of a congressman. It is meant to help the entire district or state. Also, there is no legal entitlement on the part of a citizen to a pork barrel project, such as there is with social security benefits. C is not the answer because lobbying is an activity directed towards congressmen, not one done by congressmen. A lobbyist attempts to get congressmen to support legislation that will benefit the group that the lobbyist represents. Logrolling, D, is incorrect, because it does not refer to a congressional service for constituents. It refers instead to the congressional practice of trading votes on different bills. Congressman A will vote for Congressman B's pork barrel project and in return B will vote for A's pork barrel project.

40. **D**

Children learn more from a text if the teacher helps them figure out how the book was put together. It makes the text more understandable. It also helps them to read the text critically, as part of the conversation can address the issue of what is missing in the text.

Constructed-Response Answer Earning 4 Points

For Demetrius to read this text at an independent level, he needs better word identification skills and better acquaintance with the passage's genre.

If he does not know the meaning of the word "obviously," he not only misses a clue about Jake's personality, but he also goes into decoding mode, which prevents him from enjoying the text and from making connections between the text and other experiences.

Although Demetrius has two major word identification problems—decoding words phonologically and simply not having a sufficient vocabulary to read this passage—the inability I will concentrate on here is the insufficient vocabulary. Two of the words Demetrius had trouble with—"obviously" and "resist"—should be in a fifth grader's vocabulary, and they both follow somewhat unusual phonological models.

Even with better skills in this area, however, Demetrius will still have trouble with comprehension. This passage appears to be from a science fiction book, and he definitely seems unfamiliar with the genre. Thus, his first response to Mrs. Whalen's question concerning what the passage is about is Jake's affinity for video games, which may be the only thing Demetrius grasps well about the passage. When asked what else he knows about Jake, he concentrates on Jake's trouble rather than the trouble for the human race, probably because Demetrius is more accustomed to reading books in which individuals are in trouble of their own (or maybe he's just used to being "in trouble" himself).

Both strategies that Mrs. Whalen should try could be done on either an individual basis just with Demetrius or on a class-wide (or small-group) basis, depending on how many other readers in the class are at Demetrius's level. The first strategy, to increase his vocabulary, is to work with the student(s) to analyze new and unfamiliar words in all their reading. Assuming Demetrius will be worked with on an individual basis, he should read a book that is at his current instructional level (that is he can read it independently). He should make word lists of the words that he is unfamiliar with. He should define them and try to think of (or find) other words that have similar phonemes. For instance, his words and their phonemic analogies in this passage might be "obviously ↔ previously" and "resist ↔ insist." He may need help finding meanings or analogies, so Mrs. Whalen should have occasional short conferences with him to assess whether the word lists and their analogies are useful or even possible. This strategy will theoretically increase the number of words he knows and his ability to decipher unfamiliar words as well.

A second strategy is one that Mrs. Whalen would probably want to do with the whole class, and that would be to introduce the science fiction genre. Surely many students in the class will be acquainted with science fiction at least through movies and television shows, and they will be able to list a number of standard science fiction plots. Mrs. Whalen should diagram some of these plots on a board or overhead so that students will know what to expect as they read science fiction—for example, that big matters such as human survival are often at stake.

Demetrius already shows that he can make connections between what he reads and his own life, but his connections are flawed because he relies too much on his own life and too little on the text. By learning better word-recognition strategies and by recognizing conventions of the genre he is reading, he can raise his comprehension to a higher level.

Features of the Constructed Response Scoring 4

Purpose. The purpose of the assignment has been achieved. All four bullet points listed in the assignment have been addressed in an orderly way. The essay begins by stating the two comprehension needs, then gives evidence for these needs. It goes on to discuss two strategies, with reasons that the writer expects each to have a chance for success.

Subject Matter Knowledge. By indicating specific methods for implementing both strategies, this essay shows that the writer has an idea of how to improve reading, and how to assess whether the proposed methods are successful.

Support. Specific examples from the reading assessment are cited in describing the needs, and specific examples are given for the supposed strategies.

Rationale. In a sense, the "rationale" part of the scoring is covered by the other three areas: it would be hard to give a convincing argument without answering the question, demonstrating knowledge, or supporting your points. However, this area also includes the organization of the argument, and this essay methodically elucidates its points in a manner that helps the reader keep track of the overall argument.

FOR YOUR REFERENCE ONLY—*The constructed-response item is written to assess understanding in Subarea I, Reading, which consists of the competencies listed below.*

Understand the reading process.

Understand phonological skills and strategies related to reading.

Understand skills and strategies related to word identification and vocabulary development.

Understand skills and strategies involved in reading comprehension.

Understand reading instruction and study skills in the content areas.

Understand characteristic features of children's literature and strategies to promote students' literary response and analysis.

OSAT

Oklahoma Subject Area Test
Elementary Education

Subtest 2 Review

Mathematics

Objectives

SUBAREA I—MATHEMATICS

Competency 0001

> Understand formal and informal reasoning processes, including logic and simple proofs, and apply problem-solving techniques and strategies in a variety of contexts.

> The following topics are examples of content that may be covered under this competency.
> - Judge the validity or logic of mathematical arguments.
> - Evaluate the sufficiency of information provided to solve a problem.
> - Draw a valid conclusion based on stated conditions.
> - Apply inductive reasoning to make mathematical conjectures.

Competency 0002

> Use a variety of approaches (e.g., estimation, mental math, modeling, pattern recognition) to explore mathematical ideas and solve problems.

> The following topics are examples of content that may be covered under this competency.
> - Evaluate the appropriateness of using estimation to solve a given problem.
> - Use an appropriate model to illustrate a given problem.
> - Analyze the usefulness of a specific model or mental math procedure for exploring a given mathematical idea or problem.
> - Simplify a problem to facilitate a solution.

Competency 0003

Understand mathematical communication and the historical and cultural contexts of mathematics.

The following topics are examples of content that may be covered under this competency.
* Use mathematical notation to represent a given relationship.
* Use appropriate models, diagrams, and symbols to represent mathematical concepts.
* Use appropriate vocabulary to express given mathematical ideas and relationships.
* Apply knowledge of the role of mathematics in society and the contributions of various cultures toward the development of mathematics.

Competency 0004

Understand skills and concepts related to number and numeration, and apply these skills and concepts to real-world situations.

The following topics are examples of content that may be covered under this competency.
* Use ratios, proportions, and percents to model and solve problems.
* Compare and order fractions, decimals, and percents.
* Solve problems using equivalent forms of numbers (e.g., integer, fraction, decimal, percent, exponential and scientific notation).
* Analyze the number properties used in operational algorithms (e.g., multiplication, long division).

Competency 0005

Understand and apply the principles and properties of linear algebraic relations and functions.

The following topics are examples of content that may be covered under this competency.
* Analyze mathematical relationships and patterns using tables, verbal rules, equations, and graphs.
* Derive an algebraic expression to represent a real-world relationship or pattern, and recognize a real-world relationship that is represented by an algebraic expression.
* Use algebraic functions to describe given graphs, to plot points, and to determine slopes.
* Perform algebraic operations to solve equations and inequalities.

Competency 0006

Understand the principles and properties of geometry, and apply them to model and solve problems.

The following topics are examples of content that may be covered under this competency.
- Apply the concepts of similarity and congruence to model and solve real-world problems.
- Apply knowledge of basic geometric figures to solve real-world problems involving more complex patterns.
- Apply inductive and deductive reasoning to solve real-world problems in geometry.

Competency 0007

Understand concepts, principles, skills, and procedures related to measurement, statistics, and probability; and demonstrate an ability to use this understanding to describe and compare phenomena, to evaluate and interpret data, and to apply mathematical expectations to real-world phenomena.

The following topics are examples of content that may be covered under this competency.
- Estimate and convert measurements using standard and nonstandard units.
- Solve measurement problems involving volume, time, or speed.
- Interpret graphic and nongraphic representations of frequency distributions, percentiles, and measures of central tendency.
- Determine probabilities, and make predictions based on probabilities.

Problem Solving

The ability to render some real-life quandaries into mathematical or logical problems—workable via established procedures—is a key to finding solutions. Because each quandary will be unique, so too will be your problem-solving plan of attack. Still, many real-world problems that lend themselves to mathematical solutions are likely to require one of the following strategies.

1. **Guess and check** (not the same as "wild guessing"). With this problem-solving strategy, make your best guess, and then check the answer to see whether it's right. Even if the guess doesn't immediately provide the solution, it may help to get you closer to it so that you can continue to work on the problem. An example:

   Three persons' ages add up to 72, and each person is one year older than the last person. What are their ages?

   Because the three ages must add up to 72, it is reasonable to take one-third of 72 (24) as your starting point. Of course, even though 24 + 24 + 24 gives a sum of 72, those numbers don't match the information ("Each person is one year older..."). So, you might guess that the ages are 24, 25, and 26. You check that guess by addition, and you see that the sum of 75 is too high. Lowering your guesses by one each, you try 23, 24, and 25, which indeed add up to 72, giving you the solution. There are many variations of the guess and check method.

2. **Making a sketch or a picture** can help to clarify a problem. Consider this problem:

Mr. Rosenberg plans to put a four-foot-wide concrete sidewalk around his backyard pool. The pool is rectangular, with dimensions 12' by 24'. The cost of the concrete is $1.28 per square foot. How much concrete is required for the job?

If you have exceptional visualization abilities, no sketch is needed. For most of us, however, a drawing like the one shown below may be helpful in solving this and many other real-life problems.

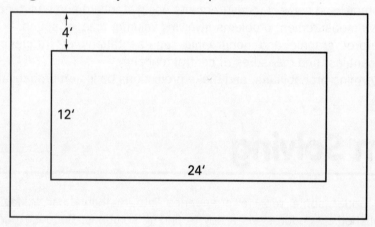

3. **Make a table or a chart.** Sometimes, *organizing* the information from a problem makes it easier to find the solution; tables and charts can be helpful.

4. **Making a list**, like making a table or chart, can help to organize information, and perhaps provide or at least hint at a solution. The strategy would work well for solving this problem: "How many different outcomes are there if you roll two regular six-sided dice?"

5. **Act it out.** Sometimes, literally "doing" a problem, with physical objects, your bodies, and so forth, can help produce a solution. A classic problem that could be solved in this manner is the following: "If five strangers meet, and if everyone shakes everyone else's hand once, how many total handshakes will there be?"

6.   **Look for patterns.** This technique encourages you to ask, "What's happening here?" Spotting a pattern would be helpful in solving a problem such as:

Nevin's weekly savings account balance for 15 weeks are as follows: $125, $135, $148, $72, $85, $96, $105, $50, $64, $74, $87, $42, $51, $60, $70. If the pattern holds, (approximately) what might Nevin's balance be the next week?

7.   **Working a simpler problem** means finding the solution to a different but simpler problem, hoping that you will spot a way to solve the harder one. *Estimating* can be thought of as working a simpler problem. If you need to know the product of 23 and 184, and no calculator or pencil and paper are handy, you could estimate the product by getting the exact answer to the simpler problem, 20 × 200.

8.   **Writing an open math sentence** (an equation with one or more variables, or "unknowns"), then solving it, is often an effective strategy. This is sometimes called "translating" a problem into mathematics. Consider this problem: "Tiana earned grades of 77%, 86%, 90%, and 83% on her first four weekly science quizzes. Assuming all grades are equally weighted, what score will she need on the fifth week's quiz in order to have an average (or mean) score of 88%?" Using the given information, you can set up the following equation, which, when solved, will answer the question:

$$\frac{(77+86+90+83+x)}{5}=88$$

9.   **Work backward.** Consider this problem: "If you add 12 to some number, then multiply the sum by 4, you will get 60. What is the number?" You can find a solution by *starting at the end*, with 60. The problem tells you that the 60 came from multiplying a sum by 4. When multiplied by 4, 15 equals 60, so 15 must be the sum referred to. And if 15 is the sum of 12 and something else, the "something else" can only be 3.

There are, of course, hybrid approaches. You can mix and match problem-solving strategies wherever you think they are appropriate. In general, attention to *reasonableness* may be most crucial to problem-solving success, especially in real-life situations.

Mathematical Communication and Mathematical Terminology, Symbols, and Representations

While a review of even basic mathematical terminology and symbolism could fill a book, there are some key points to keep in mind:

Mathematics is, for the most part, a science of precision. When working with math symbols and terminology, meticulousness is in order. For example, "less than" does not mean the same thing as "not greater than." The following two equations are *not* equivalent (every term on both sides of the first equation should be divided by 6.)

$$6m + 2 = 18$$

$$\frac{6m}{6} + 2 = \frac{18}{6}$$

All of this matters, especially in real-life problem situations.

Certain mathematical concepts and terms are frequently misunderstood. Here are a few of the "repeat offenders":

Use care with *hundreds vs. hundredths, thousands vs. thousandths*, and so forth. Remember that the "th" at the end of the word indicates a fraction. "Three hundred" means 300, whereas "three hundredths" means 0.03.

Negative numbers are those less than zero. Fractions less than zero are negative numbers, too.

The *absolute value* of a number can be thought of as its distance from zero on a number line.

Counting numbers can be shown by the set (1, 2, 3, 4, . . .). Notice that 0 is not a counting number.

Whole numbers are the counting numbers, plus 0 (0, 1, 2, . . .).

Integers are all of the whole numbers and their negative counterparts (. . . –2, –1, 0, 1, 2, . . .). Note that negative and positive fractions are not considered integers (unless they are equivalent to whole numbers or their negative counterparts).

Factors are any of the numbers or symbols in mathematics that, when multiplied together, form a product. (The whole number factors of 12 are 1, 2, 3, 4, 6, and 12.) A number with exactly two whole number factors (1 and the number itself) is a *prime number*. The first few primes are 2, 3, 5, 7, 11, 13, and 17. Most other whole numbers are *composite numbers*, because they are *composed* of several whole number factors (1 is neither prime nor composite; it has only one whole number factor).

The *multiples* of any whole number are what are produced when the number is multiplied by counting numbers. The multiples of 7 are 7, 14, 21, 28, and so on. Every whole number has an infinite number of multiples.

Recall that *decimal numbers* are simply certain fractions written in special notation. All decimal numbers are actually fractions whose denominators are powers of 10 (10, 100, 1000, etc.) 0.033, for instance, can be thought of as the fraction $\frac{33}{1000}$.

There is an agreed-upon order of operations for simplifying complex expressions.

First you compute any multiplication or division, left to right. Then you compute any addition or subtraction, also left to right. (If an expression contains any parentheses, all computation within the parentheses should be completed first.) Treat exponential expressions ("powers") as multiplication. Thus, the expression $3 + 7 \times 4 - 2$ equals 29. (Multiply 7 by 4 *before* doing the addition and subtraction.)

Exponential notation is a way to show repeated multiplication more simply. $2 \times 2 \times 2$, for instance, can be shown as 2^3, and is equal to 8. (Note: 2^3 does *not* mean 2×3.)

Scientific notation provides a method for showing numbers using exponents (although it is most useful for very large and very small numbers.) A number is in scientific notation when it is shown as a number between 1 and 10 to a power of 10. Thus, the number 75,000 in scientific notation is shown as 7.5×10^4.

Addends (or *addenda*) can be thought of as "parts of addition problems." When addends are combined, they produce *sums*. Likewise, *factors* can be seen as "parts of multiplication problems." When factors are multiplied, they produce *products*. When two numbers are divided, one into the other, the result is a *quotient*.

Equations are not the same as mathematical *expressions*. $12 + 4 = 16$ and $2x + 7 = 12$ are equations. $(144 - 18)$ and $13y^2$ are expressions. Notice that expressions are "lacking a verb," so to speak (you don't say "is equal to" or "equals" when reading expressions). Inequalities are very much like equations, but "greater than" or "less than" are added, such as in $x \le 7$.

A *trend* is a pattern over time.

Careful use of mathematical terms and ideas such as those noted above is essential to communicating mathematically.

Fast Facts

Careful use of mathematical terms and ideas is essential to communicating mathematically.

The ability to convert among various mathematical and logical representations (graphic, numeric, symbolic, verbal) is an important skill, and, as with problem solving, precision and care are keys to quality conversions. Consider this number line, which might represent ages of students who are eligible for a particular scholarship:

Are 21-year-old students eligible? No, because the conventional notation used on the number line shows a *circle* around the point at 21. That means that 21 is *not* included in the set. Converting the graphic representation to symbolism gives $18 < x < 21$.

Number Skills

Key properties of whole numbers (and some related terms) include the following:

The *Commutative Property for Addition and Multiplication* states that the order in which addends are added or factors are multiplied does not determine the sum or product. (6×9 gives the same product as 9×6, for instance.) Division and subtraction are not commutative.

The *Associative Property for Addition and Multiplication* states that "associating" three or more addends or factors in a different fashion will not change the sum or product. For example, $(3 + 7) + 5$ gives the same sum as $3 + (7 + 5)$. Division and subtraction are not associative.

The *Distributive Property of Multiplication over Addition* is shown hereafter in simple notation form:

$$a(b + c) = (a \times b) + (a \times c)$$

An illustration of the Distributive Property is this: multiplying 6 by 47 will give the same result as multiplying 6 by 40, multiplying 6 times 7, then *adding* the products. That is, $6 \times (47) = (6 \times 40) + (6 \times 7)$.

Some pairs of operations are considered to be *inverse*. Addition and subtraction are inverse operations, as are multiplication and division. The operations can be thought of as "undoing" one another: Multiplying 4 by 9 gives 36; dividing 36 by 9 "gives back" 4.

The *Multiplicative Identity Property of One* states that any number multiplied by 1 remains the same. (34 × 1 = 34, for instance.) The number 1 is called the *Multiplicative Identity*.

The *Property of Reciprocals* states that any number (except for zero) multiplied by its reciprocal gives 1. (The *reciprocal* of a number is 1 divided by that number.)

Remember that dividing by zero is considered to have no meaning; avoid doing it when computing or solving equations and inequalities.

The *Additive Identity Property of Zero* states that adding zero to any number will not change the number (87 + 0 = 87, for instance). Zero is called the *Additive Identity*.

Division is *partitive* when you know the total and the number of parts or groups but you don't how many are in each part. Consider: "You have 7 containers of bolts and a total of 98 bolts. How many bolts are in each container (assuming the same number in each)?" Arriving at the answer is an example of partitive division.

With *measurement division*, the number of groups is not known. Using the example above, if you knew that there were 14 bolts per container, and that there were 98 bolts altogether, finding the number of containers would require measurement division.

Rational Numbers, Fractions, and Decimals

A property of real numbers is *The Density Property*. It states that, given any two real numbers, there is always another real number between them. (Think of the number line: No matter how close two points are, there is always a point between them.)

Rational numbers are those that can be written as fractions. (This includes integers; 12, for instance, can be written as $\frac{12}{1}$.)

Decimals (or "decimal fractions"), which come to an end when represented exactly, are *terminating decimals* (2.125, for instance). *Repeating decimals* are those in which the digits repeat a pattern endlessly (3.333333 . . . , for example). To use shorthand notation to show repeating decimals, you can write the "repeating block" just once, putting a bar over it. The example above, for instance, can be shown as 3.3̲. (Both terminating and repeating decimals are rational numbers.)

Some numbers are real numbers, but cannot be accurately represented by fractions. The ratio of the length of the diameter of any circle to its circumference, or π, for instance, is irrational. There are useful approximations of π, such as 3.14159, but π cannot be "pinned down" in either fraction or decimal notation.

Fractions, decimal numbers, ratios, and percents can be thought of as different ways of representing values, and any given rational number can be shown any of those ways. It is useful to be able to convert from one to the other. The following are some conversion tips:

The practical method for changing a fraction into a decimal is by dividing the numerator by the denominator. For example, $\frac{1}{4}$ becomes 0.25 when 1 is divided by 4, as follows:

$$\begin{array}{r} .25 \\ 4\overline{)1.00} \\ \underline{8} \\ 20 \end{array}$$

Naturally, this can be done longhand or with a calculator. (If the decimal number includes a whole number, as with $2\frac{3}{5}$, you can ignore the whole number when doing the division.) The decimal number may terminate or repeat. Converting a simple fraction to a decimal number will never result in an irrational number.

To convert a non-repeating decimal number to a fraction in lowest terms, simply write the decimal as a fraction with the denominator a power of ten, and then reduce to lowest terms. For example, 0.125 can be written as $\frac{125}{1000}$, which reduces to $\frac{1}{8}$.

Any decimal number can be converted to a percent by shifting the decimal point two places to the right and adding the percent symbol. For example, 0.135 becomes 13.5%. (If the number before the percent symbol is a whole number, there is no need to show the decimal point.)

A percent can be converted to a decimal number by shifting the decimal point two places to the left and dropping the percent symbol: 98% becomes 0.98 as a decimal.

A percent can be converted to a fraction simply by putting the percent (without the percent symbol) over 100, then reducing. In this way 20% can be shown as $\frac{20}{100}$, which reduces to $\frac{1}{5}$.

Ratio notation is simply an alternative method for showing fractions. For example, $\frac{2}{5}$ can be rewritten as "2 to 5." Ratio notation is commonly used when you want to emphasize the relationship of one number to another. Ratios are often shown as numbers with a colon between them; 2:5 is the same ratio as 2 to 5 and $\frac{2}{5}$.

To illustrate all of the above equivalencies and conversions at once, consider the fraction $\frac{19}{20}$. Shown as a ratio, it's 19 to 20, or 19:20. As a decimal, you have 0.95; as a percent, 95%.

The rules for performing operations on rational numbers (fractions) parallel in many ways the computational rules for integers. Just as adding –3 and –11 gives –14, adding $-\frac{1}{9}$ and $-\frac{5}{9}$ gives $-\frac{6}{9}$ (or $-\frac{2}{3}$ in reduced form.)

Algebraic Concepts and Methods

An important skill is the ability to represent real problems in algebraic form, and the concept of the *variable* is key. A variable is simply a symbol that represents an unknown value. Most typically x is the letter used, although any letter can be used. By "translating" real problems to algebraic form containing one or more variables (often as equations or inequalities), solutions to many problems can be found mathematically.

Understanding the relationships among values, and being able to accurately represent those relationships symbolically, is another key to algebraic problem solving. Consider the ages of two sisters. If you don't know the age of the younger sister, but know that the older sister is three years older, you can show the information symbolically as follows: The age of the younger sister can be shown as x, and the age of the older sister as $x + 3$. If you are told that the sum of the sisters' ages is, say, 25, you can represent that information via an equation:

$$x + (x + 3) = 25$$

which can be read as "the age of the younger sister plus the age of the older sister totals 25." This sort of translation skill is crucial for using algebra for problem solving.

Some helpful *translation* tips include the following: The word *is* often suggests an equal sign; *of* may suggest multiplication, as does *product*. *Sum* refers to addition; *difference* suggests subtraction; and a *quotient* is obtained after dividing. The key when translating is to make sure that the equation accurately matches the information and relationships given in the word problem.

Operations with algebraic expressions are governed by various rules and conventions. For instance, only *like* algebraic terms can be added or subtracted to produce simpler expressions. For example, $2x^3$ and $3x^3$ can be added together to get $5x^3$ because the terms are like terms; they both have a base of $x3$. You cannot add, say, $7m^3$ and $6m^2$; m^3 and m^2 are unlike bases. (Note: To *evaluate* an algebraic expression means to simplify it using conventional rules.)

When multiplying exponential terms together, the constant terms are multiplied, but the exponents of terms with the same variable bases are *added* together, which is somewhat counterintuitive. For example, $4w^2$ multiplied by $8w^3$ gives $32w^5$ (not $32w^6$, as one might guess).

When like algebraic terms are divided, exponents are subtracted. For example,

$$\frac{2x^7}{5x^3}$$

becomes

$$\frac{2x^4}{5}$$

In algebra, you frequently need to multiply two *binomials* together. Binomials are algebraic expressions of two terms. The FOIL method is one way to multiply binomials. FOIL stands for "first, outer, inner, last": Multiply the first terms in the parentheses, then the outermost terms, then the innermost terms, then the last terms, and then add the products together. For example, to multiply $(x + 3)$ and $(2x - 5)$, you multiply x by $2x$ (the first terms), x by -5 (outer terms), 3 by $2x$ (inner terms), and 3 by 5 (last terms). The four products ($2x^2$, $-5x$, $6x$, and -15) add up to $2x^2 + x - 15$. If the polynomials to be multiplied have more than two terms (*trinomials*, for instance), make sure that *each* term of the first polynomial is multiplied by *each* term of the second.

The opposite of polynomial multiplication is factoring. Factoring a polynomial means rewriting it as the product of factors (often two binomials). The trinomial $x^2 - 11x + 28$, for instance, can be factored into $(x - 4)(x - 7)$. (You can check this by "FOILing" the binomials.)

When attempting to factor polynomials, it is sometimes necessary to find factors common to all terms first. The two terms in $5x^2 - 10$, for example, both contain the factor 5. This means that the expression can be rewritten as $5(x^2 - 2)$.

Factoring is useful when solving some equations, especially if one side of the equation is set equal to zero. Consider $2x^2 - x - 1 = 2$. It can be rewritten as $2x^2 - x - 3 = 0$. This allows the left side to be factored into $(2x - 3)(x + 1)$, giving equation solutions of $\frac{3}{2}$ and -1.

Consider all of the information above as the following problem is first "translated" into an equation, then solved.

> Three teachers who are retiring are said to have 78 years of experience among them. You don't know how many years of experience Teacher A has, but you know that Teacher B has twice as many as A, and Teacher C has three more years of experience than B. How many years of experience does each have?

You can start by calling Teacher A's years of experience x. You then consider the relationship to the other two teachers: You can call Teacher B's years of experience $2x$, which allows you to call Teacher C's years of experience (2*x* + 3). You know that the teachers' years of experience add up to 78, allowing you to write:

$$x + 2x + (2x + 3) = 78$$

Using the rules for solving such an equation, you find that *x* = 15, meaning that the teachers' years of experience are, respectively, 15, 30, and 33 years.

Geometry

A fundamental concept of geometry is the notion of a *point*. A point is a specific location, taking up no space, having no area, and frequently represented by a dot. A point is considered one-dimensional.

Through any two points there is exactly one straight line; straight lines are one-dimensional. Planes (think of flat surfaces without edges) are two-dimensional. From these foundational ideas you can move to some other important geometric terms and ideas.

A segment is any portion of a line between two points on the line. It has a definite start and a definite end. The notation for a segment extending from point *A* to point *B* is $\overline{AB}$. A ray is like a straight segment, except it extends forever in one direction. The notation for a ray originating at point *X* (an *endpoint*) through point *Y* is $\overrightarrow{XY}$.

When two rays share their endpoints, an *angle* is formed. A *degree* is a unit of measure of the angle created. If a circle is divided into 360 even slices, each slice has an angle measure of 1 degree. If an angle has exactly 90 degrees, it is called a *right* angle. Angles of less than 90 degrees are *acute* angles. Angles greater than 90 degrees are *obtuse* angles. If two angles have the same size (regardless of how long their rays might be drawn), they are *congruent*. Congruence is shown this way: ∠*m* = ∠*n* (read "angle *m* is congruent to angle *n*").

A polygon is a closed plane figure bounded by straight lines or a closed figure on a sphere bounded by arcs of great circles. In a plane, three-sided polygons are *triangles*, four-sided polygons are *quadrilaterals*, five sides make *pentagons*, six sides make *hexagons*, and eight-sided polygons are *octagons*. (Note that not all quadrilaterals are squares.) If two polygons (or any figures) have exactly the same size and shape, they are *congruent*. If they are the same shape, but different sizes, they are *similar*.

Polygons may have lines of symmetry, which can be thought of as imaginary fold lines which produce two congruent, mirror-image figures. Squares have four lines of symmetry, and non-square rectangles have two, as shown later. Circles have an infinite number of lines of symmetry; a few are shown on the circle.

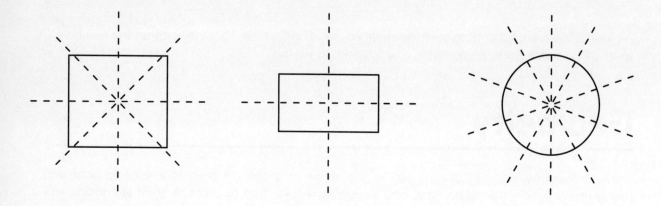

The *diameter* of a circle is a straight line segment that goes from one edge of a circle to the other side, passing through the center. The *radius* of a circle is half of its diameter (from the center to an edge). A *chord* is any segment that goes from one spot on a circle to any other spot (all diameters are chords, but not all chords are diameters).

The *perimeter* of a two-dimensional (flat) shape or object is the distance around the object.

Volume refers to how much space is inside of three-dimensional, closed containers. It is useful to think of volume as how many cubic units could fit into a solid. If the container is a rectangular solid, multiplying width, length, and height together computes the volume. If all six faces (sides) of a rectangular solid are squares, then the object is a cube.

Parallel and perpendicular are key concepts in geometry. Consider the two parallel lines that follow, and the third line (a *transversal*), which crosses them.

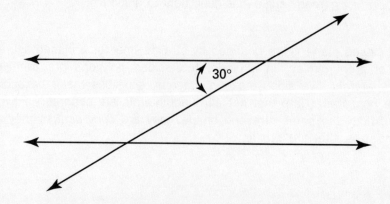

Note that among the many individual angles created, there are only two angle measures: 30° (noted in the figure) and 150° (180° − 30°).

Triangles have various properties. One is that the sum of the measures of the three angles of any triangle is 180°. If, therefore, the measures of two angles are known, the third can be deduced using addition, then subtraction. The Pythagorean theorem states that in any right triangle with legs (shorter sides) a and b, and hypotenuse (longest side) c, the sum of the squares of the sides will be equal to the square of the hypotenuse. In algebraic notation the Pythagorean theorem is given as $a^2 + b^2 = c^2$.

Two important coordinate systems are the number line and the coordinate plane, and both systems can be used to solve certain problems. A particularly useful tool related to the coordinate plane is the Distance Formula, which allows you to compute the distance between any two points on the plane. Consider points C and D in the following figure.

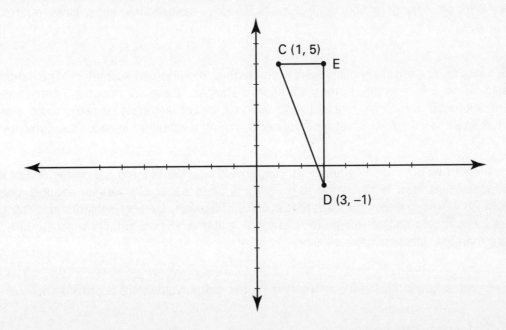

By finding the difference of the points' x coordinates (3 − 1, or 2) and the difference of their y coordinates (−1 − 5, or −6), you have found the lengths of the sides of triangle CED (2 units and 6 units—you can ignore the negative sign on the 6.) You can now use the Pythagorean theorem to find the length of the hypotenuse of triangle CED, which is the same as the length from point C to D ($2^2 + 6^2 = 40$, and the square root of 40 is approximately 6.3). Here is the distance formula in algebraic form:

$$d = \sqrt{(x_2 - x_1)^2 + (y_2 - y_1)^2}$$

Measurement

Measurement includes estimating and converting measurements within the customary and metric systems; applying procedures for using measurement to describe and compare phenomena; identifying appropriate measurement instruments, units, and procedures for measurement problems involving length, area, angles, volume, mass, time, money, and temperature; and using a variety of materials, models, and methods to explore concepts and solve problems involving measurement.

Here are some key measurement terms and ideas:

Customary units are generally the same as *U.S. units*. Customary units of length include inches, feet, yards, and miles. Customary units of weight include ounces, pounds, and tons. Customary units of capacity (or volume) include teaspoons, tablespoons, cups, pints, quarts, and gallons.

Metric units of length include millimeters, centimeters, meters, and kilometers. The centimeter is the basic metric unit of length, at least for short distances. There are about 2.5 centimeters to 1 inch. The kilometer is a metric unit of length used for longer distances. It takes more than 1.5 kilometers to make a mile. A very fast adult runner could run a kilometer in about three minutes.

Metric units of weight include grams and kilograms. The gram is the basic metric unit of mass (which for many purposes is the same as *weight*). A large paper clip weighs about 1 gram. It takes about 28 grams to make 1 ounce. Metric units of capacity include milliliters and liters. The liter is the basic metric unit of volume (or capacity). A liter is slightly smaller than a quart, so it takes more than four liters to make a gallon.

Here are some frequently used customary-to-metric ratios. Values are approximate.

1 inch = 2.54 centimeters

1 yard = 0.91 meters

1 mile = 1.61 kilometers

1 ounce = 28.35 grams

1 pound = 2.2 kilograms

1 quart = 0.94 liters

Metric-to-customary conversions can be found by taking the reciprocals of each of the factors noted above. For instance, 1 kilometer = 0.62 mile (computed by dividing 1 by 1.61).

An important step in solving problems involving measurement is to decide which area you are in; generally, such problems will fall under one of these categories: length, area, angles, volume, mass, time, money, and temperature. Solving measurement problems will likely have you calling on your knowledge in several other areas of mathematics, especially algebra. The following is one example of a measurement problem that requires knowledge of several math topics:

> Sophie's Carpet Store charges $19.40 per square yard for the type of carpeting you'd like (padding and labor included). How much will you pay to carpet your 9 foot by 12 foot room?

One way to find the solution is to convert the room dimensions to yards (3 yards by 4 yards), then multiply to get 12 square yards. Finally, multiply 12 by the price of $19.40 per square yard, for a total price of $232.80

Statistics and Probability

Measures of central tendency of a set of values include *mean*, *median*, and *mode*. The mean is found by adding all the values, then dividing the sum by the number of values. The median of a set is the middle number when the values are in numerical order. (If there is an even number of values, and therefore no middle value, the mean of the middle two values gives the median.) The mode of a set is the value occurring most often. (Not all sets of values have a single mode; some sets have more than one.) Consider the following set.

$$6 \quad 8 \quad 14 \quad 5 \quad 6 \quad 5 \quad 5$$

The mean, median, and mode of the set are 7, 6, and 5, respectively. (Note: The mean is often referred to as the average, but all three measures are averages of sorts.)

Probability theory provides models for chance variations. The *probability* of any event occurring is equal to the number of desired outcomes divided by the number of all possible events. Thus, the probability of blindly pulling a green ball out of a hat (in this case the desired outcome) if the hat contains two green and five yellow balls, is $\frac{2}{7}$ (about 29%). *Odds* are related to probability, but are different. The odds that any given event *will* occur is the ratio of the probability that the event will occur to the probability that the event *will not* occur (typically expressed as a ratio). In the example above, the odds that a green ball will be drawn are 2:5.

Statistics is the branch of mathematics that involves collecting, analyzing, and interpreting data, organizing data to describe them usefully, and drawing conclusions and making decisions. Statistics builds on probability, and typically studies "populations," meaning quantifiable groups of things. Trends and patterns not otherwise noticed may be revealed via statistics.

One key statistical concept is that of *standard deviation*. The standard deviation of a set of values tells how "tightly" all of the values are clustered around the mean of the set. When values are tightly clustered near the mean, the standard deviation is small. If values are widespread, the standard deviation is large. Here is one way to find the standard deviation of a set. Consider the set used earlier:

$$6 \quad 8 \quad 14 \quad 5 \quad 6 \quad 5 \quad 5$$

First find the mean (7). Next, find the difference of each value in the set and the mean (ignoring negative signs). This gives 1, 1, 7, 2, 1, 2, and 2. Now, you square each of those values, giving 1, 1, 49, 4, 1, 4, and 4. You next take the sum of those squares (64) and divide the sum by the number of values ($\frac{64}{7}$ = 9.14). Finally, you take the square root of 9.14, giving a standard deviation of 3.02. Think of 3.02 as the amount that the values in the set "typically" vary from the center.

Mathematical Reasoning Processes

Mathematical reasoning includes analyzing problem situations, making conjectures, organizing information, and selecting strategies to solve problems; evaluating solutions to problems; constructing arguments and judging the validity or logic of arguments; and using logical reasoning to draw and justify conclusions from given information.

Problem-solvers must rely on both formal and informal *reasoning processes*. A key informal process relies on *reasonableness*. Consider this problem:

Center Town Middle School has an enrollment of 640 students. One day, 28 students were absent. What percent of the total number of students were absent?

Even if someone forgot how to compute percents, some possible answers could be rejected instantly: 28 is a "small-but-not-tiny" chunk of 640, so answers like 1%, 18%, and 25% are *unreasonable*.

There are also formal reasoning processes, such as *deductive reasoning*. Deductive reasoning is reasoning from the general to the specific, and it is supported by deductive logic. Here is an example of deductive reasoning:

All ducks have wings (a general assertion). Donald is a duck; therefore Donald has wings (a specific proposition).

With *inductive reasoning*, a general rule is inferred from specific observations (which may be limited). Moving from the statement "All boys in this classroom are wearing jeans" (a specific but limited observation) to "All boys wear jeans" (a general assertion) is an example of inductive reasoning. Note that conclusions arrived at via deductive and inductive reasoning are not necessarily true.

Science

Chapter
12

Science, Technology, and Society

It is unworthy of excellent men to lose hours like slaves in the labor of calculation which could be relegated to anyone else if machines were used.

Gottfried Wilhelm von Leibniz (1646–1716), German polymath

Science disciplines hold to certain central values that unify them in their philosophy and methodology. Science relies on evidence collected in verifiable experiments, on conclusions validated by replication, and on theories that explain observations and that are capable of making testable predictions. Modern scientific thought traces a significant portion of its development to the work of Western European scientists, much, but far from all. It is important to recognize the contributions made by all peoples and cultures to the development of scientific knowledge. Men and women from all continents and races continue to make meaningful contributions to the advancement of science in all disciplines. Examples are readily available for enrichment and instruction from online resources.

Science can tell us how to do something, not whether we should.

Fast Facts

Technology can be loosely defined as the application of science for the benefit of mankind. For both political and economic reasons not all peoples have the same ready access to clean, safe water supplies nor to adequate food supplies, in spite of the technological capabilities that basic science has provided. Science certainly can benefit, but it too, arguably, can harm mankind and our environment. Science gives us the knowledge and tools to understand nature's principles and that knowledge can often be applied for some useful purpose. Few would debate the benefits of the wheel and axle, the electric light, the polio vaccine, or plastic. The benefits of science and technology become more complicated to evaluate when discussing the applications of gene splicing for genetically modified foods, of cloning, of nuclear energy to replace fossil fuels, or the application of atomic energy to weapons of mass destruction. Science can tell us how to do something, not whether we should.

Scientific literacy helps us participate in the decision-making process of our society as well-informed and contributing members. Real-world decisions have social, political, and economic dimensions, and scientific information is often used to both support and refute these decisions. Understanding that the inherent nature of scientific information is unbiased, and based on experimental evidence that can be reproduced by any laboratory under the same conditions can help us all make better decisions, recognize false arguments, and participate fully as active and responsible citizens.

Scientific knowledge is a body of statements of varying degrees of certainty—some most unsure, some nearly sure, but none absolutely certain . . . Now, we scientists are used to this, and we take it for granted that it is perfectly consistent to be unsure, that it is possible to live and not know.

Richard P. Feynman (1918–1988), Nobel Prize in Physics, 1965

Science education has as its goal the training of a scientifically literate public that fully participates in the economic, political, and cultural functions of our society. Scientifically literate individuals, students and teachers alike, must have knowledge that is connected and useful. The Oklahoma science curriculum, both for the preparation of preservice teachers and for K-12 instruction, is guided by this principle.

The Oklahoma curriculum operationally defines the scientifically literate individual as one who uses scientific knowledge, constructs new scientific knowledge, and reflects on scientific knowledge. Such individuals have specific science content knowledge, they build upon that knowledge through their experiences and activities, and they can evaluate objectively and critically the value and limitations of that knowledge.

SUBAREA II—SCIENCE

Competency 0008

Understand the interrelationships among the physical and life sciences and the connections among science, technology, and society.

The following topics are examples of content that may be covered under this competency.
- Apply principles of mathematics, science, and technology to model a given situation (e.g., the movement of energy and nutrients between a food chain and the physical environment).
- Analyze the effects of changes in environmental conditions (e.g., temperature, availability of water and sunlight) on plant and animal health, growth, and development.
- Analyze the effects of human activities (e.g., burning fossil fuels, clear-cutting forests) on the environment and the benefits and limitations of science and technology.
- Evaluate the use of science and technology in solving problems related to the effects of human activities on the environment (e.g., recycling, energy conservation).

Life Science

I venture to define science as a series of interconnected concepts and conceptual schemes arising from experiment and observation and fruitful of further experiments and observations. The test of a scientific theory is, I suggest, its fruitfulness.

James Bryant Conant (1893–1978), Chemist and Educator

Competency 0009

Understand the principles of life science (including biology and ecology), and use this understanding to interpret, analyze, and explain phenomena.

The following topics are examples of content that may be covered under this competency.
- Infer the life science principle (e.g., adaptation, homeostasis) illustrated in a given situation.
- Analyze relationships among the components of an ecological community.
- Analyze the factors that contribute to change in organisms and species over time.
- Analyze processes that contribute to the continuity of life (e.g., life cycles; the role of growth, repair, and maintenance).

Cells

The concept of a cell is central to our understanding of the life sciences. Cells are the simplest living unit of life, just as atoms are the building blocks of molecules, and molecules of cells. Cell Theory states that all organisms are composed of cells, that all cells arise from preexisting cells, and that the cell is the basic organizational unit of all organisms. Groups of specialized cells, or tissues, may have highly specialized characteristics and functions within an organism. A single organism may comprise only a single cell, or many billions of cells, and cells themselves range in size from the micron to many centimeters in dimension. Growth in most organisms is associated with cell division and replication, in addition to enlargement of the cells.

Classification

A dichotomous key is a tool of science that allows us to organize and classify objects by their observable traits and properties. In the life sciences, classification keys are widely used, and the simplest are based on the gross anatomy of all organisms, including plants, animals, fungi, protists, and two kingdoms of bacteria. Through comparison of the number of wings or legs, habitat, and eating habits we begin, at the earliest levels, to understand patterns in nature, constructing our own understanding of the world around us, and practice the basic elements of scientific thought and discovery.

Scientific knowledge may be classified or organized by grouping similar types of knowledge into thematic concepts. Many concepts are so broad as to find application in multiple disciplines. Cycle, for example, is a powerful concept that has widespread application throughout science, useful for both explanation and prediction. Life cycles are central to the study of biology. The recurring pattern of events in the life cycle links birth, growth, reproduction, and death. The concept of a cycle is also evident in the carbon cycle, nitrogen cycle, Krebs cycle, hydrogeologic cycle, periodic table, and many other processes, including the transformations of energy needed to sustain life. The food chain represents the complex interdependency of all plants and animals on the energy from the Sun, and the recycling of nutrients from simple to complex organisms.

Fast Facts — Life cycles are central to the study of biology.

Heredity

The discussion of life cycles brings forward the concept that the offspring of one generation bears likeness to, but also variation from, the previous generation. Some characteristics of the individual parent are passed along, while others appear not to be. We observe the connections between the visible traits of the parents and children, connections evident in all sexually reproducing organisms. It is clear that the offspring of dogs are other dogs, which generally look much like the parent dogs. Details of how such traits are conveyed through genetics are important to understand; yet instruction in these topics is allocated to the curriculum of higher grades.

Evolution

The goal of science education is to develop a scientifically literate public. At the elementary level this involves an understanding of how physical traits promote the survival of a species, how environmental changes affect species that are not adapted to those new conditions, and the role of heredity in passing and modifying the traits of successive generations. There are ample examples available to illustrate these concepts to the elementary student. A rabbit whose coat regularly turns white before the snowfall is at a temporary disadvantage, and is therefore subject to a higher degree of predation. That rabbit may not live to produce other early-white-coated rabbits. Technology, the application of knowledge for man's benefit, includes activities that are designed to select those traits that are intended to lead to healthier, stronger, and more productive crops and animals.

While the tenets of evolution as scientific theory are widely accepted, particularly as they apply to the short-term changes and adaptations within a species, the subject continues to generate some debate. To place the discussion in its proper context, some discussion of the scientific use of terms is appropriate, because the common usage of a term may differ significantly from its scientific usage. A *scientific fact* is an observation that has been repeatedly confirmed. However, scientific facts change if new observations yield new information. Frequently, the development of new, more sophisticated or precise instruments leads to such new information. A *scientific hypothesis* is a testable statement about the natural world, and as such is the starting point for most scientific experimentation. A hypothesis can generally be proven wrong, but is seldom proven right. *Scientific theories*, like atomic theory and cell theory, are well-substantiated explanations of some aspect of the natural world. A scientific theory provides a unified explanation for many related hypotheses. While a theory is generally widely accepted (e.g., through much of human history people accepted a flat Earth circled by a moving Sun), theories remain open to revision or even replacement should a better, more logical, more comprehensive or compelling explanation be found.

> A *scientific fact* is an observation that has been repeatedly confirmed.
>
> **Fast Facts**

Not all issues of our human experience are subject to the analysis and rigors of scientific experimentation and validation. Our understanding of art, poetry, philosophy, and religion rely on ways of thinking and understanding that are not necessarily subject to repeated validation through the controlled scientific experiment, or which may rely more on personal values or deference to authority. The scientifically literate individual will distinguish the role and value of scientific thought from other ways of knowing, while maintaining respect and appreciation for the ways of thinking and understanding practiced in disciplines outside of science.

Ecology

Our surroundings are a complex, interconnected system in which the living organisms exist in relationship with the soil, water, and air, linked together through chemical and physical processes, and in states of continual change or dynamic equilibrium. *Ecosystem* is the term for all the living and nonliving things in a given environment and how they interact. Scientifically literate individuals are aware of their surroundings, the interdependence of each part, and the effects that man's activities can have on those surroundings. Mutualistic and competitive relationships also exist between the organisms in an ecosystem, defining how organisms rely upon each other, and exist in competition and conflict with each other.

Energy transformations are the driving force within an ecosystem. Many organisms obtain energy from light. For example, light drives the process of photosynthesis in green plants. Solar energy also provides necessary heat for cold-blooded animals. Organisms may also derive energy from other organisms, including other plants and/or animals. When one source of energy is depleted in an ecosystem, many organisms must shift their attention to other sources of energy. For example, a bear will eat berries, fish, or nuts depending on the season. The energy pyramid for an ecosystem illustrates these relationships and identifies those organisms that are most dependent on the other organisms in the system. Higher order organisms cannot survive for long without the other organisms beneath them in the energy pyramid. The availability of adequate food within an ecosystem can be used to explain the system's functioning, the size of an animal's territory, or the effects of over-predation of a single species upon those organisms above it in the food chain.

Ecosystems change over time, both from natural processes and from the activities of man. The scientifically literate individual will be able to identify how the environment changes, how those changes impact the organisms that live there, and recognize the differences between long-term and short-term variation. Natural succession is observed when one community replaces another, for example the colonies of fungus that grow, thrive, and then are replaced by different colonies on rodent droppings held under ideal conditions.

Physical Science

All of physics is either impossible or trivial. It is impossible until you understand it, and then it becomes trivial.

Ernest Rutherford (1871–1937), Physicist, Nobel Prize for Chemistry, 1908

Competency 0010

Understand the principles of physical science (including earth science, chemistry, and physics), and use this understanding to interpret, analyze, and explain phenomena.

The following topics are examples of content that may be covered under this competency.
* Analyze factors and processes related to celestial and atmospheric phenomena (e.g., seasonal changes, the phases of the moon).
* Analyze the forces that shape the earth's surface (e.g., volcanism, erosion).

- Distinguish between physical and chemical properties of matter and between physical and chemical changes in matter.
- Infer the physical science principle (e.g., effects of common forces, conservation of energy) illustrated in a given situation.

Geosphere

Scientifically literate individuals have an understanding and appreciation for the world around them. Rocks hold an early fascination, both for their utility: as objects for throwing, skipping; and also for their beauty, texture, and diversity. Physical landforms vary considerably across the face of the Earth, revealed to the observant and thoughtful eye in road cuts, and the scenic viewpoints everywhere. On a small scale, each puddle, rivulet, and mass of sand and gravel in a yard or parking lot reveals the same actions of erosion, deposition, and graded sorting of material by size and mass that are at work on a global scale to form and reform our physical environment. The scientifically literate individual continually constructs new knowledge by study of the geosphere through direct observation, through photographs, models and samples, and through graphical representations (maps). The geosphere is the source for many natural resources essential for modern life, and the recipient of pollution caused by man's activities.

Evidence of physical changes to the geosphere is abundant, and frequently newsworthy. Each landslide, earthquake, or volcanic eruption reveals something about the Earth and its structures. Fossils, preserved remnants of or marks made by plants and animals that were once alive, are one source of evidence about changes in the environment over time. Finding fossils of marine organisms in what is now a desert is an opportunity to discuss scientific ways of knowing, of how science forms and tests hypotheses, and how theories develop to explain the reasons behind observations. The scientifically literate individual understands the concepts of uncertainty in measurement and the basis of scientific theories. Such an understanding may lead the teacher in an elementary classroom to refer to fossils and rocks simply as "very old," to dinosaurs as "living long ago," and to occasionally preface statements of scientific theory with the observation that "many scientists believe . . ."

Hydrosphere

With about seventy-five percent of the Earth's surface covered with water, the hydrosphere defines our planet and its environment. Most people live near the ocean, but few people live on, or have even experienced, the vast reaches of the world's oceans. Closer to our daily lives, and important because of the fresh water necessary to sustain life and commerce, are the rivers that pass through Oklahoma. The hydrosphere includes not just the surface waters described, but the subsurface waters of aquifers, and the water vapor present in the atmosphere. Man has a significant impact on the hydrosphere through activities that contaminate, divert, and attempt to control the flow of water. These activities can benefit one part of the environment or society while harming another.

The scientific concept of cycle is also used to describe the movement of water through its various phases, and through each part of the environment. A climate chamber formed from discarded polyethylene soda bottles can easily demonstrate these changes, and when soil, plants, and small frogs are added, a nearly complete ecosystem is formed if we count the food we add for the frog each day. In this chamber the student can observe the water cycle as liquid water evaporates, then condenses again against an ice-filled chamber to fall back to the surface. Only two phases, solid and liquid, can be observed directly, since the individual molecules of water vapor are too small to be seen by the naked eye. The white cloud visible at the tip of the teakettle, like our breath when we exhale on a cold winter day and fog, are examples of condensed water vapor (liquid water). The supply of fresh water on the Earth is limited, and water is a reusable resource that must be carefully managed. With this in mind, we are grateful for the technology to treat and purify water, which has done much to extend the human lifespan and reduce disease by providing clean and reliable sources of water in some parts of the world.

Atmosphere

The atmosphere is the layer of gases held close to the Earth by gravitational forces. In size, it has been compared with the skin on an apple. The atmosphere is densest close to the surface, where gravity holds the heavier gases and the pressure is greatest. The atmosphere becomes less dense and pressure decreases exponentially as altitude increases. All weather is contained within the lowest layer of the atmosphere (troposphere) and the temperature decreases as one rises through this layer. We can often observe the top of this layer as clouds form anvil-shaped tops when they cannot rise further than the height of the cold boundary between the lowest layer (troposphere) and the overlying layer (stratosphere).

The concept of cycle reappears in the discussion of the recurring patterns of weather, and the progression of the seasons. The basis of the seasons has much more to do with the angle of light striking the Earth, and very little to do with the distance from the Sun. Classroom weather stations and weather charts are useful learning tools, and projects to build thermometers, hygrometers, and barometers are popular in classrooms.

Density variations related to temperature drive the movement of air. Heat energy warms the air and increases water evaporation, warm air expands and rises above cooler surrounding air, rising air cools and water vapor condenses forming clouds and precipitation. Cold, heavy air settles over the polar caps and flows toward the equator, generally leading to weather trends that bring cold northerly winds into Oklahoma for part of the winter. Temperature gradients and the resulting air movement are readily observed at home where the basement is cool, the upstairs warmer, and a draft is often felt when sitting near the stairway.

Space Science

The concept of cycle again finds application in the periodic movement of the Sun and planets. The size of objects, and distances between them, are difficult to represent on the same scale. The National Mall in Washington, D.C., contains a 1/10,000,000,000th-scale solar system model in which the Sun is the size of a grapefruit, and Pluto, located some 650 yards away, is the size of a poppy seed. The openness of space is mirrored at a much smaller scale by vast open spaces between atoms and between nuclei and their electrons.

A ball rolling down the aisle of a school bus appears, to observers sitting on the bus, to swerve to the right and hit the wall as the bus makes a left-hand turn. To an observer outside the bus, the ball continued its straight-line motion until acted upon by a force, often resulting from a collision with the wall. For centuries the best science available held that the Sun rose in the east and set in the west. As scientific instruments developed and improved (telescopes for example), scientists collected new information that challenged old theories. New theories are not always well received, a fact to which Galileo would attest. We now understand that the Sun is the gravitational center of the solar system, and that the planet's motions are defined by their path along an elliptical orbit defined by its speed and its continual gravitational attraction to the Sun.

Matter and Energy

Broadly speaking, our experiences with the world involve interactions with and between matter and energy. The physical sciences give us a clearer understanding and appreciation of our surroundings and the way we interact with and affect those surroundings. Matter can be described and distinguished by its chemical and physical properties. Physical properties, such as color and density, are termed *intrinsic* when they do not change as the amount of the matter changes. Properties like mass or volume do vary when matter is added or removed, and these are termed "extrinsic properties." Mass is the amount of matter in an object, which is sometimes measured using a lever arm balance. Weight, although sometimes incorrectly used interchangeably with mass, is a measure of the force of gravity experienced by an object, often determined using a spring scale. An electronic scale may display an object's mass in grams, but it is dependant on gravity for its operation. Such a device is only accurate after using a calibration mass to adjust the electronics for the unique local gravitational force. While we may say an object is "weightless" as it floats inside the space shuttle, it is still affected by the gravitational forces from both the Earth and Sun, which keep it in orbit around each. The force of gravity is proportional to the product of the masses of the two objects under consideration divided by the square of the distance between them. Earth, being larger and more massive than Mars, has proportionally higher gravitational forces. This is the basis of the observation in H. G. Wells' *The War of the Worlds* that the Martian invaders were "the most sluggish things I ever saw crawl."

Density, the ratio of mass to volume, is an intrinsic property that depends on the matter, but not the amount of matter. Volume is defined as the amount of space an object occupies. The density of a 5-ton cube of pure copper is the same as that of a small copper penny. However, the modern penny is a thin shell of copper over a zinc plug, and the density of this coin is significantly lower than that of the older pure copper coin. Density is related to buoyancy. Objects sink, in liquids or gases alike, if they are denser than the material that surrounds them. Archimedes' principle, also related to density, states that an object is buoyed up by a force equal to the mass of the material the object displaces. Thus, a 160-lb concrete canoe will easily float in water if the volume of the submerged portion is equal to the volume of 20 gallons of water (water is approximately 8 lbs/gal × 20 gal = 160 lbs). Density is not the same as viscosity, a measure of thickness or flowability. The strength of intermolecular forces between molecules determines, for example, that molasses is slow in January, or that hydrogen bromide is a gas in any season.

All matter is composed of atoms, or combinations of atoms selected from among the more than one hundred elements. The atom is the smallest particle of an element that retains the properties of the element; similarly, the molecule is the smallest particle of a compound. Molecules cannot be separated into smaller particles (atoms or smaller) without a chemical change disrupting the chemical bonds that bind the molecule together. Physical separations, through the use of filter paper, centrifuge, or magnet for example, do not affect chemical bonds. The scientific concept of a cycle, in this case without a time dependence, is evident in the fundamental makeup of matter and reflected in the structure of the periodic table. Mendeleev is credited with the development of the modern periodic table, in part for his predicting the existence of then-unknown elements based on the repeating trends in reactivity and physical properties. The concepts associated with atoms and molecules are not found in the elementary benchmarks, but they should be well understood by the elementary teacher nonetheless, as they provide the basis of all our understanding of matter and chemical change.

Energy is loosely scientifically defined as the ability to do work. Kinetic energy is the energy of motion ($KE = 1/2mv^2$), where m is the mass and v the velocity of an object. Chemical energy is stored in the bonds of our food, held for later conversion to kinetic energy and heat in our bodies. Potential energy is held in an icicle hanging off the roof ($PE = mgh$) where m is mass, g is the gravitational force constant, and h is the height. When the icicle falls, its potential energy is converted to kinetic energy, and then to sound energy as it hits the pavement, and additional kinetic energy as the fragments skitter off. At the elementary level, students need to be able to identify the types of energy involved in various phenomena and identify the conversions between types. In the popular Rube Goldberg competitions, students use a number of sequential energy conversions to perform a simple task like breaking a balloon or flipping a pancake. Energy is conserved in each of these normal processes, converted to less useful forms (e.g., heat) but not created nor destroyed. Similarly, matter is never created or destroyed in a normal chemical reaction. Nuclear fusion is an obvious exception to both rules, following Einstein's equation $E = mc^2$; however, these reactions are generally not allowed in the classroom or school laboratory.

Students gain useful experience with energy conversions as they study simple electrical circuits and chemical dry cells. The dry cell produces electrical energy from chemical potential energy. The size of the dry cell is proportional to the amount of starting material, and thus the available current, but not the electromotive force or voltage, which is an intrinsic property. The D cell produces the same 1.5-volt potential as the AAA cell; the difference is in how long they can maintain the flow of current in the circuit. The battery is dead when when one or more of the starting materials has been depleted, or when the essential electrolytic fluid leaks or dries out. The measured cell voltage depends on the oxidation and reduction potentials and of the half-reactions involved and on the concentration of each chemical species. When a cell reaches equilibrium, the measured cell potential and free energy of the cell both reach zero.

Seldom do we find chemical reactants present in the precise quantities to match the stoichiometric ratio indicated by the chemical equation defining a reaction. In a battery, or any reaction for that matter, one of the chemicals will be depleted before the others. The concept of a limiting reactant is important in chemistry, whereby one reactant is consumed before the other, similar to the summer BBQ where hot dogs are in packages of ten, but the buns are in packages of eight. In contrast, how quickly a battery drains is linked to the rates of chemical reactions (kinetics), dependent on temperature, concentration, and the presence of a catalyst. Many chemical reactions involve multiple steps, where one step, the rate-limiting step, controls the rate of the entire process. This is much like the child in the family who is always the last one to get in the car when everyone else is in a hurry.

Simple dry cells do not pose a serious safety hazard—always an issue in hands-on activities—and are thus good for student experiments. A series connection linking dry cells in a chain increases the overall voltage, and thus the brightness of the bulb, a parallel connection with batteries placed in the circuit (like rungs in a ladder) increases the effective size of the cell but the voltage remains the same.

Changes in Matter

Scientific theories have their utility in providing a unified explanation for diverse and varied observations. Atomic theory, which views atoms and molecules as the fundamental building blocks of all matter, would be modified or abandoned if it didn't also explain other observations. Snow tracked into the kitchen quickly melts before either evaporating or being absorbed into someone's socks, which then must be hung by the fire to dry. In either of these changes the fundamental particles of water are the same, an assembly of three atoms held by covalent (shared electron) bonds in a bent molecular geometry associated with polar molecules. New attractions are possible between polar water molecules and the ions formed when some compounds are dissolved in solution. The relative strength of the new attractions to the water overcomes the attractions within the pure solid, allowing the solid to dissolve and in some cases dissociate in solution. Insoluble compounds do not dissolve because the strength of the attractions within the solid exceeds those available between the molecules and/or ions and the solvent.

Phase changes are also explained using atomic theory. Evaporation from a liquid occurs when individual molecules gain sufficient energy to break free from the intermolecular attractions in the liquid phase. The stronger the intermolecular attractions, the lower the vapor pressure and the higher the boiling point. The boiling point is the temperature at which the vapor pressure of molecules leaving solution equals the atmospheric pressure. Lowering the atmospheric pressure above a liquid makes it easier for the highest energy liquid molecules to escape, thus the boiling point is lower. Cooking while camping at high altitudes requires more time and, thus, more fuel because food cooks slower as a result of the lowered boiling temperature.

All matter has a temperature above the theoretical value of absolute zero because all matter is in continual motion. In a balloon filled with nitrogen gas, some molecules are moving relatively fast, others relatively slowly. The temperature of the gas is a measure of this motion, a measure of the average kinetic energy of the particles. Molecules are very small and fast moving, and there are vast empty spaces between them. The average speed of nitrogen molecules at 25°C is over 500 meters per second, whereas the lighter hydrogen molecules have an average speed in excess of 1,900 meters per second. One cubic centimeter of air at room temperature and normal pressure contains roughly 24,500,000,000,000,000,000 molecules (2.45×10^{19} molecules). The same quantity of water would contain roughly 3.34×10^{22} water molecules, while the same one cubic centimeter of copper would contain roughly 8.5×10^{22} copper atoms. The differences between these numbers are not nearly as large as the numbers themselves, yet the differences are readily observable. Gases have significant empty spaces between the molecules and thus can be compressed, whereas liquids and solids have less or no compressibility, respectively. If air enters the lines of hydraulic brake systems, the pedal depresses easily as the trapped gas compresses instead of having the non-compressible liquid transfer the motion into braking power.

While the atoms and molecules of all materials are in constant motion (vibrational energy), those in gases and liquids are also free to move about their own axes (rotational energy), and about the container (translational energy). Increasing the temperature of a solid imparts additional energy, which increases the vibrational energy. Once any particular atom or molecule gains sufficient energy to break free of the intermolecular attractions to the bulk solid or liquid it will slip or fly away (melt or evaporate, respectively). Hotter atoms require more space in which to vibrate. For this reason wagon wheel rims are heated in the forge to expand the metal before slipping the rim onto the wheel, basketballs left outside on a cold night don't bounce well, and in thermometers the expansion of alcohol or mercury is used to indicate temperature.

Motion

The motion of atoms and molecules is essential to our understanding of matter at the molecular level, but we have many examples of motion readily available on the macroscopic level in the world around us. Many an idle moment can be passed with a young child timing small athletic feats: for example, "How long will it take you to run to that tree and back?" or "The time to beat is 8.65 seconds; who can do it faster?" These experiences provide an informal experience with measurements of motion that serve as the basis for more scientific descriptions of speed, direction and changes of speed.

We can use time and motion to evaluate other chemical and physical phenomena. The periodic motion of a pendulum can be timed to determine the period, and experiments devised to explore the effect of pendulum mass, string length or amount of initial deflection. Hook's law can be studied by timing the vibrations of a spring. Chemical kinetics can be studied by timing reactions and observing changes in absorbance, conductivity, or pH. The growth rates of seedlings can be studied as a function of soil, water, and light conditions. Such activities provide a natural framework to teach the concepts of scientific exploration, control of variables, collection, and presentation of data.

Waves and Vibrations

Waves are one mechanism of energy transport from one location to another. We experience waves directly in the forms of light, sound and water, and indirectly through radio and TV, wireless networks, and X-rays. Waves are periodic in their nature, and the concept of periodicity (cycles) is one of the key interdisciplinary concepts that include the motions of planets, the properties of elements, life cycles of plants and animals, and many other events. Energy is transmitted through a material in a translational wave when in water. For example, particles of water move perpendicular to the direction of energy travel. A wave with greater energy has greater amplitude. AM radio refers to amplitude modulation of the radio signal, where the carrier wave amplitude is modified by adding the amplitudes of the voice or music waves to create a cumulative and more complex wave form. The receiver must subtract from this complex waveform the simple sinusoidal waveform of the carrier to leave the voice or music.

Compressional waves, like sound, are characterized by having the media move along the same axis as the direction of energy travel. The speed of sound waves is dependent on the medium through which it travels, faster in denser materials like railroad track, and faster in water than through air, yet faster in warm air than colder air. Cold air is denser, but the gas molecules in warm air move faster and more quickly convey the sound energy. Sound cannot travel in a vacuum (referring to the absence of all matter in a given space) because, as a compressional wave, it needs to have particles to compress as it travels.

Light is energy, and darkness is the absence of that energy. A shadow is not "cast" by an object, but rather the stream of light energy is blocked by the object, leaving an area of darkness. A black light behaves like any other, giving off light energy, yet at frequencies too high and wavelengths too short for our eyes to see (thus the light appears black to us). Some objects held beneath a black light absorb the energy from the ultraviolet light, and reemit this light at slightly lower wavelengths that our eyes can see, giving them the appearance that they glow in the dark. Laundry soaps with whiteners and brighteners contain additives that do something similar, converting portions of the invisible UV radiation from the Sun into lower frequency near-UV and additional visible light to make your "whites whiter." Since deer are more sensitive to near-UV wavelengths than humans, hunters are careful to launder their camouflage hunting clothes with soaps that do not contain such whiteners.

White light comprises all the visible wavelengths. Color is a property that light already has. White light passing through a prism, raindrop, or spectroscope can be separated into its constituent colors. An object appears red because it, or the dye molecules it contains, reflects the red wavelengths constituent in the white light that strike it. If a red shirt is illuminated by a blue light the shirt will appear black because there is no red light for it to reflect. Blue paint reflects blue light from a white source, and yellow paint reflects yellow. Mixing the paints gives a material that reflects blue and yellow light, and our eye sees the mixture as green. A blue filter placed before a white light allows only the blue light to pass, absorbing all other wavelengths. A red shirt, when viewed through a blue filter, will appear black because the shirt can only reflect red light, but the filter can only pass blue light. The phosphors of our TV screen are in sets of red, green, and blue, which when illuminated together release white light.

Principles and Processes of Scientific Investigations

Happy is he who gets to know the reasons for things.

Virgil (70–19 BCE), Roman poet

Competency 0011

Apply inquiry skills and processes to communicate scientific information and interpret natural phenomena.

The following topics are examples of content that may be covered under this competency.

*   Draw conclusions and make generalizations based on examination of given experimental results.
*   Interpret data presented in one or more graphs, charts, or tables to determine patterns or relationships.
*   Apply mathematical rules or formulas (including basic statistics) to analyze given experimental or observational data.
*   Evaluate the appropriateness of different types of graphic representations to communicate given scientific data.

Collecting and Presenting Data

The male has more teeth than the female in mankind, and sheep and goats, and swine. This has not been observed in other animals. Those persons which have the greatest number of teeth are the longest lived; those which have them widely separated, smaller, and more scattered, are generally more short lived.

Aristotle (384–322 BCE), Greek philosopher

Scientifically literate individuals have detailed and accurate content knowledge that is the basis of their scientific knowledge. They do not strive to recall every detail of that knowledge, but build conceptual frameworks upon which prior knowledge, as well as new learning, is added. From this framework of facts, concepts, and theories the scientifically literate individual can reconstruct forgotten facts, and use this information to answer new questions not previously considered. The scientifically literate individual is a lifelong learner who asks questions that can be answered using scientific knowledge and techniques.

Science is based upon experimentation, but not all knowledge is derived daily from first principles. The scientifically literate individual is informed by existing knowledge, and is knowledgeable about the sources, accuracy, and value of each source. Not every source is equally reliable, accurate, or valid. Classroom teachers are advised to use trusted educational sites such as those sponsored by the Oklahoma State Department of Education, which lists links at *www.sde.state.ok.us*.

Scientifically literate individuals must be able to evaluate critically the information and evidence they collect, and the conclusions or theories to which that information and evidence leads. Such analysis incorporates an understanding of the limitations to knowledge in general, and the limitations of all measurements and information based on the quality of the experimental design. The literate individual can evaluate claims for scientific merit, identify conflicting evidence and weigh the value and credibility of conflicting information. They can also recognize that not every question can be answered using scientific knowledge, valuing the contributions of other cultures and other ways of knowing, including art, philosophy, and theology.

Scientific information is communicated to nonscientific audiences in order to inform, guide policy and influence the practices that affect all of society. This information is presented through text, tables, charts, figures, pictures, models, and other representations that require interpretation and analysis. Scientifically literate individuals can read and interpret these representations, and select appropriate tools to present the information they gather.

Competency 0012

Understand principles and procedures related to the design and implementation of observational and experimental scientific investigations.

The following topics are examples of content that may be covered under this competency.
- Distinguish among the features of a given experimental design (e.g., dependent and independent variables, control and experimental groups).
- Formulate hypotheses based on reasoning and preliminary results or information.
- Evaluate the validity of a scientific conclusion in a given situation.
- Apply procedures for the care and humane treatment of animals and the safe and appropriate use of equipment in the laboratory.

Experimental Design

It is a capital mistake to theorise before one has data. Insensibly one begins to twist facts to suit theories instead of theories to suit facts.

Sherlock Holmes, the fictional creation of Arthur Conan Doyle (1859–1930), British physician and novelist

When a bat bites Gilligan, first mate of TV's ill-fated *S.S. Minnow*, he is convinced that he will turn into a vampire. Seemingly, no amount of reassurance by the Professor will convince him otherwise because, he claims, he saw the movie three times and it always came out the same way. We trust the results of experiments, both formal and informal, to help us understand our surroundings. Unfortunately, without proper control of the variables and a sound experimental design, our observations may lead us to entirely wrong-headed or incorrect conclusions.

Scientific Method

The scientific method is not a specific six-step method that is rigorously followed whenever a question arises that can be answered using the knowledge and techniques of science. Rather, it is a process of observation and analysis that is used to develop a reliable, consistent, and nonarbitrary representation and understanding of our world. We can use the scientific method (observation and description, formulation of hypotheses, prediction based on hypotheses, and tests of predictions) for many, but not all questions. The approach is best applied to situations in which the experimenter can control the variables, eliminating or accounting for all extraneous factors, and perform repeated independent tests wherein only one variable is changed at a time.

The science fair project is a common tool for instruction in the scientific method. Many formal and informal sources, often Web based, provide lists of suggested science fair topics, but not all are experiments. For the youngest students it is appropriate and useful for the focus to be upon models and demonstrations, for example the solar system model, volcano, or clay cross-section of an egg. Later the students should move to true experiments where the focus is on identifying a testable hypothesis, and controlling all experimental variables but the one of interest. Many projects may be elevated from model or demonstration to experiment. A proposal to demonstrate how windmills work can be made an experiment when the student adds quantitative measurements designed to measure one variable while varying only one other and while holding all other variables constant. For example, using an electric fan, the number of rotations per minute can be measured as a function of the fan setting (low, medium, or high). However, while keeping the fan setting constant, several different experiments could vary any one of the following variables: number of fins, size of fins, or shape of fins while in each case measuring the rotational speed.

Health and Safety

Through active, hands-on activities, science instruction is made a richer and more meaningful experience. From simple observations and activities at early grades, through detailed controlled experiments at higher grades, students who do science to learn science understand science better. While students are engaged in the process of discovery and exploration, the teacher must be engaged in protecting the health and safety of these students. The hazards vary with the discipline, and thoughtful planning and management of the activities will significantly reduce the risks to students. In all cases, students must utilize appropriate personal hygiene (hand washing) and wear personal protective equipment (goggles, gloves) while engaged in laboratory or field activities. Substitution of less hazardous materials whenever possible is a high priority. For example, in the physical sciences, replace mercury thermometers with alcohol or electronic, replace glass beakers and graduated cylinders with durable polyethylene, and eliminate or reduce the use of hazardous chemicals. In the earth sciences, rocks and minerals used in class should not contain inherently hazardous materials, students should not be allowed to taste the minerals, and reagents like HCl used for identification of carbonate minerals should be dispensed from spill-proof plastic containers. In the life sciences, special care should be given to topics such as safe practices for sharps, the safe handling of living organisms, and the care and use of microscopes. Experiments or activities involving the collection or culture of human cells or fluids should be discouraged, and proper sterilization procedures followed to prevent the growth or spread of disease agents. When they are possible, outdoor, museum, and other field activities can bring a valuable enrichment to the science curriculum in all disciplines. They also bring additional responsibilities for the safe planning and implementation of activities that increase student learning while maintaining the health and safety of the students.

Health
and Fitness

SUBAREA III—HEALTH AND FITNESS

Competency 0013

> **Understand basic principles and practices of personal, interpersonal, and community health and safety; and apply related attitudes, knowledge, and skills (e.g., decision making, problem solving) to promote personal well-being.**
>
> The following topics are examples of content that may be covered under this competency.
> * Apply decision-making and problem-solving skills and procedures in individual and group situations, including situations related to personal well-being, self-esteem, and interpersonal relationships.
> * Analyze contemporary health-related problems (e.g., HIV, teenage pregnancy, suicide, substance abuse) in terms of their causes and effects on individuals, families, and society; and evaluate strategies for their prevention.
> * Analyze the effects of specific practices (e.g., related to nutrition, exercise) and attitudes on lifelong personal health.
> * Analyze relationships between environmental conditions and personal and community health and safety.

Competency 0014

> **Understand physical education concepts and practices related to the development of personal well-being.**
>
> The following topics are examples of content that may be covered under this competency.

- Recognize activities that promote the development of motor skills (e.g., locomotor, manipulative, body mechanics), perceptual awareness skills (e.g., body awareness, spatial and directional awareness), and fitness (e.g., endurance, flexibility).
- Apply safety concepts and practices associated with physical activities (e.g., doing warm-up exercises, wearing protective equipment).
- Understand skills necessary for successful participation in given sports and activities (e.g., dodging, spatial orientation, eye-body coordination).
- Analyze ways in which participation in individual or group sports or physical activities can promote personal well-being (e.g., self-discipline, respect for self and others) and interpersonal skills (e.g., cooperation, leadership).

The health and physical education review section offers a perspective on the importance of maintaining a healthy mind and body as well as demonstrating how the two work in conjunction. This section includes discussions of cardiovascular fitness, nutrition, team sports, and the role of athletics. Preparing your mind through study will leave you in great shape to succeed on test day.

Health and Safety

Benefits of Diet and Exercise

One of the primary reasons for teaching physical education is to instill a willingness to exercise. To that end, it is important to understand the benefits of participating in a lifelong program of exercise and physical fitness.

Fortunately, it is not difficult to find justification for exercising and maintaining a consistently high level of fitness. The benefits of a consistent program of diet and exercise are many. Improved cardiac output, improved maximum oxygen intake, and improvement of the blood's ability to carry oxygen are just a few. Exercise also lowers the risk of heart disease by strengthening the heart muscle, lowering pulse and blood pressure, and lowering the concentration of fat in both the body and the blood. It can also improve appearance, increase range of motion, and lessen the risk of back problems associated with weak bones and osteoporosis.

Good Nutrition

Along with exercise, a knowledge of and participation in a healthy lifestyle are vital to good health and longevity. What constitutes good nutrition, the role of vitamins, elimination of risk factors, and strategies to control weight are all part of a healthy lifestyle.

Complex carbohydrates should constitute at least half the diet. This is important because these nutrients are the primary and most efficient source of energy. Examples of complex carbohydrates are vegetables, fruits, high-fiber breads, and cereals. Fiber in the diet is very important because it promotes digestion, reduces constipation, and has been shown to help reduce the risk of colon cancer. Another benefit of complex carbohydrates is that they are high in water content, which is vital to the functioning of the entire body.

Proteins should constitute about one-fifth of the diet. Protein builds and repairs the body. Sources of protein are beans, peas, lentils, peanuts, and other pod plants. Another source is red meat, which unfortunately contains a great deal of saturated fat.

There are two categories of fat: unsaturated, which is found in vegetables, and saturated, which comes from animals or vegetables. Cocoa butter, palm oil, and coconut oil are saturated fats that come from vegetables. Unsaturated vegetable fats are preferable to saturated fats because they appear to offset the rise in blood pressure that accompanies too much saturated fat. These fats may also lower cholesterol and help with weight loss. Whole milk products contain saturated fat, but the calcium found in them is vital to health. For this reason, most fat-limiting diets suggest the use of skim milk and low-fat cheese.

Research indicates a link between high-fat diets and many types of cancer. Diets high in saturated fats are also dangerous because fats cause the body to produce too much low-density lipoprotein in the system. Cholesterol, a substance found only in animals, is of two different kinds: LDL (low-density lipoproteins) and HDL (high-density lipoproteins). Some cholesterol is essential in order for the body to function properly. It is vital to the brain and is an important component in the creation of certain hormones. LDLs raise the probability of heart disease by encouraging the buildup of plaque in the arteries. HDLs do just the opposite. LDL can be controlled through proper diet, and HDL cholesterol levels can be raised by exercise. The body produces cholesterol in the liver. Excess cholesterol found in the blood of so many people usually comes from cholesterol in their diet rather than from internal production. Triglycerides are another form of fat found in the blood. It is important to monitor them because high triglycerides seem to be inversely proportional to HDLs.

Vitamins and Minerals

Vitamins are essential to good health. One must be careful, however, not to take too much of certain vitamins. Fat soluble vitamins—A, D, E, and K—will be stored in the body, and excessive amounts will cause some dangerous side effects. The remaining vitamins are water soluble and are generally excreted through the urinary system and the skin when taken in excess. A brief synopsis of the vitamins and minerals needed by the body follows:

- Vitamin A: Needed for normal vision, prevention of night blindness, healthy skin, resistance to disease, and tissue growth and repair. Found in spinach, carrots, broccoli and other dark green or yellow orange fruits and vegetables; also found in liver and plums.

- Vitamin D: Promotes absorption of calcium and phosphorus, and needed for normal growth of healthy bones, teeth, and nails. Formed by the action of the sun on the skin.

Also found in halibut liver oil, herring, cod liver oil, mackerel, salmon, and tuna, and is added to many milk products.

- Vitamin E: Protects cell membranes; seems to improve elasticity in blood vessels; also may prevent formation of blood clots and protect red blood cells from damage by oxidation. Found in wheat germ oil, sunflower seeds, raw wheat germ, almonds, pecans, peanut oil, and cod liver oil.

- Thiamin/B_1: Needed for functioning of nerves, muscle growth, and fertility and for production of energy, appetite, and digestion. Found in pork, legumes, nuts, enriched and fortified whole grains, and liver.

- Riboflavin/B_2: Aids in the production of red blood cells, good vision, healthy skin and mouth tissue, and production of energy. Found in lean meat, dairy products, liver, eggs, enriched and fortified whole grains, and green leafy vegetables.

- Niacin/B_3: Promotes energy production, appetite, healthy digestive and nervous system, and healthy skin.

- Pyridoxine/B_6: Promotes red blood cell formation and growth. Found in liver, beans, pork, fish, legumes, enriched and fortified whole grains, and green leafy vegetables.

- Vitamin B_{12}: Promotes healthy nerve tissue, energy production, utilization of folic acid; also aids in the formation of healthy red blood cells. Found in dairy products, liver, meat, poultry, fish, and eggs.

- Vitamin C: Promotes healing and growth, resists infection, increases iron absorption, and aids in bone and tooth formation/repair. Found in citrus fruits, cantaloupe, potatoes, strawberries, tomatoes, and green vegetables.

- Sodium: Maintains normal water balance inside and outside cells; is a factor in blood pressure regulation and electrolyte and chemical balance. Found in salt, processed foods, bread, and bakery products.

- Potassium: Prevents muscle weakness and cramping; important for normal heart rhythm and electrolyte balance in the blood. Found in citrus fruits, leafy green vegetables, potatoes, and tomatoes.

- Zinc: Taste, appetite, healthy skin, and wound healing. Found in lean meat, liver, milk, fish, poultry, whole grain cereals, and shellfish.

- Iron: Red blood cell formation, oxygen transport to the cells; prevents nutritional anemia. Found in liver, lean meats, dried beans, peas, eggs, dark green leafy vegetables, and whole grain cereals.

- Calcium: Strong bones, teeth, nails, muscle tone; prevents osteoporosis and muscle cramping; helps the nerves function and the heart beat. Found in milk, yogurt, and other dairy products, and dark leafy vegetables.

- Phosphorus: Regulates blood chemistry and internal processes; helps build strong bones and teeth. Found in meat, fish, poultry, and dairy products.

- Magnesium: Energy production, normal heart rhythm, nerve/muscle function; prevents muscle cramps. Found in dried beans, nuts, whole grains, bananas, and leafy green vegetables.

Weight Control Strategies

Statistics show that Americans get fatter every year. Even though countless books and magazine articles are written on the subject of weight control, often the classroom is the only place a student gets reliable information about diet. For example, it is an unfortunate reality that fat people do not live as long, on average, as thin ones. Being overweight has been isolated as a risk factor in various cancers, heart disease, gall bladder problems, and kidney disease. Chronic diseases such as diabetes and high blood pressure are also aggravated by, or caused by, being overweight.

Conversely, a great many problems are presented by being underweight. Our society often places too much value on losing weight, especially for women. Ideal weight as well as a good body-fat ratio is the goal when losing weight. Exercise is the key to a good body-fat ratio. Exercise helps to keep the ratio down, thus improving cholesterol levels, and helps in preventing heart disease.

In order to lose weight, calories burned must exceed calories taken in. No matter what kind of diet is tried, this principle applies. There is no easy way to maintain a healthy weight. Here again, the key is exercise. If calorie intake is restricted too much, the body goes into starvation mode and operates by burning fewer calories. Just a 250-calorie drop per day combined with a 250-calorie burn will result in a loss of one pound a week. Crash diets, which bring about rapid weight loss, are not only unhealthy but also ineffective. Slower weight loss is more lasting. Aerobic exercise is the key to successful weight loss. Exercise speeds up metabolism and causes the body to burn calories. Timing of exercise will improve the benefits. Exercise before meals speeds up metabolism and has been shown to suppress appetite. Losing and maintaining weight is not easy. Through education, people will be better able to realize that losing weight is hard work and is a constant battle.

Another aspect of health concerns awareness and avoidance of the health risks that are present in our everyday lives. Some risk factors include being overweight, smoking, using drugs, having unprotected sex, and stress. Students should learn the consequences of using drugs, both legal and illegal, and they should learn at least one of the several ways to reduce stress that are commonly used in most elementary schools. Education is the key to minimizing the presence of these risk factors. Unfortunately, because of the presence of peer pressure and the lack of parental control, the effect of education is sometimes not enough.

Family Health

The role of the family in health education deserves special consideration. The "family" includes people who provide unconditional love, understanding, long-term commitment, and encouragement. Variations in family living patterns in our society include, for example, nuclear and extended families, single-parent families, and blended families. Children from all types of families deserve equal consideration and respect; they should get it at least in the classroom, because they often do not in the larger society.

Community Health

The health of students and their families depends not only on individual and family decisions, but on the factors involving the wider society. One of these factors is advertising, which often encourages children to make unhealthy decisions. Students as young as kindergarten and first grade can learn how to recognize advertisements (e.g., for candy or sugar-laden cereal) that might lead them to unhealthy behavior, and by third or fourth grade, they should be able to demonstrate that they are able to make health-related decisions regarding advertisements in various media.

In addition, any studies of the physical environment—in science, social studies, or other subjects—should be related to health whenever possible. Examples include the effects of pollution on health, occupational-related disease (e.g., "black lung" disease and the effects of chemicals on soldiers), and the differences in health care options available to people in different parts of the world and in different economic circumstances.

Differentiation between communicable and noncommunicable disease can be taught at the youngest grade levels. Very young children should learn to wash their hands frequently, for instance. Older children should be able to explain the transmission and prevention of communicable disease, and all children should learn which diseases cannot be transmitted through casual contact.

Movement and Physical Fitness

Principles of Cardiovascular Fitness

Cardiovascular fitness, or aerobic capacity, is the ability of the entire body to work together efficiently—to be able to do the most amount of work with the least amount of effort. Cardiovascular fitness is composed of four basic components: strength and power; endurance; movement speed and flexibility; and agility. Training is required to develop consistent aerobic capacity, and training is composed of several principles. To begin, a warm-up is essential. An effective warm-up will increase body temperature and blood flow, and it will guard against strains and tears to muscles, tendons, and ligaments. A good warm-up consists of stretching exercises, calisthenics, walking, and slow jogging. Although children have trouble understanding the importance of warm-up, they should get into the habit of doing it, because it will be particularly important as they grow older.

While exercising, a student must be aware of his or her body's adaptations to the demands imposed by training. Some of these adaptations are improved heart function and circulation, improved respiratory function, and improved strength and endurance. All of these lead to improved vigor and vitality. In order to effect these adaptations, the students must exert themselves to a far greater degree than their normal daily activities. This exertion is referred to as ***overload***. Despite what this term suggests, it does not imply that children should work beyond healthy limits. However, it does imply that they must push themselves in order to see results. The rate of improvement and adaptation is directly related to the frequency, intensity, and duration of training.

In addition to regular training, you must gear your students' training toward those adaptations that are important to them. This is known as ***specificity***. Performance improves when the training is specific to the activity being performed. That is, certain activities will have more effect on cardiovascular health than on overall muscle tone and appearance, and vice versa. Therefore, you should always try to maintain a balance in the exercise you assign.

The body thrives on activity, and therefore the axiom "use it or lose it" certainly holds true. Lack of activity can cause many problems, including flabby muscles, a weak heart, poor circulation, shortness of breath, obesity, and a degenerative weakening of the skeletal system. It is important to note, however, that when many people begin a program of exercise, they expect to see results immediately. More often than not, this is not the case. Individual response to exercise varies greatly from person to person. This can be affected by heredity, age, general cardiovascular fitness, rest and sleep habits, an individual's motivation, environmental influences, and any handicap, disease, or injury that may impede the body's adaptation to training. The sum of all these factors is an individual's potential for maximizing their own cardiovascular fitness. Unfortunately, very few people live up to this full potential.

Finally, a good program of exercise always ends with a cooling-off period. Very much like the warm-up, and just as essential, the same low-impact exercises used during a warm-up may be used to cool off after a period of intense exertion. Without cooling off, blood will pool and slow the removal of waste products. With this basic introduction in mind, let's look at some more specific forms of exercise and the positive effects they have on the body.

Aerobic Exercise

Aerobic exercise involves both muscle contraction and movement of the body. Aerobic exercise requires large amounts of oxygen and, when done regularly, will condition the cardiovascular system. Some aerobic exercises are especially suited to developing aerobic training benefits, with a minimum of skill and time involved. Examples of good aerobic activities are walking, running, swimming, rope skipping, and bicycling. These activities are especially good in the development of fitness because all of them can be done alone and with a minimum of special equipment. In order to be considered true aerobic conditioning, an activity must require a great deal of oxygen, must be continuous and rhythmic, must exercise major muscle groups and burn fat as an energy source, and must last for at least 20 minutes at an individual's target heart rate. You may determine the target heart rate by subtracting 80% of your age from 220 for adolescents; healthy younger children do not need to be restricted to an arbitrary limit on heart rate during exercise.

Interval training is also a good way to develop fitness. This type of exercise involves several different aerobic activities performed at intervals to create one exercise session. If a student learns about interval training, she will be better able to create her own fitness program.

Low-Impact Aerobics

For some people, low-impact aerobics may have some advantages over traditional, or high-impact, aerobics. Because low-impact aerobic exercise is easier to perform, it is an option for all ages and levels of fitness. It is easier to monitor heart rate, and there is less warm-up and cool-down required. Because one foot is on the ground at all times, there is less chance of injury. In all other respects, such as duration and frequency, low-impact aerobic exercise is identical to high-impact.

Anatomy and Physiology

Anatomy describes the structure, position, and size of various organs. Because our bones adapt to fill a specific need, exercise is of great benefit to the skeletal system. Bones that anchor strong muscles thicken to withstand the stress. Weight-bearing bones can develop heavy mineral deposits while supporting the body. Because joints help provide flexibility and ease of movement, it is important to know how each joint moves. Types of joints are ball and socket (shoulder and hip), hinge (knee), pivot (head of the spine), gliding (carpal and tarsal bones), angular (wrist and ankle joints), partially moveable (vertebrae), and immovable (bones of the adult cranium).

Muscles are the active movers in the body. In order to teach any physical education activity properly, the functions and physiology of the muscles must be understood. Since muscles move by shortening, or contracting, proper form should be taught so the student can get the most out of an activity. It is also important to know the location of each muscle. This knowledge will help in teaching proper form while doing all physical education activities. Understanding the concept of antagonistic muscles, along with the related information concerning flexors and extensors, is also vital to the physical educator. Imagine trying to teach the proper form of throwing a ball if you do not understand the mechanics involved. Knowledge of anatomy and physiology is also necessary to teach proper techniques used in calisthenics as well as in all physical activities. Some physical education class standbys are frequently done improperly or done when the exercise itself can cause harm. Examples of these are squat thrusts, straight-leg sit-ups, straight-leg toe touches, straight-leg push-ups for girls, and double leg lifts.

Sports and Games

Individual, dual, and team sports all have a prominent place in a successful physical education curriculum. Since one of the attributes of a quality physical education program is its carryover value, it is easy to justify the inclusion of these activities in a curriculum. Learning the rules and keeping score supplies a framework for goals and for learning how to deal with both victory and defeat. Here are examples of some sports and games that are useful to achieve the aforementioned goals:

Team Sports

- Volleyball—six players, two out of three games. Winner scores 25 points with a margin of 2.

- Basketball—five players. Most points at the end of the game wins.

- Softball—9 or 10 players. Most runs at the end of seven innings wins.

- Field hockey—11 players. Most goals wins.

- Soccer—11 players. Most goals wins.

- Flag football—9 or 11 players (can be modified to fit ability and size of the class). Six points for a touchdown, one or two for a point after, and two for a safety.

Dual Sports

- Tennis—Either doubles or singles. Four "points"—15, 30, 40, and game. Tie at forty—deuce. Winner must win by a margin of two. Remember, *love* means zero points in tennis.

- Badminton—Either doubles or singles. 15 points (doubles) or 21 (singles) by a margin of 2.

- Table tennis—Either doubles or singles. 21 points by a margin of 2.

- Shuffleboard—Either singles or doubles. 50, 75, or 100 points, determined by participants before the game begins.

Individual Sports

- Swimming—Very good for cardiovascular conditioning and can be done almost anywhere there is water.

- Track and field—Scoring varies with event.

- Bowling—Scoring is unique; good math skills are encouraged.

- Weight training—No scoring involved, but the benefits are many. Muscles are toned and strengthened through the use of weight training. Either weight machines or free weights can be used. It is important for students to learn the proper techniques and principles of weight training so they can reap the benefits while avoiding injury. When weight training, participants must consider the concept of muscular balance—this is equal strength in opposing muscle groups. All opposing groups (antagonistic muscles), i.e., triceps and biceps, hamstrings and quadriceps, need to be equal or body parts may become improperly aligned. The responsibility of the physical educator is to teach accurate information about the human body as well as teach ways to prevent injury and achieve efficiency in movement. Understanding that abdominal strength is important to lower back strength can help students create an exercise program to help avoid back injuries.

- Gymnastics—Includes tumbling. Excellent activity for developing coordination and grace. Also requires strength, which is developed by the activities done. This training can begin at a very early age with tumbling activities and progress to gymnastics.

- Golf—A fantastic carryover activity that can be taught on campus, at the golf course, or both. Requires coordination, concentration, and depth perception.

- Rhythmics—Includes ball gymnastics and other activities that may require music. Rhythmics can be taught in early elementary physical education, enabling students to develop music appreciation as well as spatial awareness.

- Dance—Can be done either individually or with a partner. Dance is especially good at developing spatial awareness and the ability to follow instructions. Dance instruction should begin in elementary school. Basic steps are walk and/or skip and are suitable to teach to first and second graders. Skip, slide, and/or run are suitable for second and third graders. The more difficult step-hop can be taught to grades 3 through 6. The ability to dance can also aid in the development of social skills and teamwork. The instructor must be careful not to teach too many steps before the dance is tried with the music. Most students enjoy dance in spite of themselves.

Adaptive Physical Education

Public Law 94-142 provides the legal definition for the term "handicapped children." It includes children who have been evaluated as being mentally impaired, deaf, speech impaired, visually handicapped, emotionally disturbed, orthopedically impaired, multi-handicapped, having learning disabilities, or having other health impairments (anemia, arthritis, etc.). PL 94-142 states that these children need special education and services. The challenge in teaching physical education to handicapped children is tailoring activities to fit each child. For example, blind or partially sighted students can participate in weight lifting, dance, and some gymnastic and tumbling activities. These students can also participate in some other activities with modifications. A beeper ball can be used for softball; a beeper can be used for archery. If a beeper is not available for archery, the teacher can put the student in position and assist in aiming. Many games and activities can be modified for the handicapped. Sometimes all it takes is a little ingenuity to change activities so that handicapped students can enjoy participating.

There are many students who are only temporarily disabled who will benefit from adaptive physical education. Examples of temporary disabilities are pregnancy, broken bones, and recovery from surgery and disease.

Movement Education

Movement education is the process by which a child is helped to develop competency in movement. It has been defined as "learning to move and moving to learn." Movement competency requires the student to manage his or her body. This body management is necessary to develop both basic and specialized activities. Basic skills are needed by the child for broad areas of activity that are related to daily living and child's play. Specialized skills are required to perform sports and have very clear techniques. Basic skills must be mastered before the child can develop specialized ones. The child controls his movement during nonlocomotor (stationary) activities, in movements across the floor or field, through space, and when suspended on an apparatus. To obtain good body management skills is to acquire, expand, and integrate elements of motor control. This is done through wide experiences in movement, based on a creative and exploratory approach. It is important that children not only manage the body with ease of movement but also realize that good posture and body mechanics are important parts of their movement patterns.

Perceptual motor competency is another consideration in body management. Perceptual motor concepts that are relevant to physical education include those that give attention to balance, coordination, lateral movement, directional movement, awareness of space, and knowledge of one's own body. Basic skills can be divided into three categories: locomotor, nonlocomotor, and manipulative skills. A movement pattern might include skills from each category.

Locomotor skills involve moving the body from place to place: walking, running, skipping, leaping, galloping, and sliding. Skills that move the body upward, such as jumping or hopping, are also locomotor skills.

Nonlocomotor skills are done in place or with very little spatial movement. Examples of nonlocomotor skills are bending and stretching, pushing and pulling, raising and lowering, twisting and turning, and shaking and bouncing.

Manipulative skills are skills used when the child handles a play object. Most manipulative skills involve using the hands and the feet, but other parts of the body may be used as well. Hand-eye and foot-eye coordination are improved with manipulative objects. Throwing, batting, kicking, and catching are important skills to be developed using balls and beanbags. Starting a child at a low level of challenge and progressing to a more difficult activity is an effective method for teaching manipulative activities. Most activities begin with individual practice and later move to partner activities. Partners should be of similar ability. When teaching throwing and catching, the teacher should emphasize skill performance, principles of opposition, weight transfer, eye focus, and follow-through. Some attention should be given to targets when throwing because students need to be able to catch and throw to different levels. Reaching is a "point-to-point" arm movement that is very common in our daily activities. In fact, reaching and grasping are typically used together to serve a number of purposes, such as eating, drinking, dressing, or cooking. The reaching/grasping task requires an "eye-hand" coordination and control of movement timing for a successful attempt.

Specialized skills are related to various sports and other physical education activities such as dance, tumbling, gymnastics, and specific games. To teach a specialized skill, the instructor must use explanation, demonstration, and drill. Demonstration can be done by other students, provided the teacher monitors the demonstration and gives cues for proper form. Drills are excellent to teach specific skills but can become tedious unless they are done in a creative manner. Using game simulations to practice skills is an effective method to maintain interest during a practice session.

Teachers must always remember to use feedback when teaching a skill or activity. Positive feedback is much more conducive to skill learning than negative feedback. Feedback means correcting with suggestions to improve. If a student continually hits the ball into the net while playing tennis, he or she is aware that something is not right. The teacher should indicate what the problem is and tell the student how to succeed in getting the ball over the net.

Movement education enables the child to make choices of activity and the method they wish to employ. Teachers can structure learning situations so the child can be challenged to develop his or her own means of movement. The child becomes the center of learning and is encouraged to be creative in carrying out the movement experience. In this method of teaching, the child is encouraged to be creative and progress according to her abilities. The teacher is not the center of learning, but suggests and stimulates the learning environment. Student-centered learning works especially well when there is a wide disparity of motor abilities. If the teacher sets standards that are too high for the less talented students, they may become discouraged and not try to perform.

Basic movement education attempts to develop the children's awareness not only of what they are doing but also how they are doing it. Each child is encouraged to succeed in his or her own way according to his or her own capacity. If children succeed at developing basic skills in elementary school, they will have a much better chance at acquiring the specialized skills required for all sports activities.

Psychological and Social Aspects of Physical Education

Physical education is a very important part of a student's elementary school education. It is not only an opportunity to "blow off steam," but it is also an arena of social interaction. One psychological aspect of physical education is the enhancement of self-esteem. Often students who have limited success in other classes can "shine" in physical education. This does not happen automatically; it is up to the teacher to create situations that enable students to gain self-esteem.

Teachers must also be careful not to damage self-esteem. An example of a potentially damaging situation occurs during the exercise of choosing members of a team. Teachers should not have captains choose the teams in front of the whole class. Nothing is more demeaning than to be the last person chosen. A better method is for the teacher to select the captains (this is also a very good way to separate the superstars: have the six best athletes be the captains). The captains then go to the sidelines and pick the teams from a class list. The teacher can then post or read the team lists after mixing up the order chosen so that no one knows who were the first and last picked.

From a developmental perspective, considerable research evidence suggests that children's participation in exercise or sports results in a number of long-term benefits, including the improvement of self-esteem, or self-confidence for social interactions; the development of sport leadership and sportsmanship; and motivation for participating in lifetime physical activities.

SUBAREA IV—FINE ARTS

Competency 0015

Understand concepts, techniques, and materials associated with the visual arts; analyze works of visual art; and understand the cultural dimensions of the visual arts.

The following topics are examples of content that may be covered under this competency.
- Apply knowledge of basic tools, techniques, and technologies in creating different types of artwork.
- Analyze how the illusion of space is created in a given two-dimensional work of art (e.g., linear perspective, overlapping elements).
- Analyze a given two-dimensional or three-dimensional work of art in terms of its unifying elements.
- Analyze how given works of art reflect the cultures that produced them.

Competency 0016

Understand concepts, techniques, and materials for producing, listening to, and responding to music; analyze works of music; and understand the cultural dimensions of music.

The following topics are examples of content that may be covered under this competency.
- Compare various types of instruments (e.g., percussion, woodwind, computerized) in terms of the sounds they produce.
- Apply common musical terms (e.g., pitch, tempo).

- Relate characteristics of music (e.g., rhythm, beat) to musical effects produced.
- Analyze how different cultures have created music reflective of their own histories and societies (e.g., call-and-response songs, ballads, work songs).

Competency 0017

Understand concepts, techniques, and materials related to theater and dance; analyze works of drama and dance; and understand the cultural dimensions of drama and dance.

The following topics are examples of content that may be covered under this competency.
- Compare dramatic and theatrical forms and their characteristics (e.g., pantomime, improvisation).
- Analyze how technical aspects of drama (e.g., the use of masks, costumes, props) affect the message or overall impression created by a dramatic performance.
- Relate types of dance (e.g., ballet, folk dance) to their characteristic forms of movement, expressive qualities, and cultural roles.
- Analyze ways in which different cultures have used drama and dance (e.g., to teach moral lessons, to preserve cultural traditions, to affirm a sense of community, to entertain).

Visual Arts

Why We Create Visual Art

Visual Communication

At its most fundamental level, art—be it opera, ballet, painting, or pantomime—is a form of communication. The realm of visual art encompasses many forms of communication, including sculpture, painting and drawing, ceramics, performance art, printmaking, jewelry, fiber art, photography, and film and video. Each medium or field of specialization communicates differently than the others. Take, for instance, the difference between viewing a sculpture and a tapestry. Sculpture (in the round) requires the viewer to physically move around in space to comprehend the work, whereas a tapestry can generally be viewed from a stationary position. Sculpture is three-dimensional, encompassing height, width, and depth, whereas a tapestry is two-dimensional, encompassing only height and width. While both forms of art can have a strong visual presence, sculpture is unique in that it has the capacity to be fully physically engaging in actual space. Artists choose different disciplines and media because each method and medium has its own communicative potential.

Aesthetics

As viewers, we can be affected by visual art in ways that are difficult to define. The powerful experience of encountering, for example, a huge carved Olmec head sculpture in an outdoor garden in Villahermosa, Mexico, or contemplating a quiet, delicate Vermeer painting in The Hague, Netherlands, is sometimes termed an aesthetic moment or experience. We may try to put into words the experience of these moments—beautiful, colossal, overwhelming, transcendental—but the words often seem inadequate. What the art is communicating is perhaps hard to verbalize, but the feeling is undeniable. As viewers, we are momentarily transported so that we are no longer aware of our surroundings or ourselves. When art communicates to us in such a direct and forceful way, we consider this an aesthetic experience.

Although aesthetics has long been recognized as the branch of philosophy pertaining to beauty, it is impossible to find agreement on what is beautiful. In keeping with the root of the word, aesthetics can be understood more as a study of sensation or feeling than of beauty. This broader understanding of aesthetics has the ability to encompass the range of sensations that one can experience in viewing a work of art. Art is not always beautiful in the traditional sense of the word, and our aesthetic philosophies must be able to encompass this reality.

Current Tendencies in Visual Art

Visual art, like other forms of communication, has the capacity to convey the complexity of issues, ideas, and feelings. What generally (and traditionally) distinguishes visual art from the other disciplines in the arts is the emphasis on the visual. However, there are numerous visual artists who work entirely in sound, for example. What, then, is the factor that distinguishes visual artists from experimental sound artists, video artists from cinematographers, and performance artists from actors or dancers? The categories that distinguish one discipline from another are becoming increasingly blurred. While the traditional areas of fine art study (namely music, theatre, dance, and visual art) still exist, many artists today are what we term *interdisciplinary*. These artists are often conversant with different art disciplines while maintaining an identity in their primary field of study. The interdisciplinary crossover of art forms has opened up many exciting possibilities for music, theatre, dance, and visual art. Indeed, interdisciplinary art has the potential to capture the complexities of our present world differently than was previously possible.

Understanding Art

The Role of Visual Art in Society

From the earliest cave paintings to the most recent art installations, visual art has functioned as a form of commentary on the society from which it springs; consequently, visual art is continually changing. Over the millennia, visual art has played (and continues to play) a key role in the dissemination of aesthetic tendencies, political ideas, religious and spiritual doctrines, cultural beliefs and critiques, and societal norms and trends. Conversely, visual art has changed and adapted to these same influences. In essence, visual art has the capacity to both shape and be shaped by the society in which it exists.

Visual art has also served the vital role of empowering the artist in his or her subject matter. For example, there has been broad speculation about the functions of the animal imagery that adorns the caves of France and Spain: Some suggest that the act of representing the animals gave the creator power over the creature or the creature's soul, while others have postulated that these artistic gestures were an early form of inventory—a means to count, organize, and track the myriad animals that existed in the outside world.

The function of art as an empowering tool is as vital today as it was in past millennia. Much like the cave painters of the past, contemporary artists often use their art as a means to chart and order the complexities, wonders, and inspirations of the present-day world.

Anonymous Artist

Fast Facts The earliest examples of art known to us date back to about 40,000 BCE, and the majority of this art remains anonymous to us.

The earliest examples of art known to us date back to about 40,000 BCE, and the majority of this art remains anonymous to us. For example, all of the extant art from Egypt, of which thousands of examples survive, was created anonymously, in service to the pharaohs, gods, and society of the artists. There are instances of work crews having inscribed their names on the pyramids; however, since the form, subject matter, and imagery were determined by the dictates of that society, this seems to be more about individuals taking pride in their work than a desire for individual recognition. While this began to change during the Greek and Roman eras (wherein we begin to recognize individual artists' styles and artists more commonly signed their names), the role of the artist as an individual creator (and the subject, form, and content of art being determined by the individual artist) is a relatively recent phenomenon.

It is also important to recognize that what remains of a past society like Egypt is always incomplete. We do not have the benefit of knowing what did not survive (e.g., homes, art, and utilitarian objects of everyday life).

How We View Art

A critical aspect of understanding art requires consideration of the context in which the art has been created; indeed, by examining the specifics of an artist's milieu—geographical, political, racial, social, religious, economic, and so forth—it is possible to truly appreciate and comprehend the profound differences that occur among works of art. Moreover, the way we view art is always mitigated by all of these same factors. Throughout history, art has readily been categorized based on some of the above factors, particularly temporal, geographic, and cultural ones. For instance, we tend to distinguish pre-Colombian artifacts by time periods (classical, postclassical), regional stylistic variations (Puuc, Zapotec), and tribal or geographical distinctions (Incan, Mayan, Aztec). These categories exist as a means of organizing and distinguishing the myriad groups of people, objects, styles, and places from which visual art arises. In today's visual art world, these same categories are often incomplete or inappropriate in illuminating the distinctions between art forms: these categories alone omit or underplay the importance of specific cultural context on the work of art. Moreover, there is a long-standing tradition of Western scholars using a Eurocentric, comparative value system when examining the differences between visual arts of various cultures. This system is often biased and generally lacking in that it does not account for the contextual specifics of each culture. Some scholars have relegated or dismissed works of art as "primitive," "naïve," or simply "crude," based upon comparisons with art that is created under the aesthetic traditions of Europe. Comparing visual art from one culture to another is a rich, valuable, and worthwhile form of study, but only if cultural biases are not informing the process.

Consider the world we live in: In less than a day, one can travel to Micronesia, sub-Saharan Africa, or New Zealand. Furthermore, the Internet allows us immediate access to any person, group, country, company, or interest. Our understanding of influences in visual art has to encompass the understanding that the global network that reaches every part of the planet now influences every region of the world. In this global climate, it is not always possible to neatly categorize or even identify the influences that occur in visual art. It is possible, however, to recognize, distinguish and appreciate certain tendencies in visual art.

Concepts And Skills

Principles and Elements

In viewing and creating visual art, there are endless considerations in how to convey ideas, thoughts, and feelings in the visual realm. The elements—point, line, plane, shape, value, texture, color—and principles—balance, harmony, variety, directional thrust, focal area, and so forth—of art play an integral role in creating, viewing, and analyzing visual art. For instance, the choice of a particular color in a painting can change the whole mood of the work. Additionally, the meaning of a certain color in a work of art can change dramatically depending on the period or culture in which the work of art was created.

The color red, for instance, can simultaneously signify love, war, anger, passion, danger, warmth, death, life, and many other things depending on the cultural significance of the color, the context of the color in the work of art, and the intention of the artist. As we view and create visual art, we are constantly fine-tuning our sensibilities so that we are sensitive to the subtleties of the elements and principles of art.

Form and Meaning

As discussed previously, visual art functions as a reflection of the values, beliefs, and tendencies of an individual or society. Naturally, the *form* of art changes in relation to its function or meaning. For instance, the native carvers of Africa's Ivory Coast ascribe specific meaning to forms in the carving of their ceremonial masks. Each formal element on the mask—bulging eyes, elongated nose, perforated cheeks, and so on—serves a spiritual, cultural, and symbolic function during a ceremony, in that the mask creates a connection to the spirit world for both the performer and the tribe.

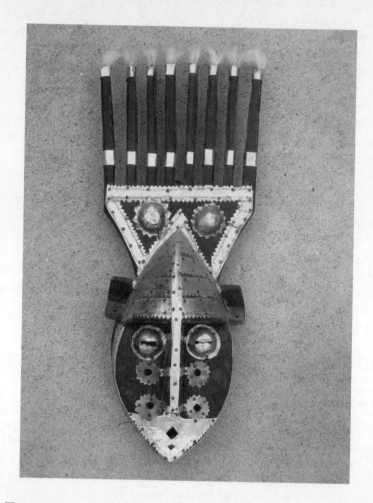

Figure 1.1   Ivory Coast Ceremonial Mask. Date unknown.

The forms on the mask, therefore, are culturally recognized, determined, and created for a specific purpose. This is very different from the view of visual art that emerged during the nineteenth century in Europe: namely, the role of form in a work of visual art was elevated to a primary level, while subject and content took an increasingly secondary role. The result of this elevation of form in visual art is what was eventually termed *formalist* art in the twentieth century in North America.

Formalism, at its peak with Post-Painterly Abstraction in the 1950s and 1960s, prided itself on its lack of meaning, symbolism, and subject matter: Simply put, it was about form or material and nothing more. It is astounding that one culture can ascribe deep, symbolic meaning to form or material while another culture can revel in its relative meaninglessness. The stark contrast between the beliefs of the Baule and the Post-Painterly Abstractionists indicates the vast differences that occur between art forms from different cultures and the importance of understanding how material associations can affect meaning in a work of art.

Deciphering Clues

Sometimes when viewing a work of art, we are unable to obtain information about the artist or the artist's intentions. In these instances, our role as viewer is akin to being a detective: We must collect as much information about the work of art as possible in order to make an educated guess about its meaning. The following mixed media drawing can be analyzed and understood based solely upon the clues we are given in the artwork.

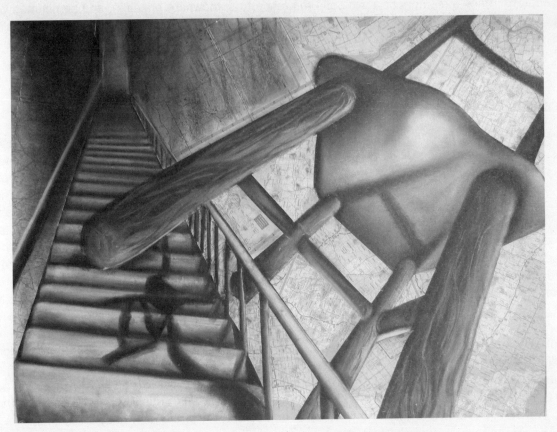

Figure 1.2   Student work by Regina Chandler

By considering aspects of the art principles and elements in the drawing, we are often able to learn about the artist's intentions. The first thing we may notice in the drawing is the chair, which for many reasons draws the attention of a viewer. It appears to be the closest object to the viewer; it is the largest object (relatively speaking) in the drawing, and it can lead one's eyes into the space behind it. Another noticeable feature is the viewer's relationship to the chair. The chair is drawn in extreme, slightly distorted three-point perspective. The initial point of view that the viewer confronts is one of ambiguity. In one way, the viewer is looking down the stairs and the chair appears to be falling away; in another way, the viewer is looking up the stairs and the chair is falling toward the viewer. Adding to the ambiguity in this drawing are the light source and shadows; indeed, the viewer is given at least two light sources that create shadows on the stairs and on the underside of the chair. Lastly, the viewer of this piece is confronted with the randomly collaged atmosphere of road maps. The predominant theme that seems to emerge from the drawing is one of confusion and ambiguity. One might assume that, based on these observations, the student's intention here was to play with the rules of perspective in order to create an indeterminate space and feeling. The drawing holds one's attention by virtue of its changeability. It is possible that the student had specific intentions about the choice of maps and the illusion of the chair (perhaps a memory or a symbolic reference to somewhere specific), and sometimes we are fortunate enough to learn the inspiration of an artist's work. Yet, in this particular example, one is able to piece together enough clues from the drawing to enjoy and appreciate the work without knowing all of the specifics of the artist's motivation.

Material Factors

Understanding the differences between works of art happens on many levels. As previously discussed, the aesthetic standards by which one assesses a work of art must take into account the many cultural factors that influence visual art. Equally important to aesthetic consideration is knowledge of the many tools, techniques, and materials that artists employ in their art. The number of potential materials for creating works of art has increased exponentially over the past 150 years or so. This situation can be attributed both to industrial innovations and to artists' broadening their scope to include found materials and unusual non-art objects and media. The foregrounding of materiality that occurred with the formalist artists in the twentieth century has further contributed to the recent expanse of materials for art making. The inclusion of uncommon materials in visual art has dramatically changed the criteria by which one assesses visual art; in fact, it is no longer unusual to be confronted with traditionally carved marble sculptures (Louise Bourgeois) and cast and licked chocolate sculptures (Janine Antoni) in the same gallery space. What becomes important in analyzing these diverse works is an understanding of the motivation behind the artwork. It is equally legitimate for one artist to pursue traditional carving in stone while another artist explores conceptual possibilities in cast and licked chocolate. One may be more attracted to one art form over another, but ultimately, it is critical for us to respect the diversity that contributes to the variety, richness and complexity of the art world.

Music

When preparing for this part of the exam, it is important to focus on the objectives to which music is primarily related. They include contexts for the music, concepts and skills involved in experiencing music, and the aesthetic and personal dimensions of music. These constitute a broad overview of the field of music and the musical experience.

One objective is to "understand historical, cultural, and societal contexts for the arts (visual arts, music, drama, dance) and the interrelationships among the arts." This suggests an integration of subject matter that is an opportunity for teachers and students to make connections between social studies, reading or language arts, and the fine arts. For example, when students are reading stories about the American Revolution, they should be aware that it occurred during the period known as the Classical Period in music history. Listening to a work by Haydn or Mozart and talking about how they reflected the "old world" and then comparing the work to a Colonial American tune of the time like "Chester" by William Billings is a great exercise. Similarly, the visual art of Andy Warhol, the music of the Beatles, the assassination of John F. Kennedy, and the war in Vietnam all share the same approximate time frame. In these and the virtually infinite number of other cases or combinations, the students can be asked to find contrasts and similarities or they can attempt to find ways that historical context affected art and ways that art affected and reflected history.

These examples from American History are easy for most to grasp quickly. However, the objective seeks to have teachers and students consider the role of the Arts, to include music, in history and culture beyond the American experience. Listening to music from China, Japan, Germany, Australia, or Africa when studying those cultures can enrich the experience and make it more memorable for students. It is even more valuable to experience live or videotaped performances of the music and dance of these cultures because often the music is performed in traditional costume with traditional instruments (sometimes very different from modern instruments) and seeing the costumes and the movement are an important part of understanding the culture.

According to the objective, merely experiencing the music is not enough. The students must be able to recognize the music or art as part of its historical context and then, through discussion or written exercises that emphasize higher order thinking, they must demonstrate an understanding of the music's place in the historical context and be able to note things that are common and things that are different from context to context—period to period, culture to culture, and so forth—appropriate to their age and level of development. For example, Haydn, Mozart, and Billings used simple melodies in their compositions, but Haydn and Mozart wrote mostly large works like symphonies and operas, whereas Billings wrote mostly psalms and songs. Students must be aware of these facts and then consider why more highly developed forms were preferred in the "old world" while basic psalms and songs were more common in the Colonies. The obvious answer is that colonists did not have the time or the resources to encourage or produce larger musical works. However, the discussion could go beyond that basic step depending on the sophistication of the students.

Another objective is to "understand concepts, techniques, and materials" for producing, listening to, and responding to music. Understanding concepts and techniques suggests more than an appreciation of these concepts and skills. The students ought to experience music making and be taught to listen as musicians listen. They should learn how to put their response to music into accepted music terminology.

Making music is a basic experience. Mothers sing to their babies. Children beat sticks together, make drums, and sing during their play. Adults whistle or sing along with tunes on the radio. People are naturally drawn to sound and music. It is an important part of culture, religious practice, and personal experience for all people. Some people become professional musicians, whereas others whistle, sing, or play for their own enjoyment and nothing more. It is important that students have the opportunity to experience as many forms of music making as possible. It is through the acquisition of basic skills in singing and playing instruments that people can grow in their ability to express themselves through music. As students develop skills, they are also exposed to basic musical concepts such as melody, harmony, rhythm, pitch, and timbre. Then, with experience, they come to make decisions about what is acceptable or not acceptable within a given cultural or historical context and thereby develop their own aesthetic awareness. There is only a very small segment of society that does not make music. These people would likely choose to make music if they could, but are unable as a result of a physical impairment or personal choice (e.g., a vow of silence). Music making is a natural part of human experience.

Listening is a skill that is often taken for granted. There is not a "right" way to listen. However, listening can be much more than allowing the sound to flow past the ears. It can be as basic as listening for melodies and analyzing for form and chord structure or as advanced as critiquing the interpretation on its musical and aesthetic merits. Listening with knowledge and understanding can make the experience of a musical performance much deeper and more meaningful. While music can be experienced and found satisfying, challenging, or beautiful without prior knowledge of a piece or an understanding of its form, cultural significance, and so forth, these things can enrich the experience.

Fast Facts **Music does not provide specific information, instructions, or reactions. People respond to it naturally.**

People respond to music naturally. They do not need prompting or help to respond. They just respond. However, in order to share that response, they must learn how to put their response to music into musical terminology. Some people call music a language, but it does not function as a spoken language. It does not provide specific information, instructions, or reactions. Rather, it sparks thoughts, feelings and emotions. In order to try to put the experience into words, musicians and artists have developed vocabulary and approaches to discussing music and art. This is not to say that there is only one way to respond to or to talk about music or art. However, it is easier to understand music and musicians, art and artists, if the students understand and can use the kind of vocabulary and approaches that musicians or artists use to discuss their work. This includes things as basic as melody and harmony and as profound as the aesthetic experience.

This objective is also about self-expression through and with regard to music. People cannot express themselves or effectively communicate if they do not understand the structures and rules that underlie the "language" that they are trying to use. Although music does not provide the kind of specific communication that spoken language does, it does have structures that can be considered and discussed to help students understand the music and express their responses to the music.

Part of meeting this objective is to understand and promote the aesthetic and personal dimensions related to music. The aesthetic experience is what draws people to music. That experience that everyone has had, but cannot describe because words seem clumsy when it comes to something that can be so profound and wonderful. The type of music or the period or the performer does not necessarily limit the aesthetic experience. It is equally possible to have an aesthetic experience when listening to a child sing a simple melody as it is when listening to a professional orchestra performing a Beethoven symphony. The important thing is to share that aesthetic experience. It is part of what makes music and art special.

There are many ways to encourage exploration of and growth through aesthetic responsiveness. A common experience is a crucial starting point. Have the students listen to several pieces of music and, after listening attentively, ask them to describe how each one made them feel. It is often best to write their response down before starting a discussion. Then, ask them if they can explain why each piece of music made them feel the way they indicated. Younger students will likely provide simple, straightforward emotional responses (e.g., "It made me feel happy!"), while older students should be exploring why it affected the feelings that it did and using both musical concepts (e.g., "It made me feel happy because it was in a major key.) and non-musical associations (e.g., "It made me feel happy because it sounded like a circus and I like to go to the circus."). Through this kind of sharing, along with teacher insights and reading about how other people have responded to music, students can explore and come to a deeper understanding of their personal responses to music, other art forms, and possibly the world. In addition, it should provide them with practical ways to express their responses or reactions to what they experience in life.

According to the objective, having an aesthetic experience, recognizing its value, and being able to grapple with discussing or sharing that experience are not enough. It is also important to promote and develop this part of the musical and artistic experience. Teachers and students must attempt to foster an appreciation for the arts and their ability to create meaning. The arts provide an opportunity to explore and express ideas and emotions through a unique view of life experiences. It is through the experience of music, or any art form, that people begin to transcend the mundane day-to-day experience and reach beyond to a richer life experience.

The objectives that deal with music include contexts for the music, concepts and skills involved in experiencing music, and the aesthetic and personal dimensions of music. Music does not exist in a vacuum. The context (e.g., historical or cultural) of a piece of music is very important. Students should know and be able to discuss the context of music through integration of subject matter. Music ought to be experienced in every way possible. Students must be given opportunities to develop basic performance skills as well as listening skills and vocabulary for responding to music. And, to pull all of these together, teachers and students should develop their aesthetic awareness and help others to do the same. While music and the musical experience can be complex, it is important to remember these basic ideas. In the end, it is not whether someone is a professional musician or an avid listener, but that they know the wonders of music and the arts.

Drama

The arts are a part of the core curriculum, both in terms of Oklahoma standards and the No Child Left Behind federal mandate. Dance, music, drama, and the visual arts are essential parts of a complete education. Study of one or more art forms develops the intellect, provides unique access to meaning, and connects individuals with works of genius, multiple cultures, and contributions to history.

Drama and theatre activities benefit students' educational growth, regardless of their future career.

Fast Facts

Drama and theatre activities offer learners opportunities to experience an art form in many different ways. Whether studying a play, mounting a production, attending a performance, or engaging in creative drama in the classroom, this subject helps students to learn about themselves and their world, develop social skills, strengthen both their verbal and nonverbal communication skills, creatively problem-solve, analyze, and collaborate. Some of the benefits inherent in this instructional methodology include developing concentration skills, analyzing content, demonstrating artistic discipline, improving listening, learning to apply research, communicating information, and making and justifying artistic choices. These are important to a student's educational growth, regardless of that individual's future career. Students who have a chance to learn about and through drama are motivated; their imaginations are engaged and their work is often quite focused.

More specific aesthetic benefits also are acquired. By participating in these activities, students learn about dramatic process and product. They acquire knowledge of theatre artists and their responsibilities. They engage in making artistic choices and learn about the personal discipline that the arts demand. Furthermore, students develop personal aesthetics that are based on informed judgments. They develop insight into cultures and communities, and better understand how this art form is manifest in both their artistic and their everyday lives.

Drama means "to do, act." Drama/theatre is an experiential way to connect to content. Students are engaged physically, mentally, and emotionally. In today's classroom, infusing these techniques into the curriculum allows for hands-on learning that is meaningful and lasting. Young people can learn not only about drama/theatre but also through the art form if it is partnered with another subject. Using these techniques helps children to understand both artistic and paired subject content.

Drama offers multiple approaches to gaining knowledge. Whether a student's preferred learning style is visual (verbal), visual (nonverbal), aural, or tactile/kinesthetic, infusing lessons with drama/theatre expands ways of knowing, especially because of the variety of activities available. Multiple approaches to knowledge acquisition and retention help to insure that all children learn. It should be no surprise, then, that in addition to students who regularly achieve in their studies, even those who generally are less successful may thrive in classrooms where drama/theatre is a regular part of their learning environment. Teaching and learning through and with dramatic art is a unique and effective approach to instruction at all educational levels and with students of varying degrees of academic achievement.

Educators teaching elementary school age children will find that understanding child drama and the continuum of activities that defines it will help them to determine what type of activity is best to use at any given time. While the following comparison helps to distinguish the two major components of this progression, it is important to recognize that one is not better than the other; they are simply different in composition and purpose. Creative drama, children's theatre, and the activities between them offer ample opportunities for integration and demonstrate that the arts are powerful partners for learning.

At one end of the drama/theatre spectrum is creative drama. In this format, process is more important than product; the benefit to the participant is paramount. Creative drama is frequently used in classrooms because it is informal drama that can work in any setting and with any number of children. Scenery, costumes, and/or props are not required. These activities move from teacher-centered to student-centered, from shorter to longer activities and sessions, from unison play to individual play, and from simple beginning activities to more complex story work. Participants need little, if any, previous experience with this approach to curriculum. Once they are introduced to this pedagogy, however, both their interests and their skills will grow.

Here are definitions for the many types of activities that are components of creative drama.

Beginning Activities: These are warm-up activities such as name games, chants, listening games, and other simple exercises designed to relax and motivate participants.

Games: These are more challenging than beginning activities and often focus upon developing players' concentration, imagination, and teamwork skills. Frequently, they are played with students seated or standing in a circle.

Sequence Games: The teacher takes a story or similar material and divides it into particular events or scenes, placing each on an index card. These are randomly distributed to players. When a student recognizes his/her cue being performed, that student goes next. Index cards should have the cue at the top and the new action at the bottom, preferably in a different font or color. The teacher should keep a master list, in order, of cues. This helps students if the correct sequence is interrupted or lost.

Pantomime: Players use their bodies to communicate rather than their voices. Pantomime sentences and stories, creative movement exercises, and miming games are common examples.

Improvisations: These are spontaneously created performances based upon at least two of the following: who (characters), what (conflict), where (setting), when (time), and how (specifics of interpretation). Performed either in pantomime or with dialogue, improvisations should not be planned or rehearsed. Interesting episodes that emerge may be further developed through story creation. Role-playing improvisations deal with problem solving. Students are exposed to differing points of view by replaying and switching roles. Role-playing should not be confused with playing in-role, which is when the teacher enters the dramatization as a character.

Stories: A number of activities can be based upon stories and can range from simple to complex. In the former category, for example, are *noisy stories*. These are simple stories that players help to tell by making sounds or saying words associated with characters. *Story creation* activities require that players develop stories, and these activities can be stimulated by various items, including props, titles, students' own writing, or true events. *Open-ended stories* are those from which students build stories given only a beginning and then share their creations either orally, in writing, or through performance. *Story dramatization* is the most complex informal dramatic activity, as it utilizes players' previously developed skills in service to playing stories. Once proficient here, students move naturally to formal theatrical endeavors.

Several types of activities bridge the gap between creative drama and theatre for youth. These include theatre-in-education (TIE), readers' theatre, and puppetry. Each can be integrated into classroom practice.

Theatre-in-Education (TIE): Originating in Britain, Theatre-in-Education is performed by actor-teachers and students. Using material based upon curriculum or social issues, players assume roles and, through these, explore and problem-solve. TIE's structure is flexible and its focus is educational.

Puppetry: Puppets can range from simple paper bag or sock creations to elaborately constructed marionettes. Puppets can be used for creative drama and theatre activities. Likewise, puppet stages can be as simple as a desktop or table, or they can be intricately constructed with artistically designed settings and theatrical trappings.

Readers Theatre: Called Theatre of the Imagination, Readers Theatre offers performance opportunities without elaborate staging. Traditionally, this type of performance has players sitting on stools, using onstage and/or offstage focus, and employing notebooks or music stands to hold scripts. A narrator may be used and readers may or may not play multiple roles. This type of performance is wedded to literature. A common misconception, however, is that this is simply expressive reading. To truly impact an audience, Readers Theatre must be more than that. Rich characterization, suggested movement, and clear interpretation of the literature are required. In their minds' eyes, audience members complete the stage pictures suggested by the interpreters.

Children's theatre is product-oriented and audience-centered. This theatre for young people can be performed by and for children, by adults for youth, or with a combined cast of adults and young people. In addition, actors can be either amateurs or professionals. Here, dialogue is memorized, the number of characters in the play determines the cast size, and scenery and costumes are generally expected production elements.

Educators may take their students to see plays or they may wish to stage plays in their classrooms or other school facilities. In addition to the familiar format, plays for young people can also be done as participation plays and as story theatre. These last two are especially adaptable to educational venues.

Traditional Theatre: In this most commonly used form of theatre, performers and audience are separate entities. Actors use character and story to communicate and the audience responds with feedback (e.g., laughing, applauding). Typically, actors perform on a stage and are supported by others who contribute the technical elements of theatre.

Participation Theatre: Children are given opportunities to use their voices and bodies within the context of the play. They might be asked for their ideas, invited to join the actors, or given chances to contribute to the play in meaningful ways.

Story Theatre: In this format, actors can function as both characters and narrators, sometimes commenting upon their own actions in role. They can play one role or multiple parts. Scenery, if used, is minimal and costume pieces can suggest a character. Story theatre is classroom friendly and closely linked to literature.

Young people benefit from exposure to theatre, whether as participant or audience member. Opportunities abound for developing vocal skills, vocabulary, imagination, understanding of dramatic structure and types of conflict, physical skills, and empathy. Theatre offers innovative instructional options.

Theatre is not a new art form; it emerged in ancient Greece as a part of religious celebrations. The fact that theatre has evolved over centuries is a testament to its nature; it is both experimental and transitional, allowing innovative elements to be absorbed into the mainstream while continuing to look for new artistic inventions. This is not its only dichotomy.

Theatre is a profession for some and an avocation for others. It is a communal and a collective art form. Regardless of its structure, theatre engages through both visual and auditory stimulation. And because it uses live actors performing for an audience that is "in the moment" with them, it can be repeated but it will never be exactly the same.

How does theatre help students to learn? Plays reflect culture. They hold up a mirror that allows us to travel to different places and time periods, learning about the conditions, people, and viewpoints that have shaped the world of the play. They challenge learners to explore and to deepen their understanding. Theatre introduces children to some characters who are like them and to some who are not. It enriches and broadens a child's way of knowing.

Using drama in the classroom may result in a lively educational environment. Teachers should welcome the energetic chatter and movement indicating students who are learning. They should also recognize that, in this type of experience, there might not be one correct answer or interpretation. Part of the joy and challenge of using drama in the classroom is that it pushes students to think creatively and independently. If teachers view themselves as co-explorers in this process, the journey they take with their students is both productive and fun!

Dance

It has been said, "to dance is human." How true! Dance is one of the most human of endeavors. Throughout history, dance has been rich with meaning and passion. It expresses the depths of humanness across all cultures.

Fast Facts

Dance expresses the depths of humanness across all cultures.

Dance plays important roles among the peoples of the world. There are many ways in which dance is a mirror of culture. Dance may be looked at as a social activity. Dance can also be a performing art. Dance is also a creative pursuit.

Dance as a Mirror of Culture

As far back into ancient times as written records or artwork exist, we have evidence that all cultures dance. From the earliest artwork to that of today, the dancing figure is the artistic subject of many cultures. When we consider why people draw, paint, or sculpt, we learn that they portray what is important to them, what their community or culture values. Dance is important enough to be represented in the art of most cultures from antiquity to today.

Cultural Values

When a culture values strength and power, their dance will show it. When a culture values the community over the individual, it is clear in the dance. When a culture values order and hierarchy in social structure, the dance will give evidence of the same structure. With an observant eye, one can learn a great deal about a culture by studying its dances. This section speaks to many dance-evident cultural values such as gender roles, sexuality, concepts of beauty and aesthetics, community solidarity, and creativity.

Religion

Most cultural dances are historically connected to religion. All over the world we can observe dances of devotion and worship of the deities where movements might include bowing in reverence, lifting arms to the heavens, and gestures of receiving of divine benefits. We can observe dances that tell stories of the power and conquests of deities (e.g., Egyptian, Greek, Indian, Japanese). These movements may include a wide, strong stance with fisted hands and stamping feet. It is also common to see the important stories of the gods told through dance and mime.

We can observe dances that appeal to the gods for survival. For hunting success (e.g., Native American, Inuit) movements may include pantomime of the animal and hunter and the inevitable killing of the animal. For fertile fields and lavish harvest (e.g., Hebrew, Egyptian, European) movements may include pantomime of the planting, tending, and harvesting, as well as lifting or expanding actions that suggest crop growth. For victory in war (e.g., Chinese, Roman, African) movements may include use of swords, spears, or shields and the miming of conflict and victory. In most cultures the power of the dance to cause the gods' positive response is unquestioned.

We can observe dances that ask for divine blessings on life events. For the birth of a child (e.g., African, Polynesian) the movements may include childbearing actions, cradling and "offering" the child up to the deity, and crawling, walking, and running to indicate growth of the child. For initiation into adulthood (e.g., Native American, African) the movements may include shows of strength and manhood for the male and swaying and nurturing gestures for the female. For marriage (in most cultures) movements are jubilant, reflect traditional gender roles for men and women, and may include movements that suggest sexuality and fertility. For funerals (e.g., Egyptian, Cambodian, Zimbabwean) movements may reenact the life story of the deceased and may include grieving as well as celebration of an afterlife. For many cultures, dance is the primary connection between people and their gods.

Gender Roles

How should a man move? How should a woman move? Each culture answers these questions in dance. Most often the rules are unwritten, but they are clear nonetheless. In the dances of the Polynesian culture of the Cook Islands, for example, men keep a pulsing rhythm in their bodies by taking a wide stance and pumping knees open and closed. Their movements are always strong and powerful. The women stand with feet together and sway softly from side to side with undulating hips and rippling arms. In their dances, the man and woman never touch. In fact, they often dance in separate gender groups. In the ballroom dancing of European and American cultures, the man leads the woman by holding her and guiding her. She follows his lead. They move in perfect synchrony and reflect the western cultural ideal of a flawless heterosexual union (led by the man) that is effortless and perfect. Each culture defines gender-specific movements and speaks volumes about the roles of men and women through its dance.

Beauty and Aesthetics

All cultures define beauty in their own way. Dances clearly reflect that ideal (aesthetic) of beauty. Some African dances, for example, feature plump and fleshy women dancers who embody health, fertility, the earth, and beauty to their people. In the European traditional form of ballet, however, the skeletal ballerina is spotlighted to reflect the fragile, ethereal, romantic ideal of female beauty. Another contrast can be made between the traditional court dances of Bali and American Modern dance. In Bali, the court dances have existed for centuries. Dancers train for many years to perform with great serenity, balance, and symmetry. They embody the ideal beauty of Balinese culture. In contemporary America, modern dance can express the very different aesthetic of a driving, off-balance asymmetry. Each image mirrors a cultural definition of what is beautiful. We can all discover many different kinds of beauty through experiencing the dances of various cultures.

Dance as a Social Activity

Social dance has a relatively short history in the human race. Dance has always drawn people together as communicants in a common religion and as celebrants of community events in the context of religion. However, the practice of dance for the primary purpose of gathering people together to enjoy each other's company is only centuries old, rather than millennia-old. When we look at the history of social dance we can clearly see changes in social structure and accepted behavior through changes in the dances.

Folk Dances around the World

Folk dances are cultural dances that have remained quite stable for a long period of time. The music has remained constant and the movements have changed little over the years. Folk dances usually reflect the national traditions of various cultures. They evoke pride in people's traditions and culture by keeping alive the dances of their ancestors. Dancers swell with pride as they perform the dances of their forebears with others that share their heritage. Folk dances are usually about the group, not the specific dancer or couple. Folk dance is a solid connection to the past and a vehicle for "belonging." When one dances a dance, one belongs to the group that has danced that dance through the ages. For some cultures that are being absorbed into western society and swallowed by global culture, such as the Inuits of northern Canada, languages are gradually lost, traditional crafts are lost and ancient religion is lost, but the dances are the last to go. People cling to their dances as the last remnant of a shared past. For the Punjab Indians who immigrated to England in the past century, the dances of their Indian culture are so important to their understanding of their cultural heritage that all children study the dances and the people perform them at social gatherings. People dance their own culture's folk dances to understand who they are and where they came from. It is also valuable to learn the folk dances of other cultures. When we dance the dances of others, we learn about them and gain respect for them by "dancing in their shoes."

Social Dances of Western Cultures

Social dances of Western cultures are usually about the couple and heterosexual courtship. In contrast with folk dance, social dances usually change over time. Through several centuries in Europe and America, changes in social dance have created a fascinating mirror of changing social attitudes toward courtship and gender. When the waltz emerged in full force on the European scene in the nineteenth century, it was soundly condemned as scandalous because the couple was for the first time dancing face to face in an embrace. However, the man continued to lead the dance and the woman followed. Each new social dance has met with similar resistance as the changes in social attitudes toward gender and sexuality have initiated new ways of moving. Embraces become closer, sexual movements become more suggestive, and clothing becomes more revealing as times and social attitudes change.

It is possible to clearly track changes in the social attitude in America by looking at the social dances of various times. The Lindy Hop of the late 1920s and 1930s is a good example. The earliest swing dance, the Lindy Hop emerged from the heart of the African-American culture of Harlem. Its popularity grew and the mainstream white culture was fascinated. White Americans began to flock to Harlem to learn the Lindy Hop. In this time of great separation between the races, the Lindy Hop forged new connections between people of different skin color. Social strictures began to marginally break down.

Another example of the power of social dance to reflect changing social attitudes is the Twist. During the 1960s in America, the Twist emerged and took the social dance scene by storm. Its impact was felt in the fact that the couple did not have to synchronize their movements. In fact, the dancers no longer had to touch each other. Each one danced alone. This dance reflects an important social change in 1960s America when women's liberation and the civil rights movements announced that each person had equal rights regardless of gender or race. The Twist was a revolutionary dance that allowed the individual to pursue her/his own movement. Neither dancer leads nor follows. What a mirror of society!

Dance as a Performing Art

Dance has played another role in history, the role of performing art. In various cultures elite groups of people are designated as dancers/performers. Their occupation is to dance before audiences. There are several examples of performing styles, old and new, among various cultures.

In Japan, Kabuki emerged as a performing art from a long history in the streets. Traditionally, men play all women's roles in elaborate makeup and costume. Highly controlled, stylized movements and lavish costumes represent favorite stories and characters. The theatre art is studied for a lifetime and the popularity of top Kabuki actors/dancers can equal the level of movie stars in Japan.

In India, the Bharata Natyam is a centuries-old dance rooted in the Hindu religion. A solo female dancer who is highly trained in this intricate form of storytelling performs the Bharata Natyam. The dancer utilizes the entire body, but especially the hands and eyes, in a very colorful and expressive dance.

From South Africa comes a style of dance called Gumboots. Out of the dark and silent goldmines and the oppressive lives of the slave laborers emerges a style of dance performed by groups of men wearing miners' gumboots. The dancers leap, turn, and stamp their boots in well-grounded group formations. Their rhythmic and exuberant dance tells of solidarity within adversity and of the workers' amazing endurance.

Finally, out of Irish step-dancing traditions and American innovation comes the Riverdance phenomenon. In this vertically lifted, stylized Irish dancing, the dancers hold their arms tightly at their sides while making quick explosive movements of the legs. They balance mainly on their toes while creating lightning-fast tap rhythms with their hard-soled shoes in kaleidoscopic group patterns.

In Europe and America, the primary performance styles of dance are ballet, modern, jazz, and tap dance.

Ballet, a stylized form in which the body is elongated and extended into space, emerges from the royal courts of Renaissance Europe. Female dancers, or ballerinas, study for years to be able to dance "en pointe," on the tips of their toes. The romantic ballet literally elevates the ballerina to an otherworldly figure unhampered by gravity. Ballet has a long history as an elite form of dance that contains elements of the affectations of royalty. Modern forms of ballet, however, have stretched the limits of the traditional form to include many more movement possibilities.

Modern dance emerged around the turn of the twentieth century, primarily in America, as a reaction against the style restrictions of ballet. It is a "freer" form of dance in which the dancer explores and creates dance with very few stylistic limits. Modern, and now postmodern, dancers and choreographers use many existing movement styles and combine them in innovative ways to create new forms.

Jazz and tap dance emerged in America from a similar source. They both meld the dance styles of Europe, Africa, and various other cultures. Both grow from the fertile cross-cultural ground of nineteenth and twentieth century America to create new dance blends and hybrids. Jazz dance is a performing style that also borrows from American social dance and uses contemporary music, physical power, body-part isolations, and gravity to create strong and rhythmic dances. Tap dance uses metal taps attached to the toes and heels of dance shoes to create intricate and complex rhythms. These four western performing styles have greatly influenced each other throughout the twentieth and into the twenty-first centuries. Choreographers and dancers borrow from each other, style lines become blurred, and new blends between styles are common and exciting. Performing forms are constantly changing through time, but each has a cherished tradition.

Dance as a Creative Pursuit

Creative Problem-Solving

Arguably the earliest creative act of a human being is movement. Long before mastering poetry, visual art, or music, a child creates movement. Fundamentally, in all creative pursuits, we are practicing problem solving. Creative problem solving includes: contemplating a problem, considering various solutions, trying various solutions, choosing one solution, altering and fine-tuning the solution, and finally evaluating the solution. Development of creative problem solving skills is important in human life. All education programs profess the importance of problem solving, and the arts are no exception. The more we use creative movement in the classroom, the greater the learning potential. As students create, they learn about the world, about others, and about themselves.

The Body as the Medium

Dance is an art that requires only the human body, standard equipment for all children. No pen, paintbrush, or musical instrument is needed. As children explore the basics of movement (body, space, time, and relationship), they gain the movement vocabulary to express themselves more and more eloquently. Mastery of the body as a creative medium should be a primary goal in dance education.

Dance Content

Usually, dances are about something. They often have identifiable content. Most dances create meaning in some form, even when quite abstract. When a human being creates a dance, he or she may be expressing such diverse ideas as: community, literary conflict, properties of magnets, regular or irregular rhythms, mathematical patterns, or visual design. A dancer/choreographer may be exploring feelings such as: alienation, comfort, precision, smooth or bumpy flow, anger, or peace. A choreographer may also be sharing experiences through dance by telling a story or by creating an environment that arises from their life experience. Students are encouraged to create meaning in dance by expressing ideas, exploring feelings, or sharing experiences learn a great deal about themselves while developing their creative problem-solving skills.

Dance in the Classroom and across the Curriculum

Why isn't there more dancing in the schools? General classroom teachers may feel inadequate to teach dance but maybe they define dance too narrowly as merely patterns of intricate steps. Dance in the elementary schools should be about creative movement. Any sensitive teacher can guide students through creative movement that builds upon classroom learning.

For example, in language arts, students can learn spelling and vocabulary words by groups spelling words with their bodies or acting out the meaning of the word. They can *embody* the concept of opposites, for example, by exploring (alone or with a partner) heavy/light, near/far, curved/angular, or symmetrical/asymmetrical. Students can also dance the character or mime the story they are studying.

Movement and math also share much ground. Creative movement studies can use repetition and rhythm to count in multiples or can use partner body sculptures to reflect symmetry and asymmetry, for example.

Science studies can include exploration of gravity, creating a group machine, demonstrating the flow of electrical currents and circuits, or moving within the properties of various types of clouds.

Social studies supply many rich ideas for creative movement, too. Some movement ideas include drawing a map of the classroom and creating a movement "journey" or exploring various occupations, transportation forms, or types of communities through creative movement. Folk dances are always a powerful means to experience other cultures.

Summary

Dance is a powerful force in human life that can express and teach about others, our world, and our selves. Dance is a mirror of culture, cultural values, religion, gender roles, and concepts of beauty. Dance is a social activity that draws people together into belonging and expresses community through folk dance and social dance. Dance is a performing art in many cultures, reflecting cultural ideals through choreography and performance. And finally, dance is a creative pursuit that uses creative problem solving to transform body movement into meaning: expressing ideas, exploring feelings, and sharing experiences. Dance is a powerful teaching tool that can bridge the disciplines of the curriculum.

OSAT

Oklahoma Subject Area Test
Elementary Education

Practice Subtest 2

SUBTEST DIRECTIONS

A sample of the general directions for the OSAT is shown in the box below. You may want to familiarize yourself with the directions, as similar versions will be used for the actual examination.

You should have in front of you:

(1) a test booklet for the test for which you registered (check the field name on the front cover);

(2) an answer document (be sure you have signed your answer document and filled in the required information on pages 1 and 3); and

(3) a No. 2 lead pencil.

IF YOU DO NOT HAVE ALL OF THESE MATERIALS, PLEASE INFORM THE TEST ADMINISTRATOR. REMOVE ALL OTHER MATERIALS FROM YOUR DESK.

GENERAL DIRECTIONS

This test booklet contains two sections: a selected-response section and a writing assignment. You may complete the sections in the order you choose, but it is suggested that you complete the selected-response section of the test first. The directions for each section appear immediately before that section.

Each selected-response question in this booklet has four answer choices. Read each question carefully and choose the ONE best answer. Record your answer on the answer sheet in the space that corresponds to the question number. Completely fill in the space having the same letter as the answer you have chosen. *Use only a No. 2 lead pencil.*

Sample Question:

1. Which of these cities is farthest north?

    A. Oklahoma City

    B. Muskogee

    C. Tulsa

    D. Lawton

The correct answer to this question is C. You would indicate that on the answer sheet as follows:

1. Ⓐ Ⓑ ● Ⓓ

You should answer all questions. Even if you are unsure of an answer, it is better to guess than not to answer a question at all. You may use the margins of the test booklet for scratch paper, but all of your answers must be recorded in your answer document. Answers that are written in the test booklet will **NOT** be scored.

The words "End of Section" indicate you have completed a section. After you have completed one section, you may go on to the other section. You may go back and review your answers but be sure you have answered all selected-response questions and rechecked all the information in your answer document, particularly your identification information on pages 1 and 3, before you raise your hand for dismissal. Your test materials must be returned to a test administrator when you finish the test.

FOR TEST SECURITY REASONS, YOU MAY NOT TAKE NOTES OR REMOVE ANY OF THE TEST MATERIALS FROM THE ROOM.

This session will last four hours. You may work at your own pace on the different sections of the test. If you have any questions, please ask them now before you begin the test.

STOP

DO NOT GO ON UNTIL YOU ARE TOLD TO DO SO.

Answer Sheet

1. (A)(B)(C)(D)	11. (A)(B)(C)(D)	21. (A)(B)(C)(D)	31. (A)(B)(C)(D)
2. (A)(B)(C)(D)	12. (A)(B)(C)(D)	22. (A)(B)(C)(D)	32. (A)(B)(C)(D)
3. (A)(B)(C)(D)	13. (A)(B)(C)(D)	23. (A)(B)(C)(D)	33. (A)(B)(C)(D)
4. (A)(B)(C)(D)	14. (A)(B)(C)(D)	24. (A)(B)(C)(D)	34. (A)(B)(C)(D)
5. (A)(B)(C)(D)	15. (A)(B)(C)(D)	25. (A)(B)(C)(D)	35. (A)(B)(C)(D)
6. (A)(B)(C)(D)	16. (A)(B)(C)(D)	26. (A)(B)(C)(D)	36. (A)(B)(C)(D)
7. (A)(B)(C)(D)	17. (A)(B)(C)(D)	27. (A)(B)(C)(D)	37. (A)(B)(C)(D)
8. (A)(B)(C)(D)	18. (A)(B)(C)(D)	28. (A)(B)(C)(D)	38. (A)(B)(C)(D)
9. (A)(B)(C)(D)	19. (A)(B)(C)(D)	29. (A)(B)(C)(D)	39. (A)(B)(C)(D)
10. (A)(B)(C)(D)	20. (A)(B)(C)(D)	30. (A)(B)(C)(D)	40. (A)(B)(C)(D)

Practice Test

DIRECTIONS: Use the information below to answer the three questions that follow.

An experiment is planned to test the effect of microwave radiation on the success of seed germination. One hundred corn seeds will be divided into four sets of twenty-five each. Seeds in Group 1 will be microwaved for one minute, seeds in Group 2 for two minutes, and seeds in Group 3 for ten minutes. Seeds in Group 4 will not be placed in the microwave. Each group of seeds will be soaked overnight and placed between the folds of water-saturated newspaper.

1. When purchasing the seeds at the store no single package contained enough seeds for the entire project, most contain about thirty seeds per package. Which of the following is an acceptable approach for testing the hypotheses?

   I. Purchase one packet from each of four different brands of seed, one packet for each test group
   II. Purchase one packet from each of four different brands of seed and divide the seeds from each packet equally among the four test groups
   III. Purchase four packets of the same brand, one packet for each test group
   IV. Purchase four packets of the same brand, and divide the seeds from each packet equally among the four test groups.

   A. I and II only

   B. II and IV only

   C. III and IV only

   D. IV only

2. During the measurement of seed and root length it is noted that many of the roots are not growing straight. Efforts to manually straighten the roots for measurement are only minimally successful as the roots are fragile and susceptible to breakage. Which of the following approaches is consistent with the stated hypothesis?

   A. At the end of the experiment, straighten the roots and measure them

   B. Use a string as a flexible measuring instrument for curved roots

   C. Record the mass instead of length as an indicator of growth

   D. Record only the number of seeds that have sprouted, regardless of length

3. In presenting the results of this experiment, which of the following could be used to present the data to confirm or refute the hypothesis?

    I. A single bar graph with one bar for each test group indicating the number of days until the first seed sprouts.

    II. A pie chart for each test group showing the percent of seeds in that group that sprouted.

    III. A line graph plotting the total number of sprouted seeds from all test groups vs. time (experiment day).

    IV. A line graph plotting the number of germinated seeds vs. the minutes of time exposed to the microwave.

A. I only

B. II only

C. II and IV only

D. III and IV only

4. Which equation could be used to answer the following question?

Together, a pen and a pencil cost $2.59 (ignoring tax). The pen cost $1.79 more than the pencil. What was the cost of the pencil?

A. $x = (2.59 - 1.79) \times 2$

B. $2.59 = x - 1.79$

C. $2.59 = x + (x + 1.79)$

D. $x = 2.59 - 1.79$

5. Bemus School is conducting a lottery to raise funds for new band uniforms. Exactly 1000 tickets will be printed and sold. Only one ticket stub will be drawn from a drum to determine the single winner of a big-screen television. All tickets have equal chances of winning. The first 700 tickets are sold to 700 different individuals. The remaining 300 tickets are sold to Mr. Greenfield.

Given the information above, which of the following statements are true?

    I. It is impossible to tell in advance who will win.

    II. Mr. Greenfield will probably win.

    III. Someone other than Mr. Greenfield will probably win.

    IV. The likelihood that Mr. Greenfield will win is the same as the likelihood that someone else will win.

A. I and II only

B. I and III only

C. II and IV only

D. III and IV only

DIRECTIONS: The following two questions are based upon this excerpt from Jules Verne's 1870 work *From the Earth to the Moon and Round the Moon* pp. 39–40 (Dodd, Mead & Company 1962), where plans are made to construct a cannon 900 feet long to shoot a projectile to the Moon.

The problem before us is how to communicate an initial force of 12,000 yards per second to a shell of 108 inches in diameter, weighing 20,000 pounds. Now when a projectile is launched into space, what happens to it? It is acted upon by three independent forces: the resistance of the air, the attraction of the earth, and the force of impulsion with which it is endowed. Let us examine these three forces. The resistance of the air is of little importance. The atmosphere of the earth does not exceed forty miles. Now, with the given rapidity, the projectile will have traversed this in five seconds, and the period is too brief for the resistance of the medium to be regarded otherwise than as insignificant. Proceeding, then, to the attraction of the earth, that is, the weight of the shell, we know that this weight will diminish in the inverse ratio of the square of the distance. When a body left to itself falls to the surface of the earth, it falls five feet in the first second; and if the same body were removed 257,542 miles farther off, in other words, to the distance of the moon, its fall would be reduced to about half a line in the first second.

6. Propelling such a large projectile requires a massive force. The "initial force of 12,000 yards per second" is really a reference to the projectile's initial speed. The calculation of force required to move an object with a mass of 20,000 pounds from rest to a speed of 12,000 yards per second in a time span of 0.05 seconds is reflected in which of the following:

    A. $20,000 \times 12,000 / 0.05$

    B. $20,000 \times 12,000 \times 0.05$

    C. $(20,000 \times 9.8) / (20,000 \times 0.05)$

    D. $(20,000 / 9.8) \times (12,000 / 0.05)$

7. The acceleration due to gravity is generally accepted as 9.8 m/sec^2 for objects near the Earth's surface, and the Earth's radius is approximately 4,000 miles. Given that the proposed projectile weighs 20,000 lbs at the surface, what would be the approximate mass at a distance of 8,000 miles from the surface of the Earth?

    A.   20,000 lbs / 2

    B.   20,000 lbs / 4

    C.   20,000 lbs / 8

    D.   20,000 lbs / 16

8. The primary and most efficient energy source of the body comes from

   A. proteins.

   B. fats.

   C. complex carbohydrates.

   D. simple sugars.

9. Which of the following is a locomotor skill?

   A. bouncing

   B. catching

   C. throwing

   D. leaping

10. Which is NOT a principle of aerobic conditioning?

    A. requires oxygen

    B. continuous and rhythmic

    C. burns protein for energy

    D. uses major muscle groups

11. Dance can be a mirror of culture. Which of the following is not an illustration of this statement?

    A. Women in the Cook Islands dance with their feet together and sway, while the men take a wide stance and flap their knees.

    B. Movement basics include body, space, time, and relationship.

    C. In Africa, the birth of a child is an occasion for a dance that asks for divine blessings.

    D. The court dancers of Bali study for many years to achieve the balance, beauty, and serenity of their dance.

Use the image below to answer the two questions that follow.

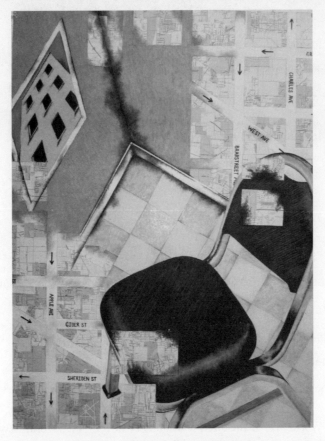

Student work by Sara Goodrich

12.   As shown in the figure, the technique of gluing imagery to a two-dimensional surface is referred to as

   A.   montage.

   B.   frottage.

   C.   collage.

   D.   assemblage.

13.   In the above image, the chair is the focal point of the drawing. Why?

   A.   It is large, frontal, and drawn in high contrast.

   B.   It is highly simplified and minimally detailed.

   C.   It is asymmetrically balanced in the drawing.

   D.   It is drawn in three-point perspective.

14. In order to achieve lasting weight loss, students should

    A. enter a commercial diet program.

    B. combine permanent dietary changes with exercise.

    C. cut calories to below 1,000 per day.

    D. exercise for two hours a day.

15. Which of the following vitamins is not fat soluble?

    A. Vitamin D

    B. Vitamin C

    C. Vitamin E

    D. Vitamin K

16. Of the following, which test does NOT measure muscular strength and endurance in children?

    A. Pull-ups

    B. Flexed arm hang

    C. Grip strength test

    D. Sit-and-reach test

17. Around the time of World War II the chemical industry developed several new classes of insecticide that were instrumental in protecting our soldiers from pest-borne diseases common to the tropic regions they were fighting in. These same insecticides found widespread use at home to increase production of many agricultural crops by reducing the damage from insects like cotton weevils and grasshoppers. While farmers continued to use the same levels of insecticide, over time it was found that the insect population was increasing. Identify the best explanation for this observation:

    A. Insecticides, like most chemicals, lose their potency when stored.

    B. The insect population was increasing to reach the carrying capacity of a given ecosystem.

    C. The initial doses of pesticide were too low to effectively kill the insects.

    D. Insects with a tolerance to insecticide survived the initial doses and lived to produce insecticide resistant offspring.

18. Which of the following types of pollution or atmospheric phenomena are correctly matched with their underlying causes?

      I.   global warming – carbon dioxide and methane
     II.   acid rain – sulfur dioxide and nitrogen dioxide
    III.   ozone depletion – chlorofluorocarbons and sunlight
    IV.   aurora borealis – solar flares and magnetism

    A.   I and II only

    B.   II and III only

    C.   I and IV only

    D.   I, II, III, and IV

19. Which of the following characteristics of a sound wave is associated with its pitch?

      I.   Amplitude
     II.   Frequency
    III.   Wavelength
    IV.   Speed

    A.   I only

    B.   II only

    C.   II and III only

    D.   IV only

20. Which of the following statements correctly describes each group of vertebrates?

      I.   Amphibians are cold-blooded, spending part of their life cycle in water and part on land.
     II.   Reptiles are generally warm-blooded, having scales that cover their skin.
    III.   Fish are cold-blooded, breathing with gills, and covered by scales.
    IV.   Mammals are warm-blooded with milk glands and hair.

    A.   I and IV only

    B.   I, III, and IV only

    C.   IV only

    D.   I, II, III, and IV

21. Pitch is the relative _____ of a musical sound.

    A.   duration or length

    B.   loudness or softness

    C.   highness or lowness

    D.   rhythm

22. Dance can reflect the religion of a culture by
    I.   offering adoration and worship to the deity.
    II. appealing to the deity for survival in war.
    III. asking the deity for success in the hunt.
    IV. miming the actions of planting and harvesting crops.

    A. I and II only

    B. I and III only

    C. II, III, and IV only

    D. I, II, III, and IV

23. Which of the following do the dances of Waltz, Lindy Hop, and Twist have in common?

    A. They became popular in the nineteenth century.

    B. They are forms of "swing" dance.

    C. They reflect changes in social attitudes of their time.

    D. They are danced by couples touching each other.

24. Which of the following is NOT a characteristic of cholesterol?

    A. Cholesterol plays a role in the function of the brain.

    B. Cholesterol is a component in the creation of certain hormones.

    C. Cholesterol is produced in the liver.

    D. Excess cholesterol found in the blood of many people usually comes from internal production.

25. A table tennis game is scored to

    A. 15 points.

    B. 15 points, with a margin of two.

    C. 21 points, with a margin of two.

    D. 21 points.

26. Matt earned the following scores on his first six weekly mathematics tests: 91%, 89%, 82%, 95%, 86%, and 79%.

    He had hoped for an average (mean) of 90% at this point, which would just barely give him an A– in math class on his first report card. How many more total percentage points should Matt have earned over the course of those six weeks to qualify for an A–?

    A. 87

    B. 3

    C. 90

    D. 18

27. The floor of a rectangular room is to be covered in two different types of material. The total cost of covering the entire room is $136.00. The cost of covering the inner rectangle is $80.00. The cost of covering the shaded area is $56.00.

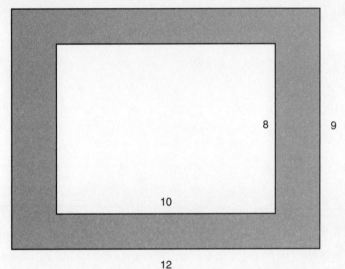

    We wish to determine the cost of material per square foot used to cover the shaded area. What information given below is unnecessary for this computation?

        I.   The total cost of covering the entire room.
        II. The cost of covering the inner rectangle.
        III. The cost of covering the shaded area.

    A. I only

    B. II only

    C. I and II

    D. I and III

28. Which of the following is an important reason why music should be included in every child's daily classroom activities?

    A. The imagination, creativity, and aesthetic awareness of a child can be developed through music for more creative living in our mechanized society.

    B. Students need an opportunity to stay current with today's popular music culture.

    C. Making and listening to music is part of our cultural experience and provides opportunities for personal aesthetic growth.

    D. Participating in creatively planned musical activities helps build a child's self-esteem and understanding of others.

29. Harmony results when a melody is accompanied by
    I.   a rhythm instrument.
    II. a guitar.
    III. another instrument or singer playing or singing the melody.
    IV. another instrument playing chords.

    A. I and II only

    B. I and III only

    C. II and III only

    D. II and IV only

30. Identify the incorrect statement from the following:

    A. Heredity is the study of how traits are passed from parent to offspring.

    B. The chemical molecule that carries an organism's genetic makeup is called DNA.

    C. Sections of the DNA molecule that determine specific traits are called chromosomes.

    D. The genetic makeup of an organism is altered through bioengineering.

31. Which of the following sources of energy is nonrenewable?

    A. hydrogen-cell

    B. geothermal

    C. nuclear

    D. hydroelectric

32. To move a heavy book across a tabletop at a constant speed, a person must continually exert a force on the book. This force is primarily used to overcome which of the following forces?

   A.   The force of gravity

   B.   The force of air resistance

   C.   The force of friction

   D.   The weight of the book

33. To complete an effective aerobic workout, exercise should be performed at an individual's target heart rate for a minimum of

   A.   15 minutes.

   B.   20 minutes.

   C.   30 minutes.

   D.   45 minutes.

34. Which of the following statements is not true?

   A.   Infectious diseases are caused by viruses, bacteria, or protists.

   B.   Cancers and hereditary diseases can be infectious.

   C.   Environmental hazards can cause disease.

   D.   The immune system protects the body from disease.

35. Nelson's Menswear Shop was selling sweaters for $40 at the beginning of the year. In March, the price of the sweaters was raised by 10%. In September, the price was raised by an additional 15%. Ignoring tax, what was the price of the sweaters in September?

   A. $50.00

   B. $65.40

   C. $59.00

   D. $50.60

36. Three pounds of cherries cost $4.65. What would five pounds cost (at the same price per pound)?

   A. $7.75

   B. $7.50

   C. $23.00

   D. $23.25

37. You have stepped into an art museum and are drawn to a painting you know nothing about. In order to appreciate the painting, it is helpful to

      I. know all of the details of the artist's intentions and motivations.
      II. study the clues in the artwork for potential meaning.
      III. determine the cultural significance of every visual clue in the painting.
      IV. consider the art elements and principles in the work of art.

    A. I and II only

    B. I and III only

    C. II and IV only

    D. III and IV only

38. Which one of the following statements is most true regarding the materials of visual art?

    A. Industrial innovations in art-making materials have improved art in the past 150 years.

    B. The use of uncommon materials in art-making has improved art in the past 150 years.

    C. The use of unusual materials in art-making has changed the standards by which we view art.

    D. Industrial innovations in art-making materials have had little influence on visual art.

39. How many ten thousands are there in one million?

    A. 100

    B. 10

    C. 1,000

    D. 10,000

40. An owner of twin Siamese cats knows the following data:

      I. Cost of a can of cat food

      II. Volume of a can of cat food

      III. Number of cans of cat food eaten each day by one cat

      IV. The weight of the cat food in one can

Which of the data above can be used to determine the cost of cat food for 7 days for the 2 cats?

    A. I and II only

    B. I and III only

    C. I and IV only

    D. III and IV only

OSAT

Oklahoma Subject Area Test
Elementary Education

Answers:
Practice Subtest 2

Answer Key

1. (B)	11. (B)	21. (C)	31. (C)
2. (D)	12. (C)	22. (D)	32. (C)
3. (C)	13. (A)	23. (C)	33. (B)
4. (C)	14. (B)	24. (D)	34. (B)
5. (B)	15. (B)	25. (C)	35. (D)
6. (A)	16. (D)	26. (D)	36. (A)
7. (B)	17. (D)	27. (C)	37. (C)
8. (C)	18. (D)	28. (C)	38. (C)
9. (D)	19. (C)	29. (D)	39. (A)
10. (C)	20. (B)	30. (C)	40. (B)

Practice Subtest

Detailed Explanations of Answers

1. **B**

   The experiment requires a control of all variables other than the one identified in the hypothesis—exposure to microwave radiation. Seeds from different suppliers may be different; for example, one brand may be treated with a fungicide or a different fungicide. While it is likely that item III might be acceptable, without confirming that all packages are from the same year and production run, the four packages may be significantly different from each other. The best solution is to randomly divide the available seeds equally between the four test groups. Item II allows the experiment to also compare the germination rates between the different brands, but only if the seeds from each packet are isolated within each test group, and the number of seeds large enough to create a statistically significant sample.

2. **D**

   The hypothesis is to evaluate seed germination as a function of microwave irradiation. Recording the overall growth or length of the seed root, while interesting, is not the stated hypothesis. Item C would be a good approach if the hypothesis were to relate seed growth to some variable, as it would more accurately reflect the growth of thicker or multiple roots in a way that root length might not measure.

3. **C**

   Item I will not reflect the success of seed germination overall, one seed in a given sample may germinate early. Reporting the time until the last seed germinates would also not be useful. Item III combines the number of all the sprouted seeds, losing the differentiation of the test groups. Items II and IV maintain the distinction between test groups and indicate the overall success rate of the germination.

4. **C**

The total price of the two items is given as $2.59, hinting that equation B or C may be correct. (In both cases, $2.59 is shown as the sum of two values.)

Examine the right side of equation C: You note that one value is $1.79 higher than the other. That is, in equation C, x could stand for the price of the pencil, and (x + 1.79) could stand for the price of the more expensive pen. Hence, equation C is the right one. None of the others fit the information given.

5. **B**

Statement I is true because the winner could be Mr. Greenfield and it could be someone else. Statement II is not true, even though Mr. Greenfield bought many more tickets than any other individual. He still has a block of only 300; there are 700 ticket stubs in the drum that aren't his. This tells us that statement III is true.

Finally, statement IV is false. Don't confuse the true statement "all tickets have an equal chance of winning" with the false statement that "all persons have an equal chance of winning."

6. **A**

Force is equal to mass multiplied by acceleration (F = ma). The force needed is the product of the object's mass (20,000 lbs) and the acceleration. Acceleration is the change in speed per unit of time. The projectile's acceleration is thus (12,000 yards/second – 0 yards/second) / 0.05 seconds).

7. **B**

The force of gravity is inversely proportional to the square of the distance; thus, doubling the distance reduces the gravitational force by a factor of 4. The mass reduction for this object at the top of the atmosphere, just forty miles above the surface, would be insignificant. However, experience tells us that objects are "weightless" in the space shuttle. This apparent weightlessness is a result of a balance between the forward motion of the shuttle and the gravitational attraction of the Earth. Both the shuttle and the objects in it are moving forward together at a high rate of speed, and falling together under the force of gravity. They are "weightless" only relative to each other. Were the shuttle to cease forward motion it would fall directly and precipitously to Earth under the unrelenting force of gravity.

8. **C**

Complex carbohydrates are the most efficient energy source for the body. While other choices provide some energy, they are not nearly as efficient as complex carbohydrates.

9. **D**

Leaping is the only locomotor skill listed. Bouncing (A), catching (B), and throwing (C) are manipulative movements.

10. **C**

A, B, and D are principles of aerobic conditioning. C is not.

11. **B**

The statement "Movement basics include body, space, time, and relationship" is the correct answer because this describes only the dimensions of dance movement; in no way does it speak to how dance reflects the culture of which it is part.

12. **C**

Choice C is the correct answer. This is a collage.

13. **A**

It is large, frontal, and drawn in high contrast.

14. **B**

Permanent dietary changes and exercise are the only way to produce lasting weight loss. Commercial diets (A) do not always include a program of exercise, but rather concentrate on diet. Radically reducing calorie intake (C) will cause the body to go into starvation mode and slow down digestion to conserve energy. Two hours of daily exercise (D) is not very practical and without controlling calorie intake, it would be ineffective.

15. **B**

Vitamin C is water soluble—the remaining choices are fat soluble.

16. **D**

The grip strength test (C), pull-ups (for boys) (A), and flexed arm hang (for girls) (B), are all tests to measure muscular strength and endurance. The sit-and-reach test measures flexibility.

17. **D**

Early doses of pesticide were strong enough to kill most of the insects; only a few survived who, perhaps because of some genetic trait, had a slightly higher tolerance to the poison. When these pesticide-tolerant insects reproduced they passed the tolerance to their offspring, so D is correct. Higher doses of pesticide are initially effective, but again a few individuals survive with tolerance to that new level. Control of pest populations generally requires access to a variety of pesticides that work through different mechanisms, and which are applied in such a way as to minimize buildup of tolerance in the insect population.

18. **D**

All are correctly matched.

19. **C**

The frequency of a wave is associated with pitch. Middle C has a frequency of 440 cycles per second. However, wavelength and frequency are directly related by the relationship $v = c / \lambda$ where v (nu) is the frequency, c is the speed of sound, and λ (lambda) is wavelength.

20. **B**

Reptiles are not generally warm-blooded, so II is incorrect; all other statements are correct.

21. **C**

This question focuses on a specific but very basic musical concept, pitch. Answer C is the best answer and the only correct answer. Answer A refers indirectly to the basic concept of rhythm. This relates to answer D, which is totally wrong because it is another concept and not a descriptor of the concept of pitch. Answer B is wrong because it refers directly to the basic concept of dynamics.

22. **D**

The correct choice is D, statements I, II, III, and IV. Dance can reflect the religion of a culture in many ways on account of its deep historical roots in religious tradition.

23. **C**

The Waltz, Lindy Hop, and the Twist each reflect changes in social attitudes of their time.

24. **D**

Excess cholesterol found in the blood typically comes from cholesterol in a diet rather than internal production. Cholesterol, which is produced in the liver (C), plays a vital role in brain function (A) and is important for creating certain hormones (B).

25. **C**

Table tennis is scored to 21 and must be won by a margin of two points. In doubles play for badminton, the winner must score 15 points (A). Singles badminton is also scored to 21 points with a margin of two points needed for victory.

26. **D**

It is helpful to compute Matt's current average. Adding up his scores, you get 522. Dividing that by 6 (the number of scores), you find that his average is 87%. Similarly, you can multiply 90 by

6 to compute the number of total points it would take to have an average of 90 (90 × 6 = 540). Matt only earned 522 points, so he was 18 shy of the A−.

27. **C**

The total area of the larger rectangle is

base × height = 12 × 9 = 108 sq. ft.

Therefore, the area of the shaded portion surrounding the inner rectangle is

108 sq. ft. − 80 sq. ft. = 28 sq. ft.

If the total cost of material used to cover the shaded area is $56 and we have 28 sq. ft., the cost per square foot is $\frac{\$56}{28 \text{ sq. ft.}}$ = $2.00 per square foot.

Answers A, B, and D are incorrect. Neither I nor II is necessary to determine the cost per square foot of the shaded area. D is incorrect because III is needed to determine the cost per sq foot.

28. **C**

This question is focused on the music objective as stated in the Oklahoma standards. Therefore, it is important to look for the answer that best reflects the objective. Answer C is the best answer because it covers all parts of the objective in at least a minimal way and is the only one that mentions music's cultural dimensions. Answer A is a good answer and the second best answer because it deals with one of the objectives, but the focus on creativity rather than culture keeps it from being the best answer. Answers B and D are not good answers because they do not deal with the objectives.

29. **D**

This question focuses on a basic musical concept, "harmony." Harmony is the performance of two or more different pitches simultaneously. Therefore, when looking at the answers provided, it is good to begin by eliminating answers that have nothing to do with pitch. A rhythm instrument is a non-pitched instrument in almost all cases, so choice I is not pitch-related and that means that answers A and B are eliminated because they both include choice I. Since two or more different pitches must be performed simultaneously to have harmony, choice III can also be eliminated because there are two performers, but not two different pitches. That eliminates answer C and leaves answer D as the best and correct answer.

30. **C**

Genes are the sections of the DNA molecule that determine specific traits.

31. **C**

Nuclear energy is nonrenewable. Nuclear energy has potential advantages in providing large quantities of energy from a small amount of source material, but once started the process of radioactive decay is nonreversible.

32. **C**

The force of friction between the book and the table is the primary force that must be overcome to move the book. An experiment to study these frictional forces could keep all other variables (size and weight of the book, speed of travel) constant while measuring the force needed to move the book using a spring scale. Different experiments could change the surface of the book by covering the book with wax paper, construction paper, or sandpaper.

33. **B**

Exercising cardiovascularly for a minimum of 20 minutes per session, as part of an exercise program, will lead to effective physical results with a proper nutritional diet. Forty-five minutes (D) is an effective time period when performing a weight-lifting exercise session.

34. **B**

Diseases caused by viruses, bacteria, or protists that invade the body are called infectious diseases. These disease-causing organisms are collectively referred to as germs. Cancers and hereditary diseases are not infectious.

35. **D**

The first price increase is for 10%. That's the same as one-tenth, and one-tenth of $40 is $4. Adding $4 to $40 gives $44 as the March price.

The next increase is 15% of $44. Multiplying 44 by 0.15 (0.15 being another way to represent 15%) gives 6.6, which is read as $6.60. You then increase the March price of $44 by $6.60, giving you $50.60.

Note that you cannot arrive at the answer by adding the individual percent increases (10 + 15 = 25) and then multiplying by 40.

36. **A**

Finding the answer by setting up a proportion works well here:

$$\frac{3}{4.65} = \frac{5}{x}$$

Proportions often are two fractions set equal to each other, with one "corner" being the unknown value, or x. The equation above can be read as "3 is to 4.65 as 5 is to what?"

One way to solve a proportion (that is; to find the value of x), is to cross-multiply the two corners that have known values (in this case 4.65 and 5). That gives 23.25, which is then divided by the remaining known value (3), giving 7.75.

37. **C**

Choice C, statements II and IV, is correct. You would want to study the clues in the artwork for potential meaning and consider the art elements and principles in the work of art. The more you know about the context in which the artist worked, the more you can appreciate the work itself. Not everything will be immediately evident, so you will want to assume the role of detective.

38. **C**

Choice C is the correct answer. The use of uncommon materials has dramatically changed the criteria by which one assesses visual art.

39. **A**

You know that ten thousand contains 4 zeros, or 10^4 in place value. One million contains 10^6, or six zeros. Thus, 10^6 divided by 10^4 is 10^2 or 100. You may divide out 10,000 into one million, but that is the laborious way to solve this. Choice A is correct.

40. **B**

You are challenged to analyze which data you would need to calculate the cost of feeding 2 cats for 7 days. If you calculate the cost for one cat for 7 days, then double the answer, you will have an approximate cost for 2 cats. The total cost for one cat is the cost of a can of food, times the number of cans of food eaten each day by one cat, times 7 days.

Your Test-Day Checklist

☑ Get a good night's sleep. Tired test-takers consistently perform poorly.

☑ Wake up early.

☑ Dress comfortably. Keep your clothing temperature appropriate. You'll be sitting in yout test clothes for hours. Clothes that are itchy, tight, too warm, or too cold take away from your comfort level.

☑ Eat a good breakfast.

☑ Take these with you to the test center:
- Several sharpened No. 2 pencils. Pencils are not provided at the test center
- Admission ticket
- Proper indentification: current, government-issued identification bearing your photograph and signature, and one additional piece of identification

☑ Arrive at the test center early. Remember, no one is allowed into a test session after the test has begun.

☑ Compose your thoughts and try to relax before the test.

Remember that eating, drinking, and smoking are prohibited. Calculators, dictionaries, textbooks, notebooks, briefcases, and packages are also prohibited.

Index

Speaking process, 239–240

Squinting modifiers, 38

Stalin, Josef, 122

Standard deviation, statistical concept of, 82, 314

Statistical concepts, 81–84, 313–314

Storytelling, 227

Story Theatre, 361

Straight line
equation for, 98
parallel lines, 105, 310–311

Study skills and strategies, 224–226

Subject-verb agreement, 63–67

Subordinating conjunction, 40, 47

Summarization questions, 24–25

Support questions, 21–22

Surrealism, 115

T

Tables, 30–31
as study aids, 225

Tap dance, 366–367

Tapestry, 348

Teaching models, in science education, 109

Team sports, 343

Technology, 318. *See also* Science education

Theatre. *See* Drama

Theatre-in-Education, 360

Theatre of the Imagination. *See* Readers Theatre

Theories, scientific, 321

Traditional literature, 227

Traditional Theatre, 361

Trends in data, 80, 303

Triangles, 102, 104, 311
similarity transformation, 105

Trinomials, 90

The Twist, 365

U

United States of America
and the Cold War, 123
democracy, ideals of, 247
World Trade Center, 2001 attacks, 123

V

Variation, statistical concept of, 82

Venn diagram, 224

Verbs
subject-verb agreement, 63–67
tense sequence, 61–62

Vibrational energy, 328

Vietnam War, 123

Visual aids, 240

Visual arts
anonymous artists, 350
categorization, 350–351
concepts and skills, 351–354
purposes of, 348–349
role in society, 349–350
Western, history of, 114–115

Vitamins, 337–338

Vocabulary skills, 220–222

Volume, 103–104, 310

W

Water cycle, 324

Waves, 328–329

Weather patterns, 324

Weight control strategies, 339

Weight training, 343

Western visual arts, history of, 114–115

White light, 329

Whole-language approach to reading, 220

Whole numbers, 302–303, 304

Word choice, 71–73
transitional words and phrases, 132–133

Wordiness, 72

Word problems, 88, 89–90, 307, 308–309, 313

World War I, 122

World War II, 122

Writing
audience, importance of, 131
for constructed response, 253–255
essays, 128–129, 234–237
process of, 130–136, 231–233
thesis, proof of, 129

Y

Yugoslavia, breaking up of, 123

NOTES

NOTES

NOTES

NOTES

NOTES

NOTES

REA's Test Preps
The Best in Test Preparation

- REA "Test Preps" are **far more** comprehensive than any other test preparation series
- Each book contains up to **eight** full-length practice tests based on the most recent exams
- **Every** type of question likely to be given on the exams is included
- Answers are accompanied by **full** and **detailed** explanations

REA publishes over 70 Test Preparation volumes in several series. They include:

Advanced Placement Exams (APs)
Biology
Calculus AB & Calculus BC
Chemistry
Economics
English Language & Composition
English Literature & Composition
European History
Government & Politics
Physics B & C
Psychology
Spanish Language
Statistics
United States History

College-Level Examination Program (CLEP)
Analyzing and Interpreting Literature
College Algebra
Freshman College Composition
General Examinations
General Examinations Review
History of the United States I
History of the United States II
Human Growth and Development
Introductory Sociology
Principles of Marketing
Spanish

SAT Subject Tests
Biology E/M
Chemistry
English Language Proficiency Test
French
German

SAT Subject Tests (cont'd)
Literature
Mathematics Level 1, 2
Physics
Spanish
United States History
Writing

Graduate Record Exams (GREs)
Biology
Chemistry
Computer Science
General
Literature in English
Mathematics
Physics
Psychology

ACT - ACT Assessment

ASVAB - Armed Services Vocational Aptitude Battery

CBEST - California Basic Educational Skills Test

CDL - Commercial Driver License Exam

CLAST - College Level Academic Skills Test

COOP & HSPT - Catholic High School Admission Tests

ELM - California State University Entry Level Mathematics Exam

FE (EIT) - Fundamentals of Engineering Exams - For both AM & PM Exams

FTCE - Florida Teacher Certification Exam

GED - High School Equivalency Diploma Exam (U.S. & Canadian editions)

GMAT - Graduate Management Admission Test

LSAT - Law School Admission Test

MAT - Miller Analogies Test

MCAT - Medical College Admission Test

MTEL - Massachusetts Tests for Educational Licensure

NJ HSPA - New Jersey High School Proficiency Assessment

NYSTCE: LAST & ATS-W - New York State Teacher Certification

PLT - Principles of Learning & Teaching Tests

PPST - Pre-Professional Skills Tests

PSAT / NMSQT

SAT

TExES - Texas Examinations of Educator Standards

THEA - Texas Higher Education Assessment

TOEFL - Test of English as a Foreign Language

TOEIC - Test of English for International Communication

USMLE Steps 1,2,3 - U.S. Medical Licensing Exams

U.S. Postal Exams 460 & 470

RESEARCH & EDUCATION ASSOCIATION   website: www.rea.com
61 Ethel Road W. • Piscataway, New Jersey 08854 • Phone: (732) 819-8880

Please send me more information about your Test Prep books

Name _____

Address _____

City _____ State _____ Zip _____

REA's Test Prep Books Are The Best!
(a sample of the <u>hundreds of letters</u> REA receives each year)

" The gem of the book is the tests. They were indicative of the actual exam.
The explanations of the answers are practically another review session. "
Student, Fresno, CA

" I just wanted to thank you for helping me get a great score
on the AP U.S. History... Thank you for making great test preps! "
Student, Los Angeles, CA

" Your Fundamentals of Engineering Exam book was the absolute best
preparation I could have had for the exam, and it is one of the major
reasons I did so well and passed the FE on my first try. "
Student, Sweetwater, TN

" I used your book to prepare for the test and found that the advice and the
sample tests were highly relevant... Without using any other material, I earned
very high scores and will be going to the graduate school of my choice. "
Student, New Orleans, LA

" What I found in your book was a wealth of information sufficient to shore up my basic
skills in math and verbal.... The practice tests were challenging and the
answer explanations most helpful. It certainly is the Best Test Prep for the GRE! "
Student, Pullman, WA

" I really appreciate the help from your excellent book. Please keep
up with your great work. "
Student, Albuquerque, NM

" I used your *CLEP Introductory Sociology* book and rank it 99%– thank you! "
Student, Jerusalem, Israel

(more on next page)

REA's Test Prep Books Are The Best!
(a sample of the <u>hundreds of letters</u> REA receives each year)

" I used [*the REA study guide*] to study for the LSAT and ATS-W tests—and passed them both with *perfect scores*. This book provided excellent preparation ... "
Student, New York, NY

" The reviews in [the REA book] were outstanding ... If it wasn't for your excellent prep, I would not have stood a chance [of passing the NYSTCE]. "
Student, Elmira, New York

" I did well because of your wonderful prep books... I just wanted to thank you for helping me prepare for these tests. "
Student, San Diego, CA

" My students report your chapters of review as the most valuable single resource they used for review and preparation. "
Teacher, American Fork, UT

" Your book was such a better value and was so much more complete than anything your competition has produced—and I have them all! "
Teacher, Virginia Beach, VA

" Compared to the other books that my fellow students had, your book was the most helpful in helping me get a great score. "
Student, North Hollywood, CA

" Your book was responsible for my success on the exam, which helped me get into the college of my choice... I will look for REA the next time I need help. "
Student, Chesterfield, MO

" Just a short note to say thanks for the great support your book gave me in helping me pass the test... I'm on my way to a B.S. degree because of you! "
Student, Orlando, FL

(more on previous page)